Let Dai

Vol. 2

Sooyeon Won

NETCOMICS

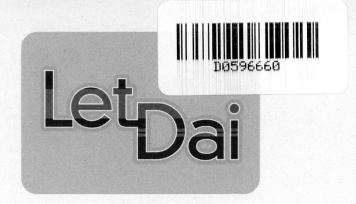

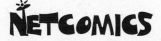

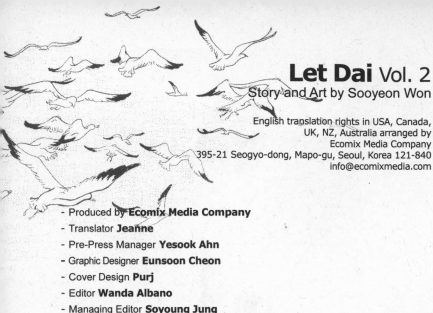

Let Dai Vol. 2
Story and Art by Sooyeon Won

English translation rights in USA, Canada,
UK, NZ, Australia arranged by
Ecomix Media Company
395-21 Seogyo-dong, Mapo-gu, Seoul, Korea 121-840
info@ecomixmedia.com

- Produced by **Ecomix Media Company**
- Translator **Jeanne**
- Pre-Press Manager **Yesook Ahn**
- Graphic Designer **Eunsoon Cheon**
- Cover Design **Purj**
- Editor **Wanda Albano**
- Managing Editor **Soyoung Jung**
- President & Publisher **Heewoon Chung**

NETCOMICS

P.O.Box 16484, Jersey City, NJ 07306
info@netcomics.com
www.NETCOMICS.com

ISBN: 1-60009-006-0

First printing: March 2006
10 9 8 7 6 5 4 3 2 1
Printed in Korea

Let Dai

Vol. 2

Sooyeon Won

SOOYEON'S BOOKSHELF

2005 Full House Part II

Let Dai vol. 15: Final

2004 AZUR: Illustrations

2003 Elio & Yvette: Collector's Edition

Want You vol. 1

2002~2003 Banana vol. 1~4

1995 Let Dai vol. 1

1993 Full House vol. 1

1992 Humanoid E.O.

1990 A Beautiful Hunt

1988~1992 Have You Ever Seen The Rain

Hammer Picnic

A Man Too Good For You

1988 Dances of Time

1987 Against The Shadow One Afternoon

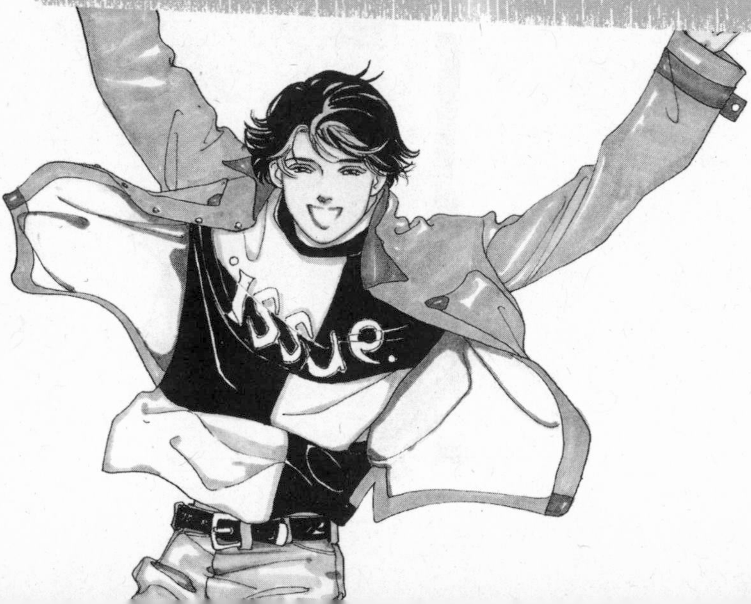

blue.

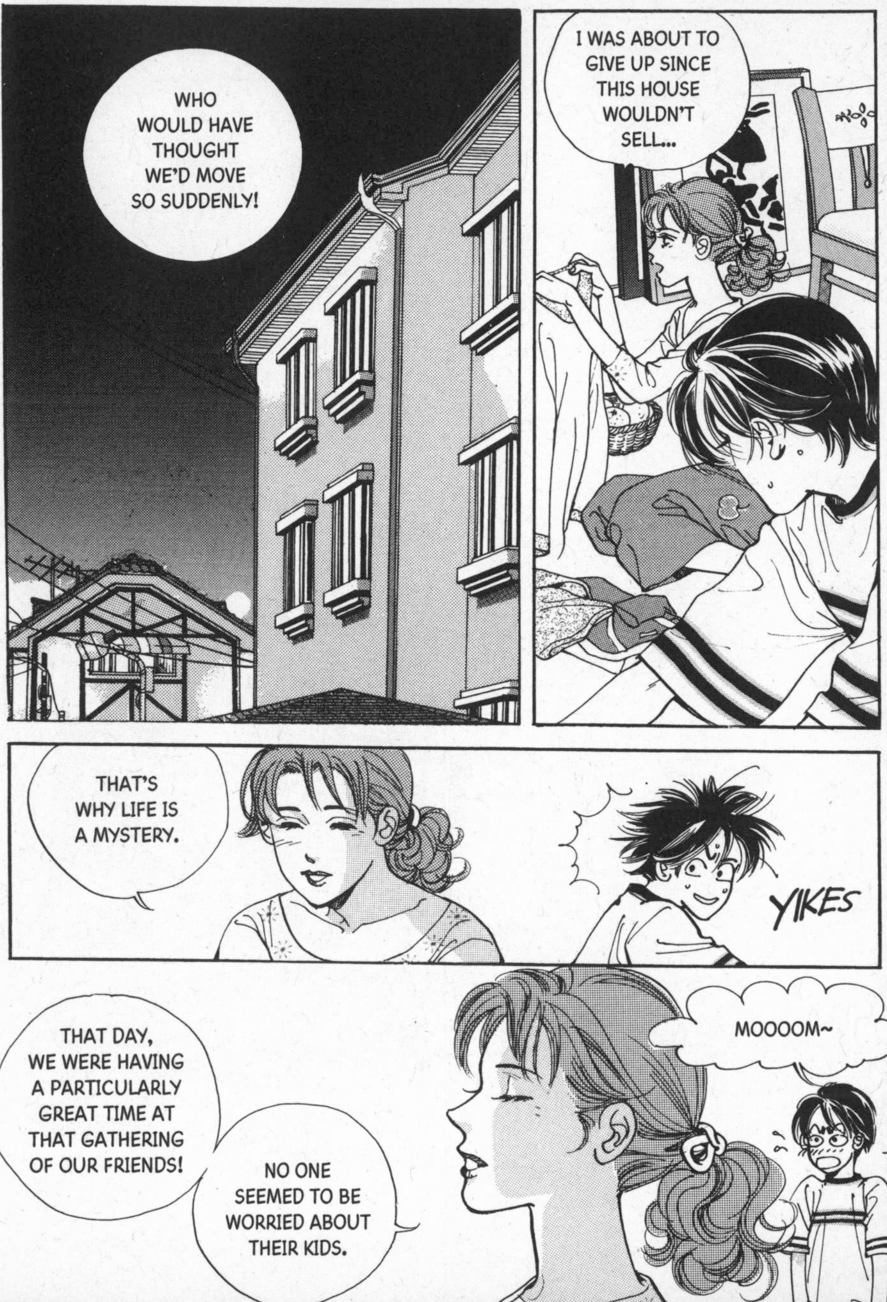
WHO WOULD HAVE THOUGHT WE'D MOVE SO SUDDENLY!
I WAS ABOUT TO GIVE UP SINCE THIS HOUSE WOULDN'T SELL...
THAT'S WHY LIFE IS A MYSTERY.
YIKES
THAT DAY, WE WERE HAVING A PARTICULARLY GREAT TIME AT THAT GATHERING OF OUR FRIENDS!
NO ONE SEEMED TO BE WORRIED ABOUT THEIR KIDS.
MOOOOM~

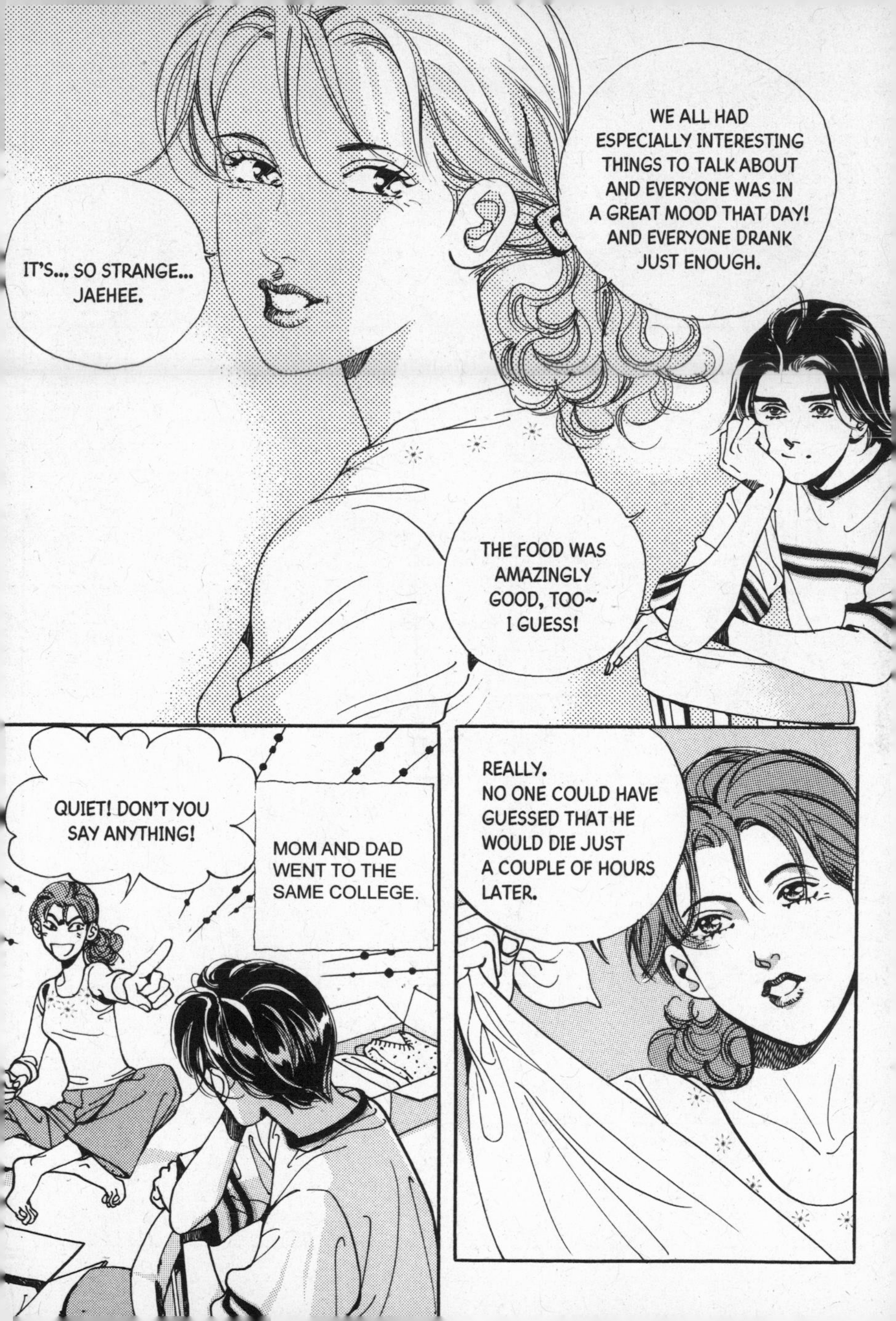
IT'S... SO STRANGE... JAEHEE.
WE ALL HAD ESPECIALLY INTERESTING THINGS TO TALK ABOUT AND EVERYONE WAS IN A GREAT MOOD THAT DAY! AND EVERYONE DRANK JUST ENOUGH.
THE FOOD WAS AMAZINGLY GOOD, TOO~ I GUESS!
QUIET! DON'T YOU SAY ANYTHING!
MOM AND DAD WENT TO THE SAME COLLEGE.
REALLY. NO ONE COULD HAVE GUESSED THAT HE WOULD DIE JUST A COUPLE OF HOURS LATER.

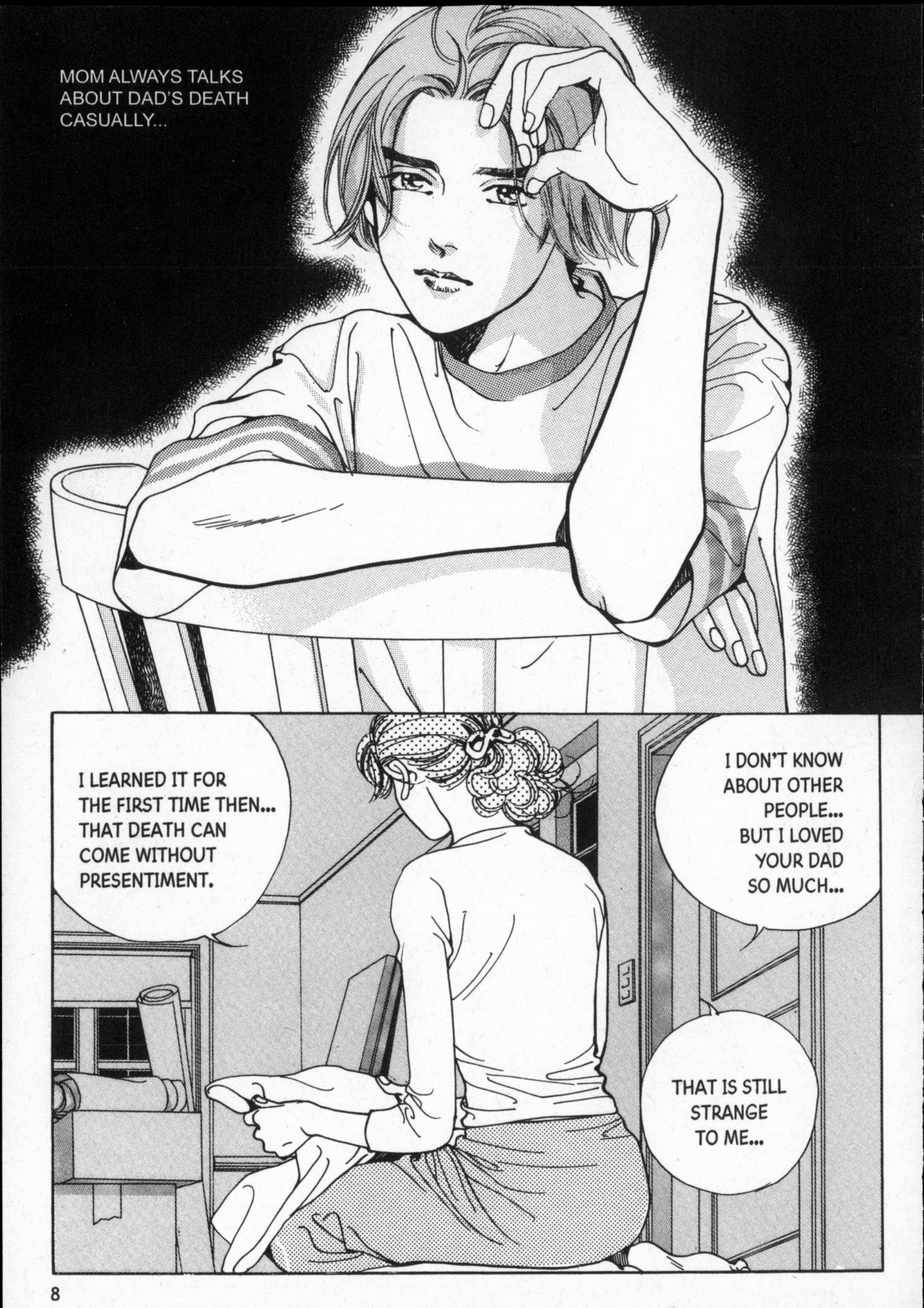
MOM ALWAYS TALKS ABOUT DAD'S DEATH CASUALLY...
I LEARNED IT FOR THE FIRST TIME THEN... THAT DEATH CAN COME WITHOUT PRESENTIMENT.
I DON'T KNOW ABOUT OTHER PEOPLE... BUT I LOVED YOUR DAD SO MUCH...
THAT IS STILL STRANGE TO ME...

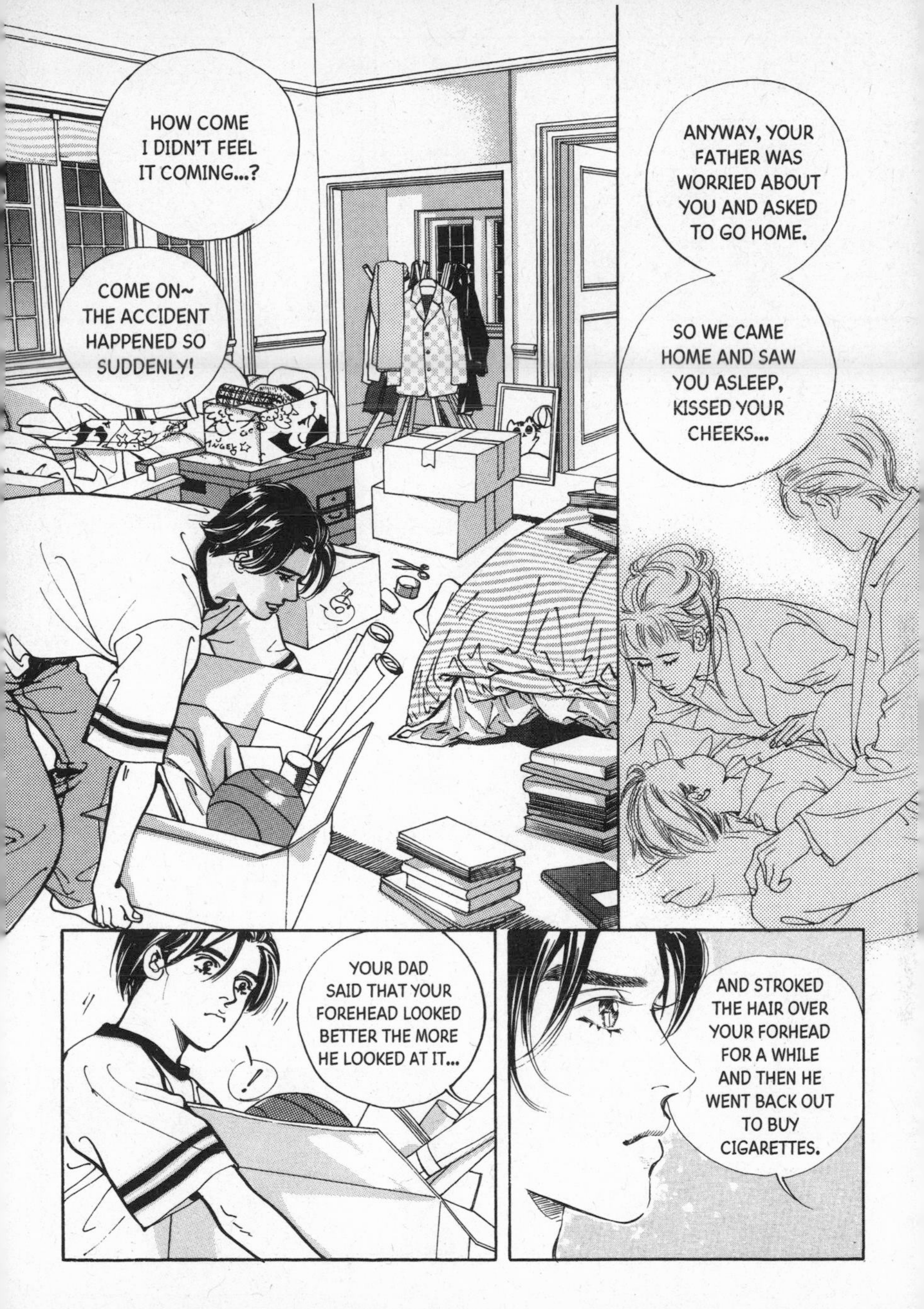
HOW COME I DIDN'T FEEL IT COMING...?
COME ON~ THE ACCIDENT HAPPENED SO SUDDENLY!
ANYWAY, YOUR FATHER WAS WORRIED ABOUT YOU AND ASKED TO GO HOME.
SO WE CAME HOME AND SAW YOU ASLEEP, KISSED YOUR CHEEKS...
YOUR DAD SAID THAT YOUR FOREHEAD LOOKED BETTER THE MORE HE LOOKED AT IT...
!
AND STROKED THE HAIR OVER YOUR FORHEAD FOR A WHILE AND THEN HE WENT BACK OUT TO BUY CIGARETTES.

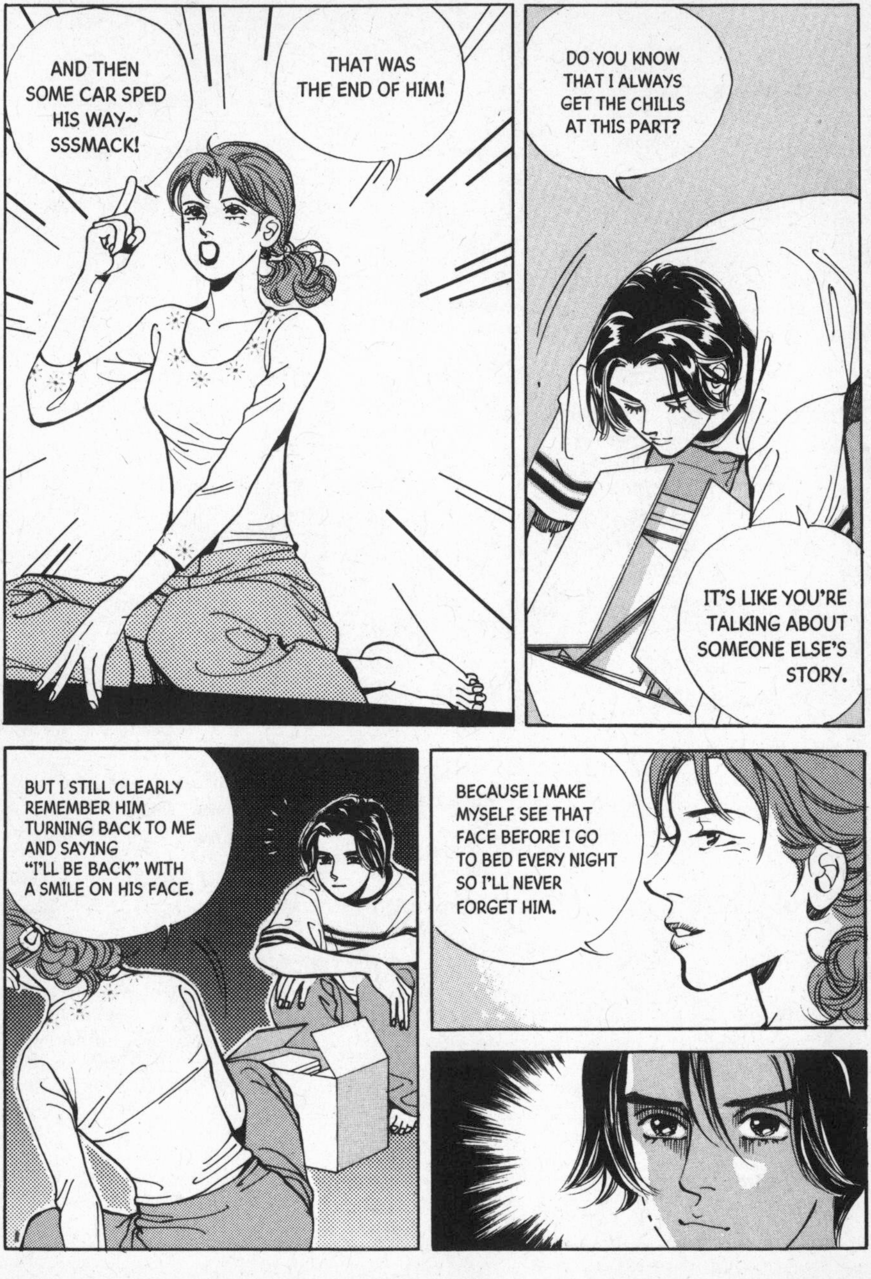
AND THEN SOME CAR SPED HIS WAY~ SSSMACK!
THAT WAS THE END OF HIM!
DO YOU KNOW THAT I ALWAYS GET THE CHILLS AT THIS PART?
IT'S LIKE YOU'RE TALKING ABOUT SOMEONE ELSE'S STORY.
BUT I STILL CLEARLY REMEMBER HIM TURNING BACK TO ME AND SAYING "I'LL BE BACK" WITH A SMILE ON HIS FACE.
BECAUSE I MAKE MYSELF SEE THAT FACE BEFORE I GO TO BED EVERY NIGHT SO I'LL NEVER FORGET HIM.

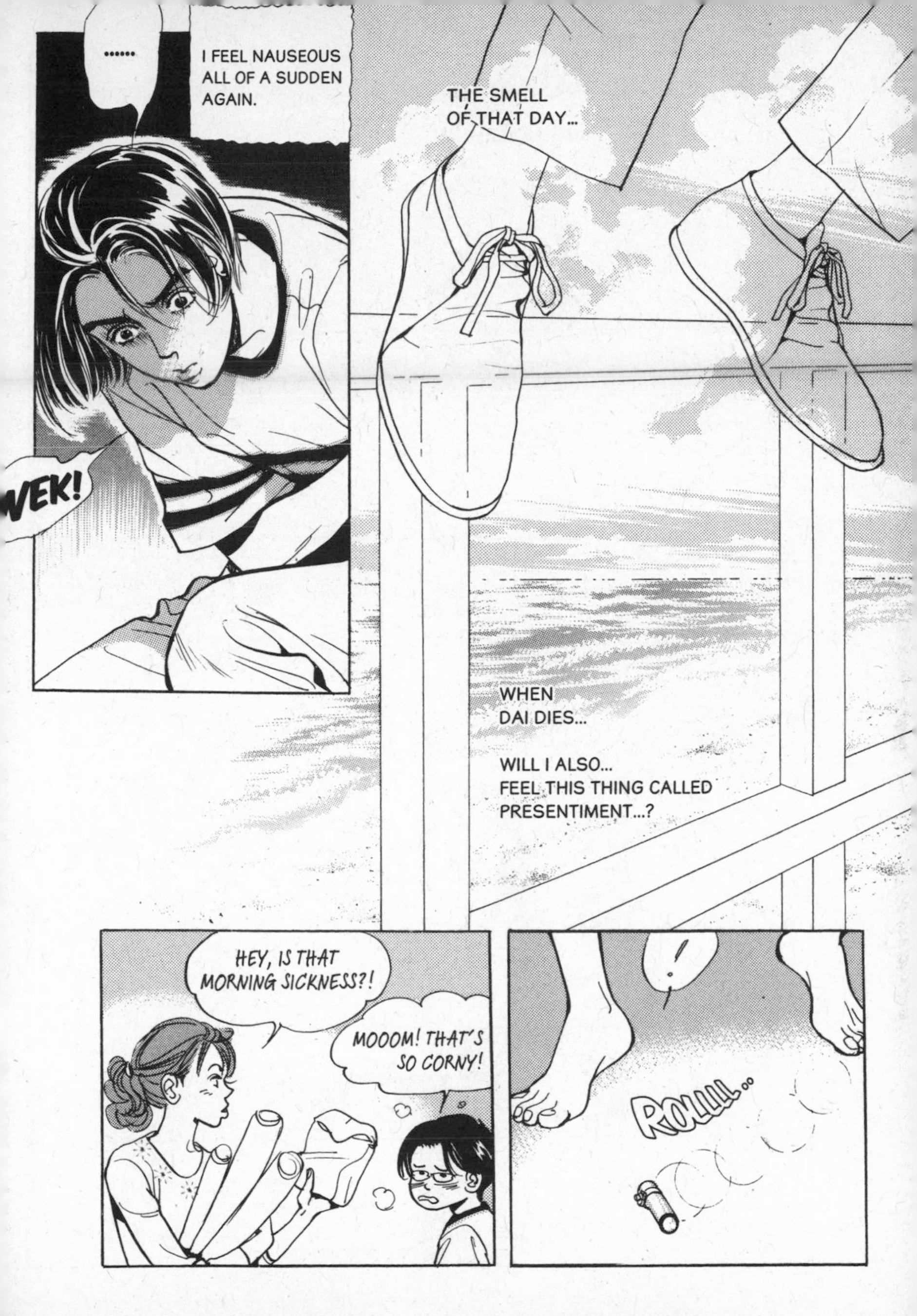
......
I FEEL NAUSEOUS ALL OF A SUDDEN AGAIN.
WEK!
THE SMELL OF THAT DAY...
WHEN DAI DIES...
WILL I ALSO... FEEL THIS THING CALLED PRESENTIMENT...?
HEY, IS THAT MORNING SICKNESS?!
MOOOM! THAT'S SO CORNY!
!
ROLLLL..

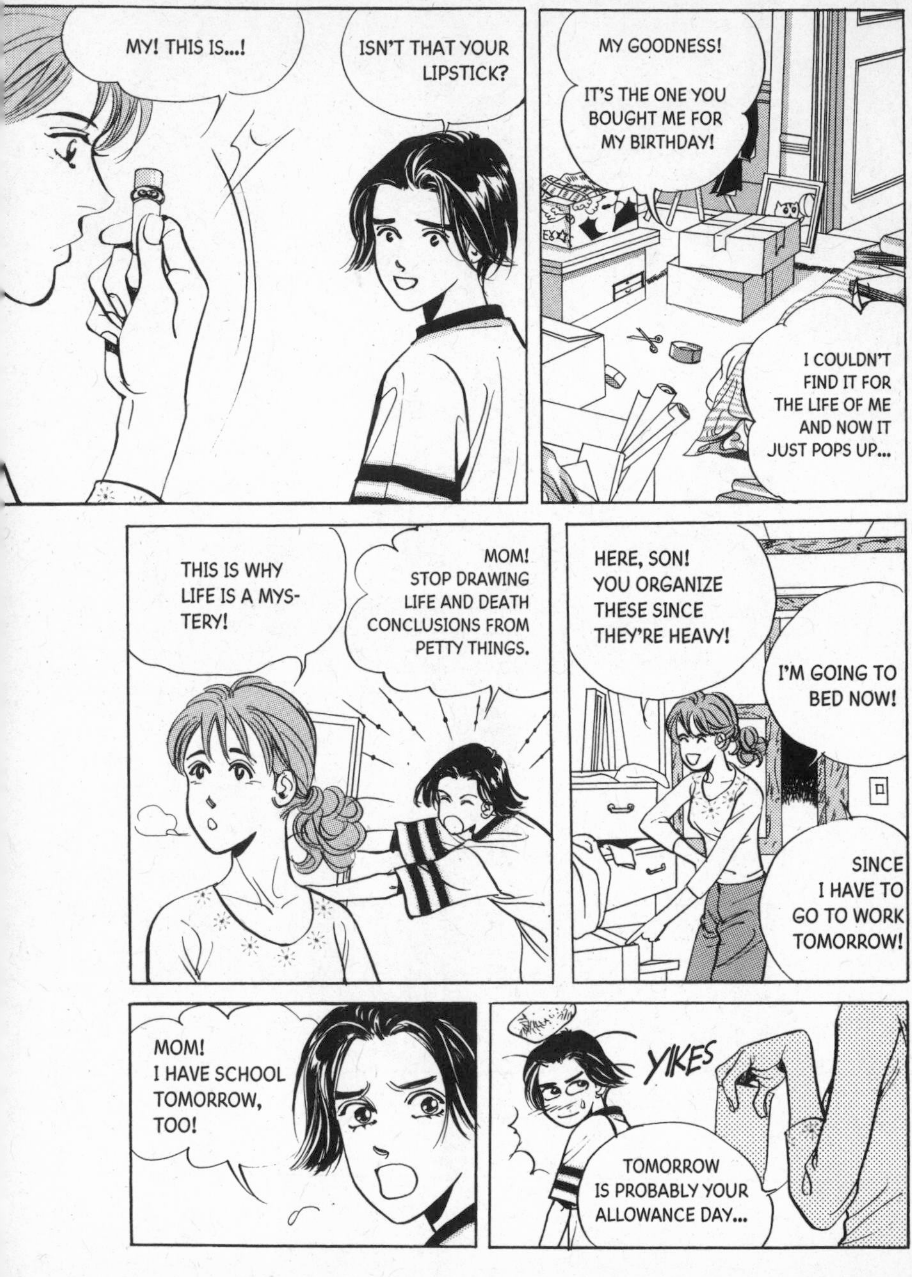
MY! THIS IS...!
ISN'T THAT YOUR LIPSTICK?
MY GOODNESS!
IT'S THE ONE YOU BOUGHT ME FOR MY BIRTHDAY!
I COULDN'T FIND IT FOR THE LIFE OF ME AND NOW IT JUST POPS UP...
THIS IS WHY LIFE IS A MYS-TERY!
MOM! STOP DRAWING LIFE AND DEATH CONCLUSIONS FROM PETTY THINGS.
HERE, SON! YOU ORGANIZE THESE SINCE THEY'RE HEAVY!
I'M GOING TO BED NOW!
SINCE I HAVE TO GO TO WORK TOMORROW!
MOM! I HAVE SCHOOL TOMORROW, TOO!
YIKES
TOMORROW IS PROBABLY YOUR ALLOWANCE DAY...

JEEEEEZ~! I DON'T KNOW IF I'M A SON OR A FARM SERVANT.

ALRIGHT!

WHO DO YOU THINK GETS MORE MONEY, A SON OR A FARM SERVANT?

A FARM SERVANT!

YOU SURE ARE SMART. YOU ARE A VOLUNTEER FARM SERVANT.

I'M GOING TO LEAVE THIS RIGHT HERE.

SINCE THAT DAY...

THERE HAVE BEEN MANY CHANGES IN US.

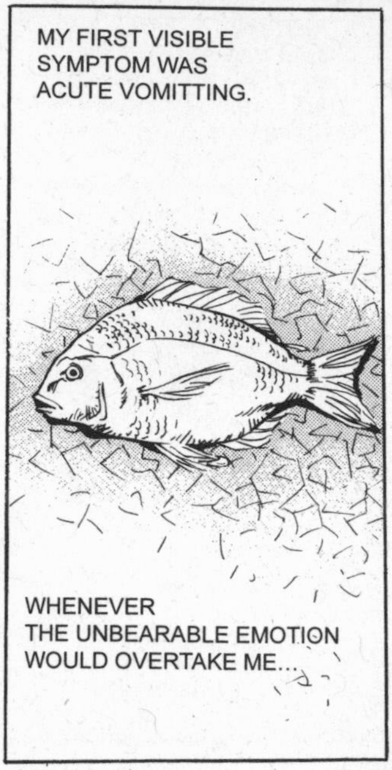
MY FIRST VISIBLE SYMPTOM WAS ACUTE VOMITTING.
WHENEVER THE UNBEARABLE EMOTION WOULD OVERTAKE ME...
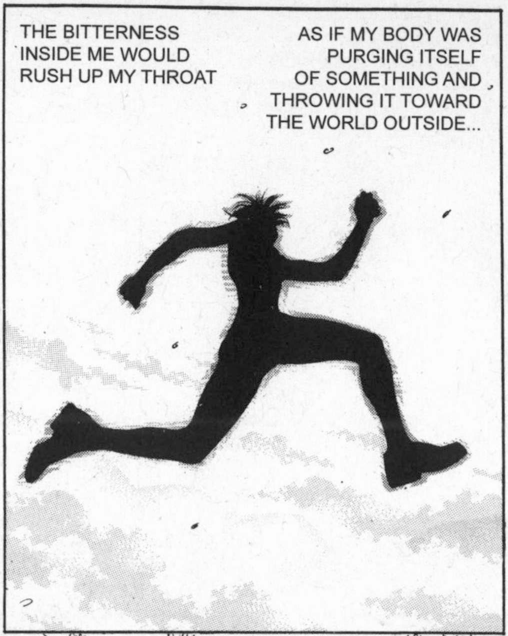
THE BITTERNESS INSIDE ME WOULD RUSH UP MY THROAT
AS IF MY BODY WAS PURGING ITSELF OF SOMETHING AND THROWING IT TOWARD THE WORLD OUTSIDE...
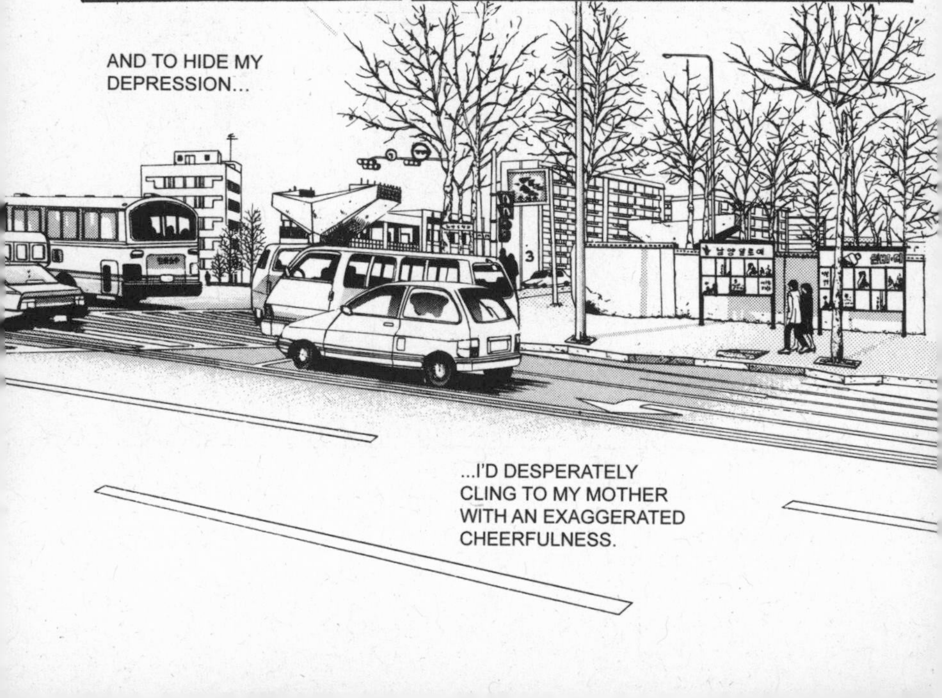
AND TO HIDE MY DEPRESSION...
...I'D DESPERATELY CLING TO MY MOTHER WITH AN EXAGGERATED CHEERFULNESS.

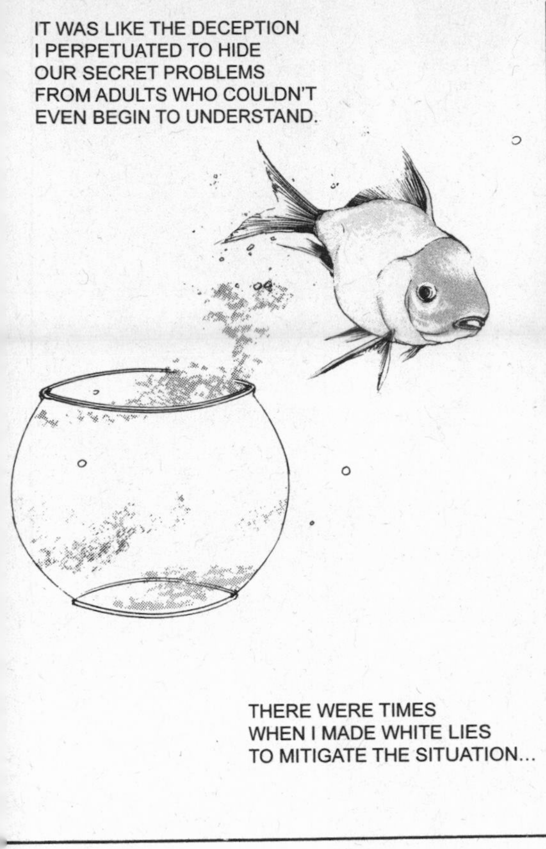
IT WAS LIKE THE DECEPTION I PERPETUATED TO HIDE OUR SECRET PROBLEMS FROM ADULTS WHO COULDN'T EVEN BEGIN TO UNDERSTAND.
THERE WERE TIMES WHEN I MADE WHITE LIES TO MITIGATE THE SITUATION...
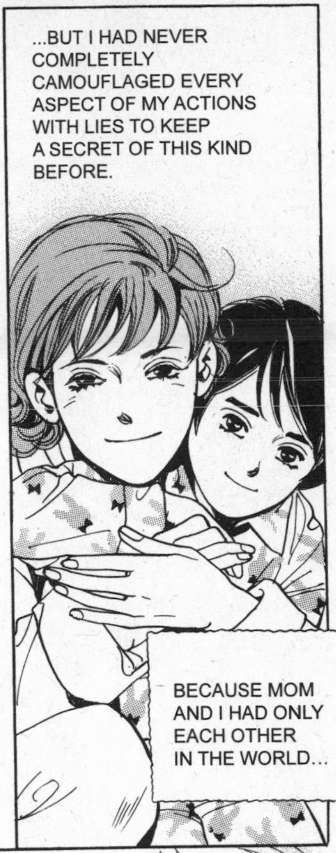
...BUT I HAD NEVER COMPLETELY CAMOUFLAGED EVERY ASPECT OF MY ACTIONS WITH LIES TO KEEP A SECRET OF THIS KIND BEFORE.
BECAUSE MOM AND I HAD ONLY EACH OTHER IN THE WORLD...
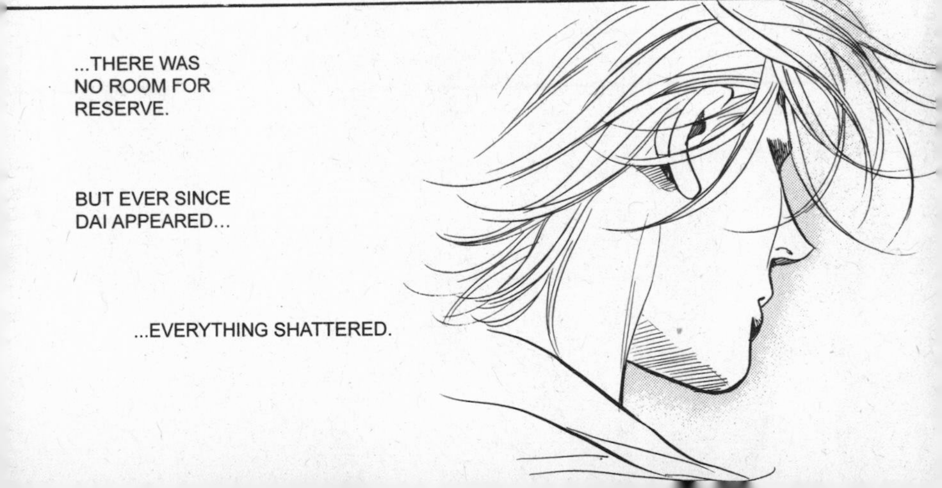
...THERE WAS NO ROOM FOR RESERVE.
BUT EVER SINCE DAI APPEARED...
...EVERYTHING SHATTERED.

THE NIGHT
I STABBED DAI
WITH A KNIFE...

I HAD
A TERRIBLE
DREAM.

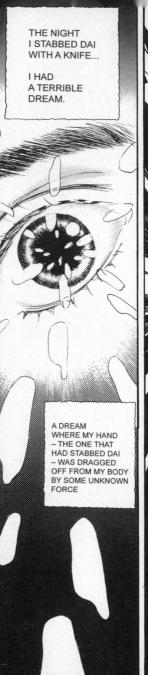

A DREAM
WHERE MY HAND
— THE ONE THAT
HAD STABBED DAI
— WAS DRAGGED
OFF FROM MY BODY
BY SOME UNKNOWN
FORCE

AND WAS
BRUTALLY CUT
INTO PIECES...

PERHAPS
THE MOMENT
MY STRENGTH
WAS ADDED...

TO DAI'S HAND
THAT WAS PULLING
MY HAND HOLDING
A KNIFE...

I HAD BEGUN TO LIVE
LIFE ON A DIFFERENT
PLANE.

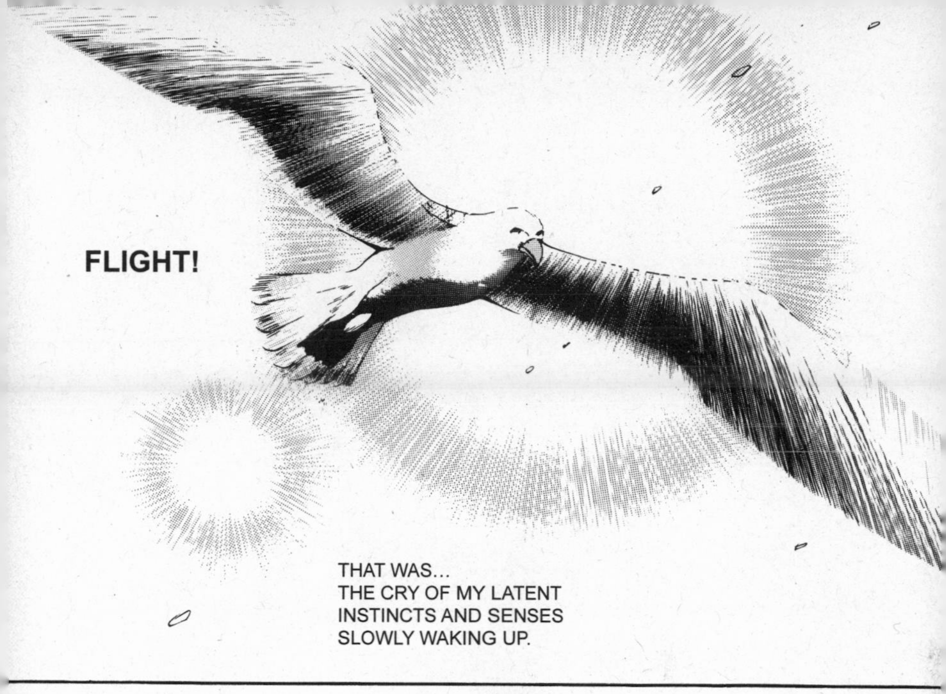
FLIGHT!
THAT WAS... THE CRY OF MY LATENT INSTINCTS AND SENSES SLOWLY WAKING UP.
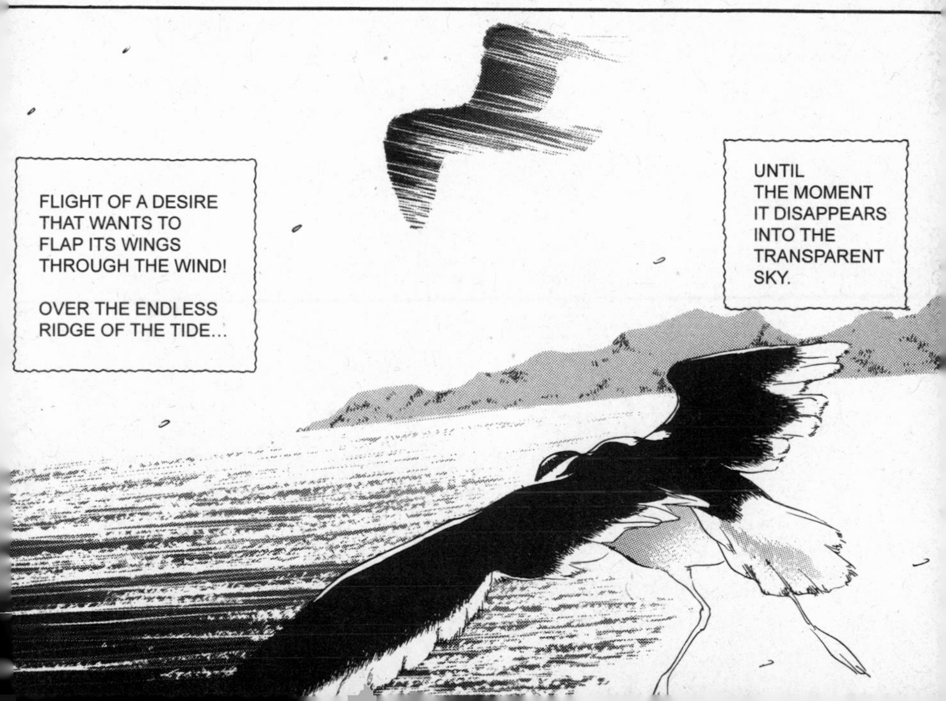
FLIGHT OF A DESIRE THAT WANTS TO FLAP ITS WINGS THROUGH THE WIND!
OVER THE ENDLESS RIDGE OF THE TIDE...
UNTIL THE MOMENT IT DISAPPEARS INTO THE TRANSPARENT SKY.

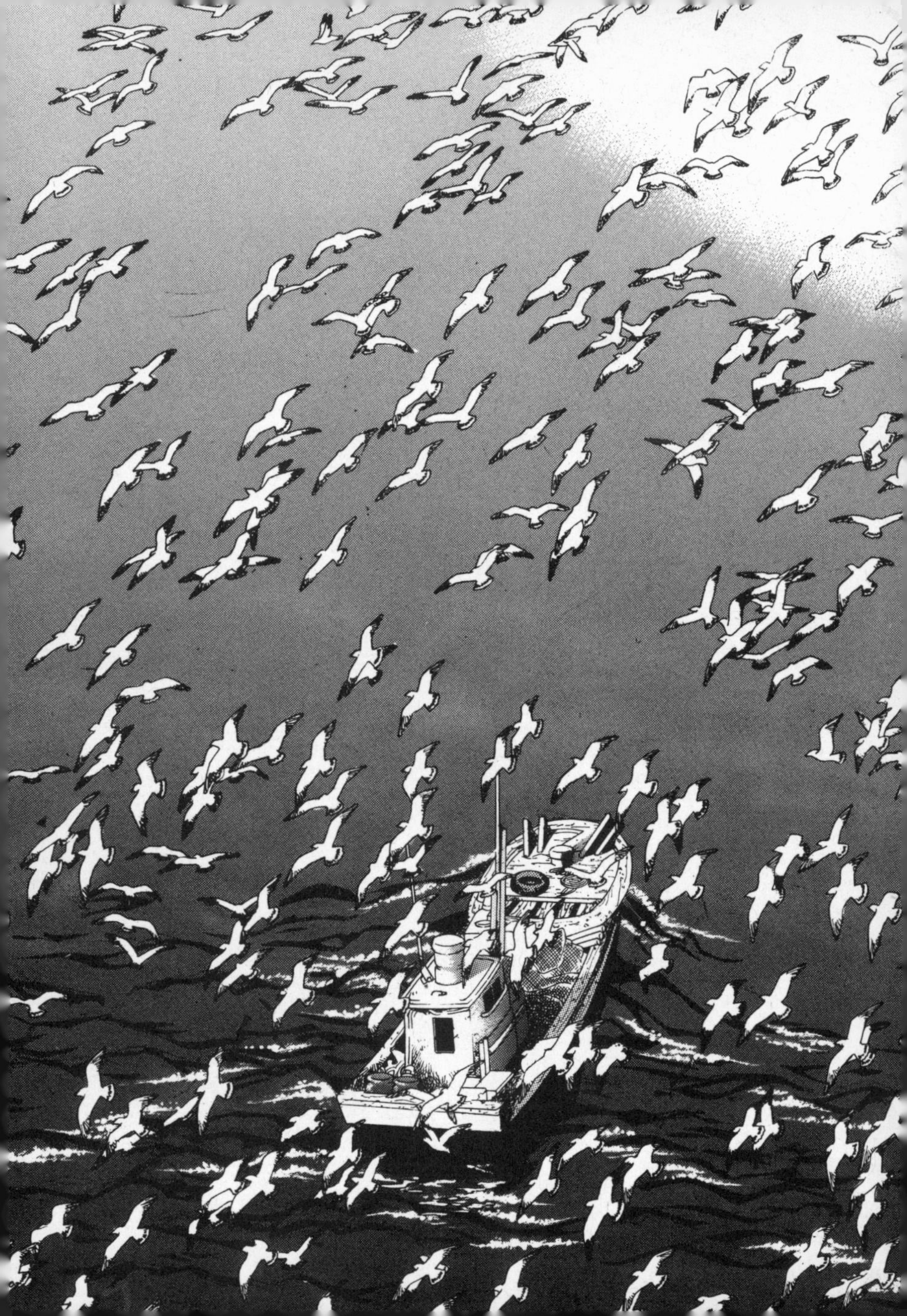

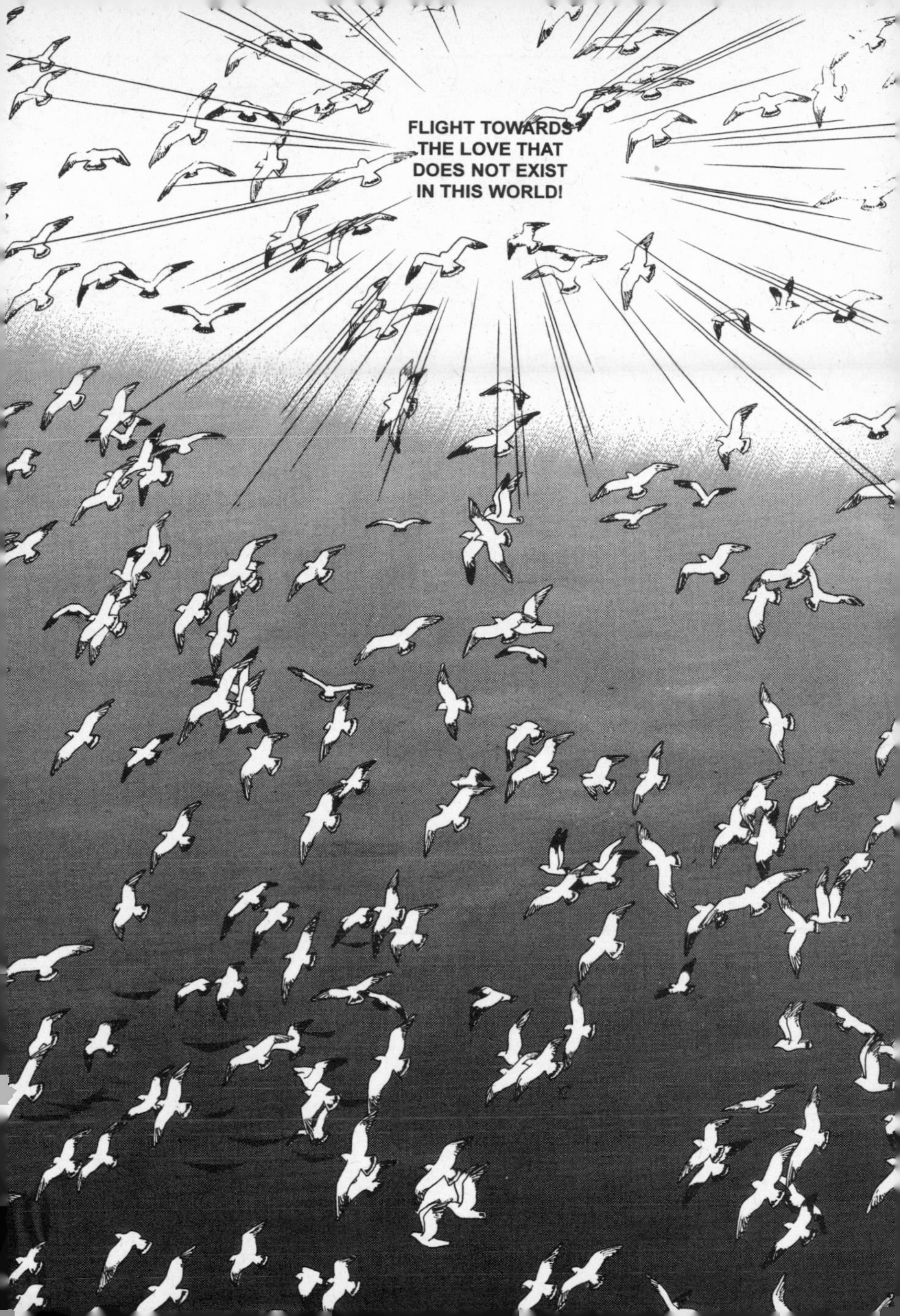
FLIGHT TOWARDS THE LOVE THAT DOES NOT EXIST IN THIS WORLD!

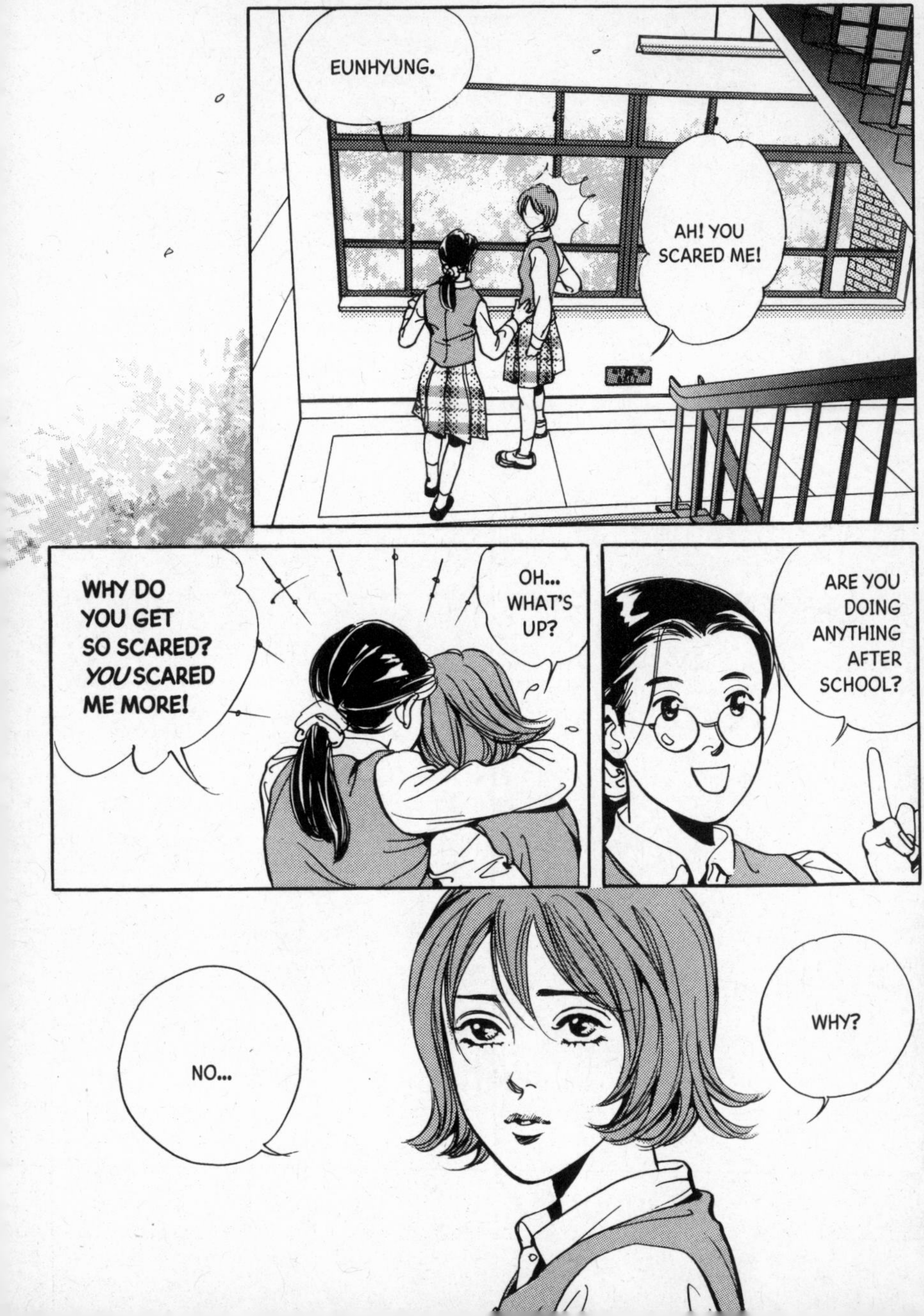
EUNHYUNG.
AH! YOU SCARED ME!
WHY DO YOU GET SO SCARED? *YOU* SCARED ME MORE!
OH... WHAT'S UP?
ARE YOU DOING ANYTHING AFTER SCHOOL?
NO...
WHY?

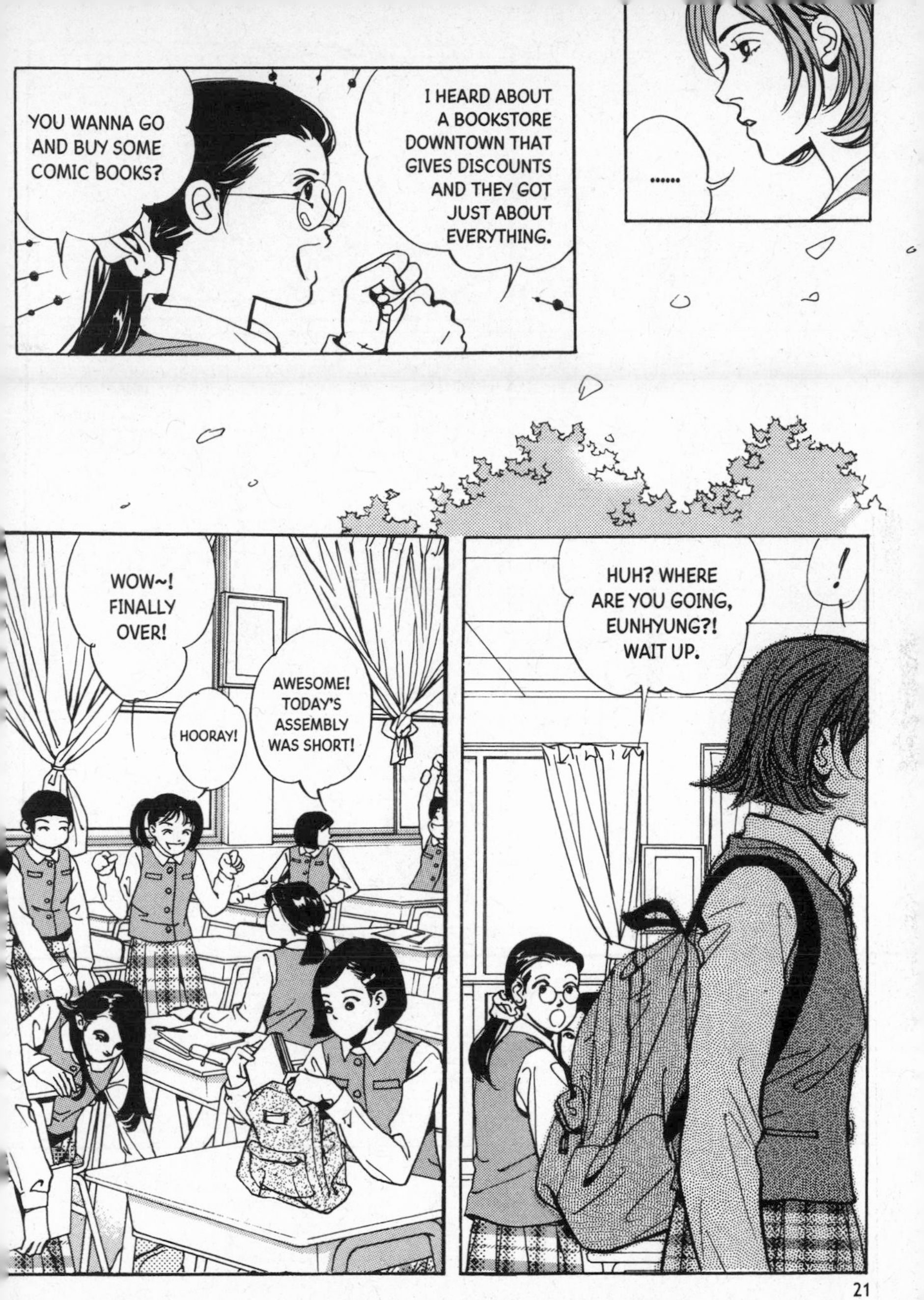

YOU WANNA GO AND BUY SOME COMIC BOOKS?
I HEARD ABOUT A BOOKSTORE DOWNTOWN THAT GIVES DISCOUNTS AND THEY GOT JUST ABOUT EVERYTHING.
......
WOW~! FINALLY OVER!
HOORAY!
AWESOME! TODAY'S ASSEMBLY WAS SHORT!
HUH? WHERE ARE YOU GOING, EUNHYUNG?! WAIT UP.
!

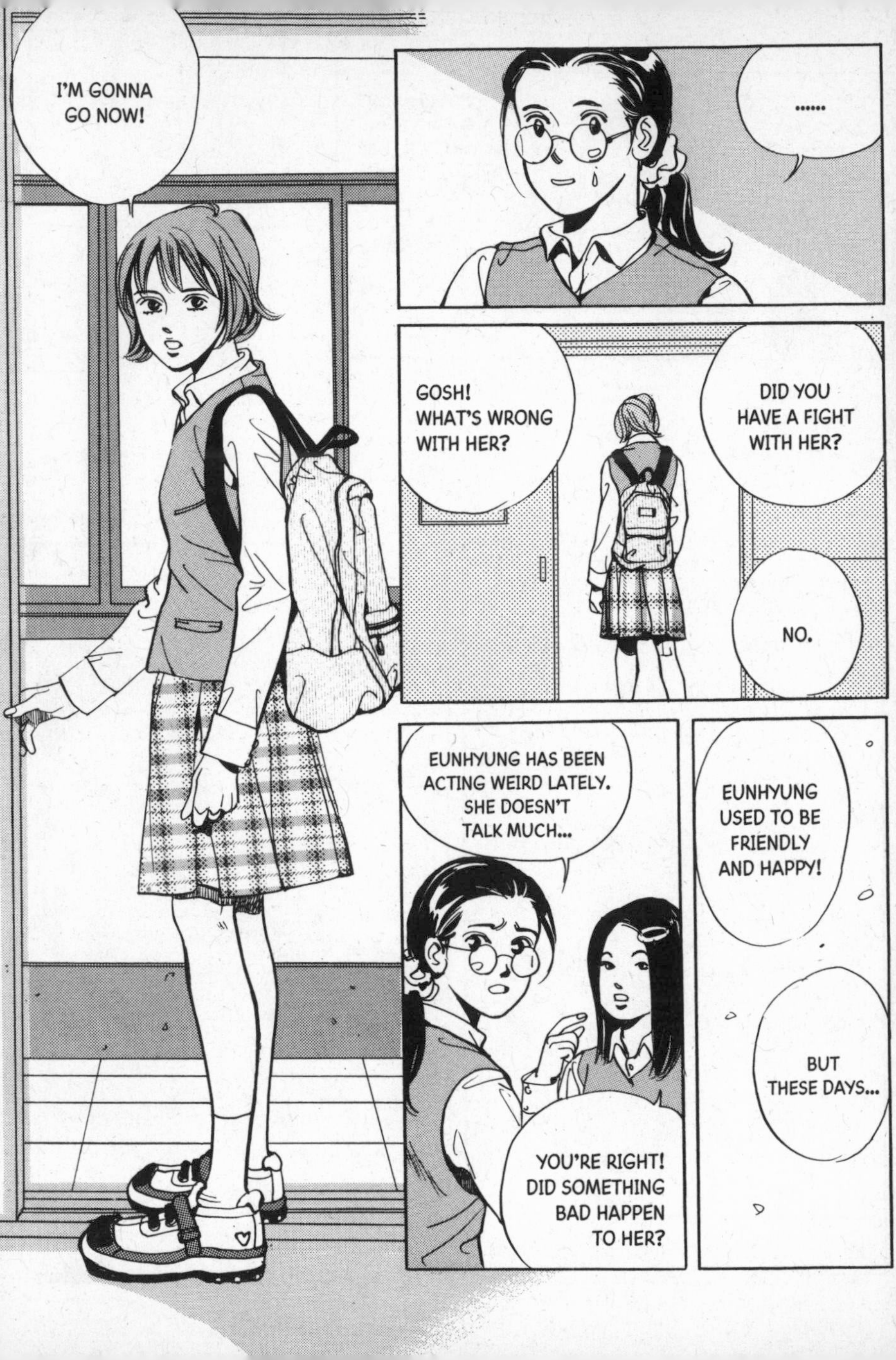
I'M GONNA GO NOW!
......
GOSH! WHAT'S WRONG WITH HER?
DID YOU HAVE A FIGHT WITH HER?
NO.
EUNHYUNG HAS BEEN ACTING WEIRD LATELY. SHE DOESN'T TALK MUCH...
YOU'RE RIGHT! DID SOMETHING BAD HAPPEN TO HER?
EUNHYUNG USED TO BE FRIENDLY AND HAPPY!
BUT THESE DAYS...

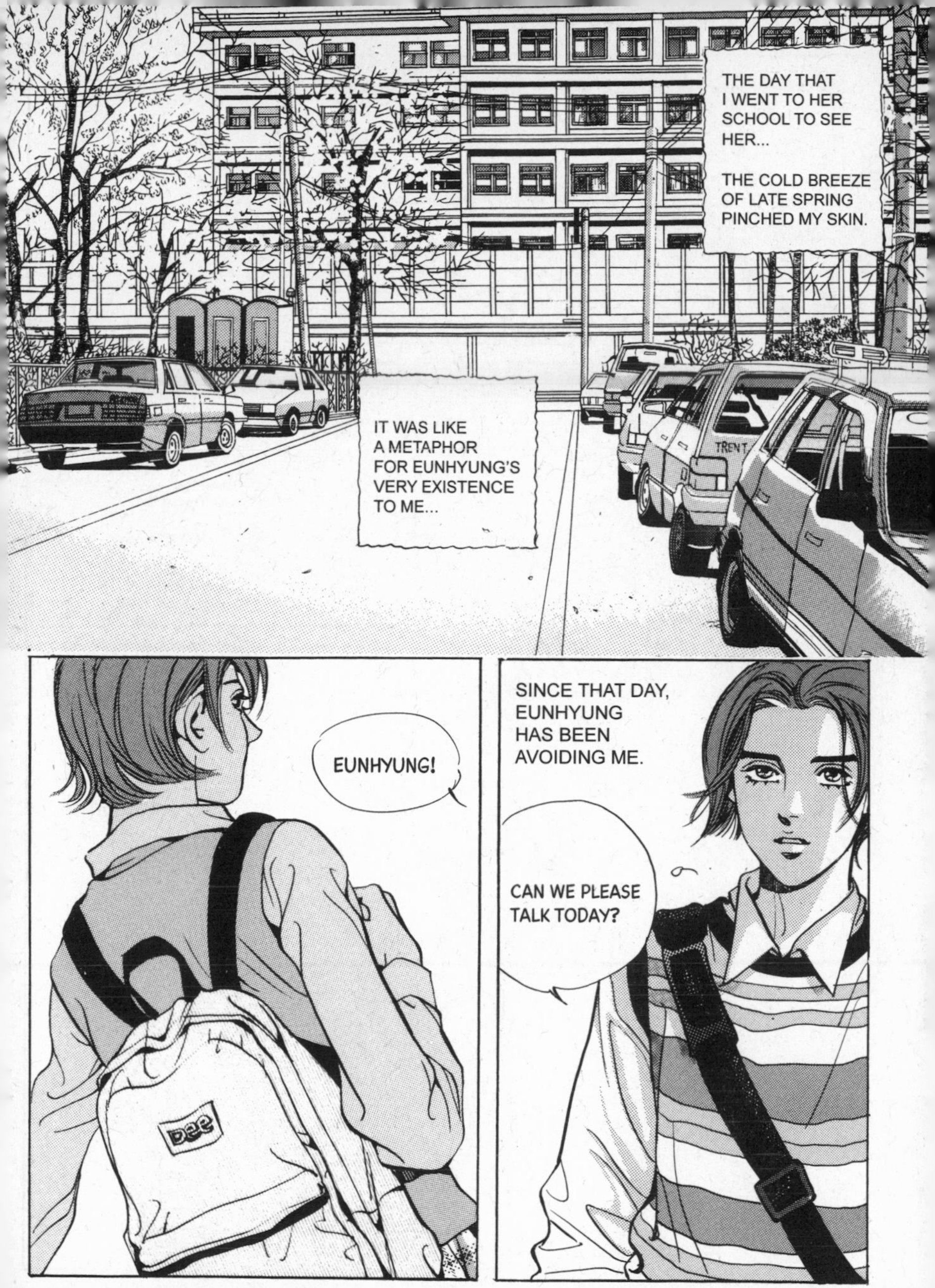
THE DAY THAT I WENT TO HER SCHOOL TO SEE HER...
THE COLD BREEZE OF LATE SPRING PINCHED MY SKIN.
IT WAS LIKE A METAPHOR FOR EUNHYUNG'S VERY EXISTENCE TO ME...
TRENT
EUNHYUNG!
SINCE THAT DAY, EUNHYUNG HAS BEEN AVOIDING ME.
CAN WE PLEASE TALK TODAY?

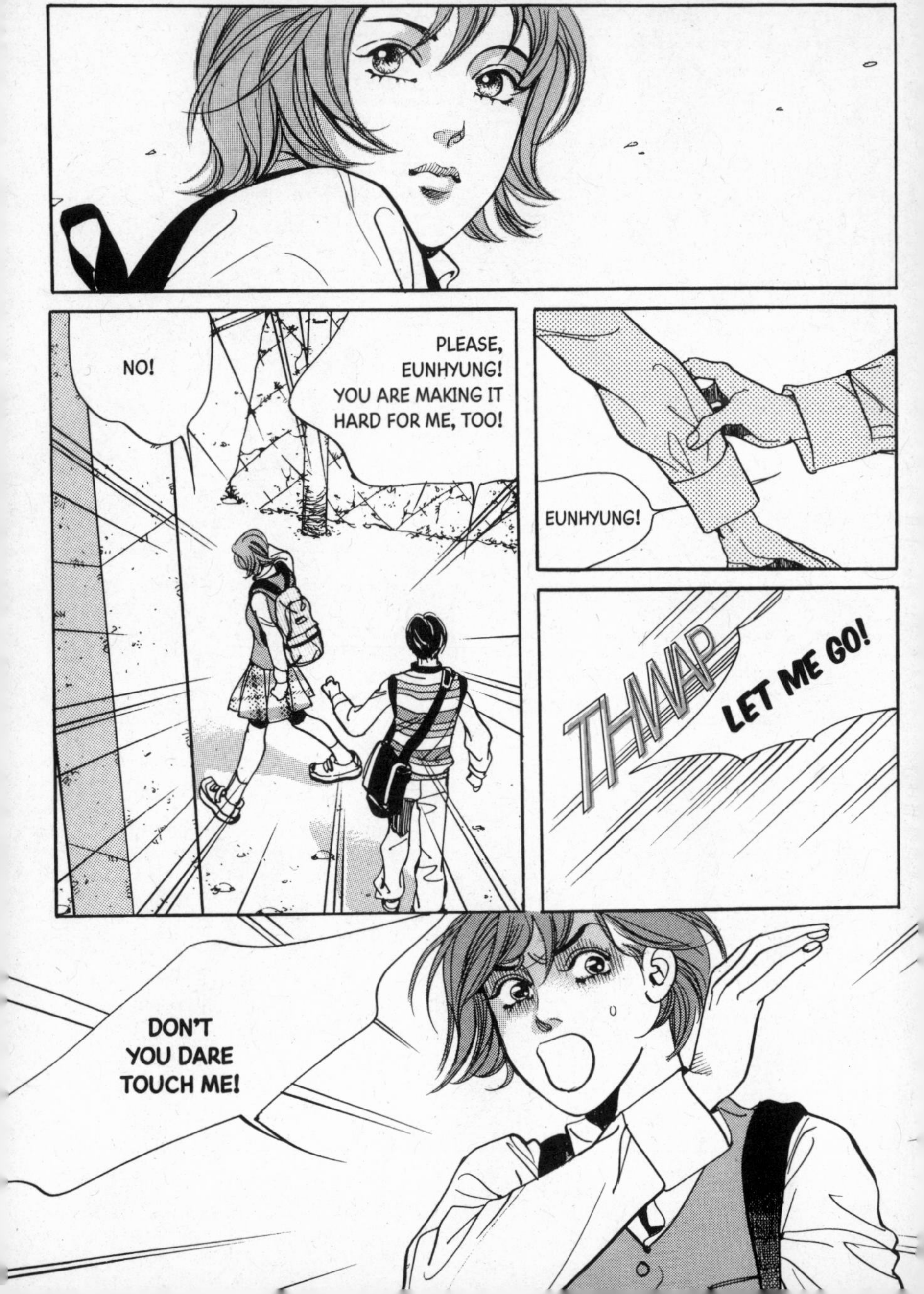
NO!
PLEASE, EUNHYUNG! YOU ARE MAKING IT HARD FOR ME, TOO!
EUNHYUNG!
THWAP
LET ME GO!
DON'T YOU DARE TOUCH ME!

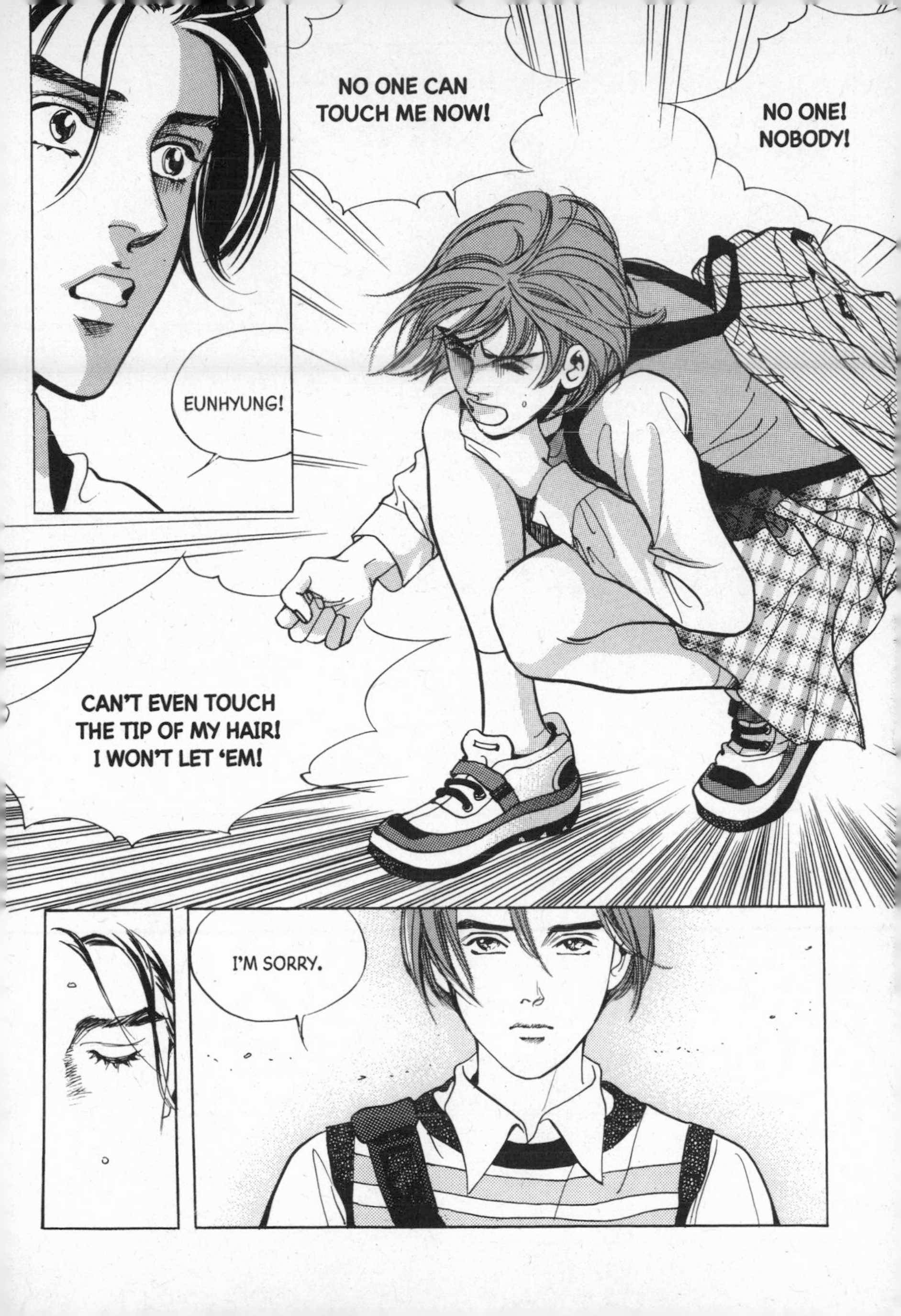
EUNHYUNG!
NO ONE CAN TOUCH ME NOW!
NO ONE! NOBODY!
CAN'T EVEN TOUCH THE TIP OF MY HAIR! I WON'T LET 'EM!
I'M SORRY.

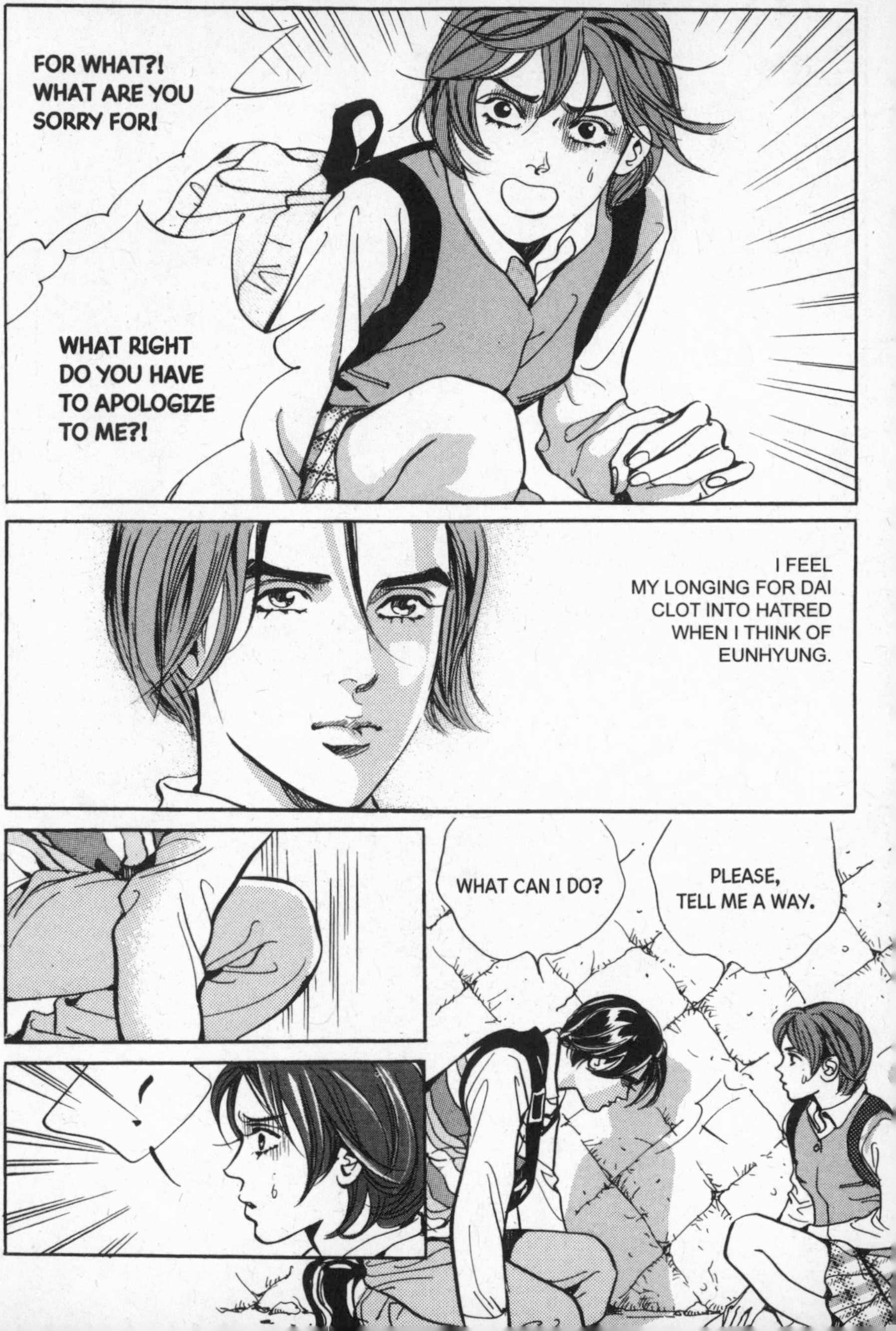
FOR WHAT?! WHAT ARE YOU SORRY FOR!
WHAT RIGHT DO YOU HAVE TO APOLOGIZE TO ME?!
I FEEL MY LONGING FOR DAI CLOT INTO HATRED WHEN I THINK OF EUNHYUNG.
WHAT CAN I DO?
PLEASE, TELL ME A WAY.

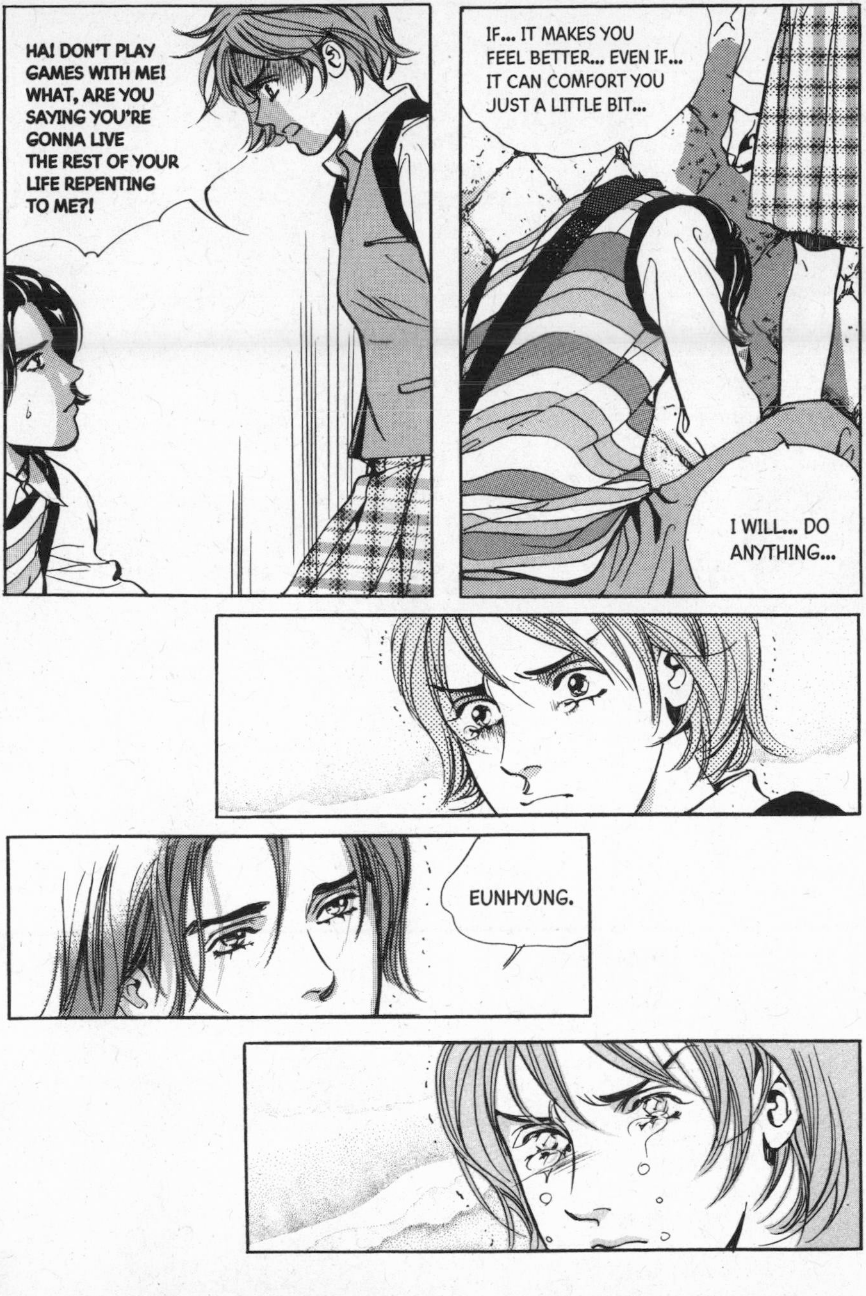
HA! DON'T PLAY GAMES WITH ME! WHAT, ARE YOU SAYING YOU'RE GONNA LIVE THE REST OF YOUR LIFE REPENTING TO ME?!
IF... IT MAKES YOU FEEL BETTER... EVEN IF... IT CAN COMFORT YOU JUST A LITTLE BIT...
I WILL... DO ANYTHING...
EUNHYUNG.

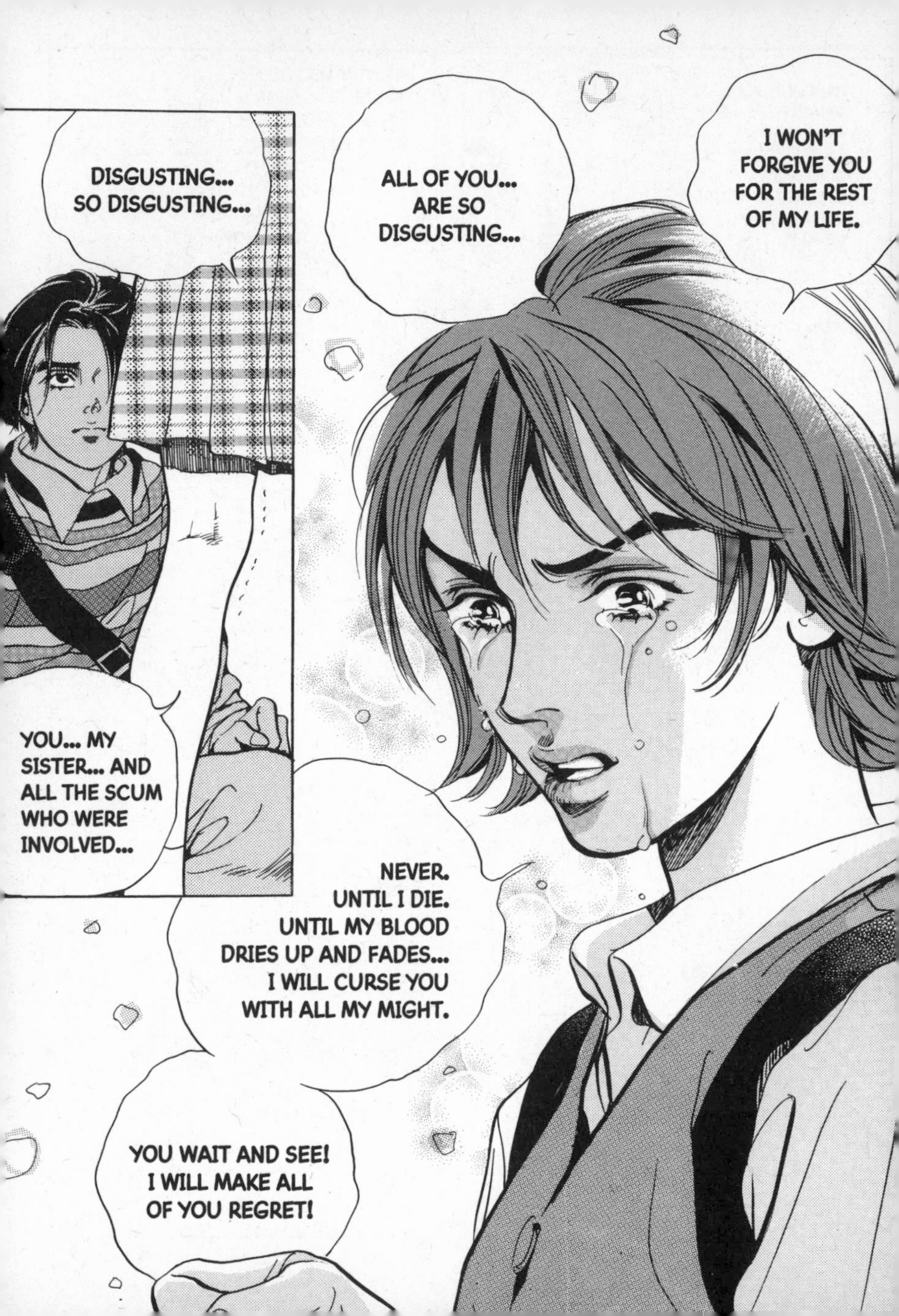
DISGUSTING... SO DISGUSTING...
YOU... MY SISTER... AND ALL THE SCUM WHO WERE INVOLVED...
ALL OF YOU... ARE SO DISGUSTING...
I WON'T FORGIVE YOU FOR THE REST OF MY LIFE.
NEVER. UNTIL I DIE. UNTIL MY BLOOD DRIES UP AND FADES... I WILL CURSE YOU WITH ALL MY MIGHT.
YOU WAIT AND SEE! I WILL MAKE ALL OF YOU REGRET!

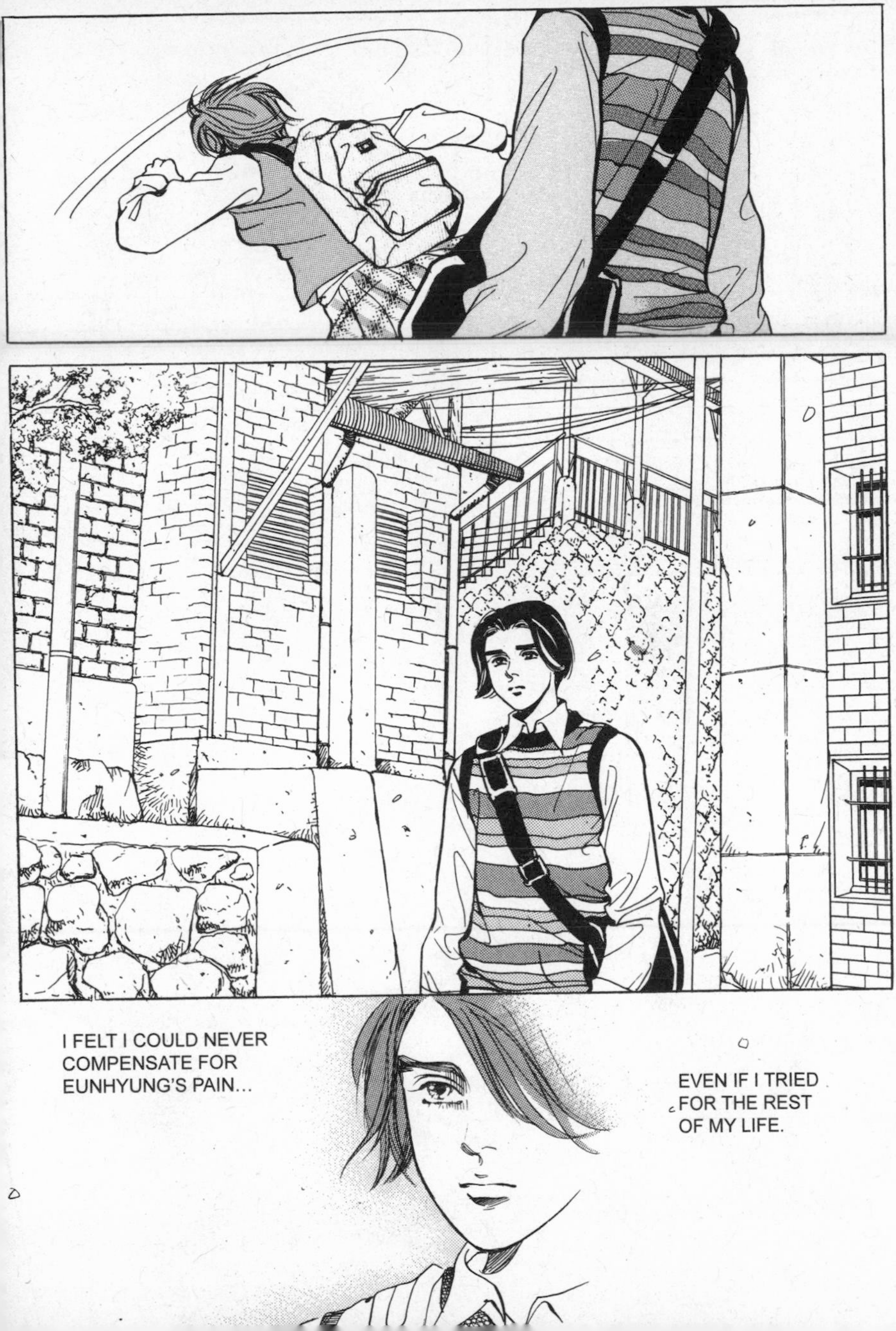
I FELT I COULD NEVER COMPENSATE FOR EUNHYUNG'S PAIN...
EVEN IF I TRIED FOR THE REST OF MY LIFE.

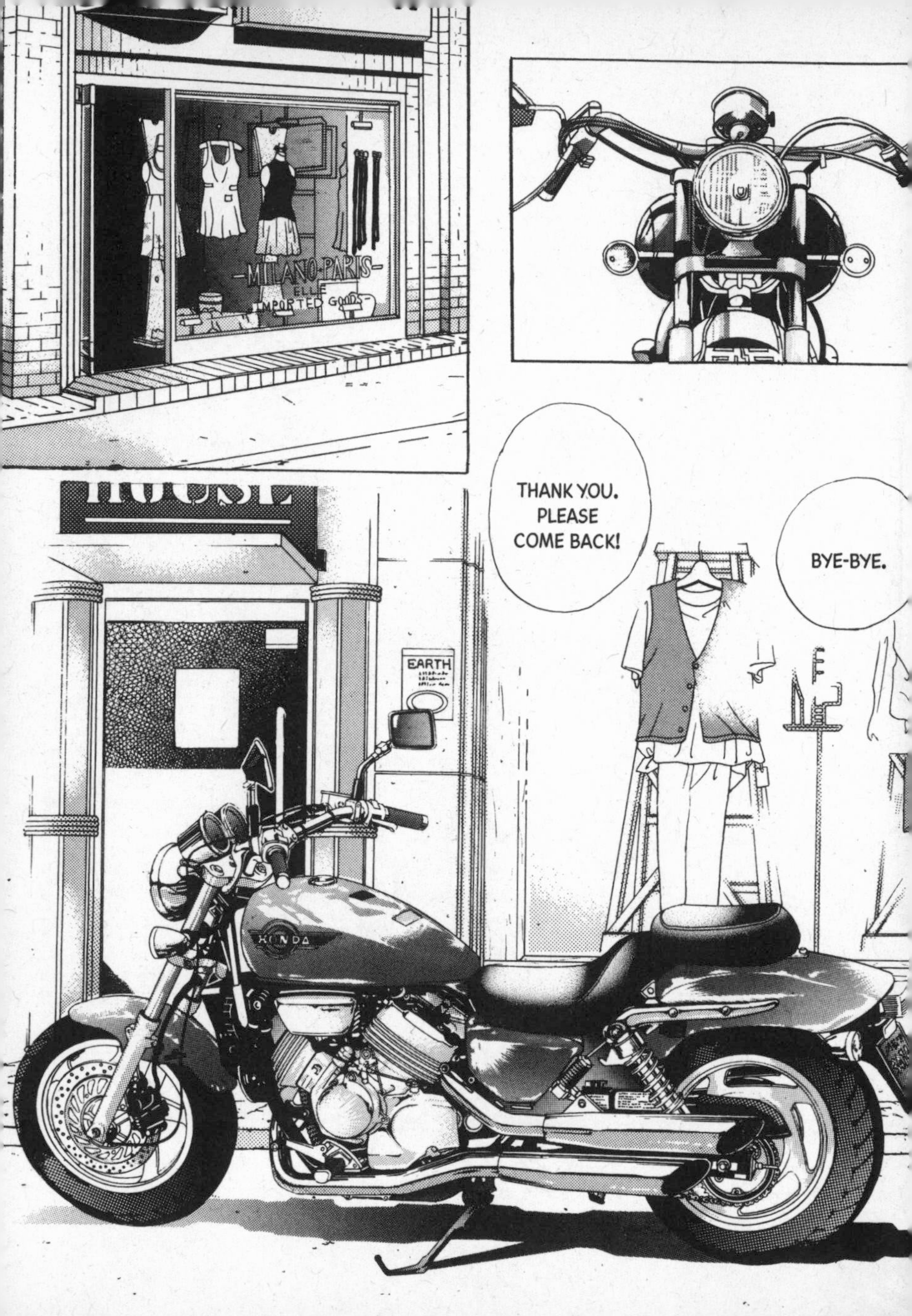

-MILANO-PARIS-
ELLE
IMPORTED GOODS
EARTH
HONDA
THANK YOU. PLEASE COME BACK!
BYE-BYE.

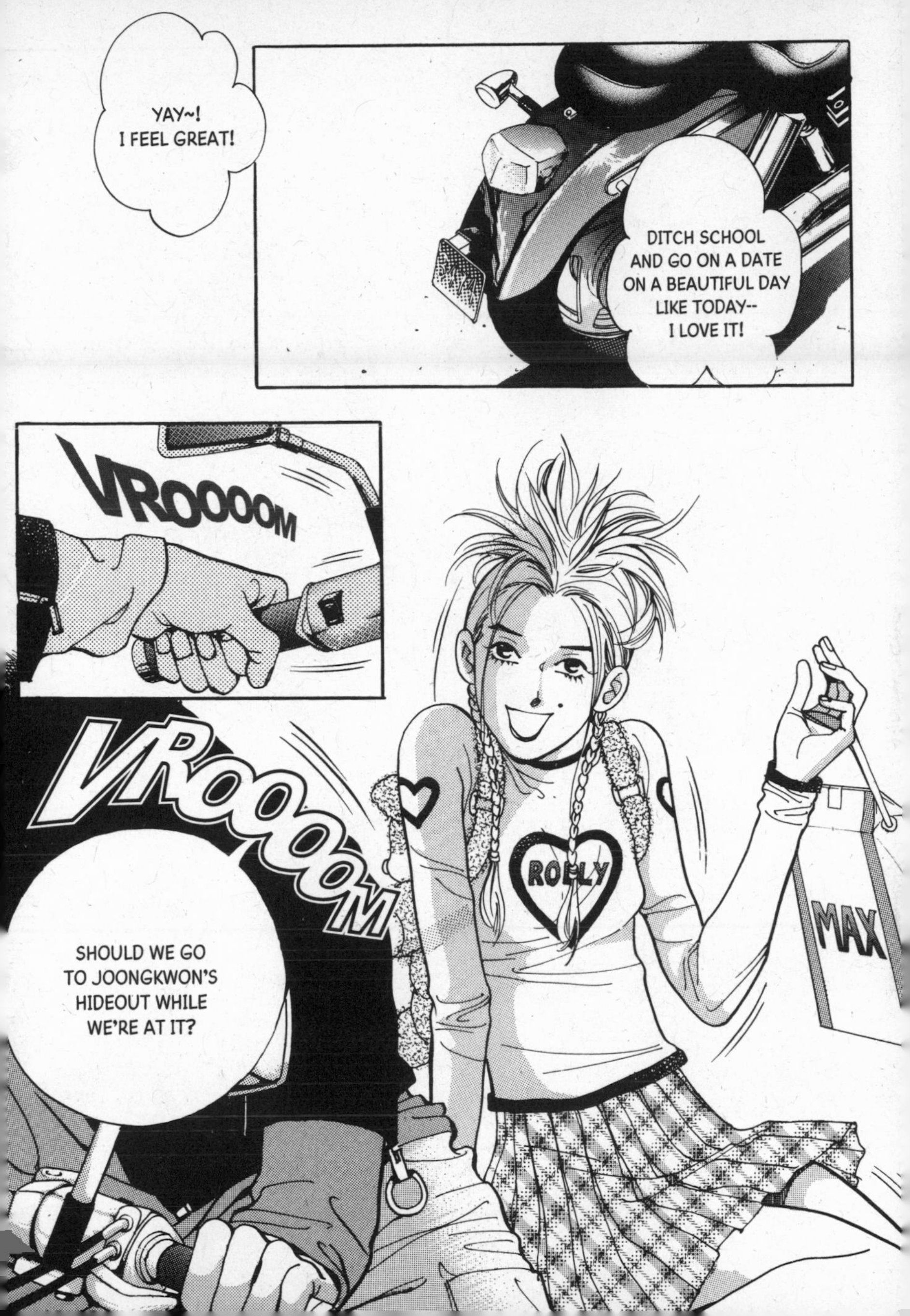
YAY~! I FEEL GREAT!
DITCH SCHOOL AND GO ON A DATE ON A BEAUTIFUL DAY LIKE TODAY-- I LOVE IT!
VROOOOM
VROOOOM
SHOULD WE GO TO JOONGKWON'S HIDEOUT WHILE WE'RE AT IT?
MAX

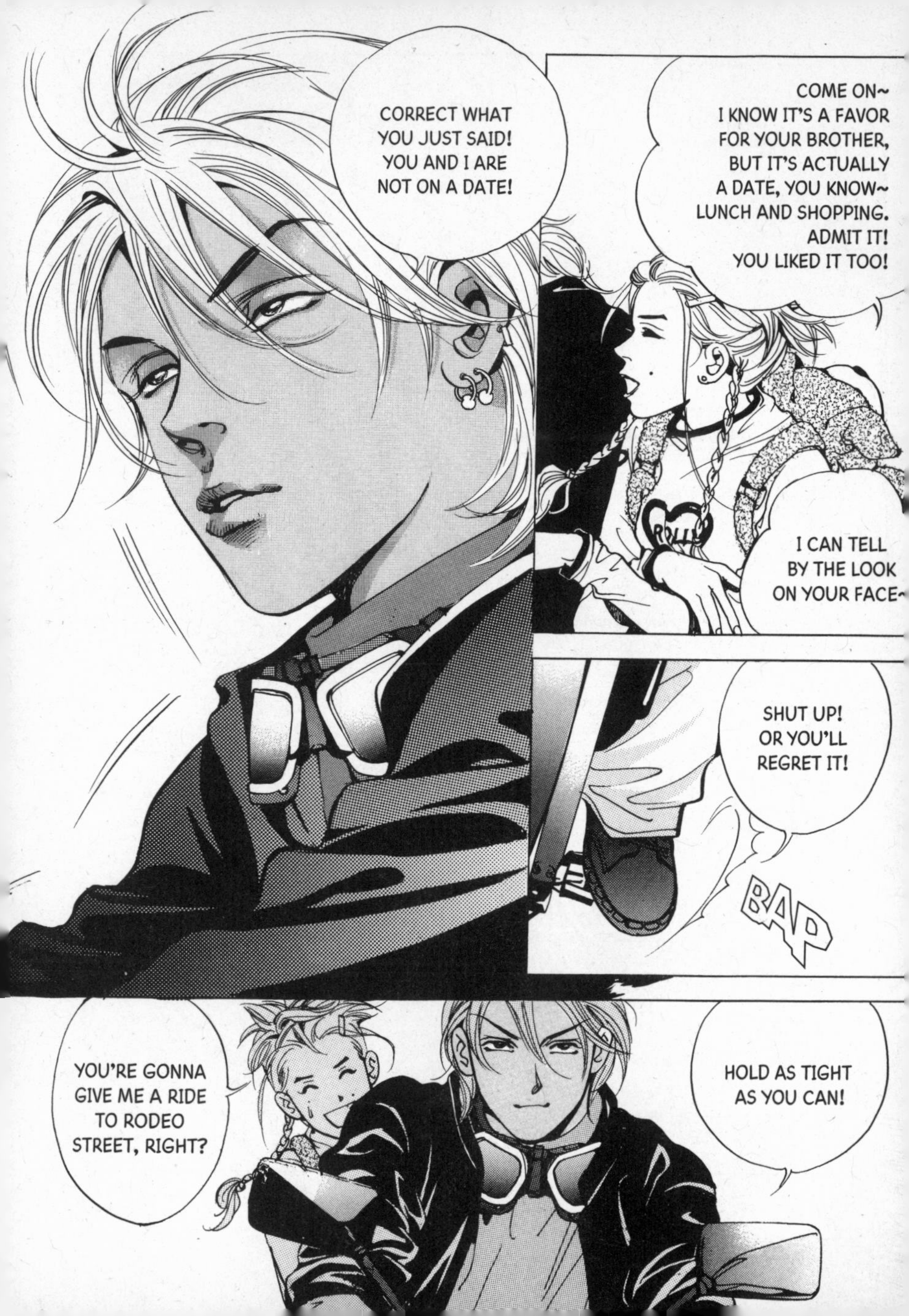
CORRECT WHAT YOU JUST SAID! YOU AND I ARE NOT ON A DATE!
COME ON~ I KNOW IT'S A FAVOR FOR YOUR BROTHER, BUT IT'S ACTUALLY A DATE, YOU KNOW~ LUNCH AND SHOPPING. ADMIT IT! YOU LIKED IT TOO!
I CAN TELL BY THE LOOK ON YOUR FACE~
SHUT UP! OR YOU'LL REGRET IT!
BAP
YOU'RE GONNA GIVE ME A RIDE TO RODEO STREET, RIGHT?
HOLD AS TIGHT AS YOU CAN!

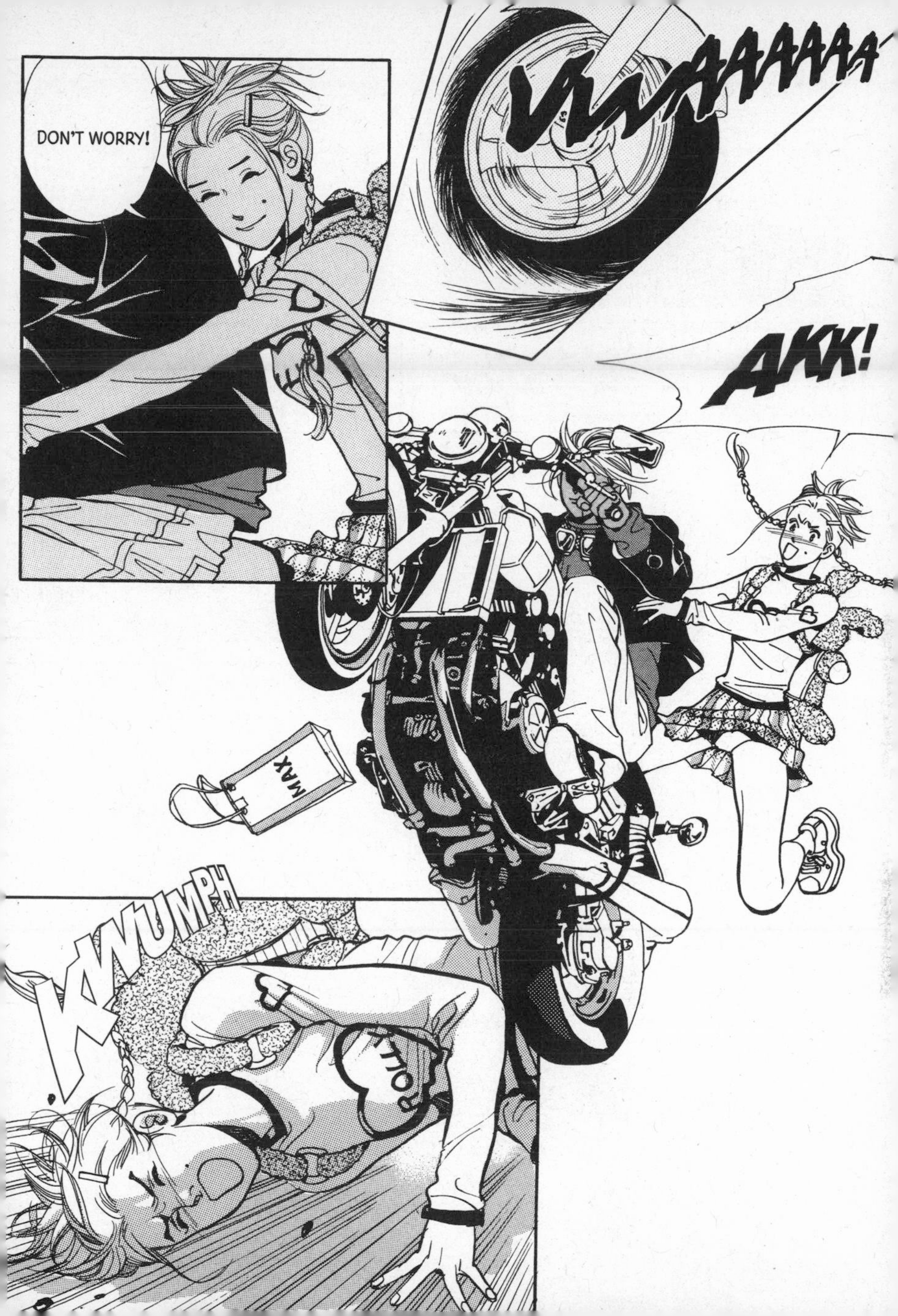
DON'T WORRY!
VRAAAAAAA
AKK!
MAX
KWUMPH
JOLLY

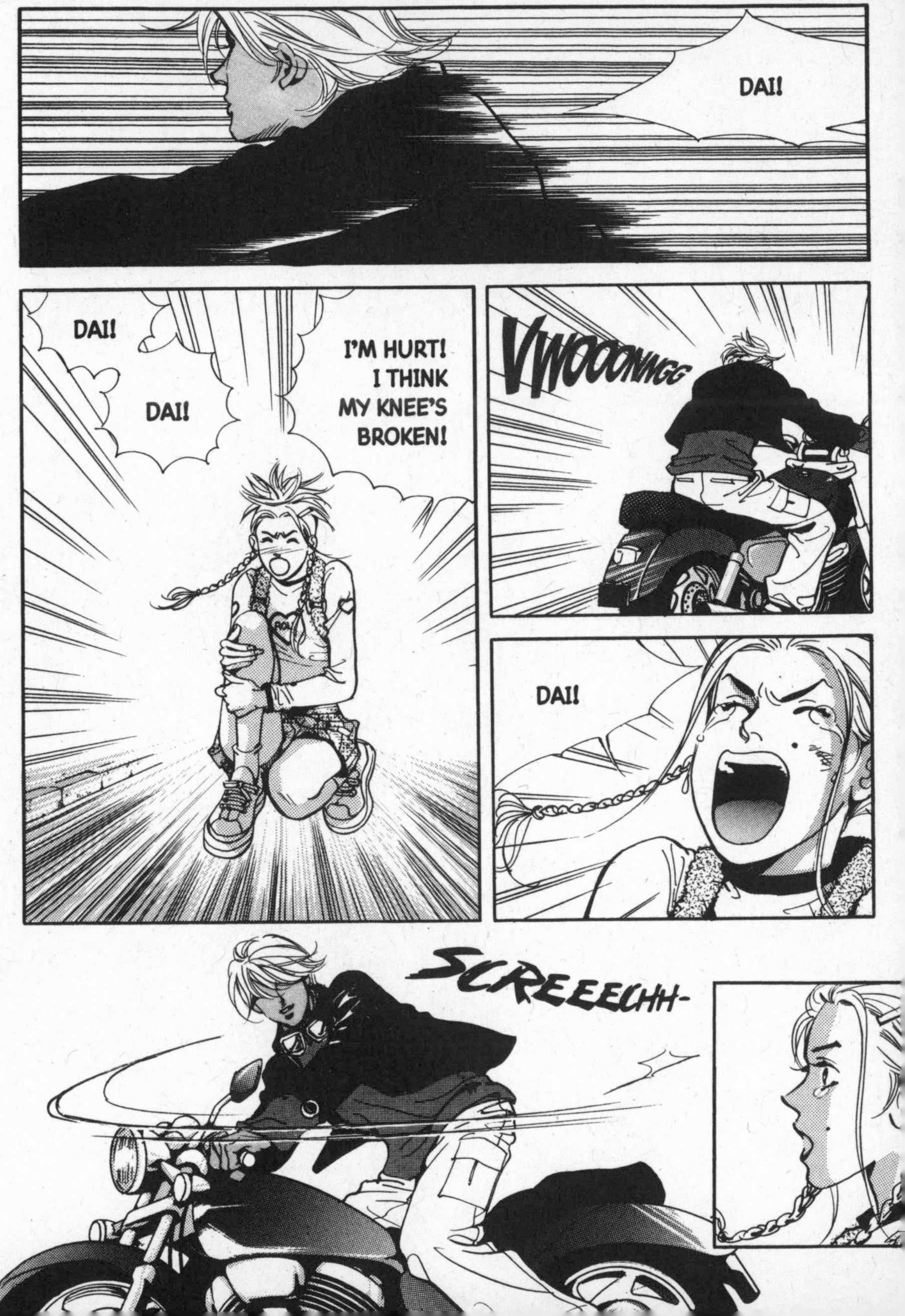
DAI!
DAI!
DAI!
I'M HURT! I THINK MY KNEE'S BROKEN!
VWOOONNGG
DAI!
SCREEECHH-

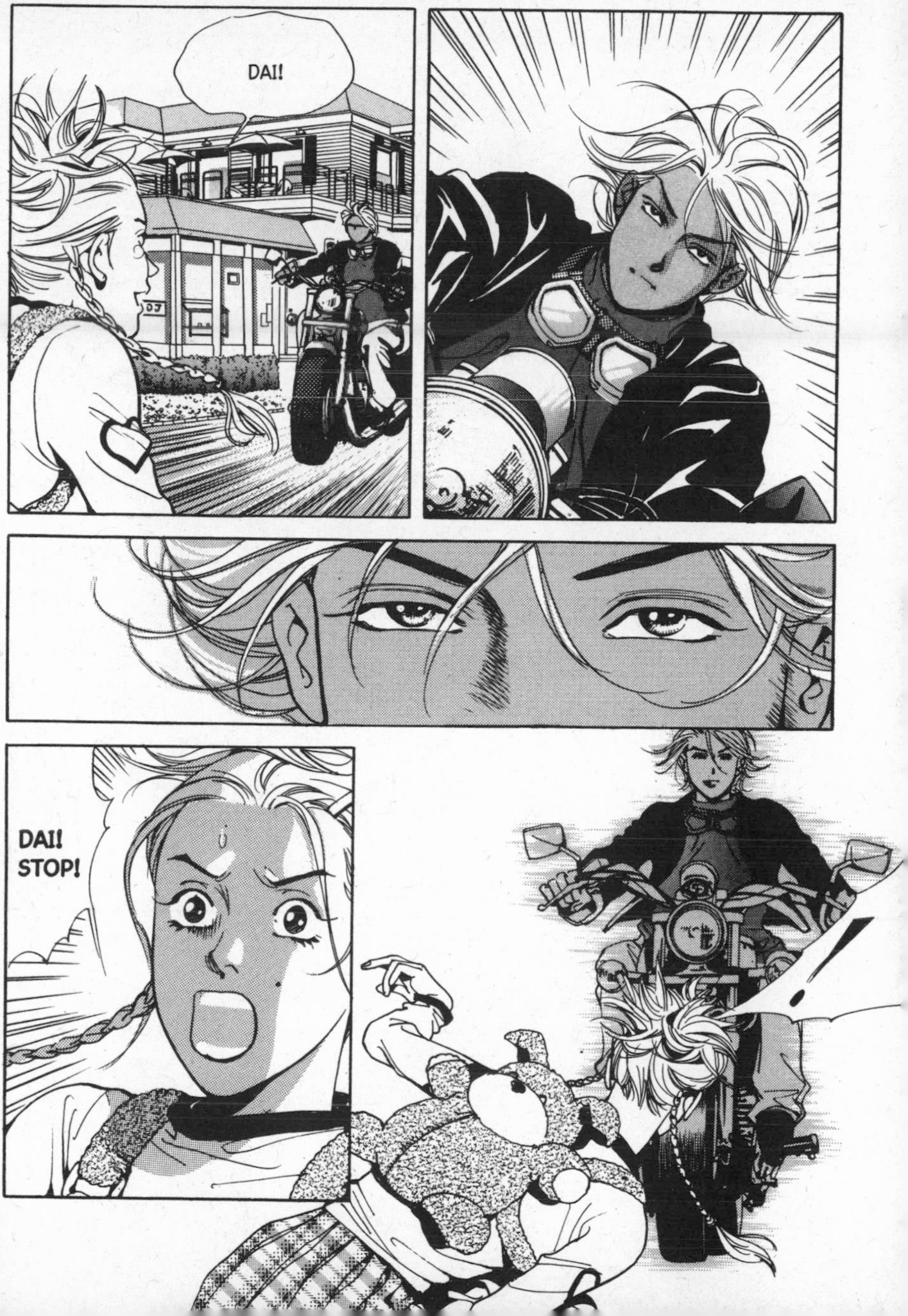
DAI!
DAI! STOP!
!

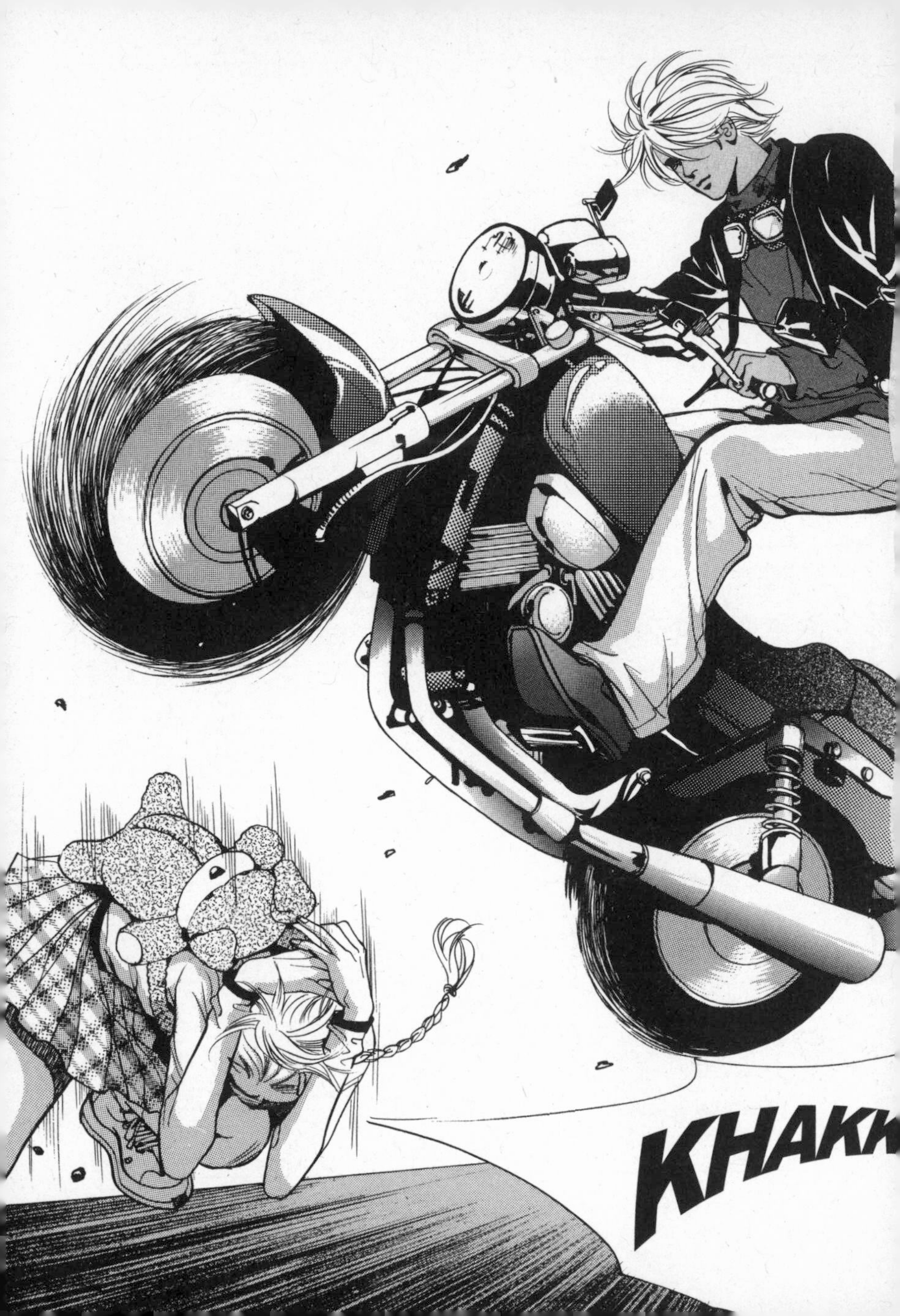
KHAKK

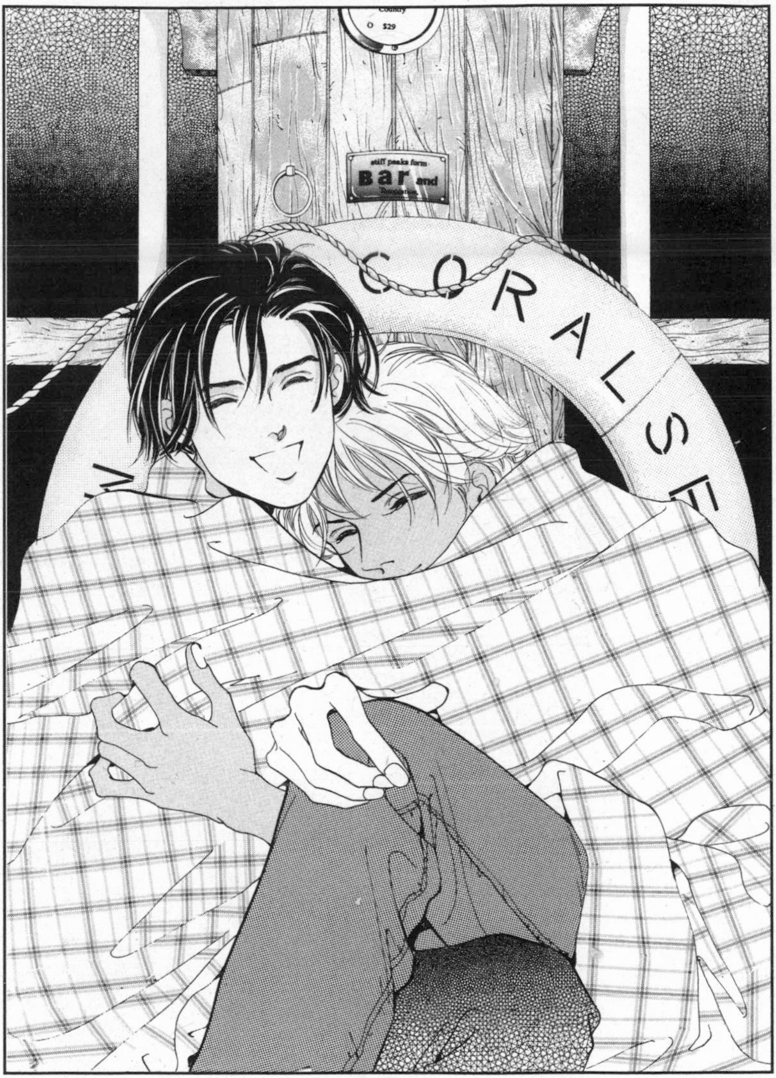
Country
$29
stiff peaks form
Bar and
CORALSE

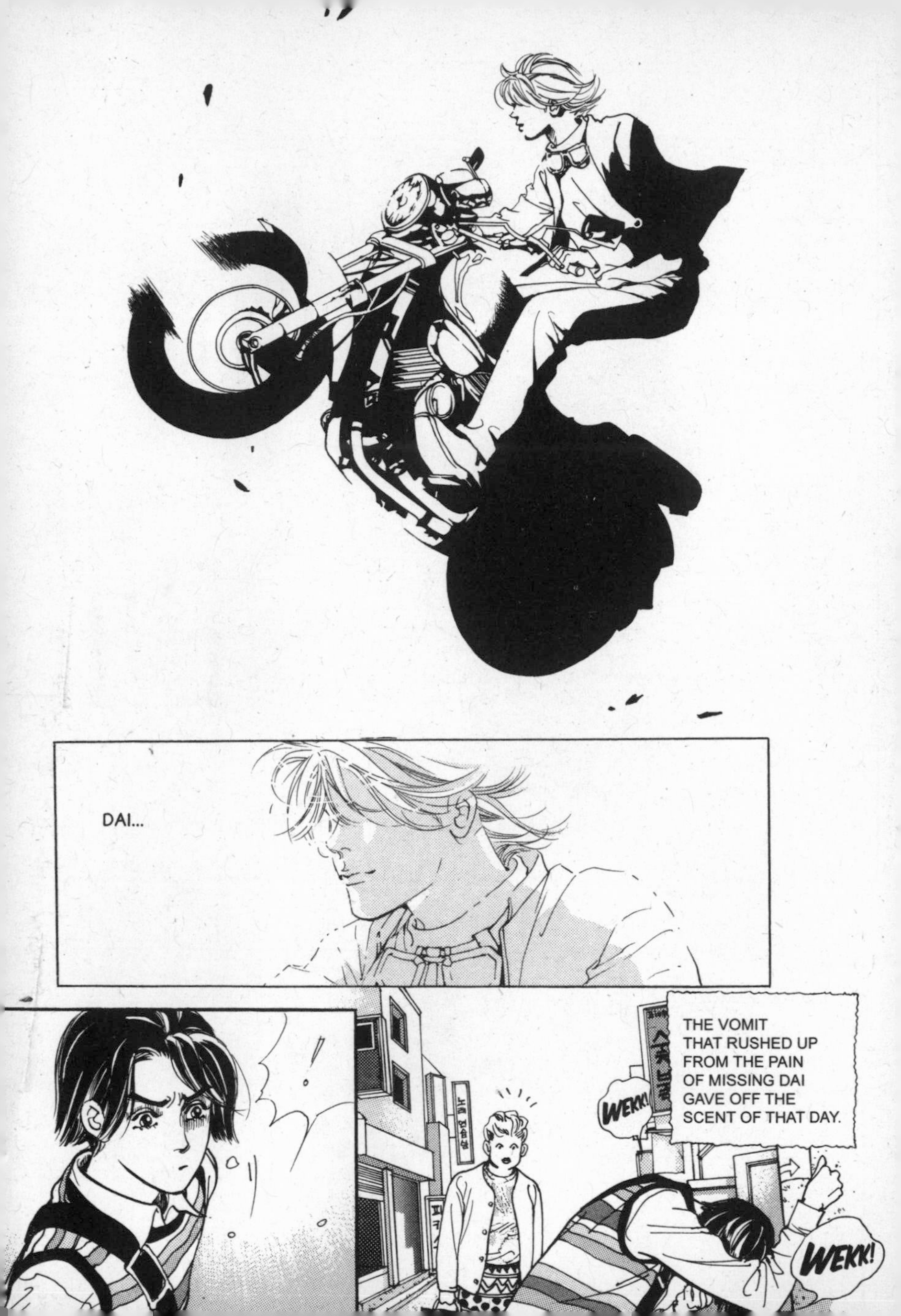
DAI...
THE VOMIT THAT RUSHED UP FROM THE PAIN OF MISSING DAI GAVE OFF THE SCENT OF THAT DAY.
WEKK!
WEKK!

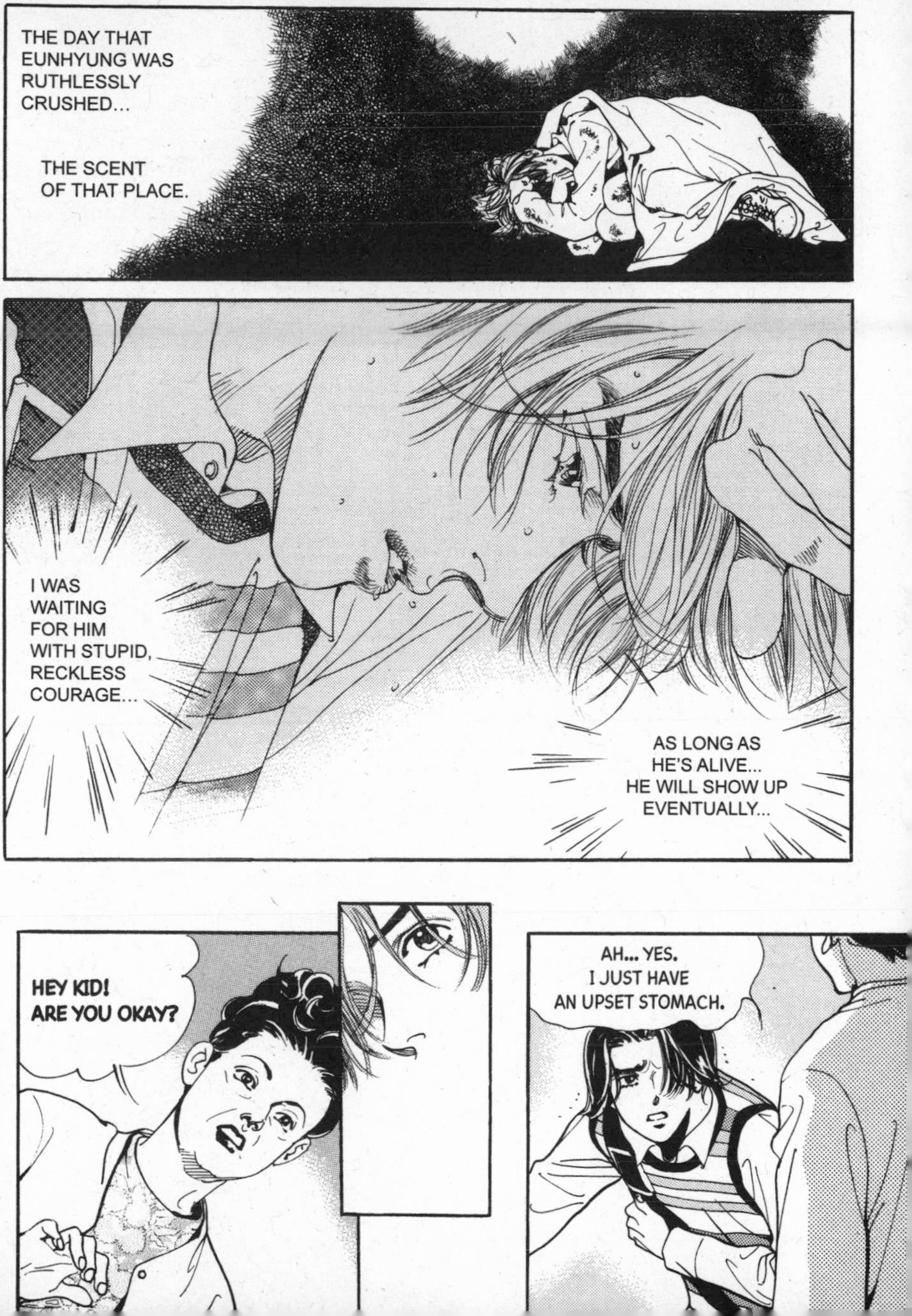
THE DAY THAT EUNHYUNG WAS RUTHLESSLY CRUSHED...
THE SCENT OF THAT PLACE.
I WAS WAITING FOR HIM WITH STUPID, RECKLESS COURAGE...
AS LONG AS HE'S ALIVE... HE WILL SHOW UP EVENTUALLY...
HEY KID! ARE YOU OKAY?
AH... YES. I JUST HAVE AN UPSET STOMACH.

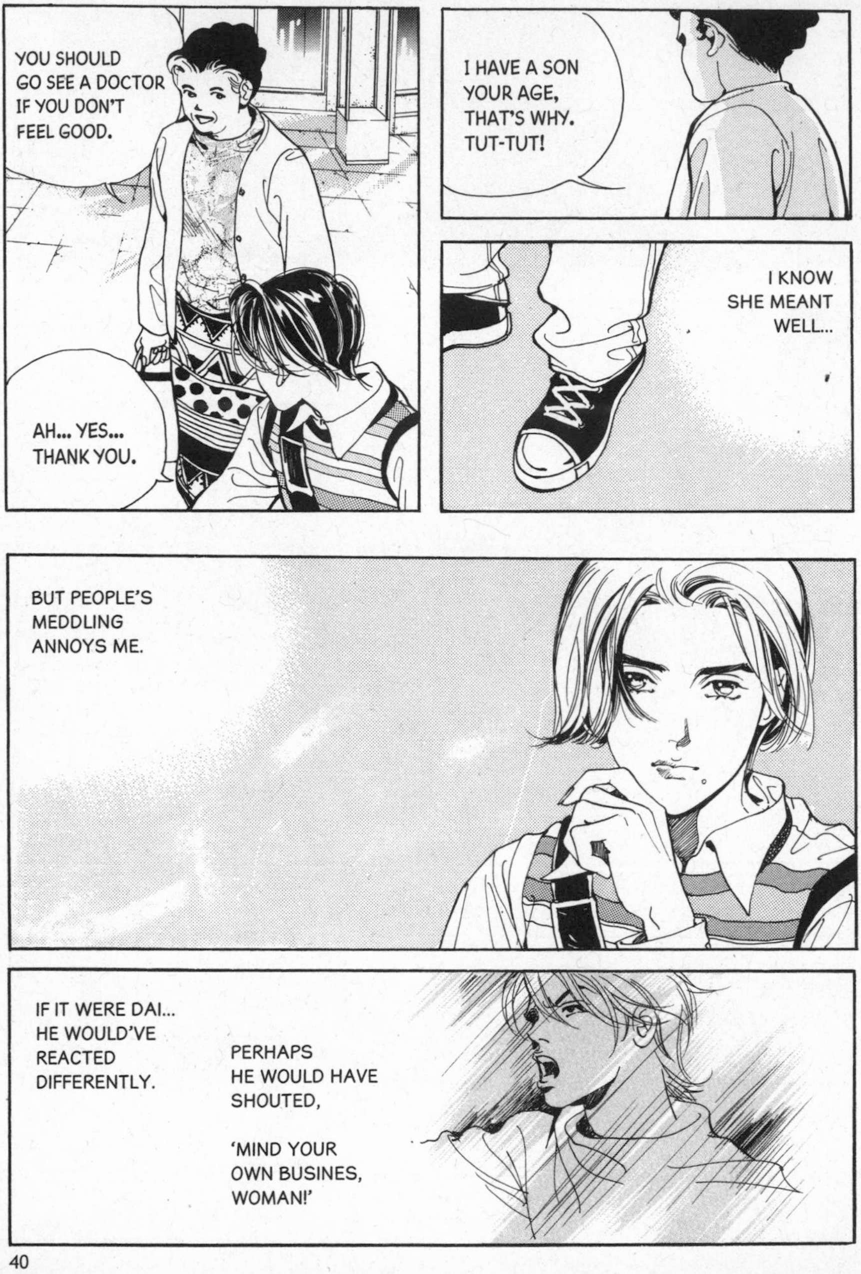
YOU SHOULD GO SEE A DOCTOR IF YOU DON'T FEEL GOOD.
AH... YES... THANK YOU.
I HAVE A SON YOUR AGE, THAT'S WHY. TUT-TUT!
I KNOW SHE MEANT WELL...
BUT PEOPLE'S MEDDLING ANNOYS ME.
IF IT WERE DAI... HE WOULD'VE REACTED DIFFERENTLY.
PERHAPS HE WOULD HAVE SHOUTED,
'MIND YOUR OWN BUSINES, WOMAN!'

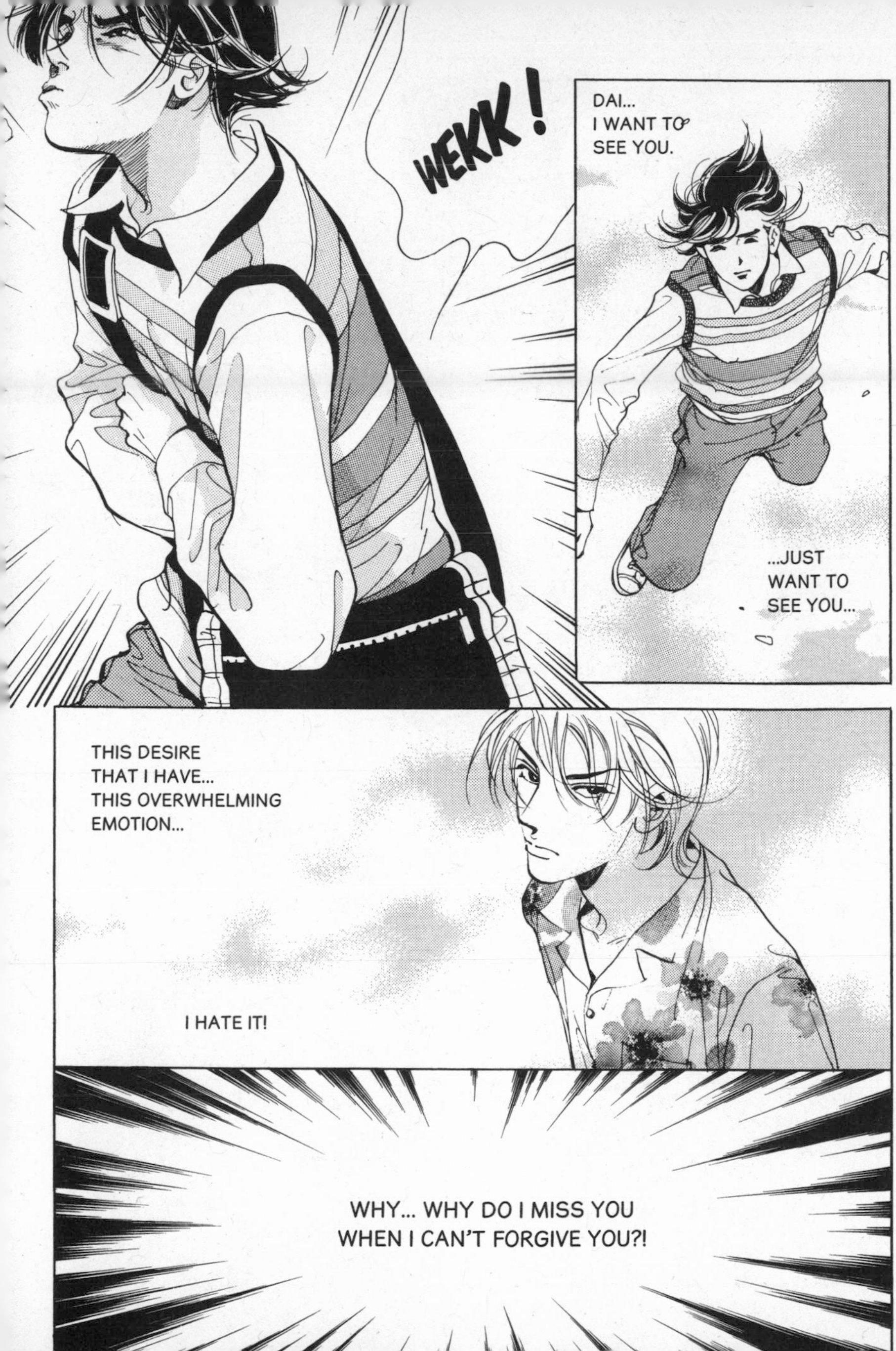
WEKK!
DAI...
I WANT TO
SEE YOU.
...JUST
WANT TO
SEE YOU...
THIS DESIRE
THAT I HAVE...
THIS OVERWHELMING
EMOTION...
I HATE IT!
WHY... WHY DO I MISS YOU
WHEN I CAN'T FORGIVE YOU?!

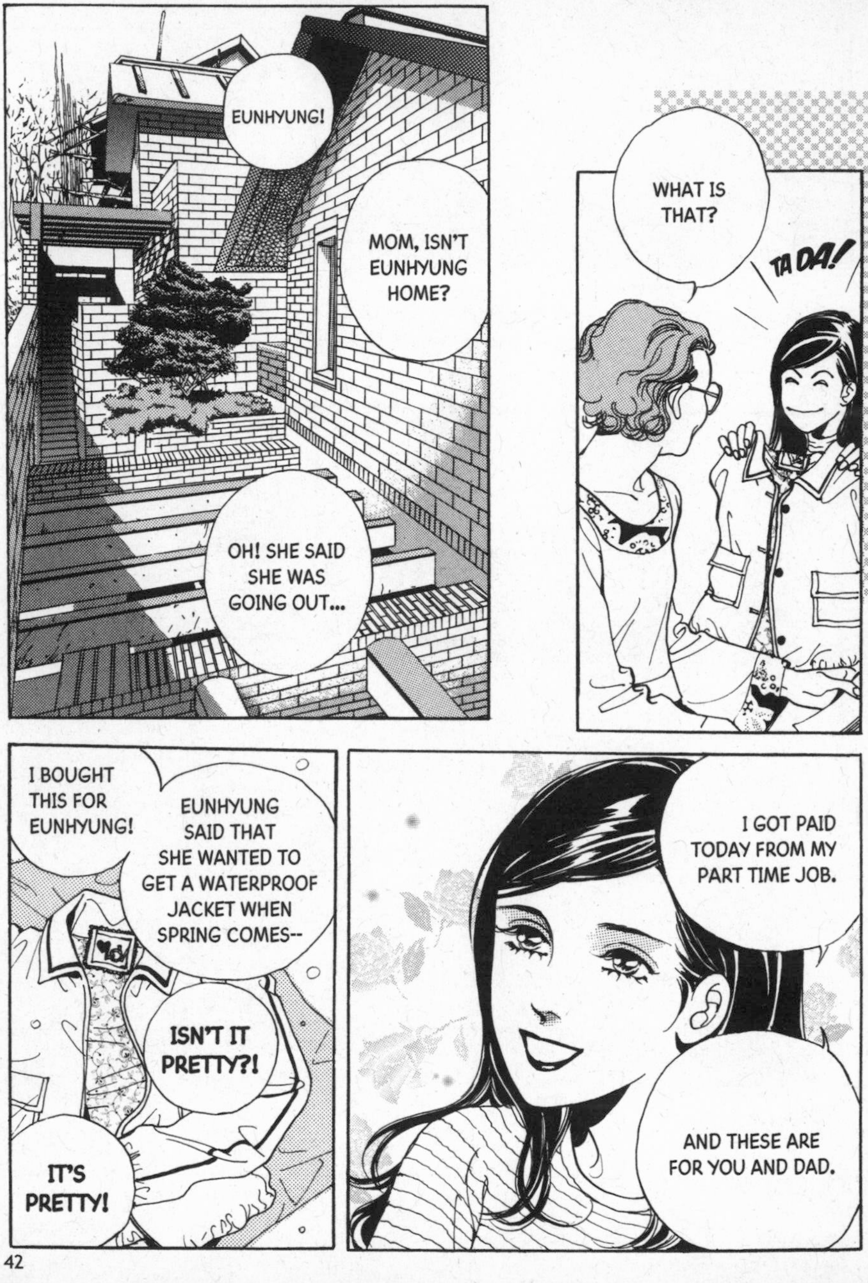
EUNHYUNG!
MOM, ISN'T EUNHYUNG HOME?
OH! SHE SAID SHE WAS GOING OUT...
WHAT IS THAT?
TA DA!
I BOUGHT THIS FOR EUNHYUNG!
EUNHYUNG SAID THAT SHE WANTED TO GET A WATERPROOF JACKET WHEN SPRING COMES--
ISN'T IT PRETTY?!
IT'S PRETTY!
I GOT PAID TODAY FROM MY PART TIME JOB.
AND THESE ARE FOR YOU AND DAD.

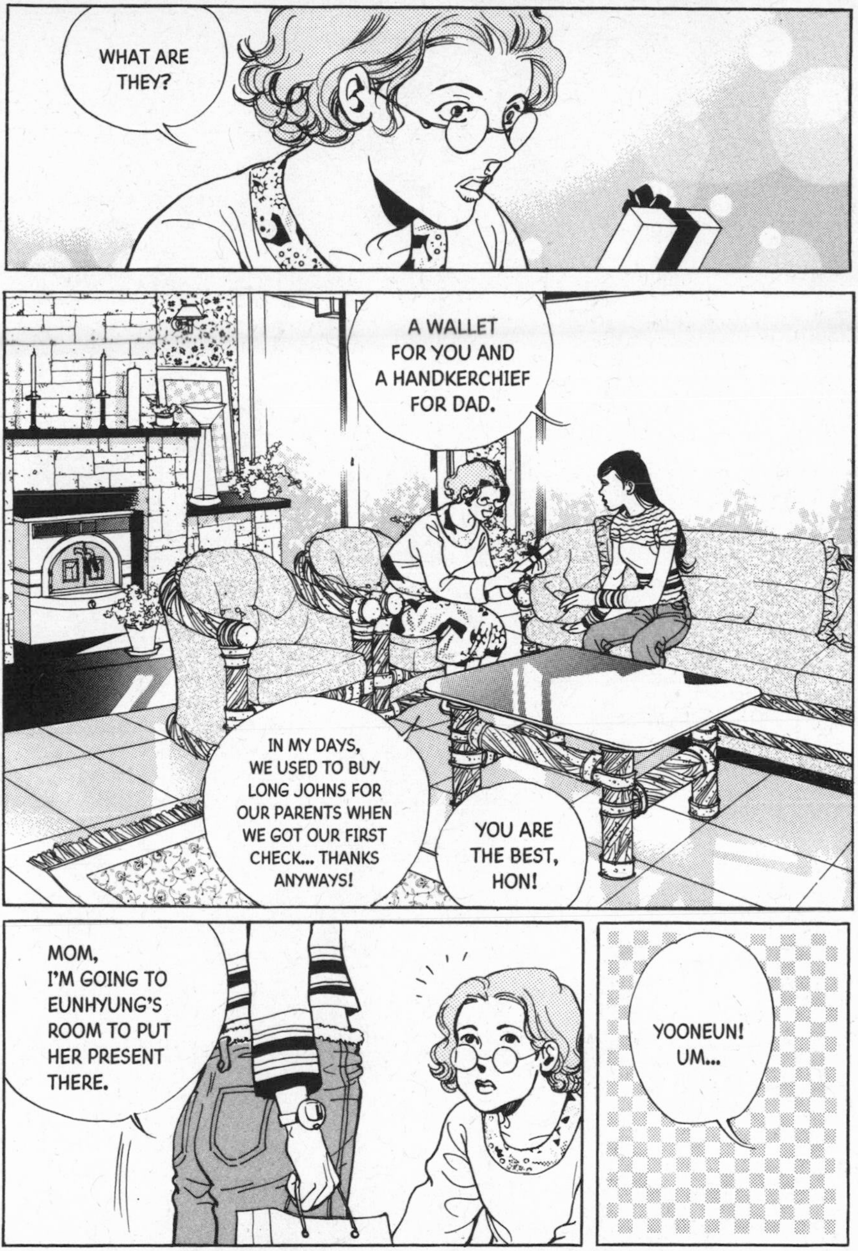
WHAT ARE THEY?
A WALLET FOR YOU AND A HANDKERCHIEF FOR DAD.
IN MY DAYS, WE USED TO BUY LONG JOHNS FOR OUR PARENTS WHEN WE GOT OUR FIRST CHECK... THANKS ANYWAYS!
YOU ARE THE BEST, HON!
MOM, I'M GOING TO EUNHYUNG'S ROOM TO PUT HER PRESENT THERE.
YOONEUN! UM...

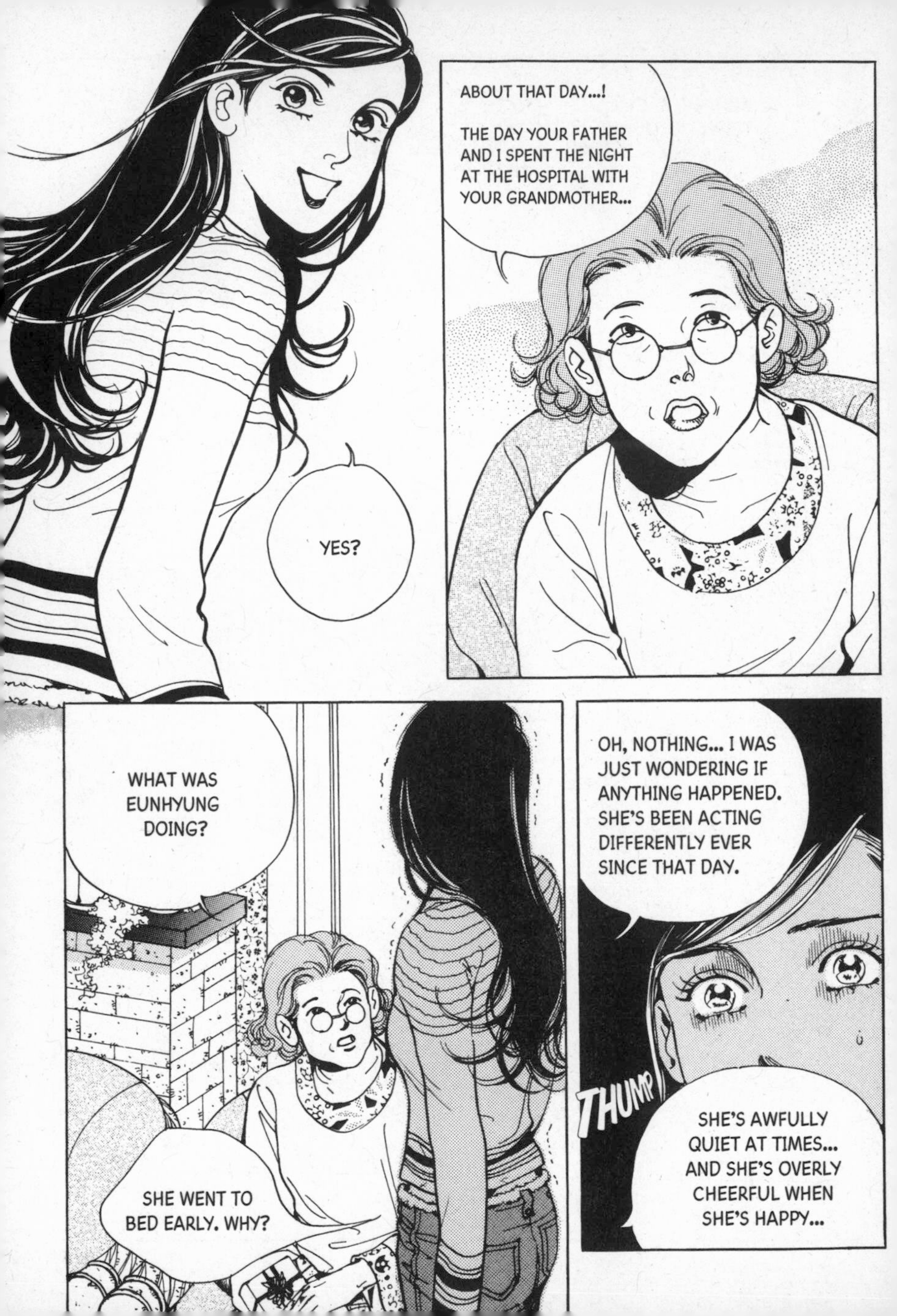
YES?
ABOUT THAT DAY...!
THE DAY YOUR FATHER AND I SPENT THE NIGHT AT THE HOSPITAL WITH YOUR GRANDMOTHER...
WHAT WAS EUNHYUNG DOING?
SHE WENT TO BED EARLY. WHY?
OH, NOTHING... I WAS JUST WONDERING IF ANYTHING HAPPENED. SHE'S BEEN ACTING DIFFERENTLY EVER SINCE THAT DAY.
THUMP
SHE'S AWFULLY QUIET AT TIMES... AND SHE'S OVERLY CHEERFUL WHEN SHE'S HAPPY...

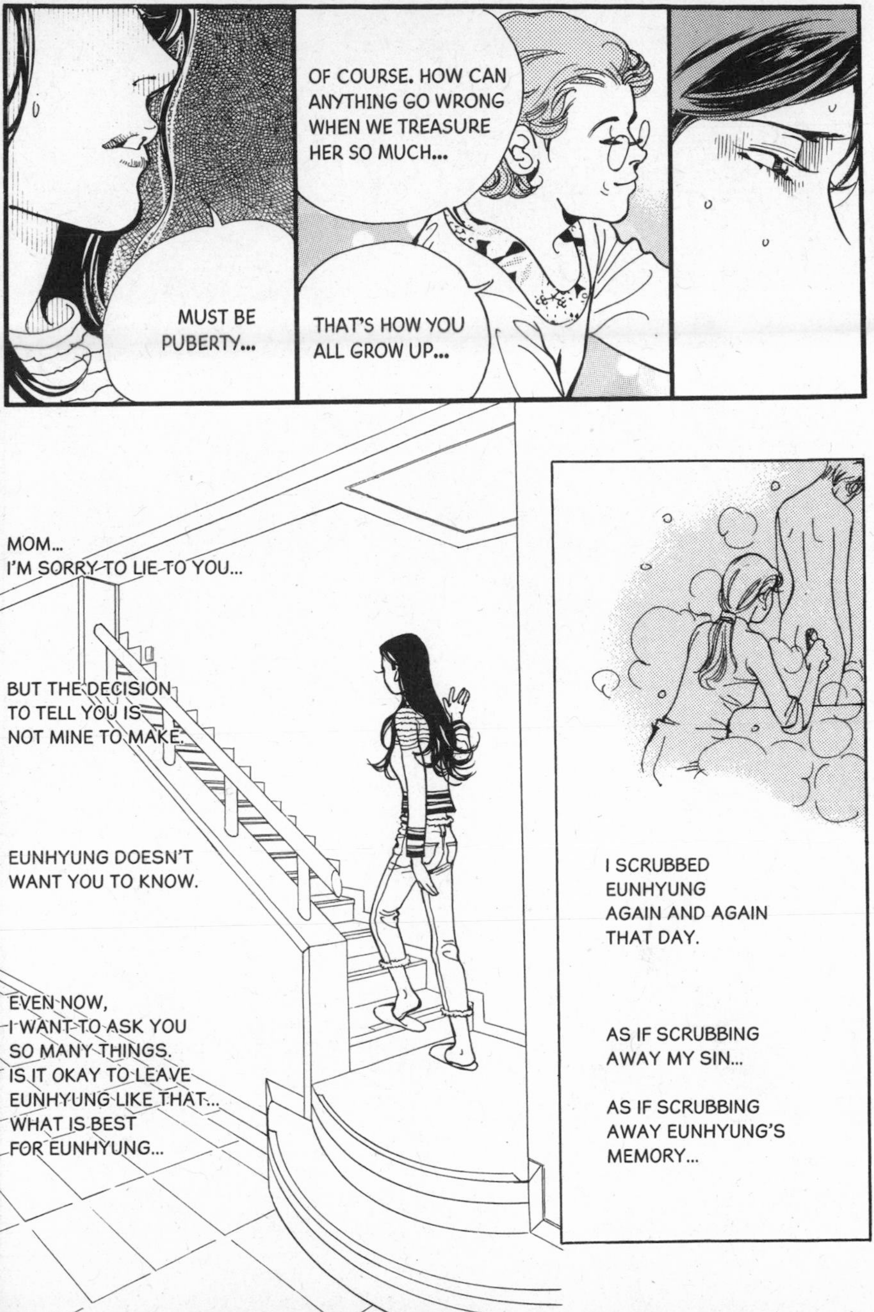
MUST BE PUBERTY...
OF COURSE. HOW CAN ANYTHING GO WRONG WHEN WE TREASURE HER SO MUCH...
THAT'S HOW YOU ALL GROW UP...
MOM... I'M SORRY TO LIE TO YOU...
BUT THE DECISION TO TELL YOU IS NOT MINE TO MAKE.
EUNHYUNG DOESN'T WANT YOU TO KNOW.
EVEN NOW, I WANT TO ASK YOU SO MANY THINGS. IS IT OKAY TO LEAVE EUNHYUNG LIKE THAT... WHAT IS BEST FOR EUNHYUNG...
I SCRUBBED EUNHYUNG AGAIN AND AGAIN THAT DAY.
AS IF SCRUBBING AWAY MY SIN...
AS IF SCRUBBING AWAY EUNHYUNG'S MEMORY...

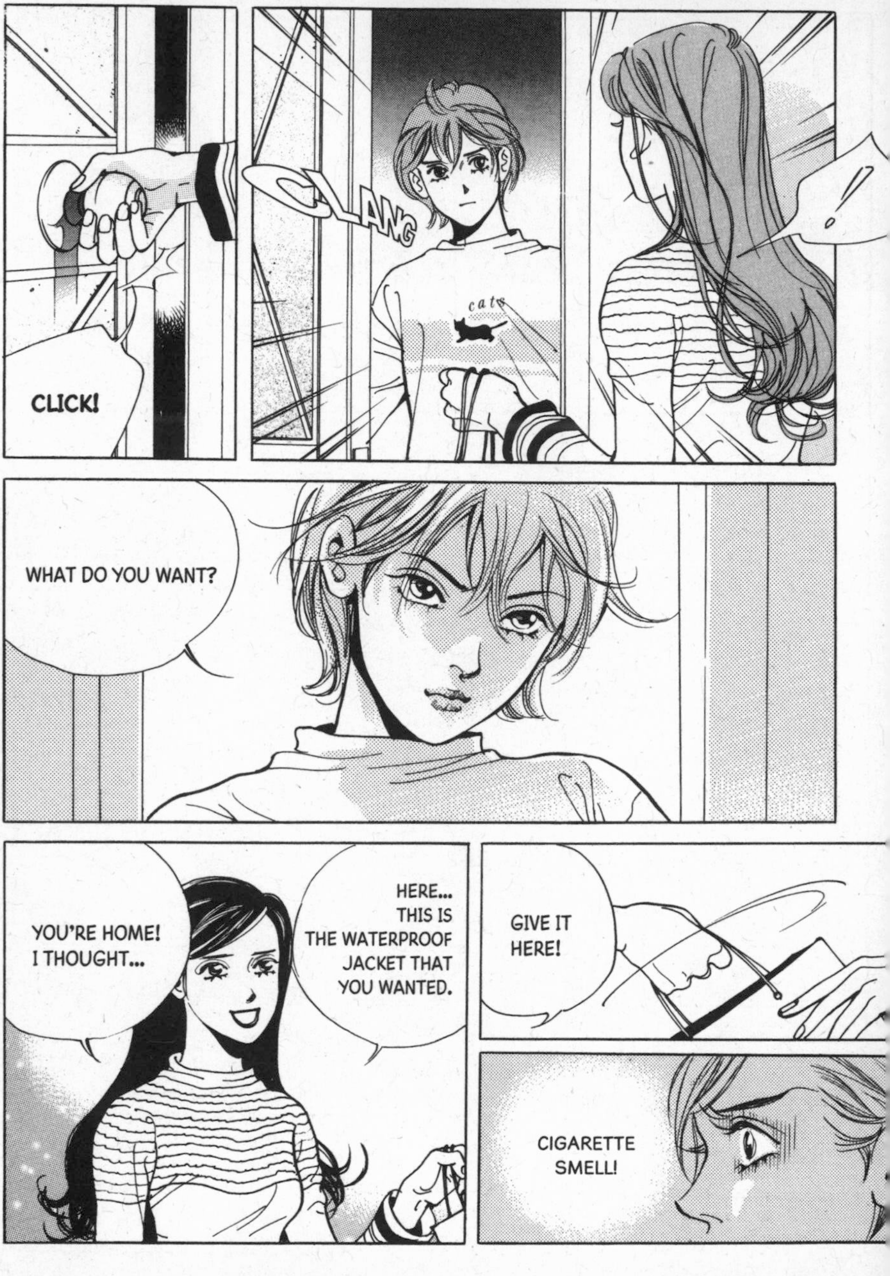
CLICK!
CLANG
!?
WHAT DO YOU WANT?
YOU'RE HOME! I THOUGHT...
HERE... THIS IS THE WATERPROOF JACKET THAT YOU WANTED.
GIVE IT HERE!
CIGARETTE SMELL!

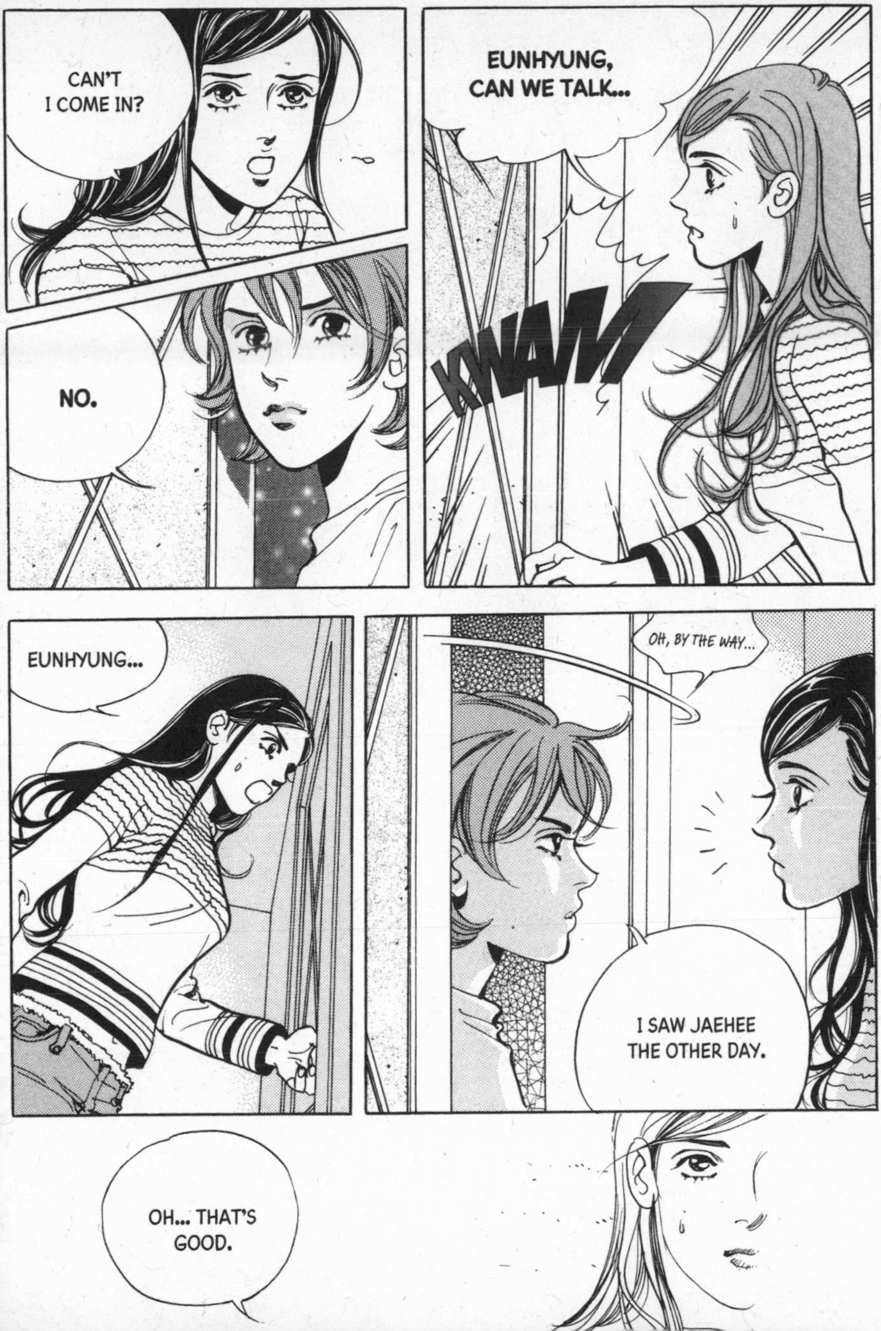
CAN'T I COME IN?
NO.
EUNHYUNG, CAN WE TALK...
KWAM
EUNHYUNG...
OH, BY THE WAY...
I SAW JAEHEE THE OTHER DAY.
OH... THAT'S GOOD.

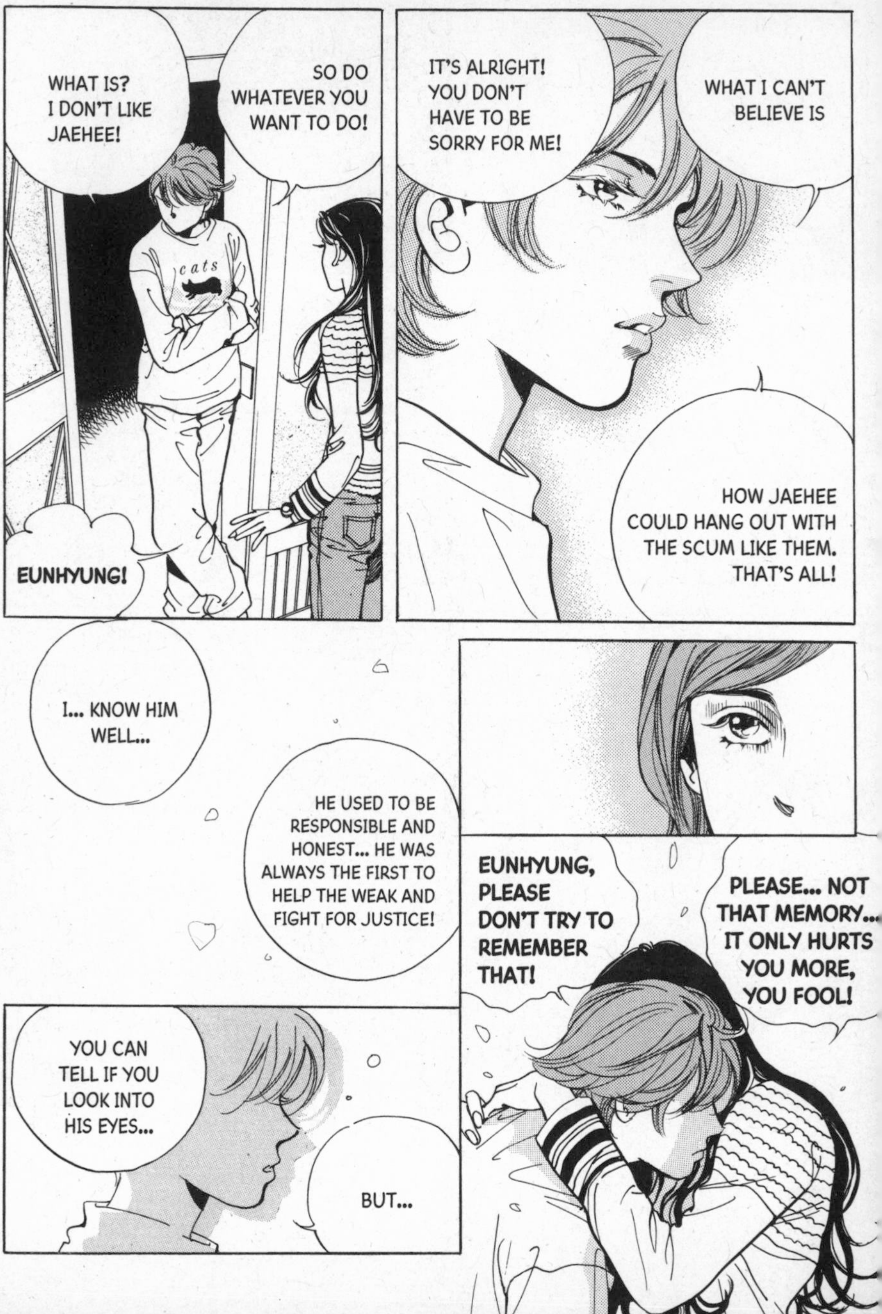
WHAT IS? I DON'T LIKE JAEHEE!
SO DO WHATEVER YOU WANT TO DO!
EUNHYUNG!
IT'S ALRIGHT! YOU DON'T HAVE TO BE SORRY FOR ME!
WHAT I CAN'T BELIEVE IS
HOW JAEHEE COULD HANG OUT WITH THE SCUM LIKE THEM. THAT'S ALL!
I... KNOW HIM WELL...
HE USED TO BE RESPONSIBLE AND HONEST... HE WAS ALWAYS THE FIRST TO HELP THE WEAK AND FIGHT FOR JUSTICE!
YOU CAN TELL IF YOU LOOK INTO HIS EYES...
BUT...
EUNHYUNG, PLEASE DON'T TRY TO REMEMBER THAT!
PLEASE... NOT THAT MEMORY... IT ONLY HURTS YOU MORE, YOU FOOL!

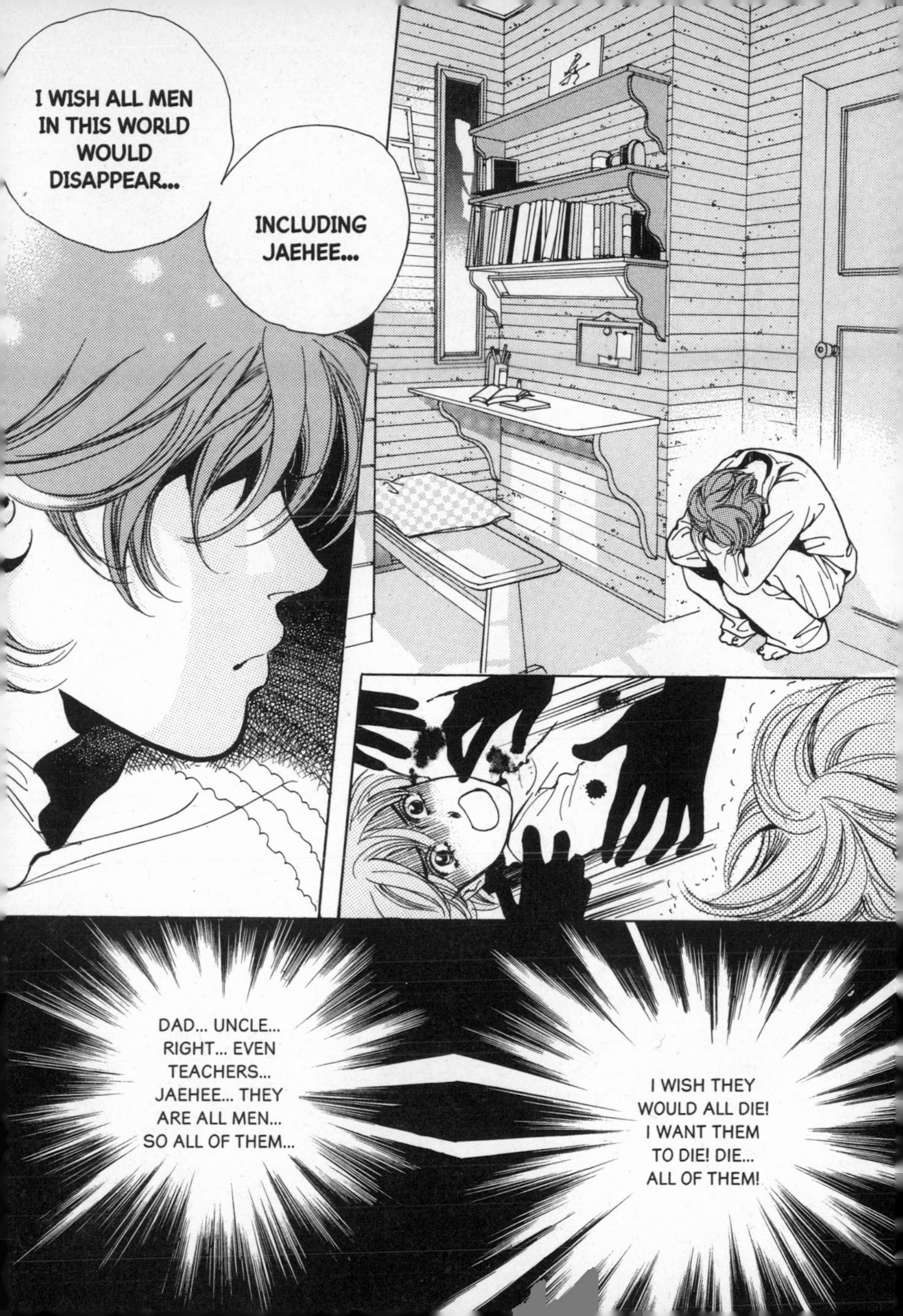
I WISH ALL MEN IN THIS WORLD WOULD DISAPPEAR...
INCLUDING JAEHEE...
DAD... UNCLE... RIGHT... EVEN TEACHERS... JAEHEE... THEY ARE ALL MEN... SO ALL OF THEM...
I WISH THEY WOULD ALL DIE! I WANT THEM TO DIE! DIE... ALL OF THEM!

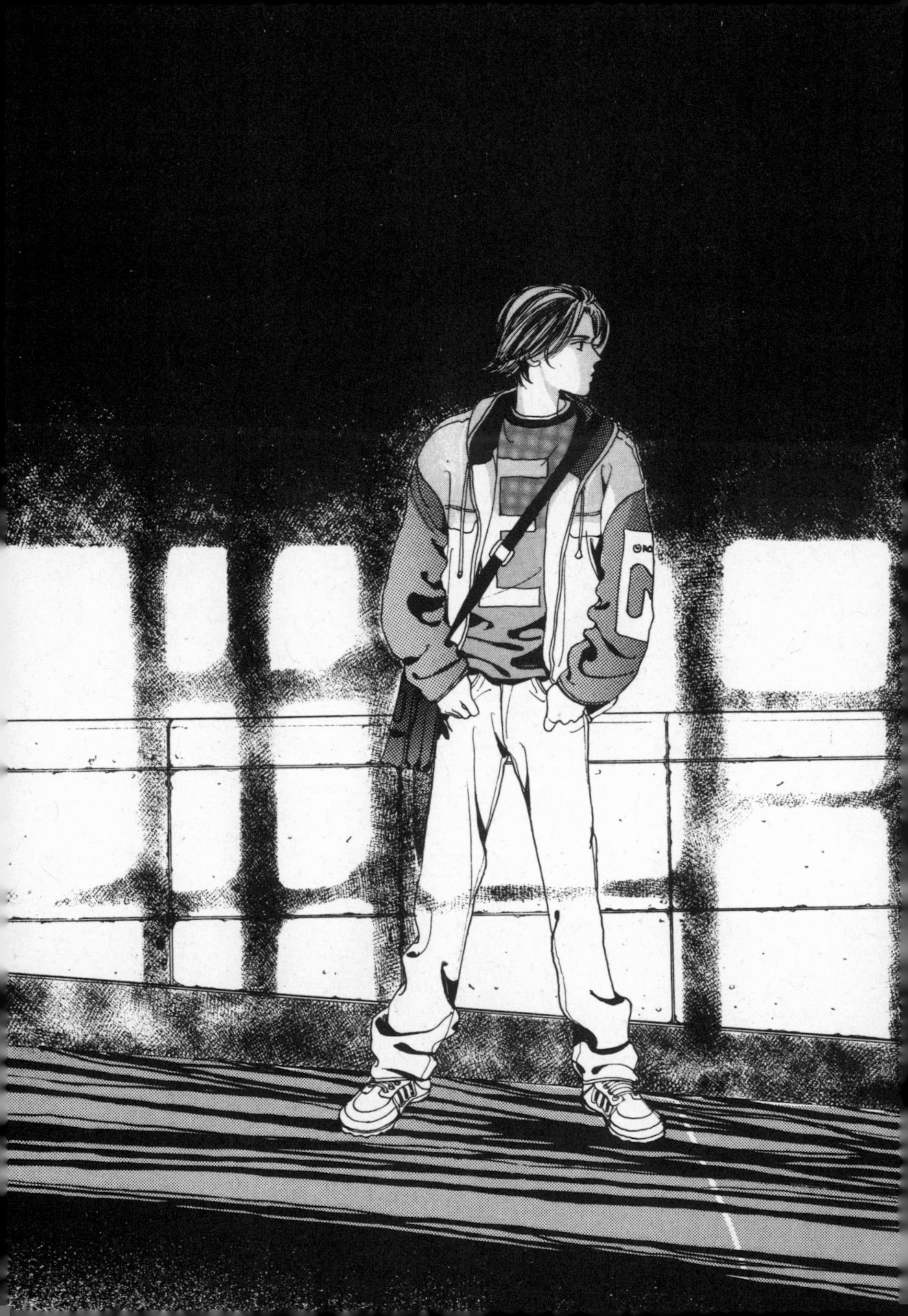

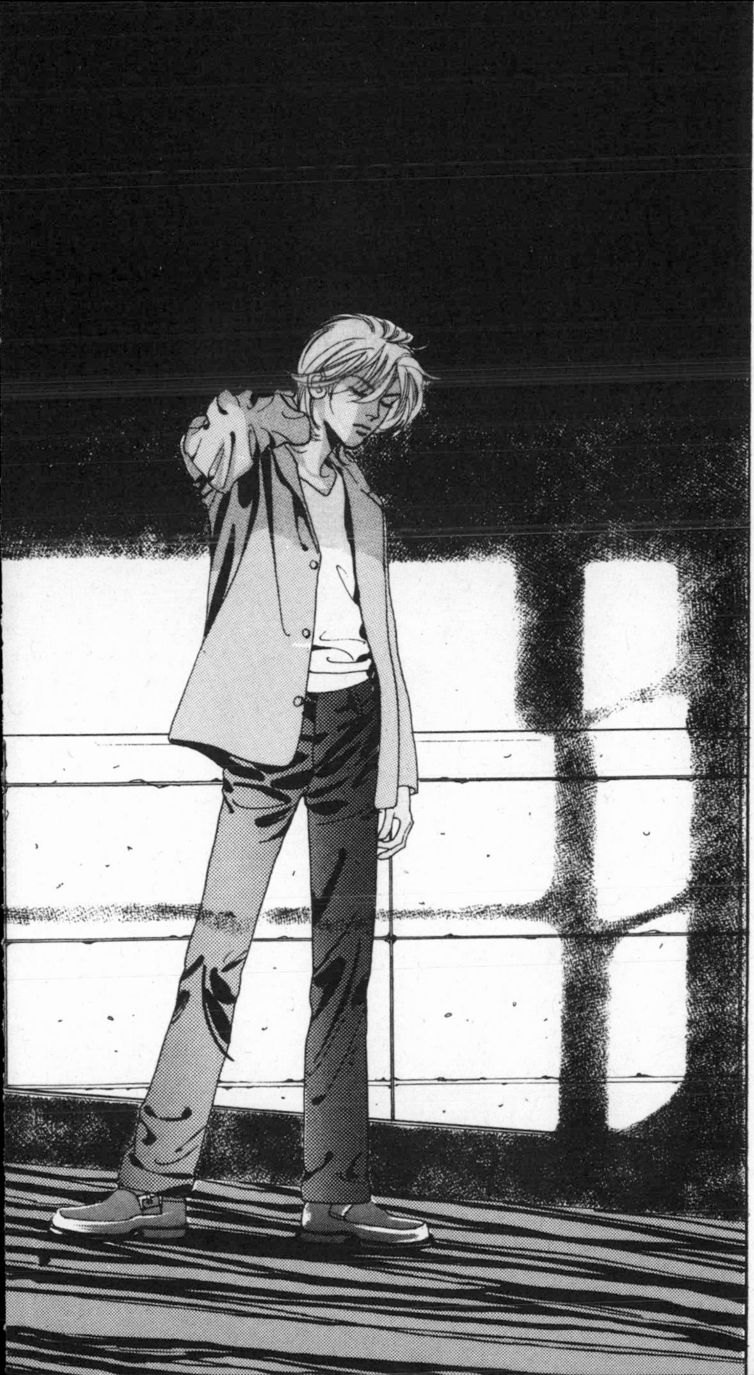

VIEW 1.
CRASHING SPRING

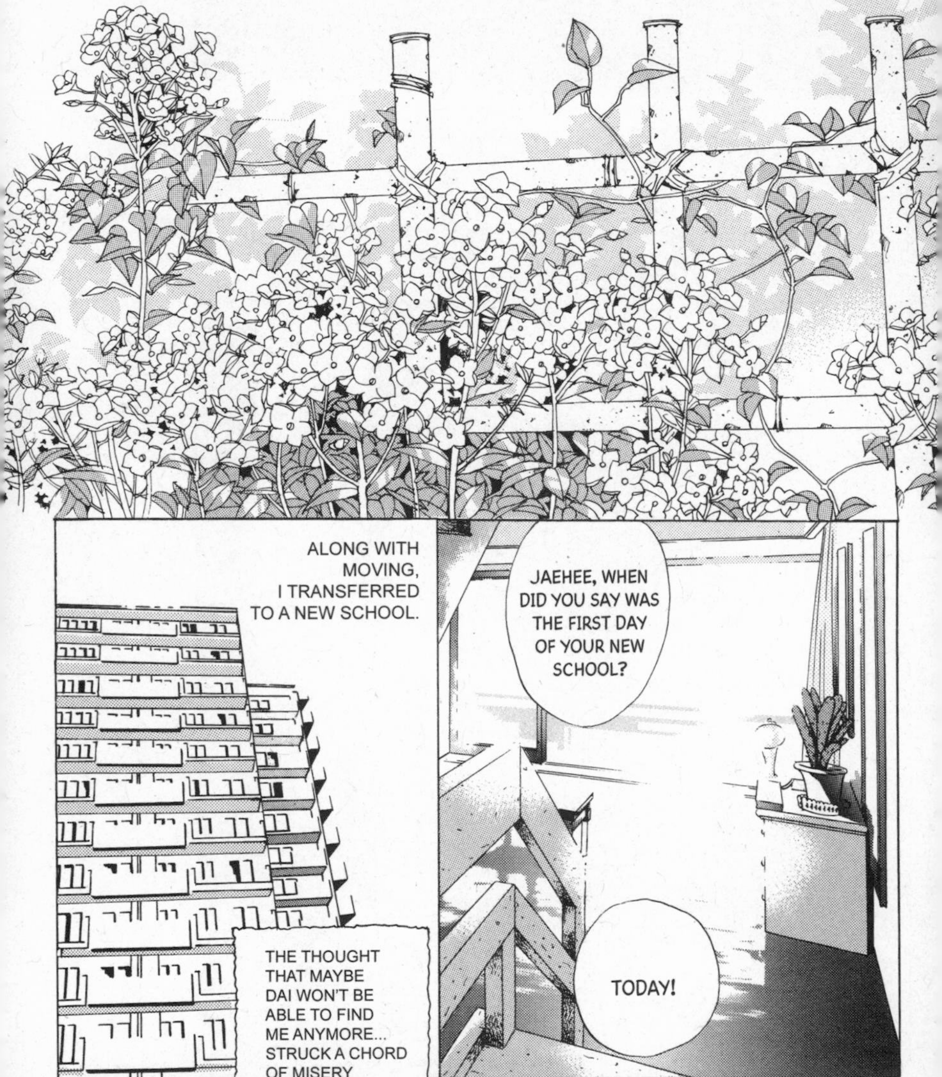

ALONG WITH MOVING, I TRANSFERRED TO A NEW SCHOOL.
THE THOUGHT THAT MAYBE DAI WON'T BE ABLE TO FIND ME ANYMORE... STRUCK A CHORD OF MISERY IN MY HEART.
JAEHEE, WHEN DID YOU SAY WAS THE FIRST DAY OF YOUR NEW SCHOOL?
TODAY!

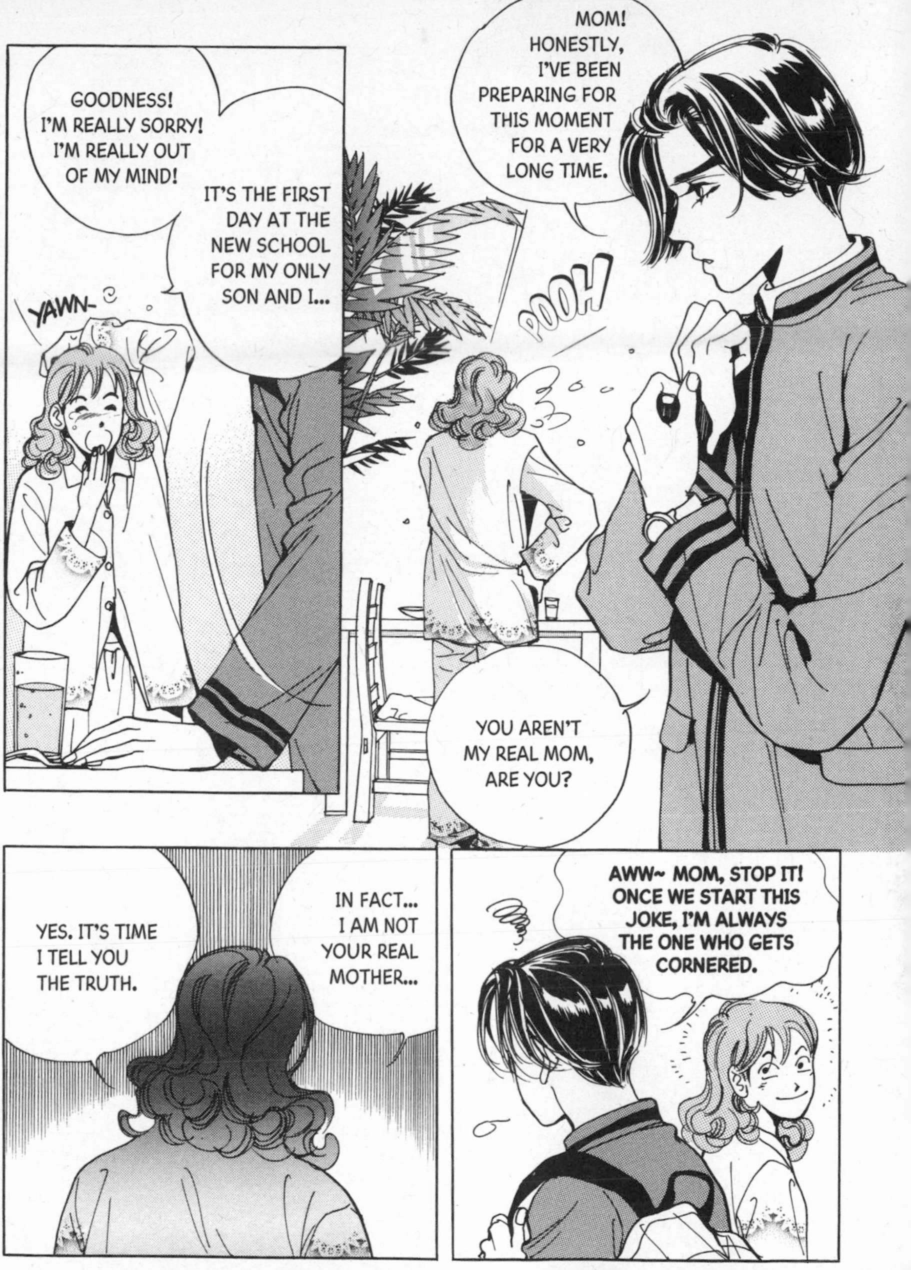
GOODNESS! I'M REALLY SORRY! I'M REALLY OUT OF MY MIND!
IT'S THE FIRST DAY AT THE NEW SCHOOL FOR MY ONLY SON AND I...
YAWN-
MOM! HONESTLY, I'VE BEEN PREPARING FOR THIS MOMENT FOR A VERY LONG TIME.
POOH
YOU AREN'T MY REAL MOM, ARE YOU?
YES. IT'S TIME I TELL YOU THE TRUTH.
IN FACT... I AM NOT YOUR REAL MOTHER...
AWW~ MOM, STOP IT! ONCE WE START THIS JOKE, I'M ALWAYS THE ONE WHO GETS CORNERED.

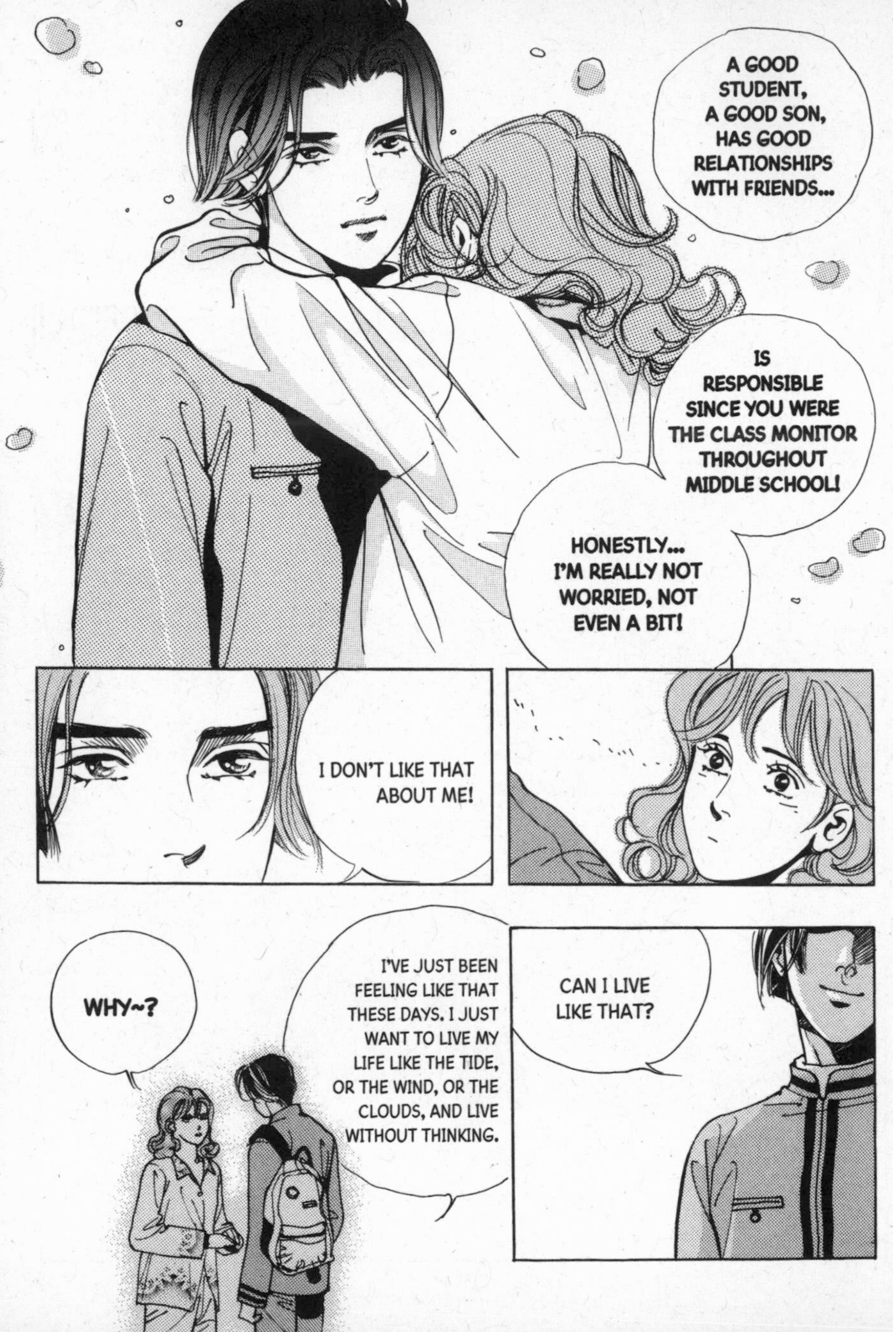
A GOOD STUDENT, A GOOD SON, HAS GOOD RELATIONSHIPS WITH FRIENDS...
IS RESPONSIBLE SINCE YOU WERE THE CLASS MONITOR THROUGHOUT MIDDLE SCHOOL!
HONESTLY... I'M REALLY NOT WORRIED, NOT EVEN A BIT!
I DON'T LIKE THAT ABOUT ME!
WHY~?
I'VE JUST BEEN FEELING LIKE THAT THESE DAYS. I JUST WANT TO LIVE MY LIFE LIKE THE TIDE, OR THE WIND, OR THE CLOUDS, AND LIVE WITHOUT THINKING.
CAN I LIVE LIKE THAT?

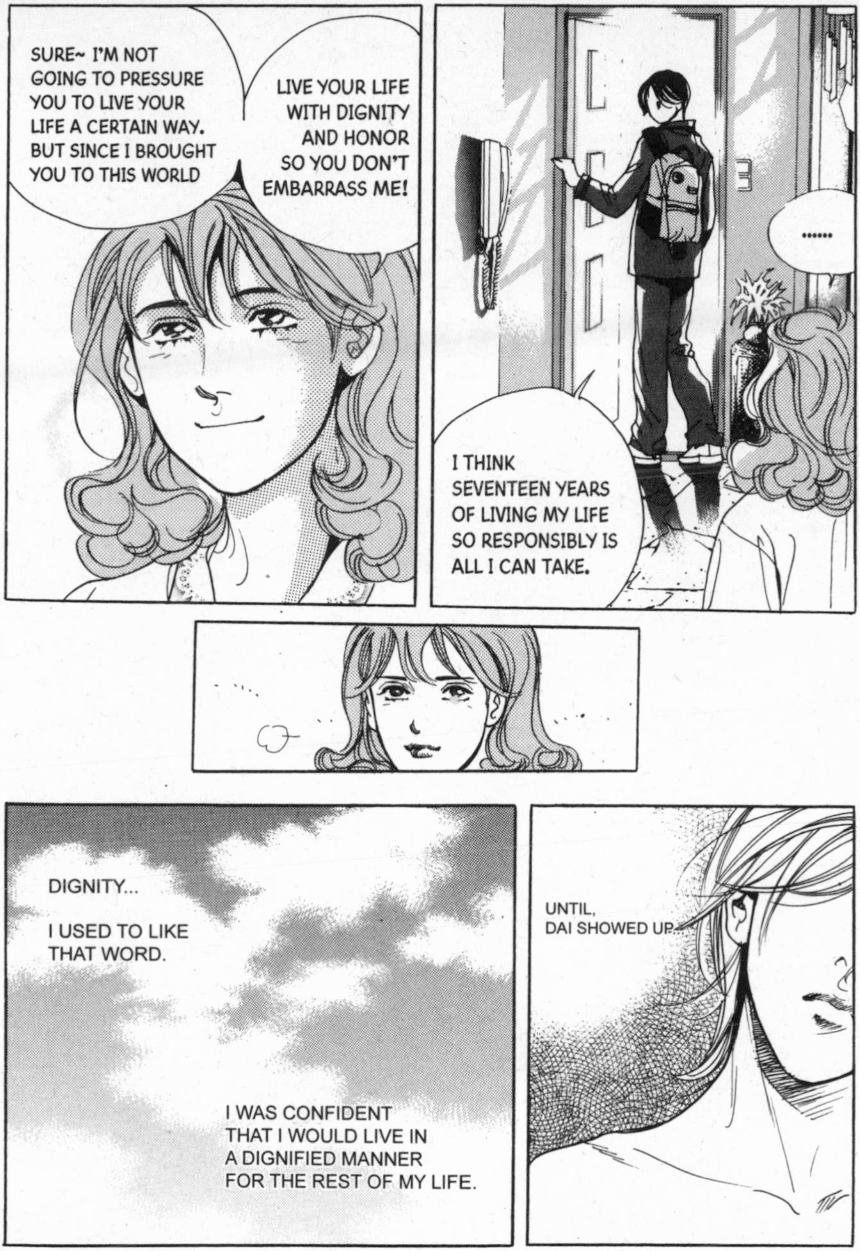

SURE~ I'M NOT GOING TO PRESSURE YOU TO LIVE YOUR LIFE A CERTAIN WAY. BUT SINCE I BROUGHT YOU TO THIS WORLD
LIVE YOUR LIFE WITH DIGNITY AND HONOR SO YOU DON'T EMBARRASS ME!
......
I THINK SEVENTEEN YEARS OF LIVING MY LIFE SO RESPONSIBLY IS ALL I CAN TAKE.
DIGNITY...
I USED TO LIKE THAT WORD.
I WAS CONFIDENT THAT I WOULD LIVE IN A DIGNIFIED MANNER FOR THE REST OF MY LIFE.
UNTIL, DAI SHOWED UP...

MOM WOULD
NEVER UNDERSTAND.

NO,
SHE'LL GET HURT INSTEAD.

MORE SO BECAUSE
I'M HER ONLY SON.

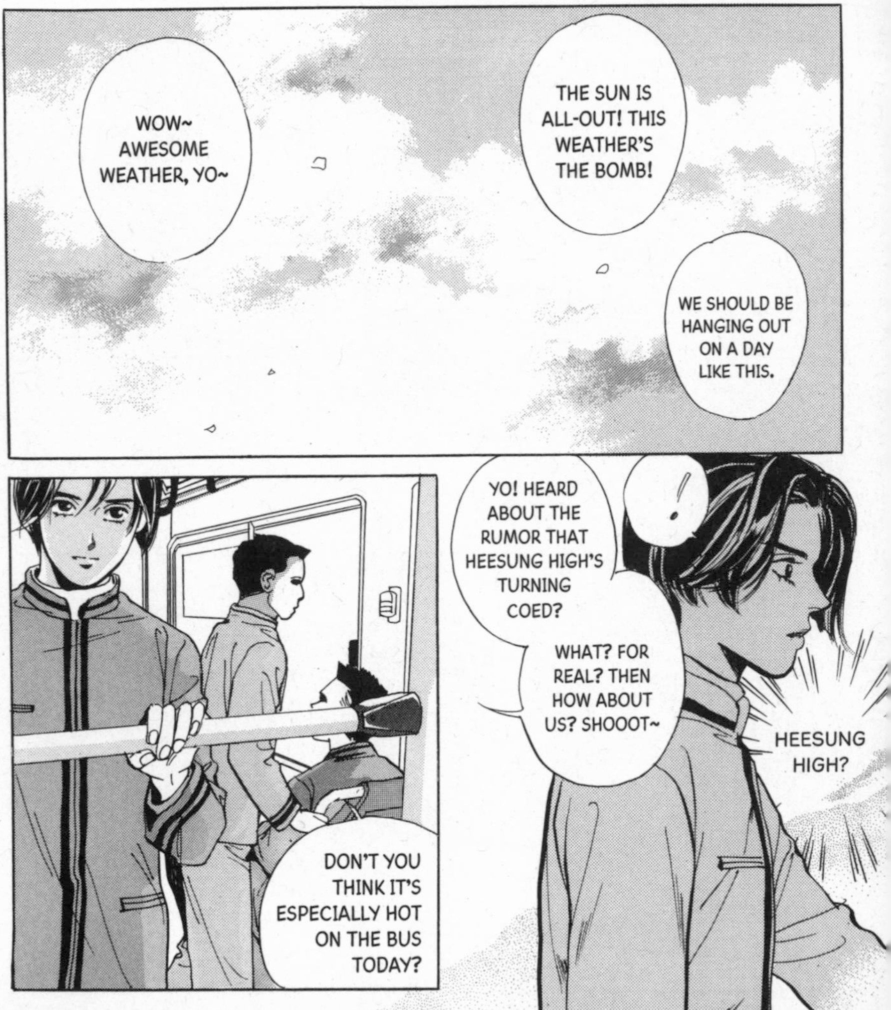

WOW~ AWESOME WEATHER, YO~
THE SUN IS ALL-OUT! THIS WEATHER'S THE BOMB!
WE SHOULD BE HANGING OUT ON A DAY LIKE THIS.
DON'T YOU THINK IT'S ESPECIALLY HOT ON THE BUS TODAY?
YO! HEARD ABOUT THE RUMOR THAT HEESUNG HIGH'S TURNING COED?
!
WHAT? FOR REAL? THEN HOW ABOUT US? SHOOOT~
HEESUNG HIGH?

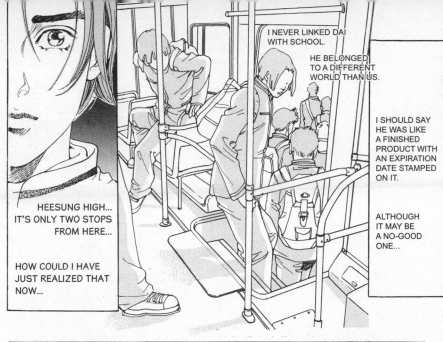

HEESUNG HIGH... IT'S ONLY TWO STOPS FROM HERE...
HOW COULD I HAVE JUST REALIZED THAT NOW...
I NEVER LINKED DAI WITH SCHOOL.
HE BELONGED TO A DIFFERENT WORLD THAN US.
I SHOULD SAY HE WAS LIKE A FINISHED PRODUCT WITH AN EXPIRATION DATE STAMPED ON IT.
ALTHOUGH IT MAY BE A NO-GOOD ONE...
New York
Plaza
THE SUNLIGHT ON THAT SPRING DAY FLOWED ON THE STREETS, CUTTING OPEN A CURTAIN OF FOG.
THE SUN SHONE SO BRIGHTLY THAT IT BLINDED ME AND MADE THE ASPHALT AND WHITE BLOCKS ON THE ROAD GLISTEN LIKE MIRRORS.

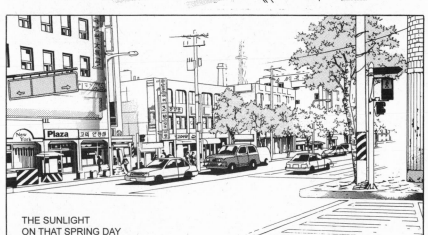

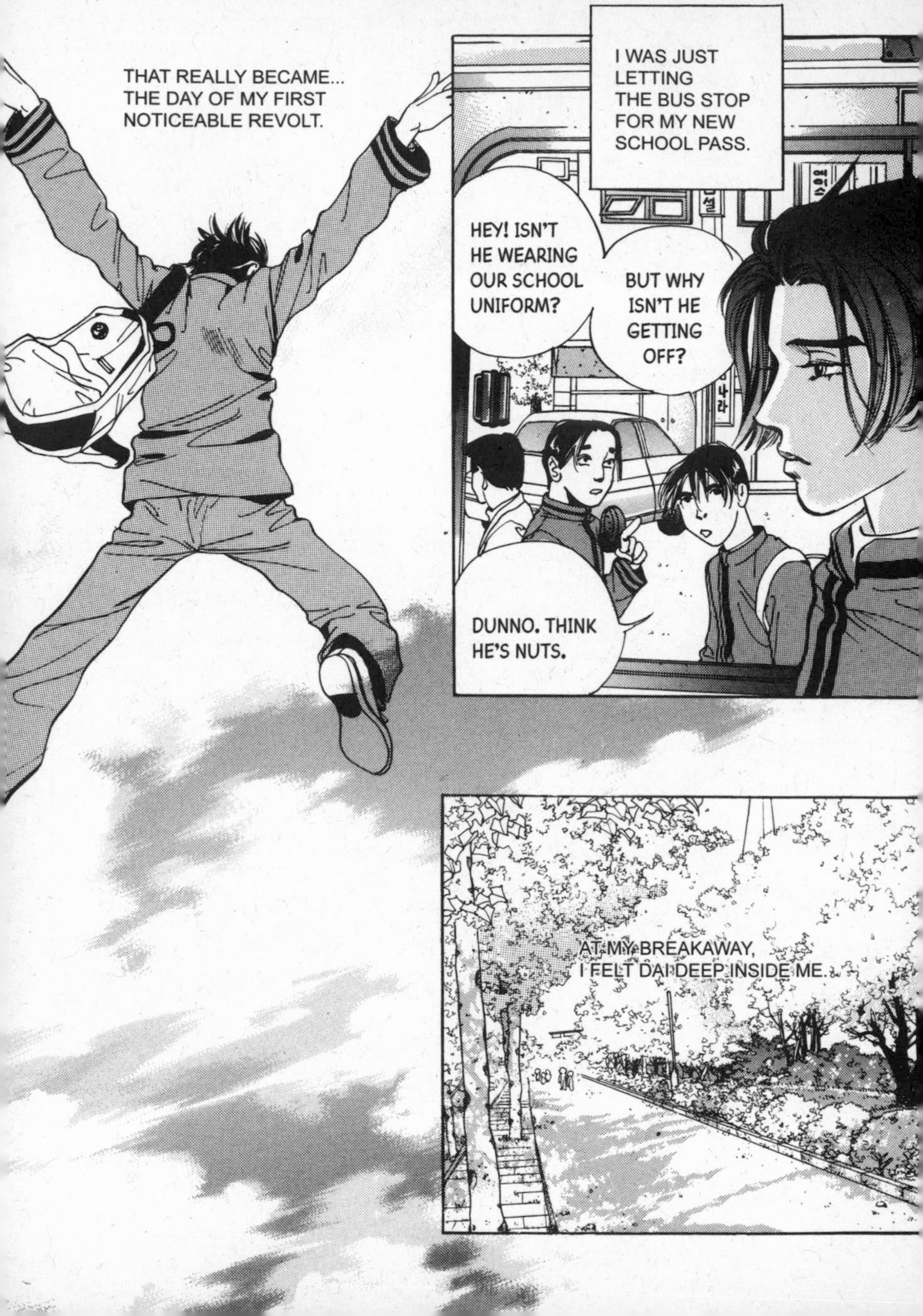
THAT REALLY BECAME... THE DAY OF MY FIRST NOTICEABLE REVOLT.
I WAS JUST LETTING THE BUS STOP FOR MY NEW SCHOOL PASS.
HEY! ISN'T HE WEARING OUR SCHOOL UNIFORM?
BUT WHY ISN'T HE GETTING OFF?
DUNNO. THINK HE'S NUTS.
AT MY BREAKAWAY, I FELT DAI DEEP INSIDE ME.

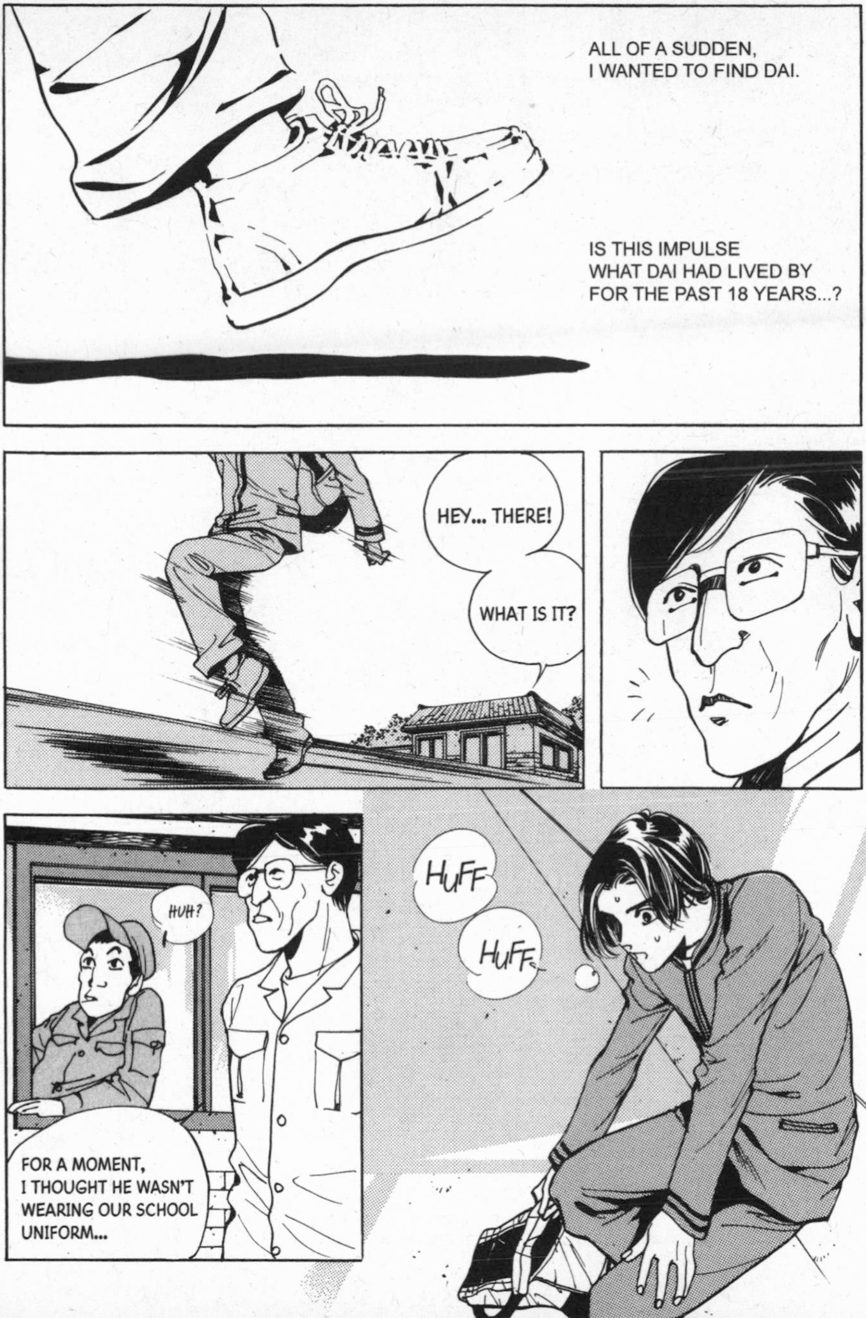
ALL OF A SUDDEN,
I WANTED TO FIND DAI.
IS THIS IMPULSE
WHAT DAI HAD LIVED BY
FOR THE PAST 18 YEARS...?
HEY... THERE!
WHAT IS IT?
HUH?
FOR A MOMENT,
I THOUGHT HE WASN'T
WEARING OUR SCHOOL
UNIFORM...
HUFF
HUFF

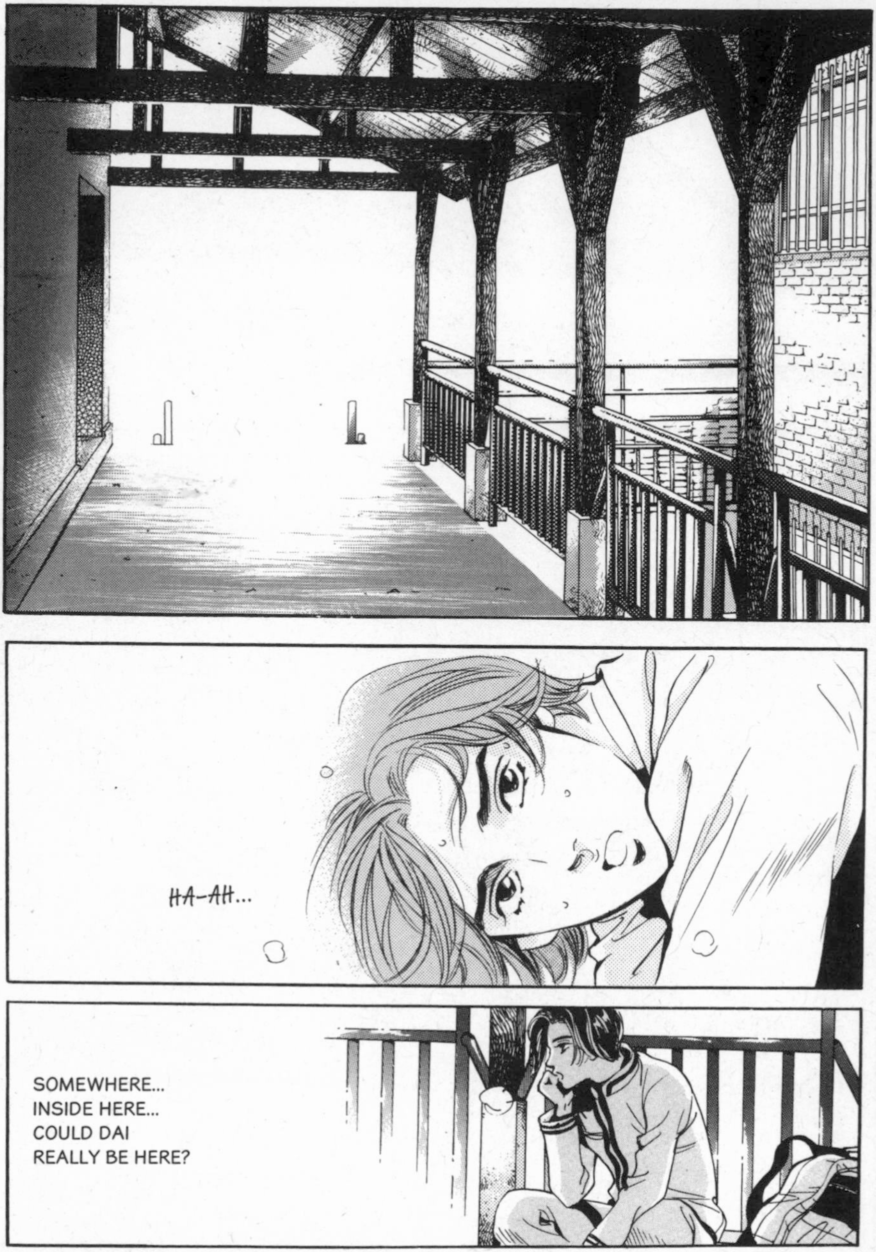
HA-AH...
SOMEWHERE... INSIDE HERE... COULD DAI REALLY BE HERE?

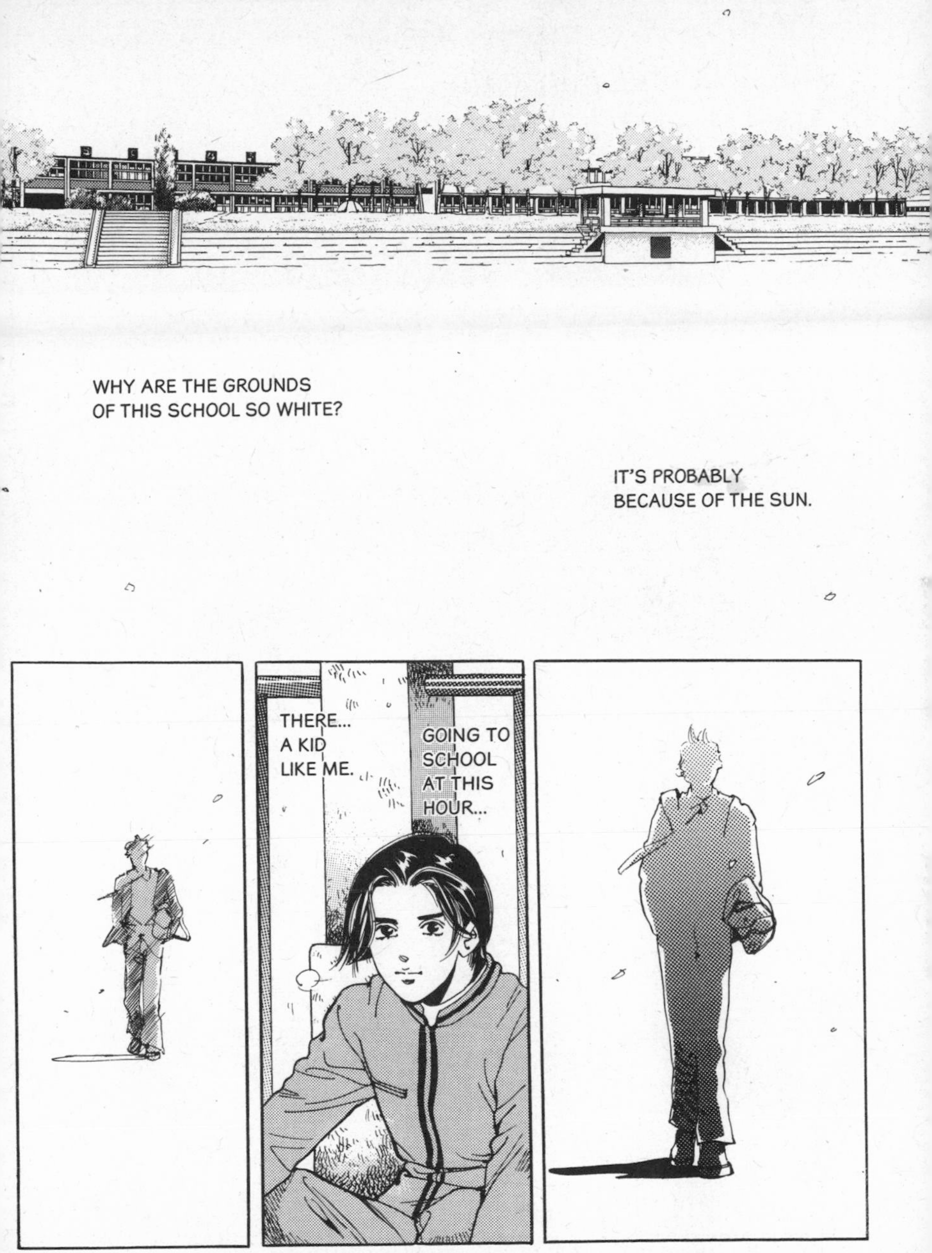
WHY ARE THE GROUNDS OF THIS SCHOOL SO WHITE?
IT'S PROBABLY BECAUSE OF THE SUN.
THERE... A KID LIKE ME.
GOING TO SCHOOL AT THIS HOUR...

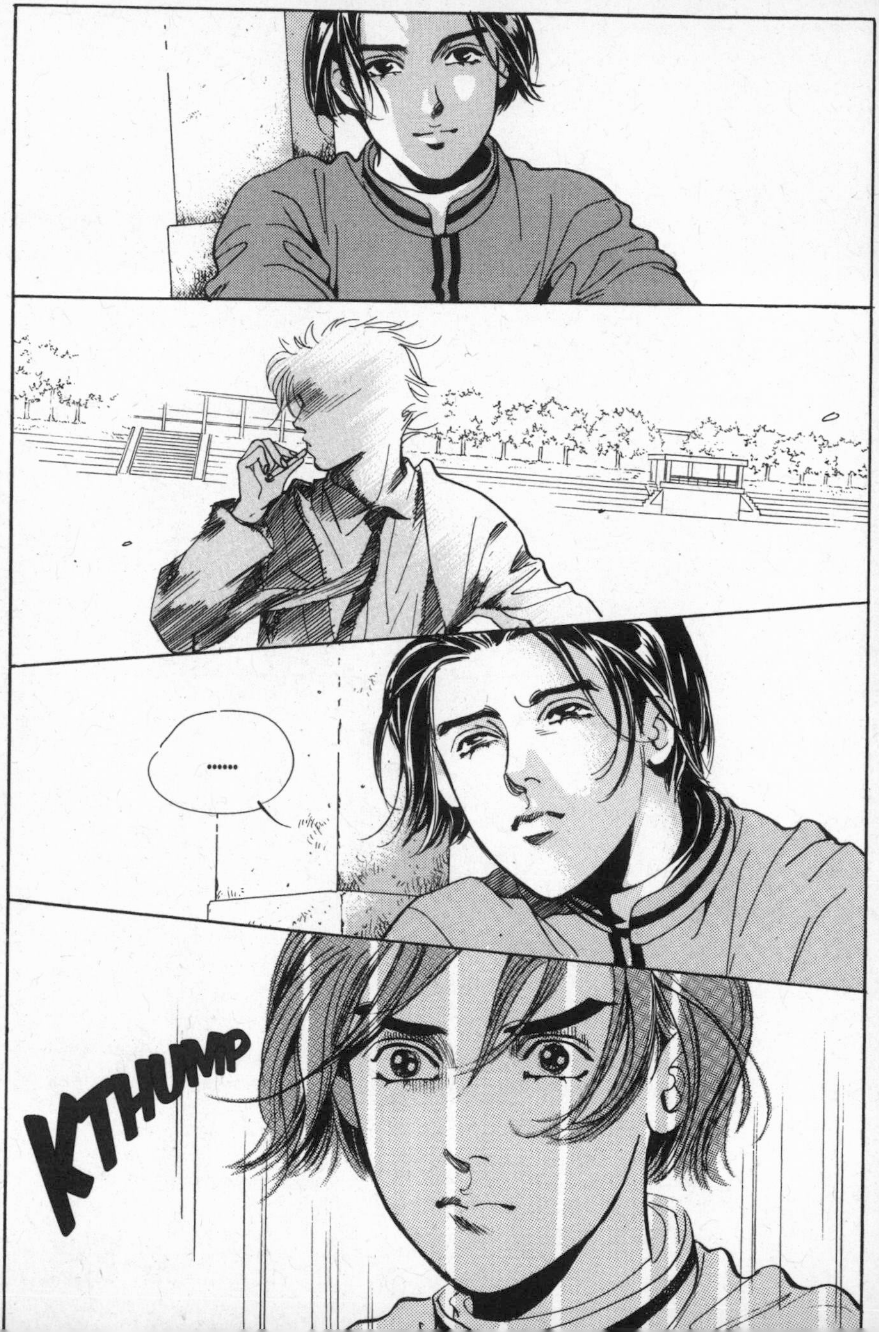
......
KTHUMP

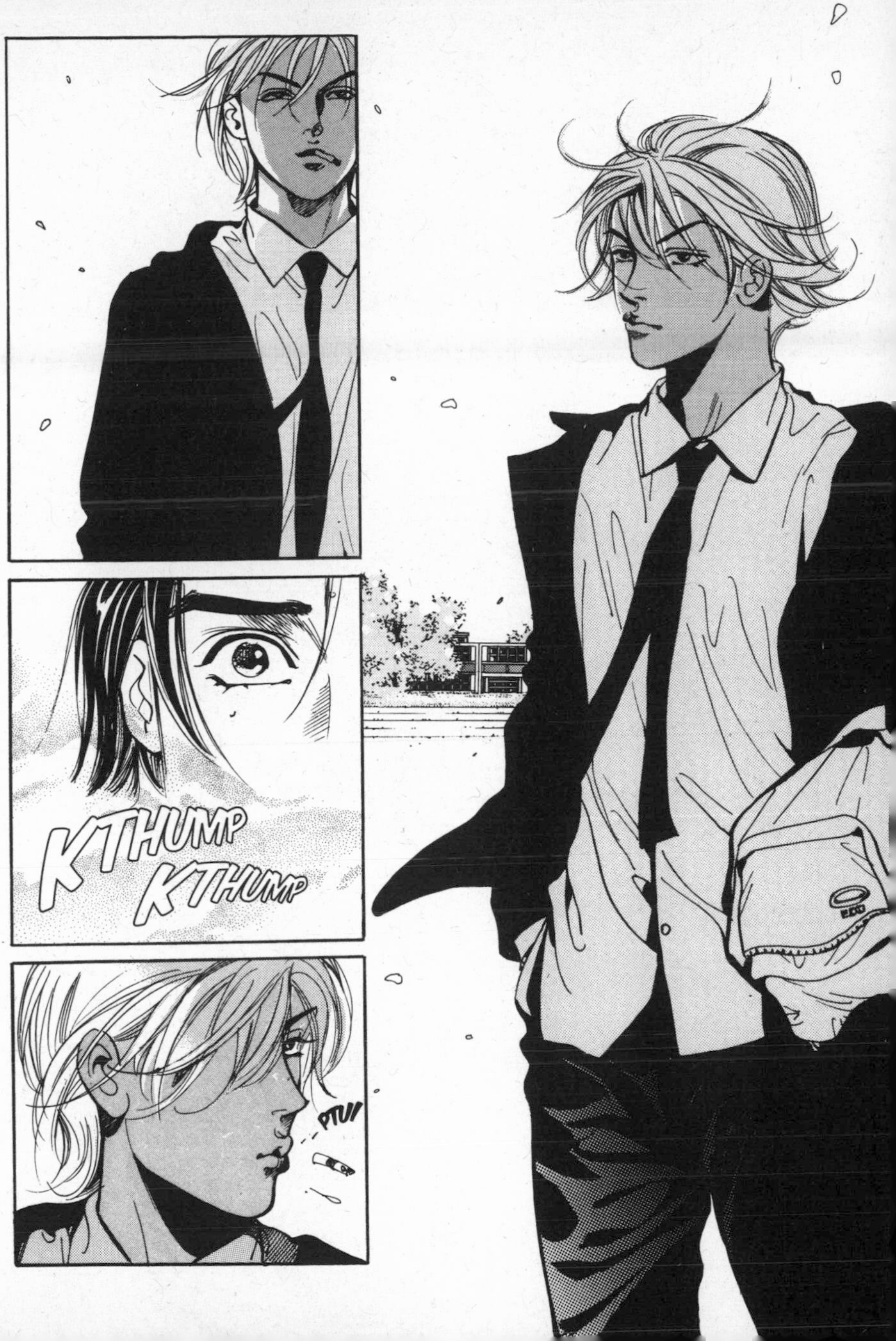
KTHUMP
KTHUMP
PTUI

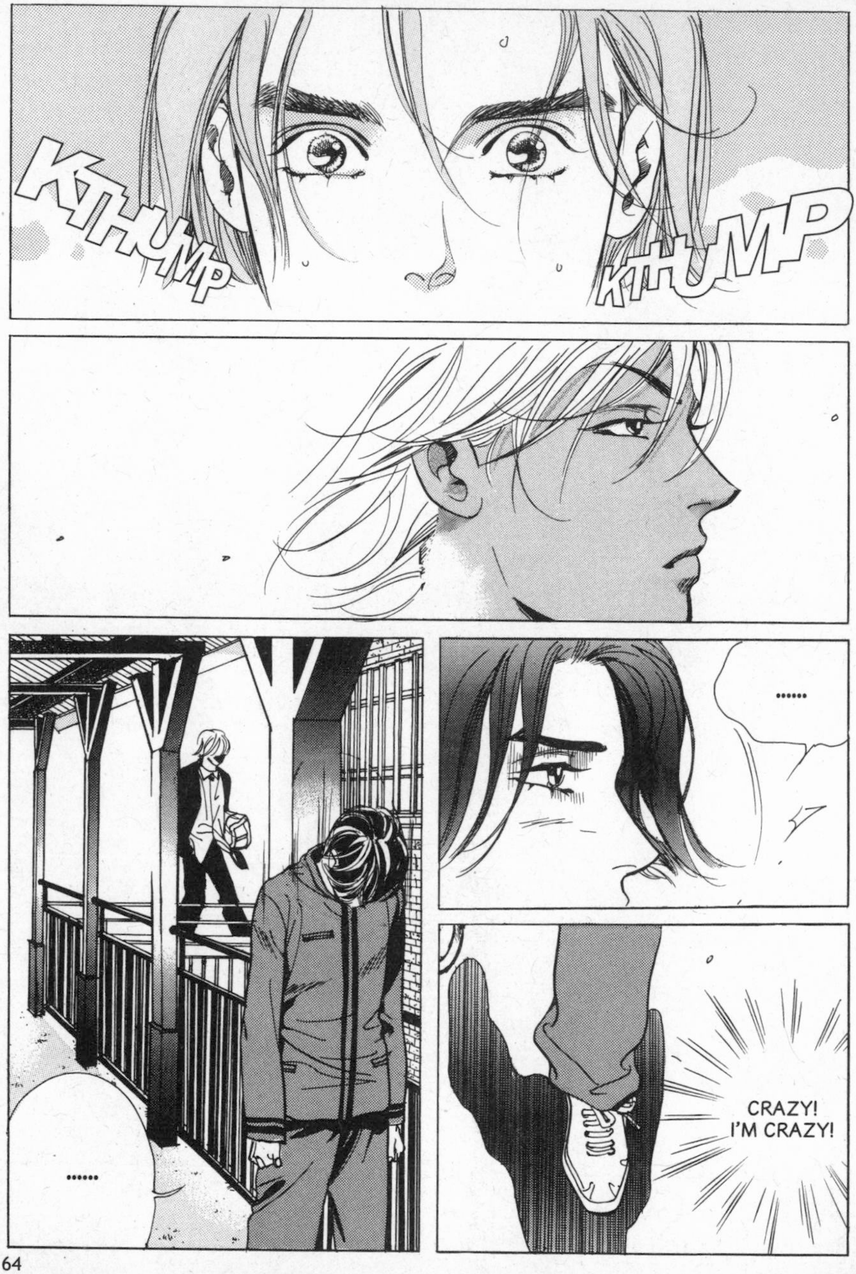
KTHUMP
KTHUMP
......
......
CRAZY! I'M CRAZY!

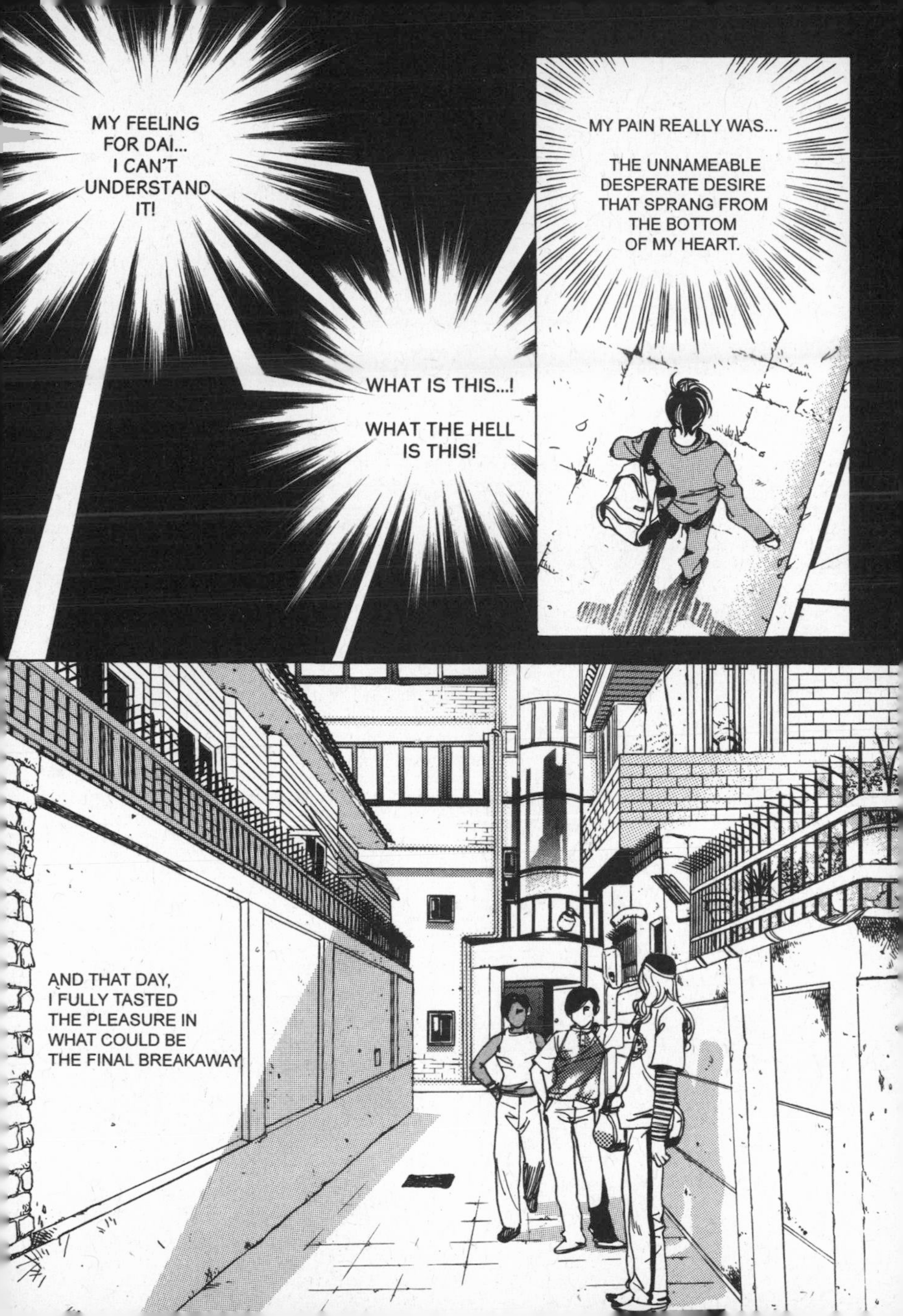
MY FEELING FOR DAI... I CAN'T UNDERSTAND IT!
WHAT IS THIS...!
WHAT THE HELL IS THIS!
MY PAIN REALLY WAS...
THE UNNAMEABLE DESPERATE DESIRE THAT SPRANG FROM THE BOTTOM OF MY HEART.
AND THAT DAY, I FULLY TASTED THE PLEASURE IN WHAT COULD BE THE FINAL BREAKAWAY

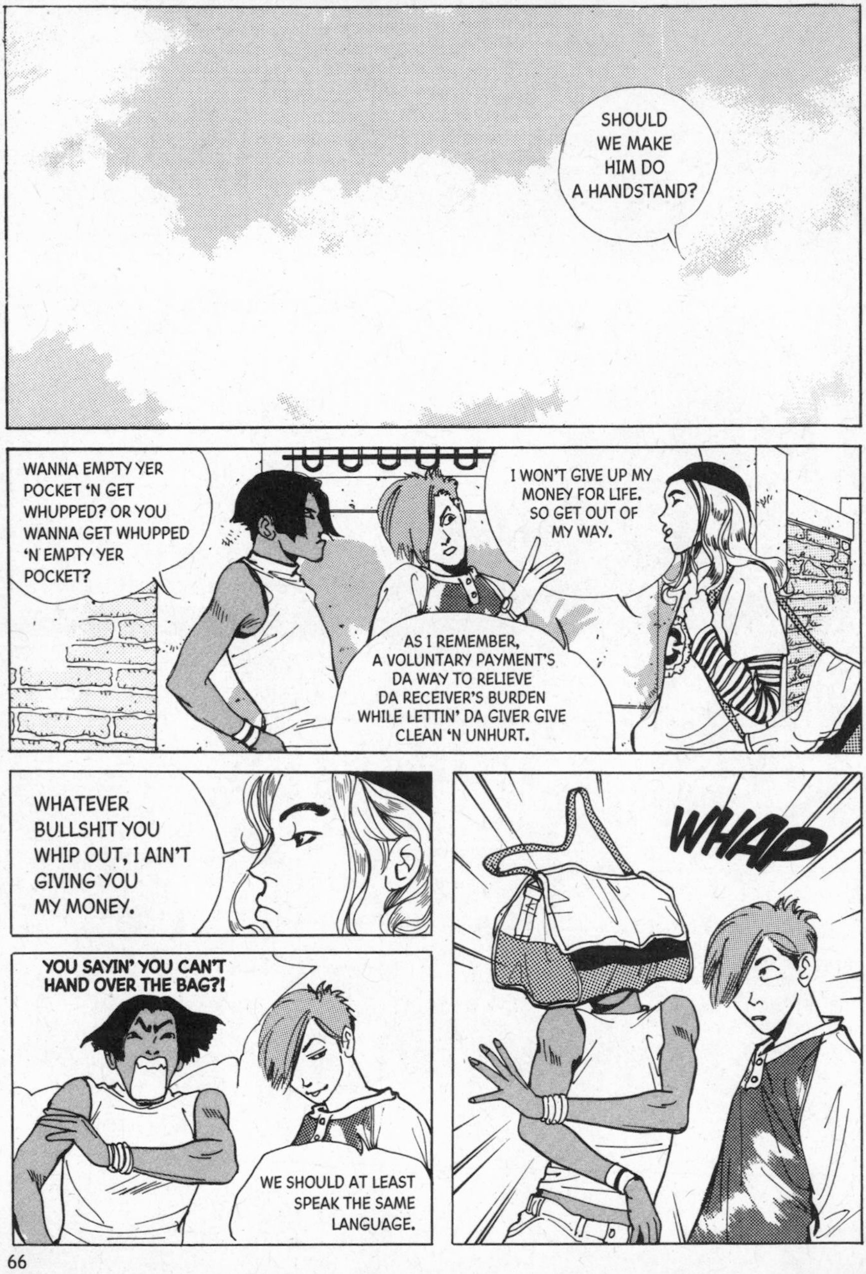
SHOULD WE MAKE HIM DO A HANDSTAND?
WANNA EMPTY YER POCKET 'N GET WHUPPED? OR YOU WANNA GET WHUPPED 'N EMPTY YER POCKET?
I WON'T GIVE UP MY MONEY FOR LIFE. SO GET OUT OF MY WAY.
AS I REMEMBER, A VOLUNTARY PAYMENT'S DA WAY TO RELIEVE DA RECEIVER'S BURDEN WHILE LETTIN' DA GIVER GIVE CLEAN 'N UNHURT.
WHATEVER BULLSHIT YOU WHIP OUT, I AIN'T GIVING YOU MY MONEY.
YOU SAYIN' YOU CAN'T HAND OVER THE BAG?!
WE SHOULD AT LEAST SPEAK THE SAME LANGUAGE.
WHAP

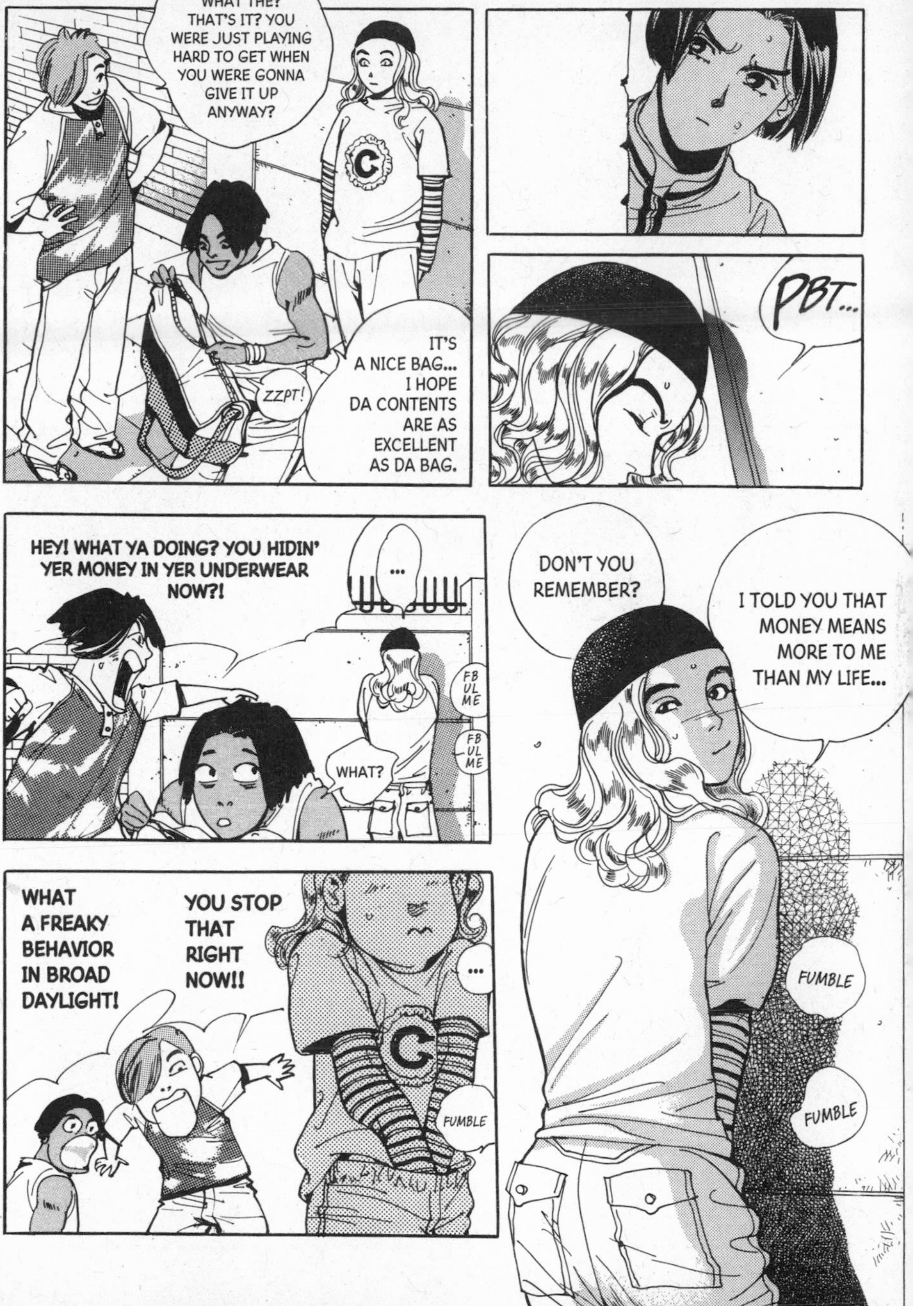
WHAT THE? THAT'S IT? YOU WERE JUST PLAYING HARD TO GET WHEN YOU WERE GONNA GIVE IT UP ANYWAY?
ZZPT!
IT'S A NICE BAG... I HOPE DA CONTENTS ARE AS EXCELLENT AS DA BAG.
PBT...
HEY! WHAT YA DOING? YOU HIDIN' YER MONEY IN YER UNDERWEAR NOW?!
...
FBULME
FBULME
WHAT?
WHAT A FREAKY BEHAVIOR IN BROAD DAYLIGHT!
YOU STOP THAT RIGHT NOW!!
...
FUMBLE
DON'T YOU REMEMBER?
I TOLD YOU THAT MONEY MEANS MORE TO ME THAN MY LIFE...
FUMBLE
FUMBLE

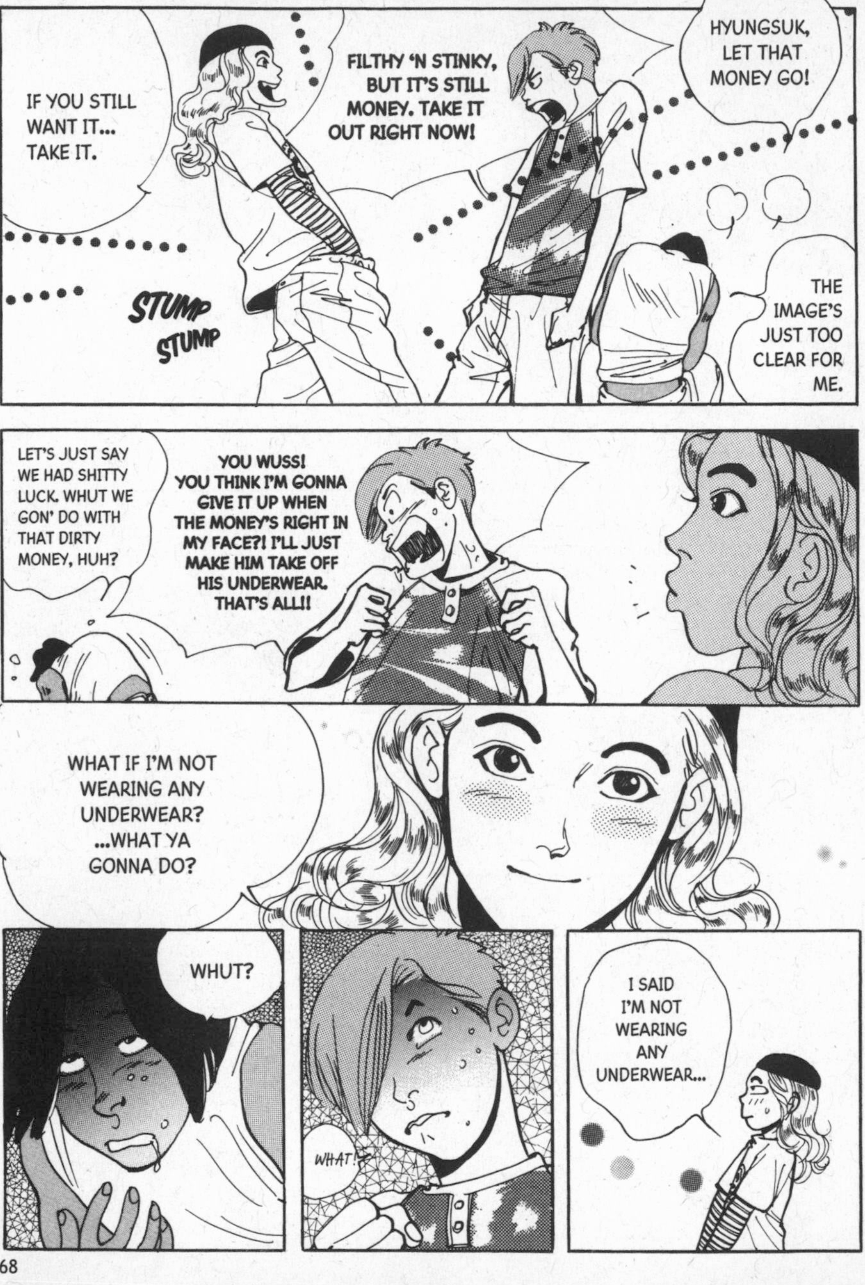

IF YOU STILL WANT IT... TAKE IT.
FILTHY 'N STINKY, BUT IT'S STILL MONEY. TAKE IT OUT RIGHT NOW!
HYUNGSUK, LET THAT MONEY GO!
STUMP STUMP
THE IMAGE'S JUST TOO CLEAR FOR ME.
LET'S JUST SAY WE HAD SHITTY LUCK. WHUT WE GON' DO WITH THAT DIRTY MONEY, HUH?
YOU WUSS! YOU THINK I'M GONNA GIVE IT UP WHEN THE MONEY'S RIGHT IN MY FACE?! I'LL JUST MAKE HIM TAKE OFF HIS UNDERWEAR. THAT'S ALL!!
WHAT IF I'M NOT WEARING ANY UNDERWEAR? ...WHAT YA GONNA DO?
WHUT?
WHAT!
I SAID I'M NOT WEARING ANY UNDERWEAR...

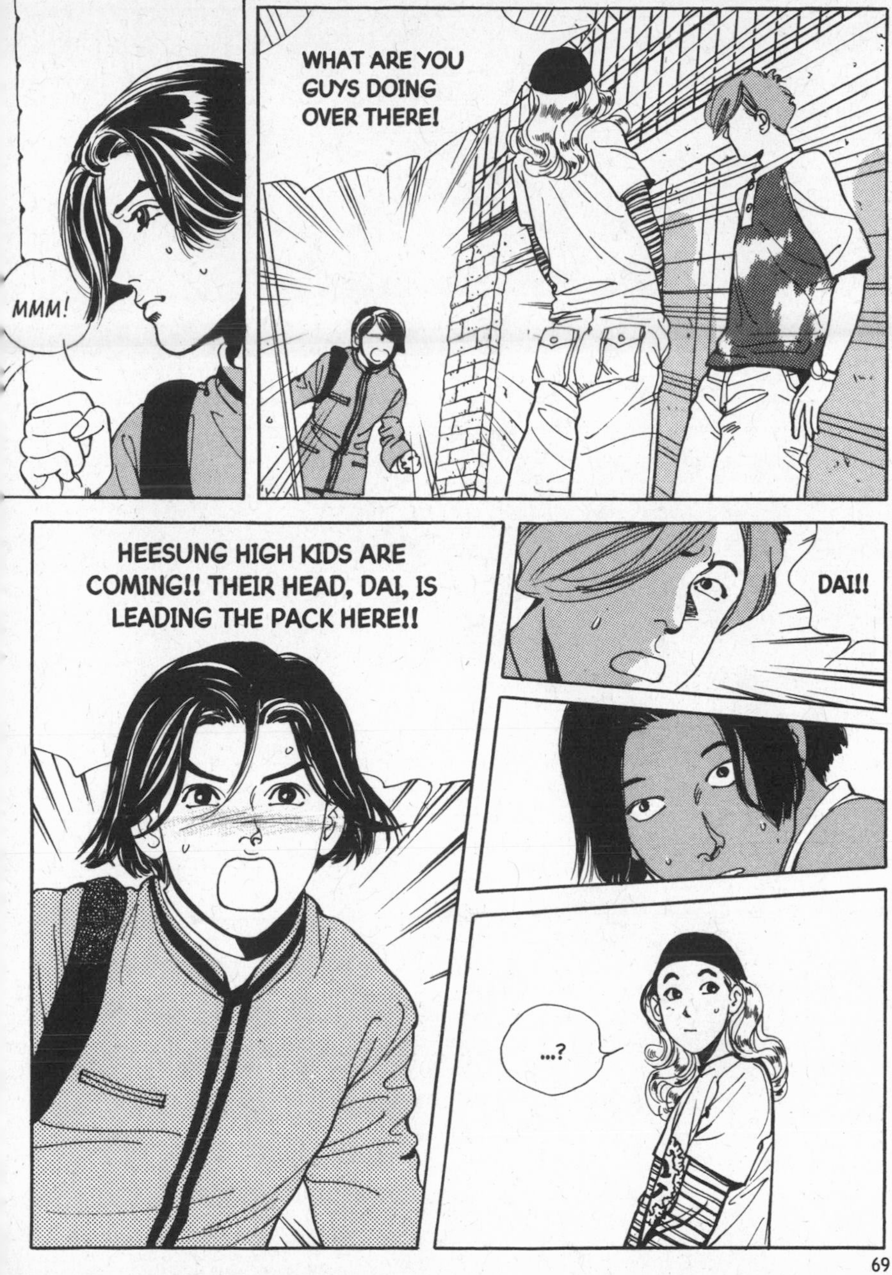
MMM!
WHAT ARE YOU GUYS DOING OVER THERE!
HEESUNG HIGH KIDS ARE COMING!! THEIR HEAD, DAI, IS LEADING THE PACK HERE!!
DAI!!
...?

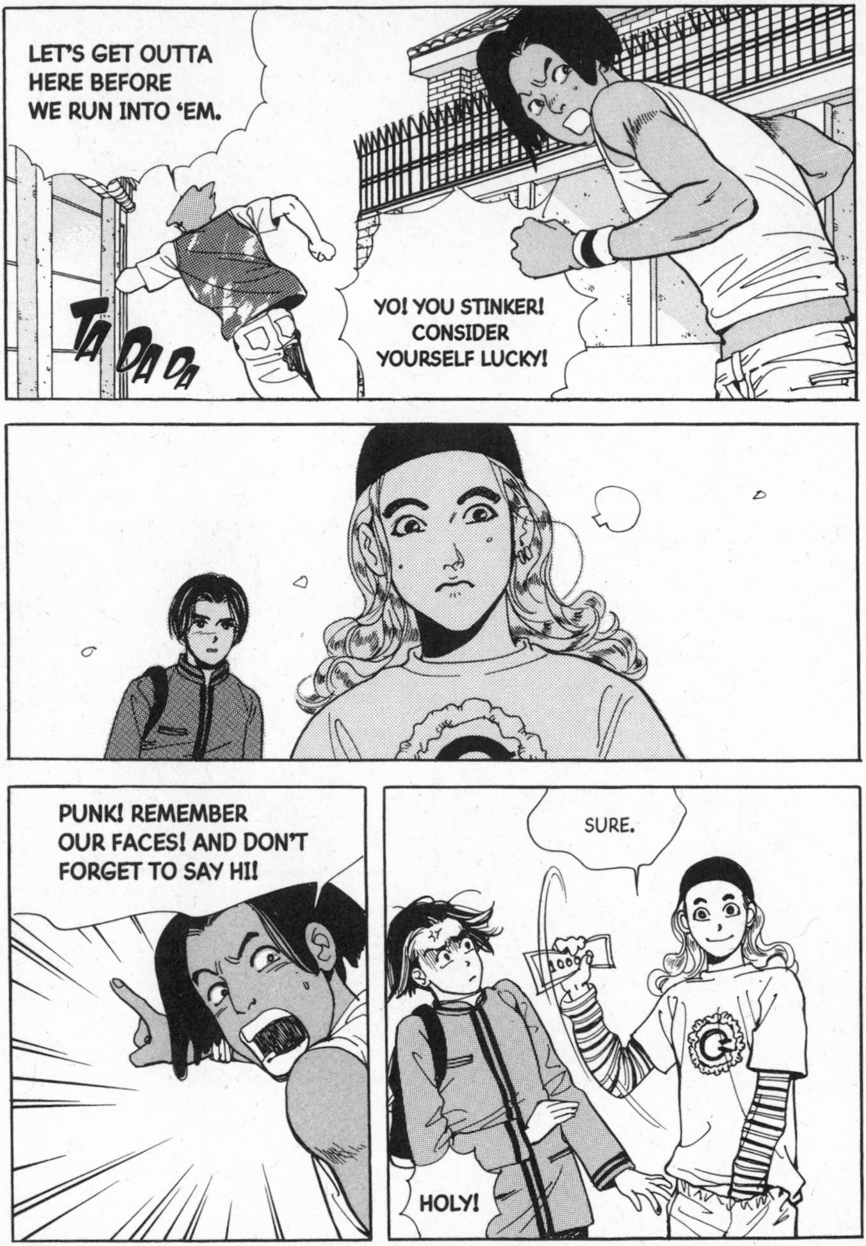
LET'S GET OUTTA HERE BEFORE WE RUN INTO 'EM.
TA DA DA
YO! YOU STINKER! CONSIDER YOURSELF LUCKY!
PUNK! REMEMBER OUR FACES! AND DON'T FORGET TO SAY HI!
SURE.
HOLY!

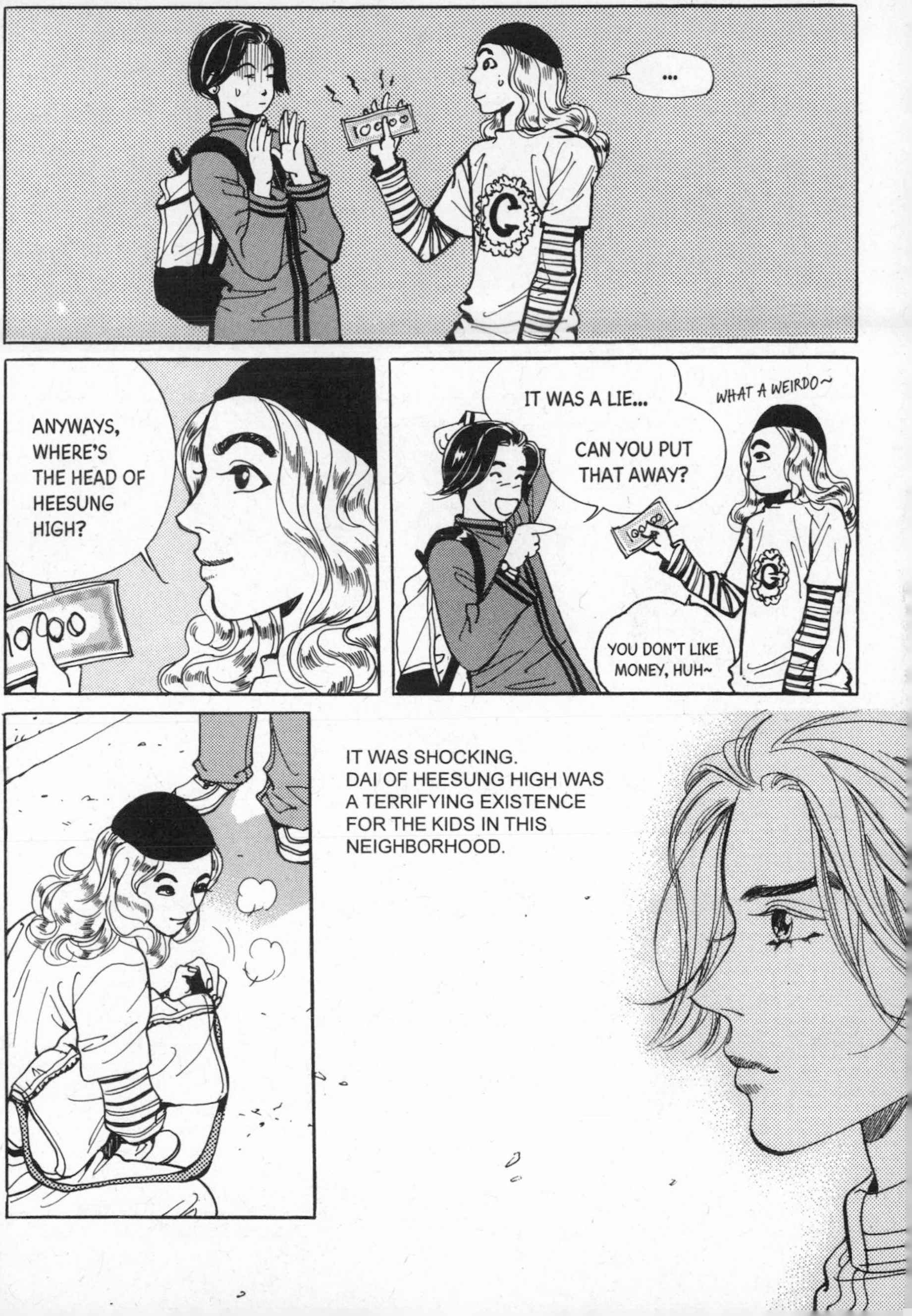
...
ANYWAYS, WHERE'S THE HEAD OF HEESUNG HIGH?
IT WAS A LIE...
CAN YOU PUT THAT AWAY?
WHAT A WEIRDO~
YOU DON'T LIKE MONEY, HUH~
IT WAS SHOCKING.
DAI OF HEESUNG HIGH WAS A TERRIFYING EXISTENCE FOR THE KIDS IN THIS NEIGHBORHOOD.

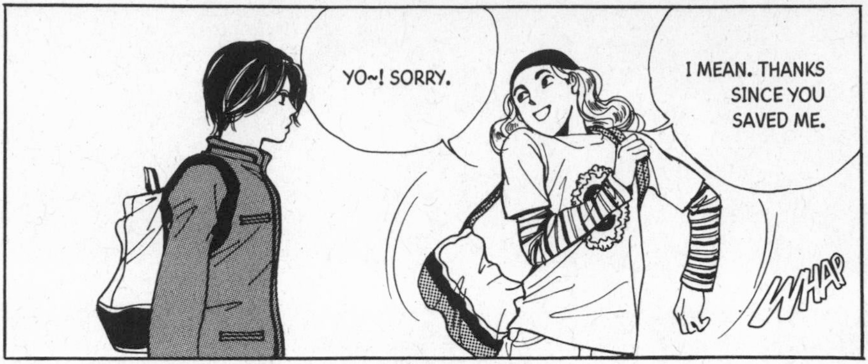
YO~! SORRY.
I MEAN. THANKS SINCE YOU SAVED ME.
WHAP

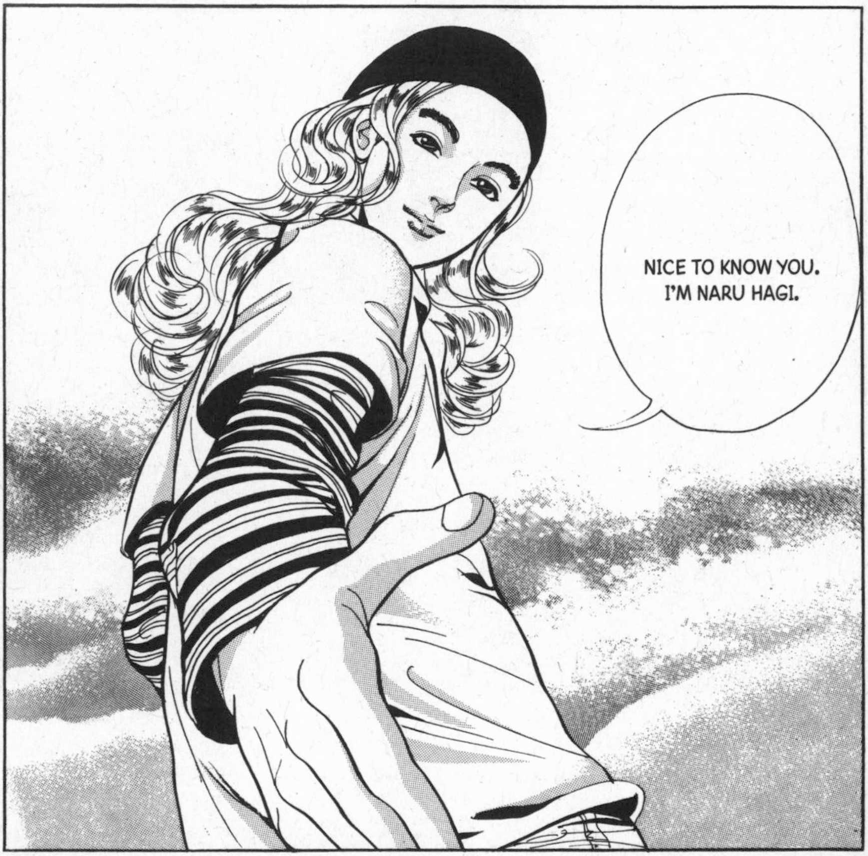
NICE TO KNOW YOU. I'M NARU HAGI.

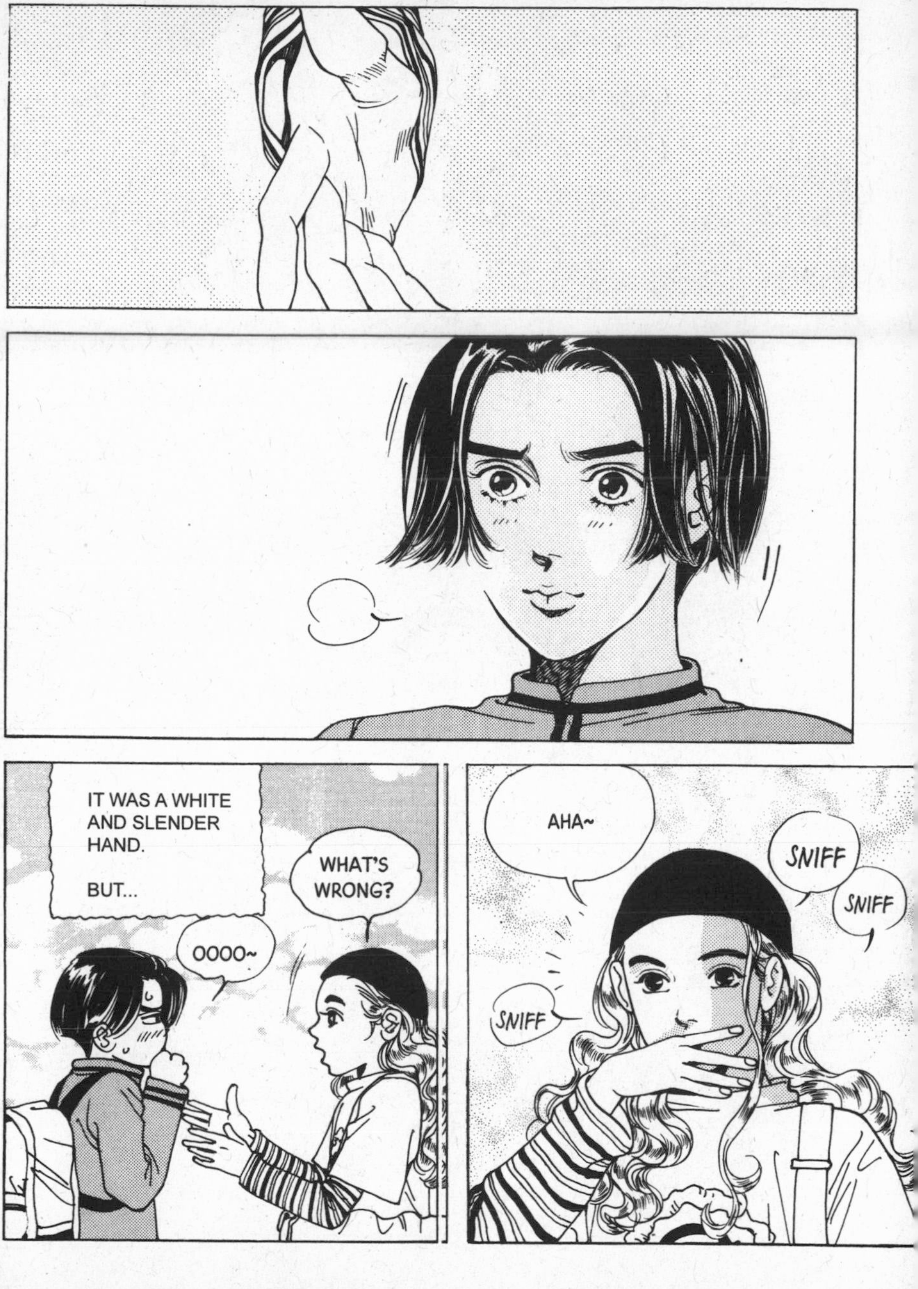
IT WAS A WHITE AND SLENDER HAND.
BUT...
WHAT'S WRONG?
OOOO~
AHA~
SNIFF
SNIFF
SNIFF

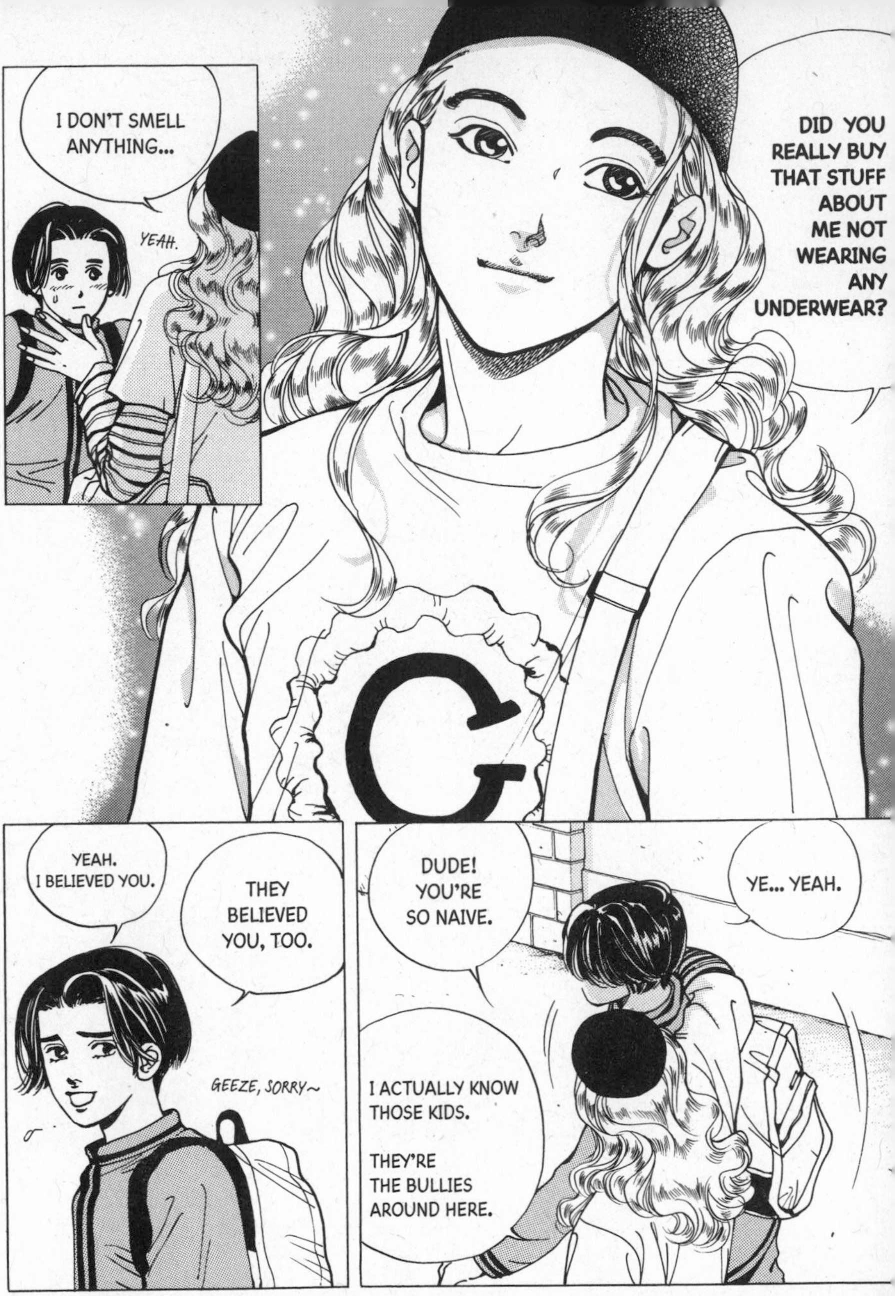
I DON'T SMELL ANYTHING...
YEAH.
DID YOU REALLY BUY THAT STUFF ABOUT ME NOT WEARING ANY UNDERWEAR?
YEAH. I BELIEVED YOU.
THEY BELIEVED YOU, TOO.
GEEZE, SORRY~
DUDE! YOU'RE SO NAIVE.
YE... YEAH.
I ACTUALLY KNOW THOSE KIDS.
THEY'RE THE BULLIES AROUND HERE.

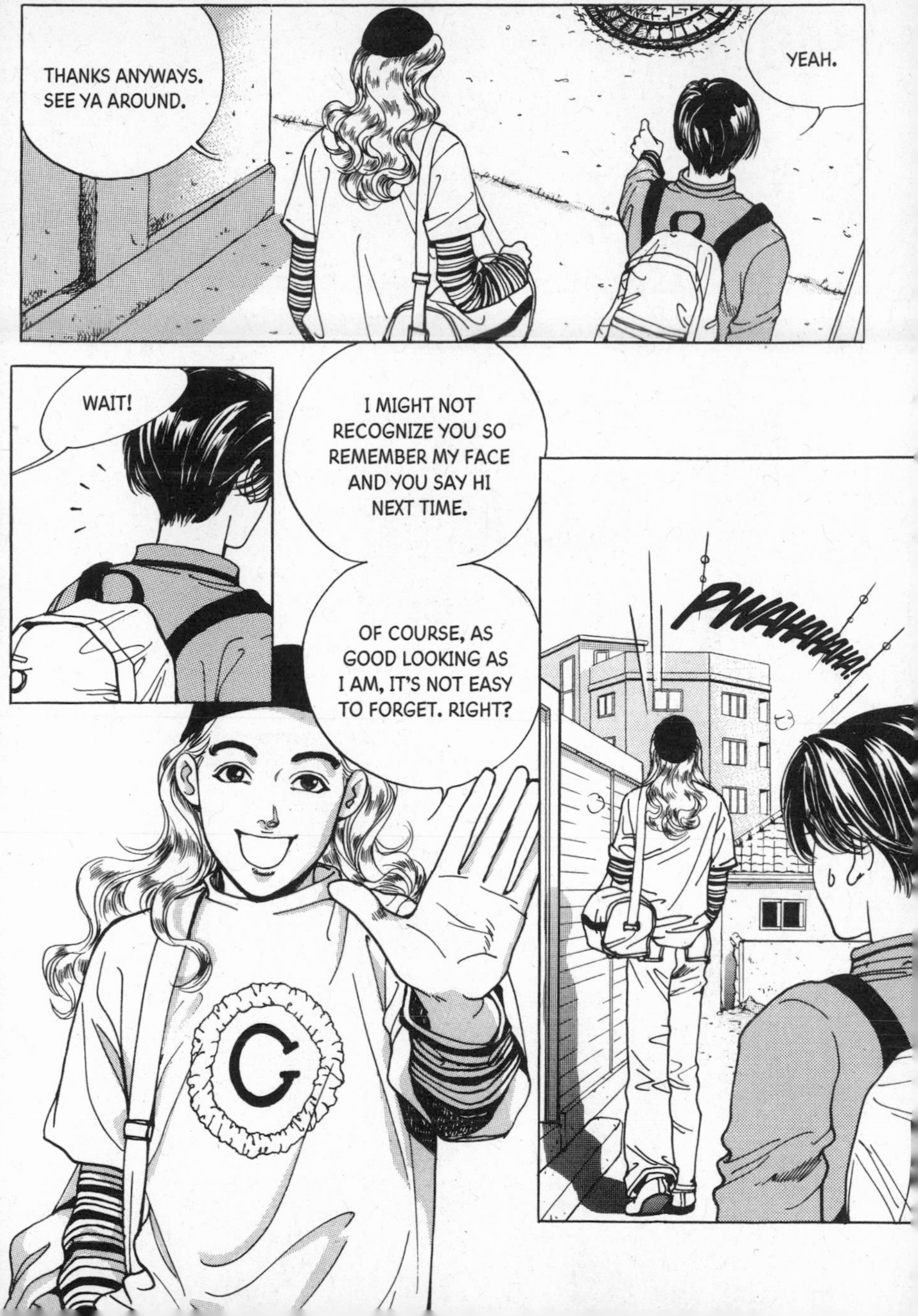
THANKS ANYWAYS. SEE YA AROUND.
YEAH.
WAIT!
I MIGHT NOT RECOGNIZE YOU SO REMEMBER MY FACE AND YOU SAY HI NEXT TIME.
OF COURSE, AS GOOD LOOKING AS I AM, IT'S NOT EASY TO FORGET. RIGHT?
PWAHAHAHAHA!

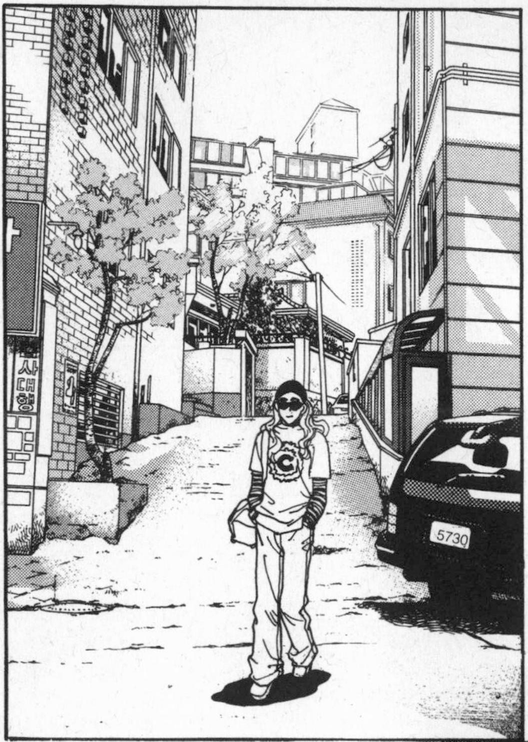
5730

NARU HAGI.

HE WAS AN ODDLY
STRIKING PAL.

THERE WAS
AN ALMOST CHAOTIC
FREEDOM IN HIM.

AND NARU WAS
THE KIND OF SPARK
THAT ALLOWED ME
TO EXPERIENCE
MY KEEN SENSE OF
SMELL WITH MY EYES.

A RELAXED
CONFIDENCE...

THAT IS NOT CHAINED
TO ANYTHING.

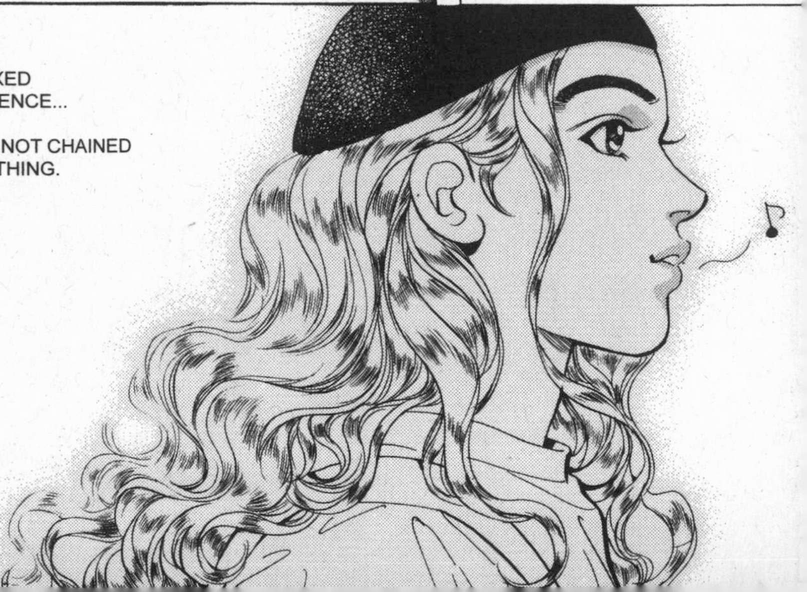

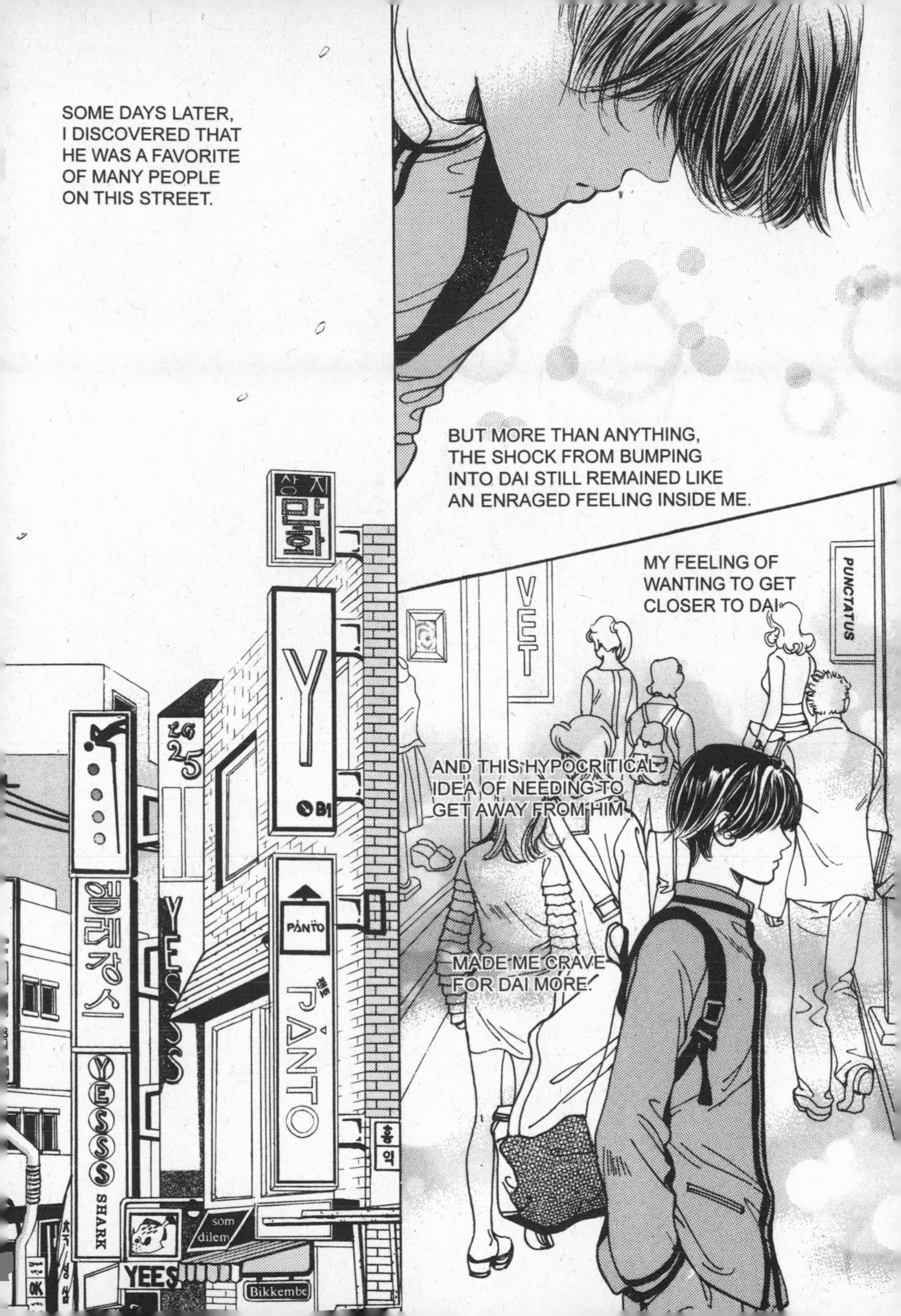
SOME DAYS LATER, I DISCOVERED THAT HE WAS A FAVORITE OF MANY PEOPLE ON THIS STREET.
PÀNTO
PÀNTO
YESSS
SHARK
Bikkembe
BUT MORE THAN ANYTHING, THE SHOCK FROM BUMPING INTO DAI STILL REMAINED LIKE AN ENRAGED FEELING INSIDE ME.
MY FEELING OF WANTING TO GET CLOSER TO DAI
VET
PUNCTUATUS
AND THIS HYPOCRITICAL IDEA OF NEEDING TO GET AWAY FROM HIM
MADE ME CRAVE FOR DAI MORE.

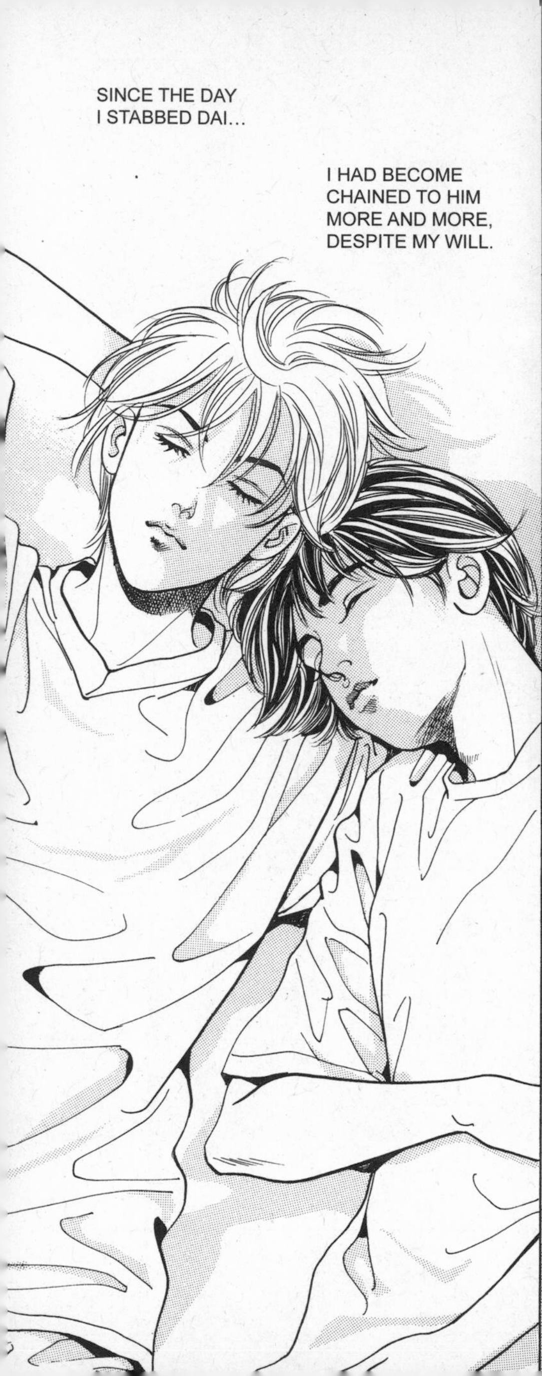
SINCE THE DAY I STABBED DAI…
I HAD BECOME CHAINED TO HIM MORE AND MORE, DESPITE MY WILL.

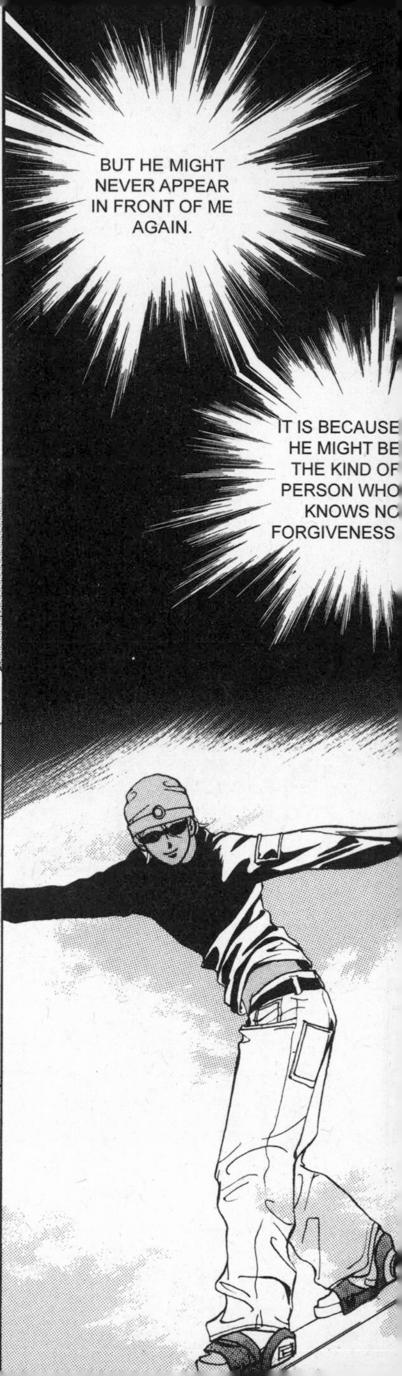
BUT HE MIGHT NEVER APPEAR IN FRONT OF ME AGAIN.
IT IS BECAUSE HE MIGHT BE THE KIND OF PERSON WHO KNOWS NO FORGIVENESS

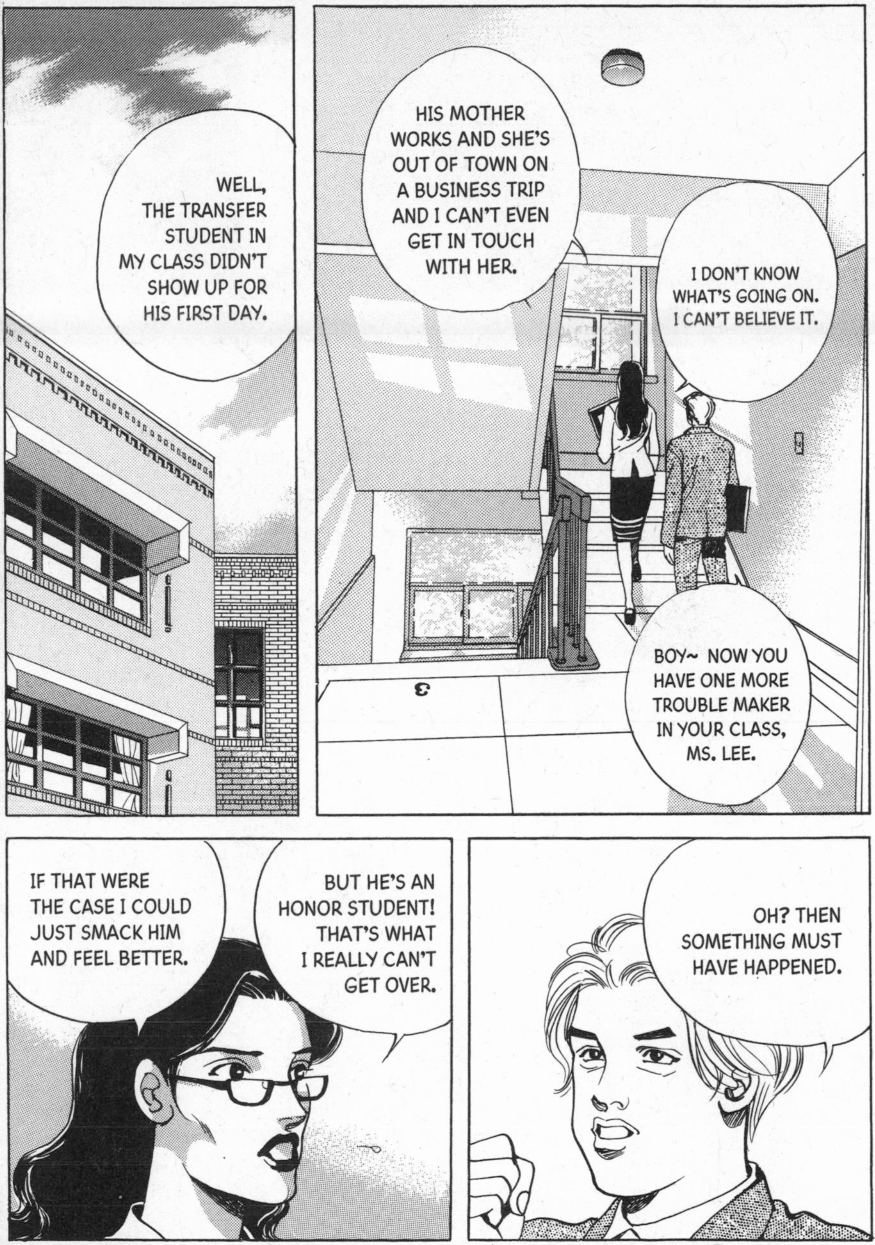
WELL, THE TRANSFER STUDENT IN MY CLASS DIDN'T SHOW UP FOR HIS FIRST DAY.
HIS MOTHER WORKS AND SHE'S OUT OF TOWN ON A BUSINESS TRIP AND I CAN'T EVEN GET IN TOUCH WITH HER.
I DON'T KNOW WHAT'S GOING ON. I CAN'T BELIEVE IT.
BOY~ NOW YOU HAVE ONE MORE TROUBLE MAKER IN YOUR CLASS, MS. LEE.
IF THAT WERE THE CASE I COULD JUST SMACK HIM AND FEEL BETTER.
BUT HE'S AN HONOR STUDENT! THAT'S WHAT I REALLY CAN'T GET OVER.
OH? THEN SOMETHING MUST HAVE HAPPENED.

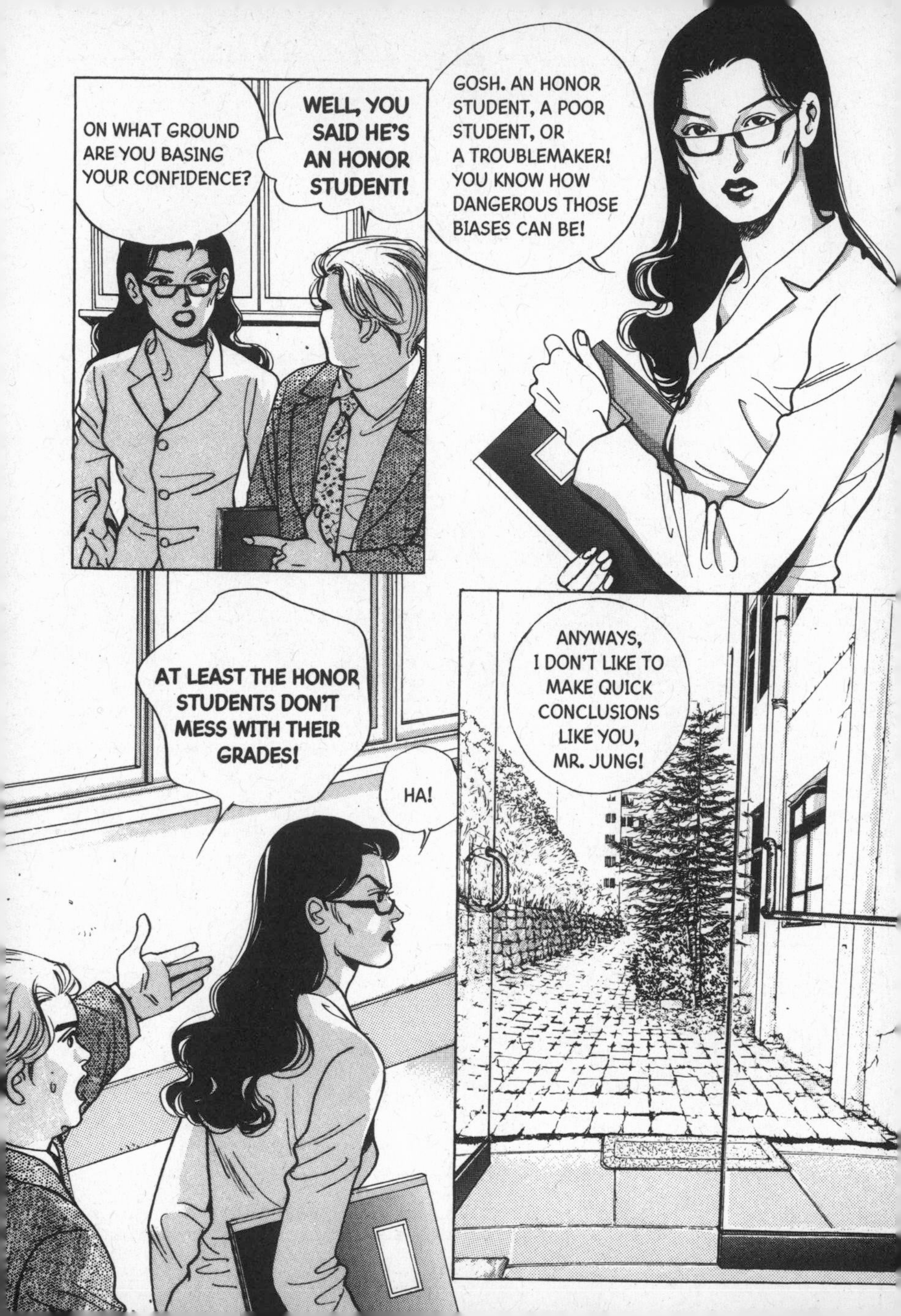
ON WHAT GROUND ARE YOU BASING YOUR CONFIDENCE?
WELL, YOU SAID HE'S AN HONOR STUDENT!
GOSH. AN HONOR STUDENT, A POOR STUDENT, OR A TROUBLEMAKER! YOU KNOW HOW DANGEROUS THOSE BIASES CAN BE!
AT LEAST THE HONOR STUDENTS DON'T MESS WITH THEIR GRADES!
HA!
ANYWAYS, I DON'T LIKE TO MAKE QUICK CONCLUSIONS LIKE YOU, MR. JUNG!

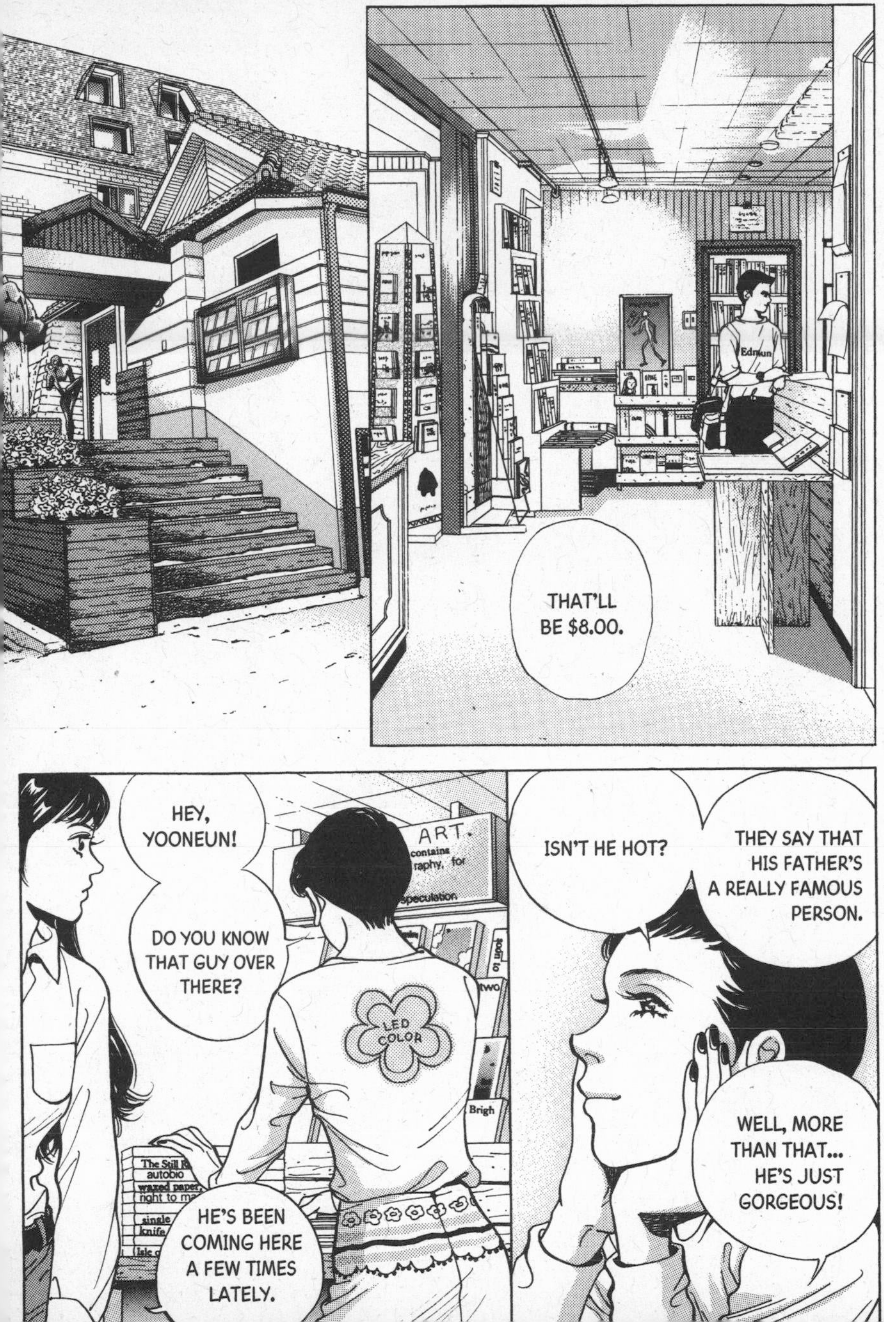
THAT'LL BE $8.00.
HEY, YOONEUN!
DO YOU KNOW THAT GUY OVER THERE?
ART
LED COLOR
HE'S BEEN COMING HERE A FEW TIMES LATELY.
ISN'T HE HOT?
THEY SAY THAT HIS FATHER'S A REALLY FAMOUS PERSON.
WELL, MORE THAN THAT... HE'S JUST GORGEOUS!

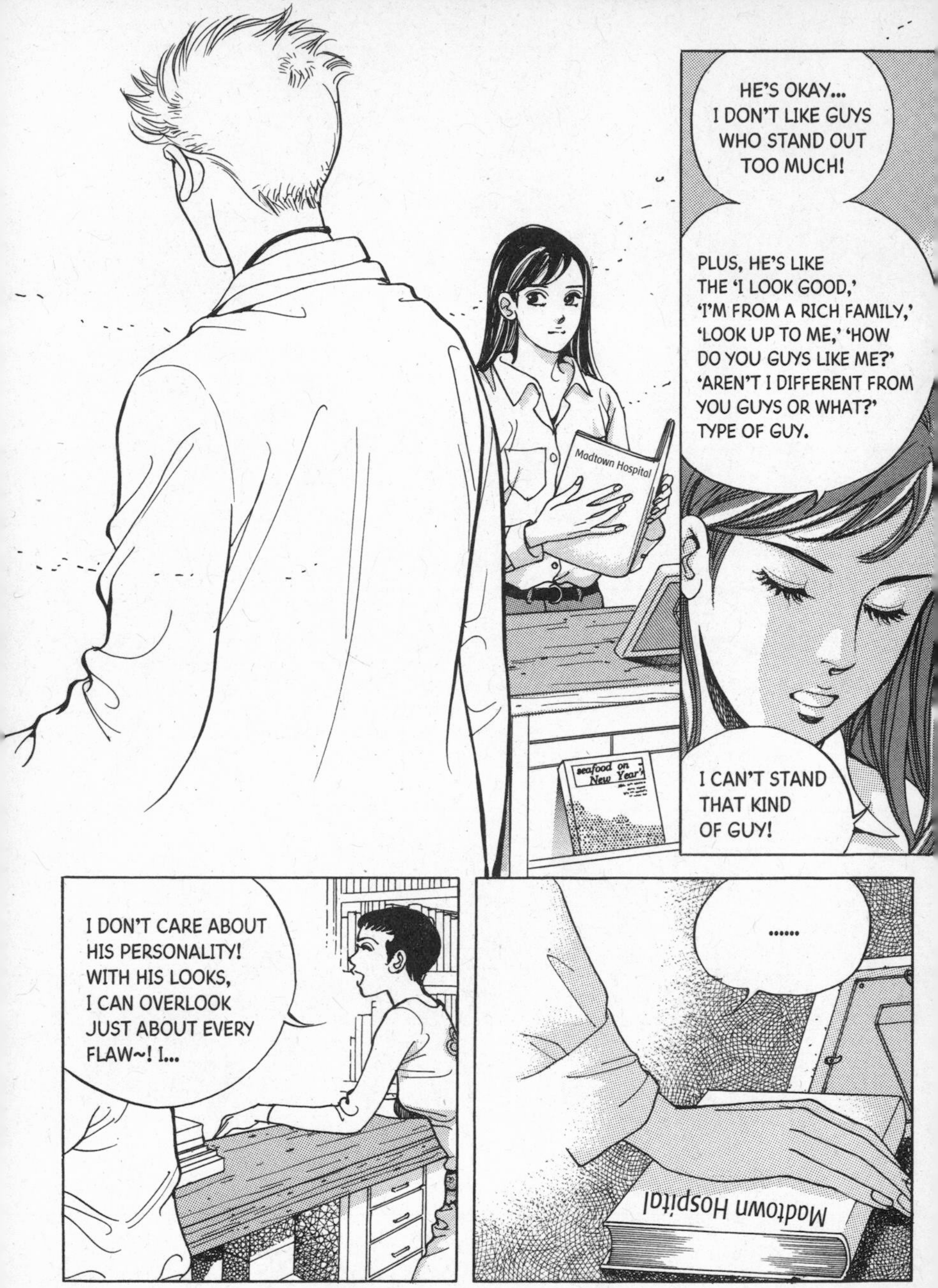
Madtown Hospital
seafood on New Year's
HE'S OKAY... I DON'T LIKE GUYS WHO STAND OUT TOO MUCH!
PLUS, HE'S LIKE THE 'I LOOK GOOD,' 'I'M FROM A RICH FAMILY,' 'LOOK UP TO ME,' 'HOW DO YOU GUYS LIKE ME?' 'AREN'T I DIFFERENT FROM YOU GUYS OR WHAT?' TYPE OF GUY.
I CAN'T STAND THAT KIND OF GUY!
I DON'T CARE ABOUT HIS PERSONALITY! WITH HIS LOOKS, I CAN OVERLOOK JUST ABOUT EVERY FLAW~! I...
......
Madtown Hospital

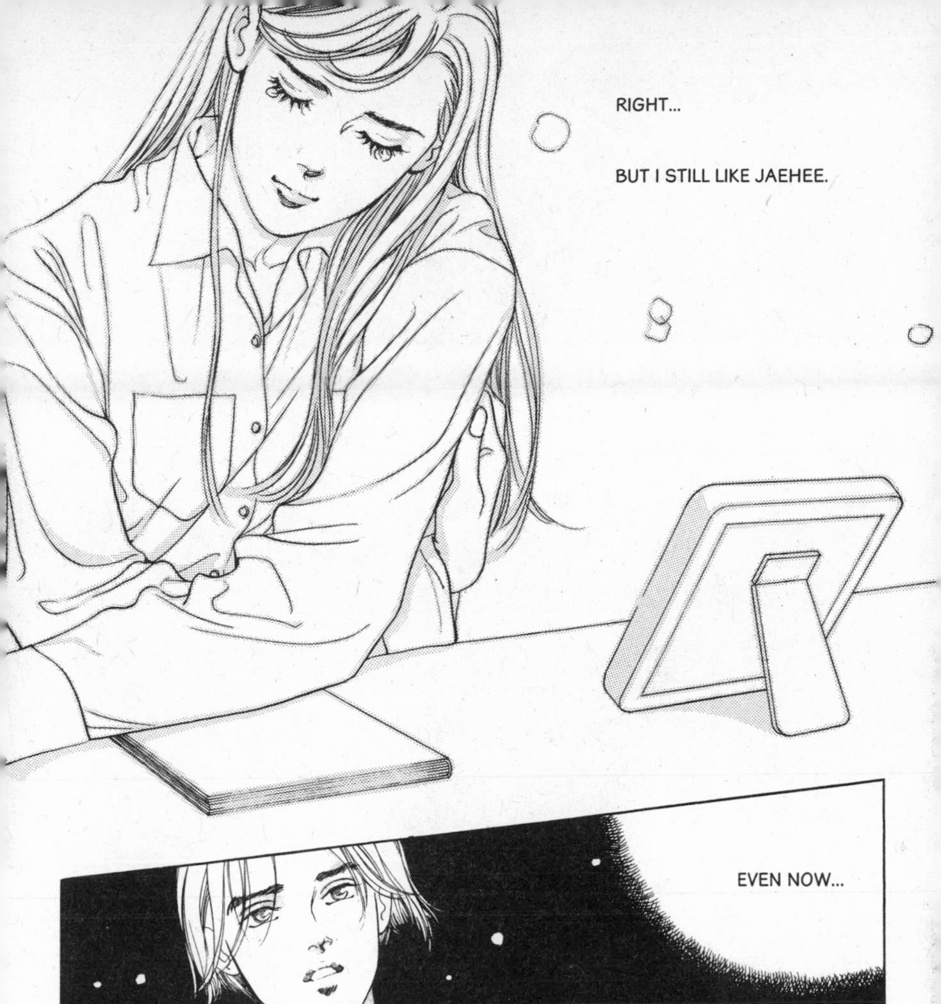
RIGHT...
BUT I STILL LIKE JAEHEE.

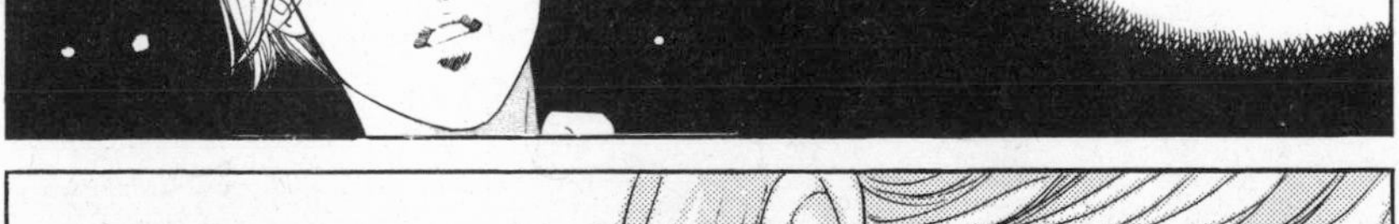
EVEN NOW...

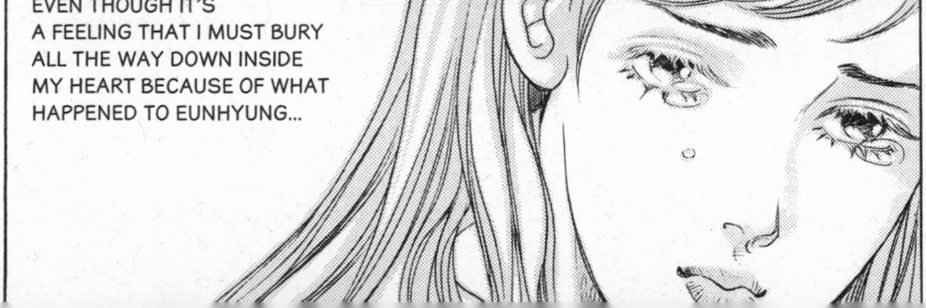
EVEN THOUGH IT'S A FEELING THAT I MUST BURY ALL THE WAY DOWN INSIDE MY HEART BECAUSE OF WHAT HAPPENED TO EUNHYUNG...

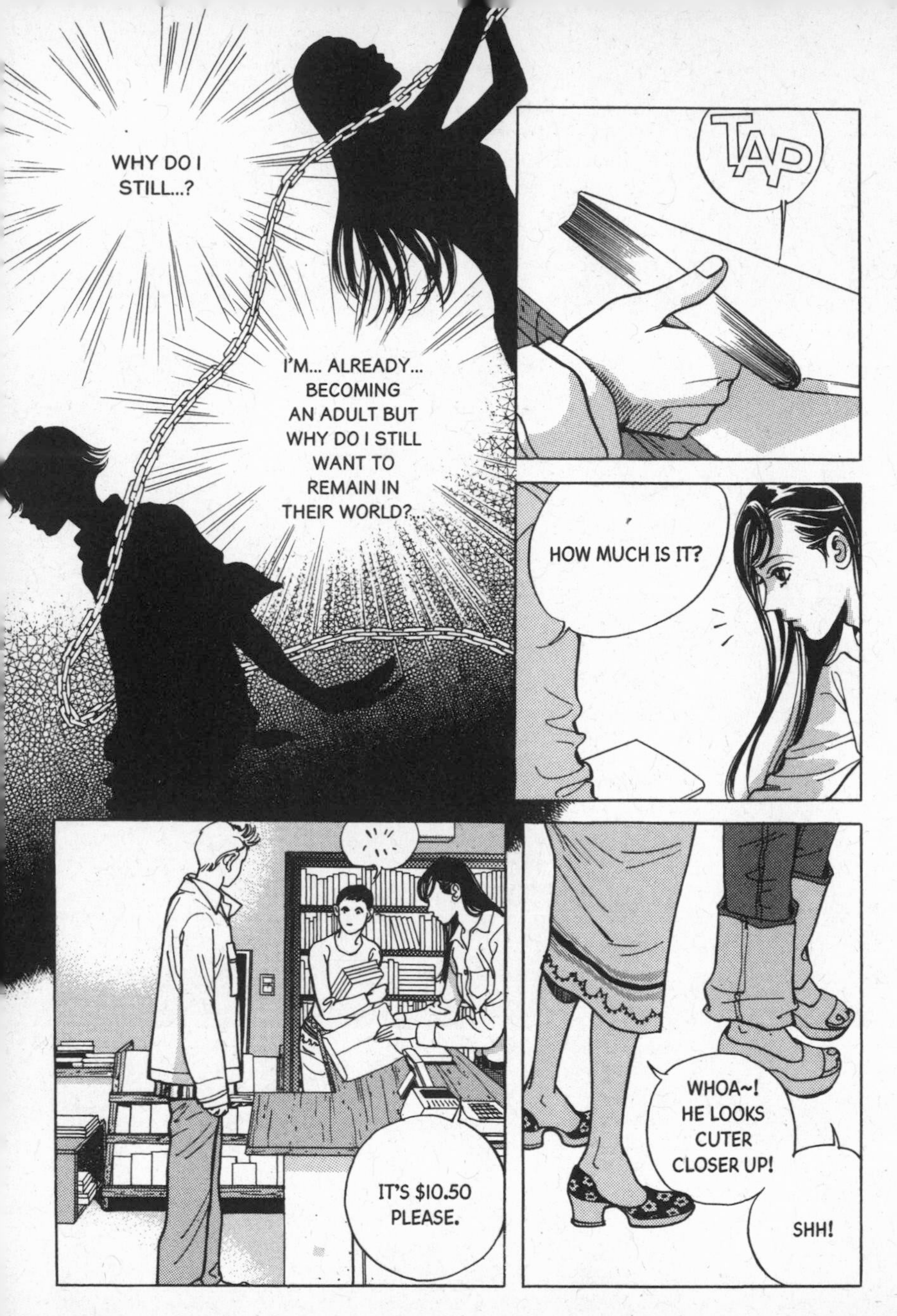
WHY DO I STILL...?
I'M... ALREADY... BECOMING AN ADULT BUT WHY DO I STILL WANT TO REMAIN IN THEIR WORLD?...
TAP
HOW MUCH IS IT?
!
IT'S $10.50 PLEASE.
WHOA~! HE LOOKS CUTER CLOSER UP!
SHH!

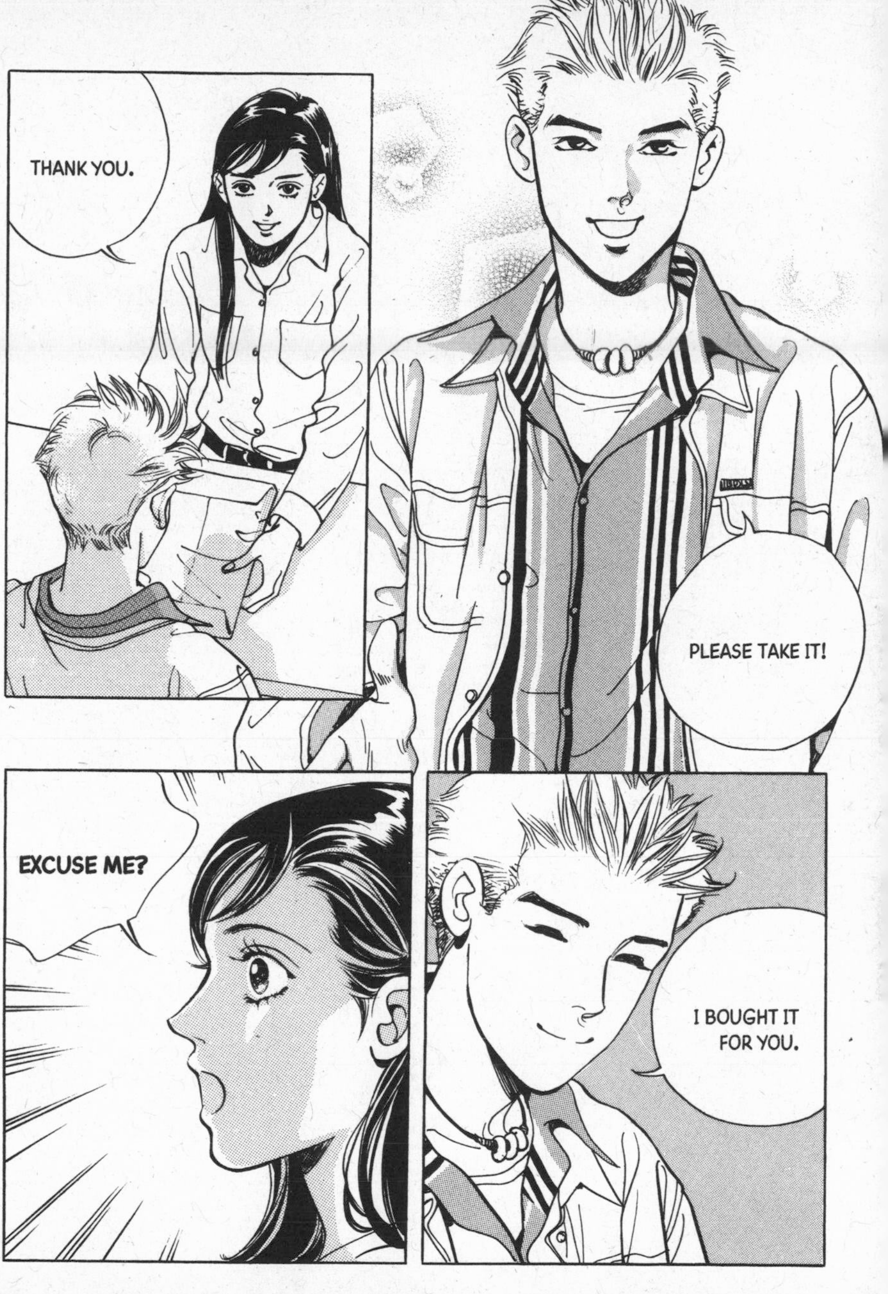
THANK YOU.
PLEASE TAKE IT!
EXCUSE ME?
I BOUGHT IT FOR YOU.

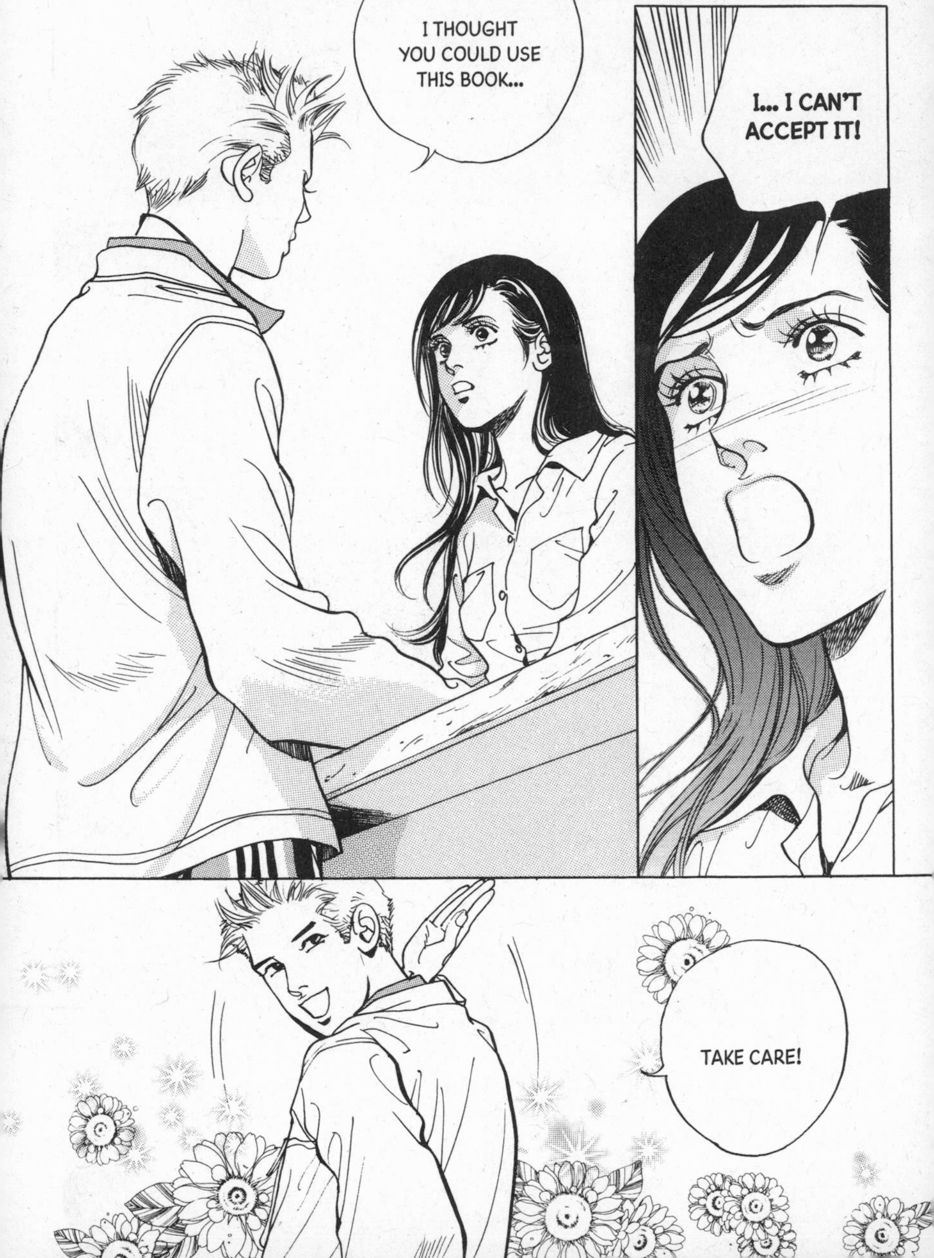
I THOUGHT YOU COULD USE THIS BOOK...
I... I CAN'T ACCEPT IT!
TAKE CARE!

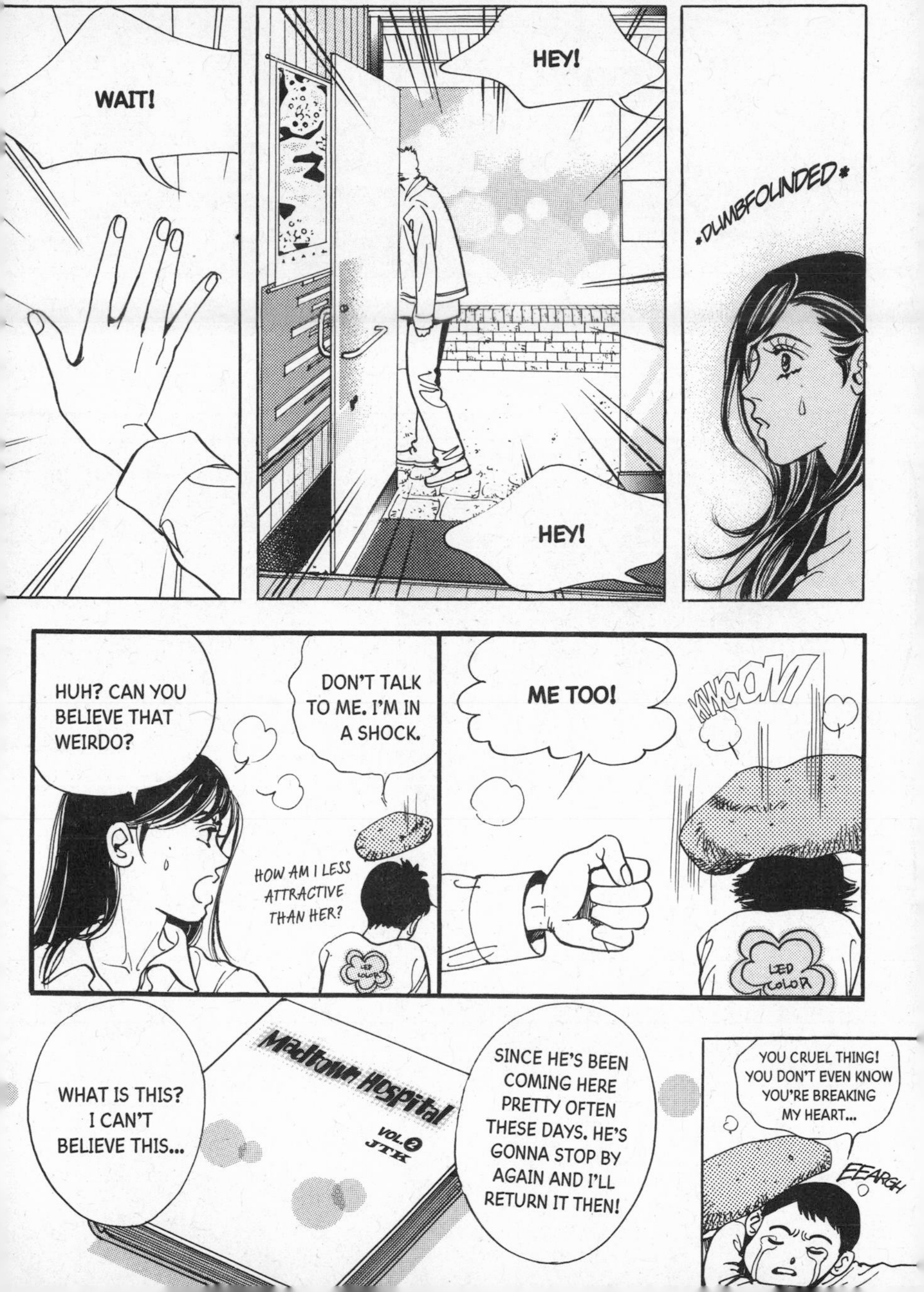
WAIT!
HEY!
HEY!
DUMBFOUNDED
HUH? CAN YOU BELIEVE THAT WEIRDO?
DON'T TALK TO ME. I'M IN A SHOCK.
HOW AM I LESS ATTRACTIVE THAN HER?
LED COLOR
ME TOO!
KWOOM
LED COLOR
WHAT IS THIS? I CAN'T BELIEVE THIS...
Madtown Hospital
VOL. 2
JTK
SINCE HE'S BEEN COMING HERE PRETTY OFTEN THESE DAYS. HE'S GONNA STOP BY AGAIN AND I'LL RETURN IT THEN!
YOU CRUEL THING! YOU DON'T EVEN KNOW YOU'RE BREAKING MY HEART...
EEARGH

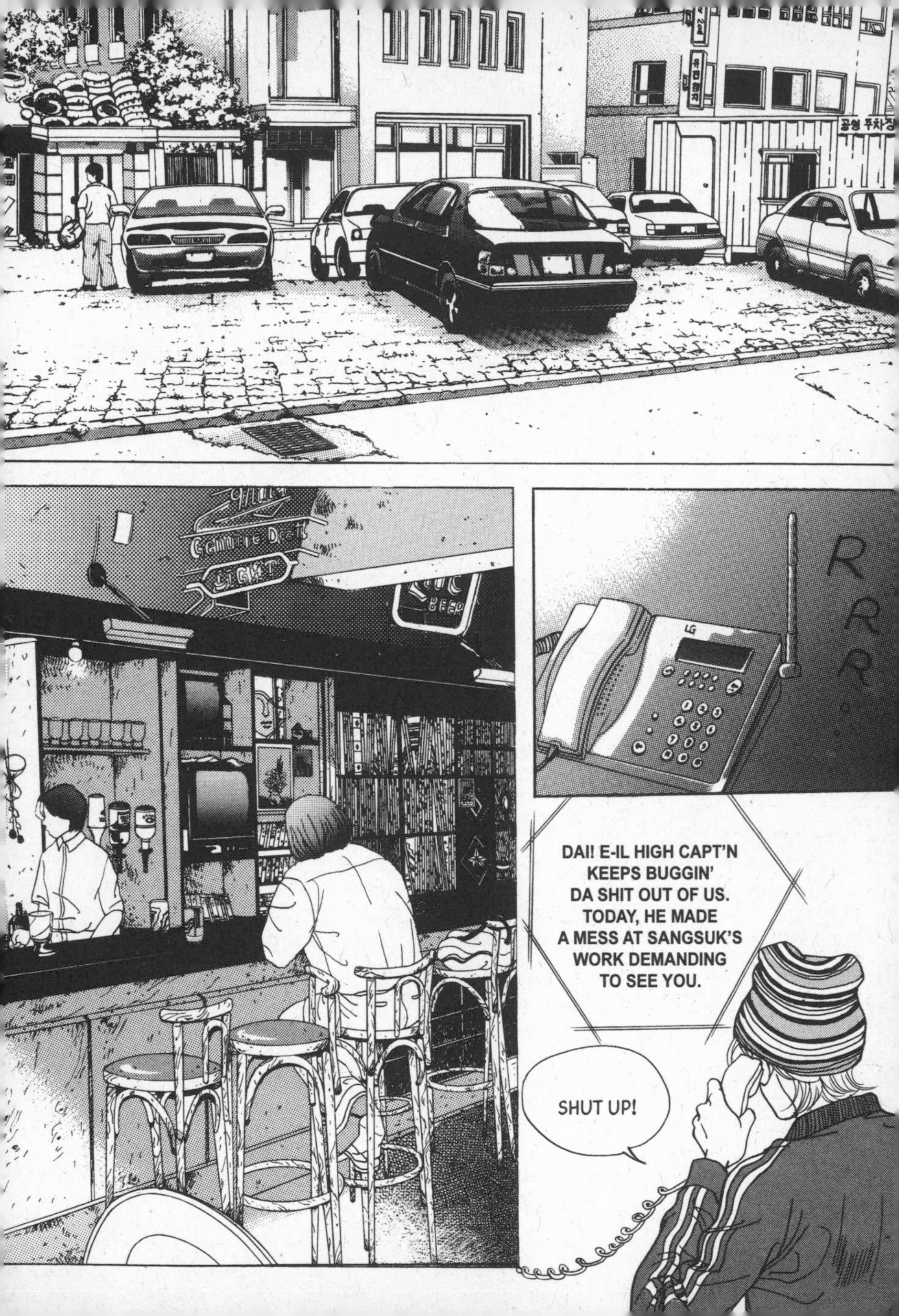

공영 주차장
Genuine Draft
LIGHT
BEER
RRR
DAI! E-IL HIGH CAPT'N KEEPS BUGGIN' DA SHIT OUT OF US. TODAY, HE MADE A MESS AT SANGSUK'S WORK DEMANDING TO SEE YOU.
SHUT UP!

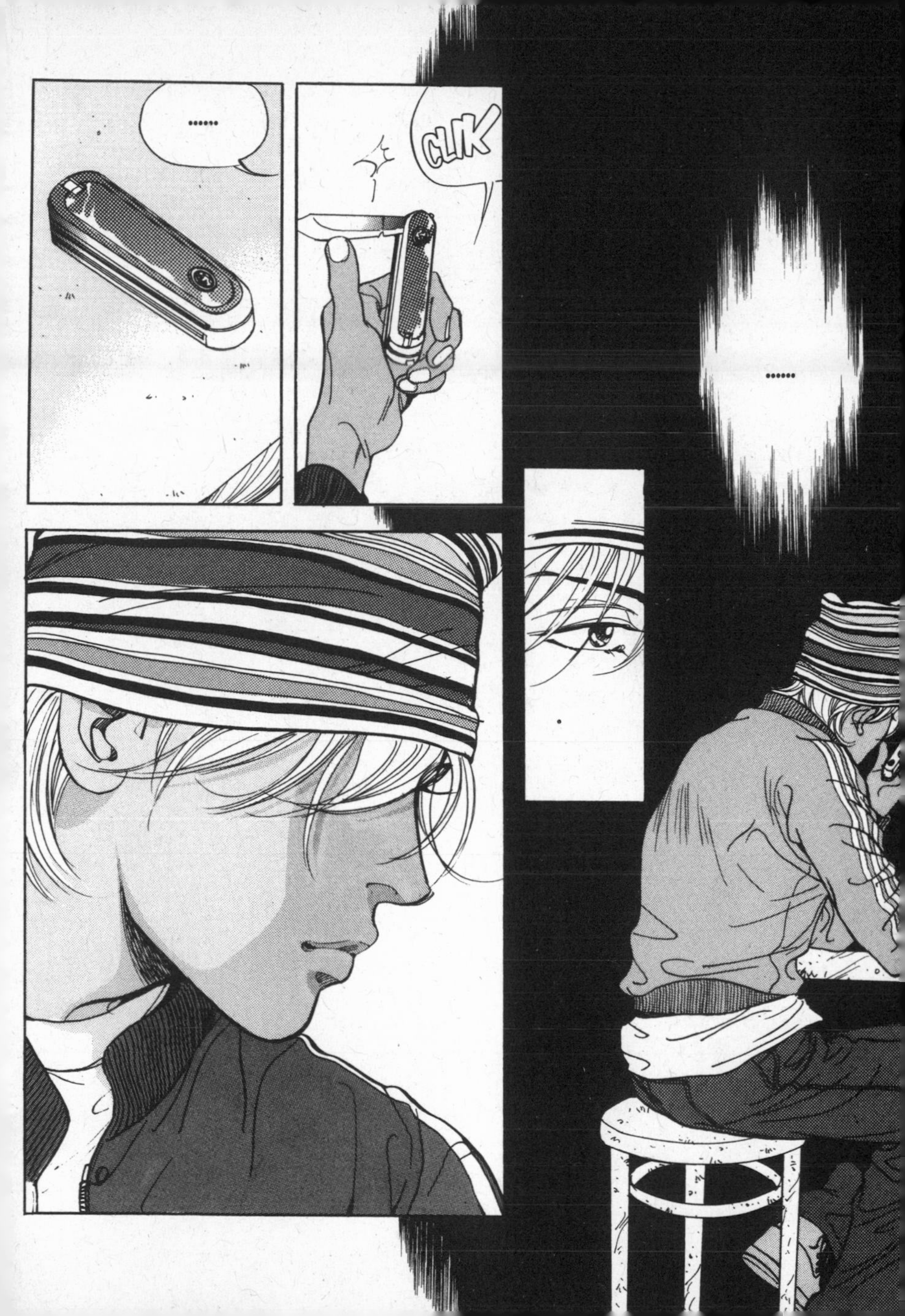
......
CLIK
......

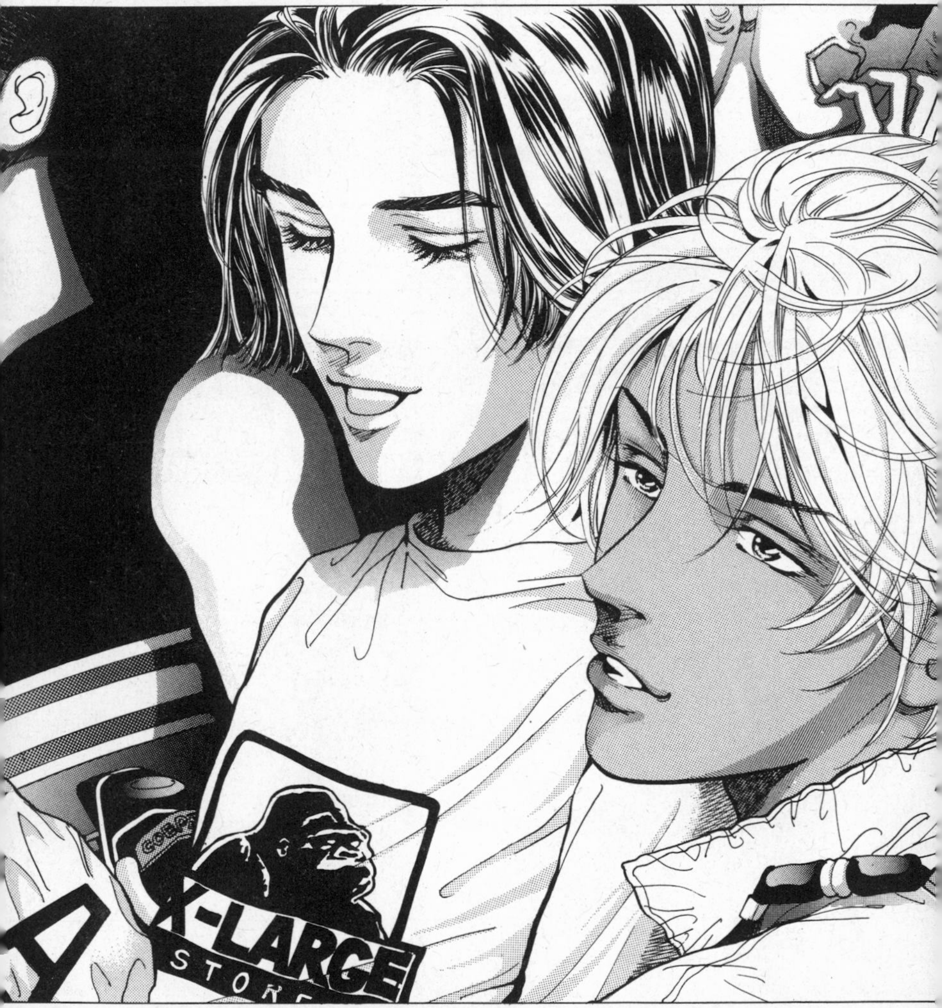
X-LARGE

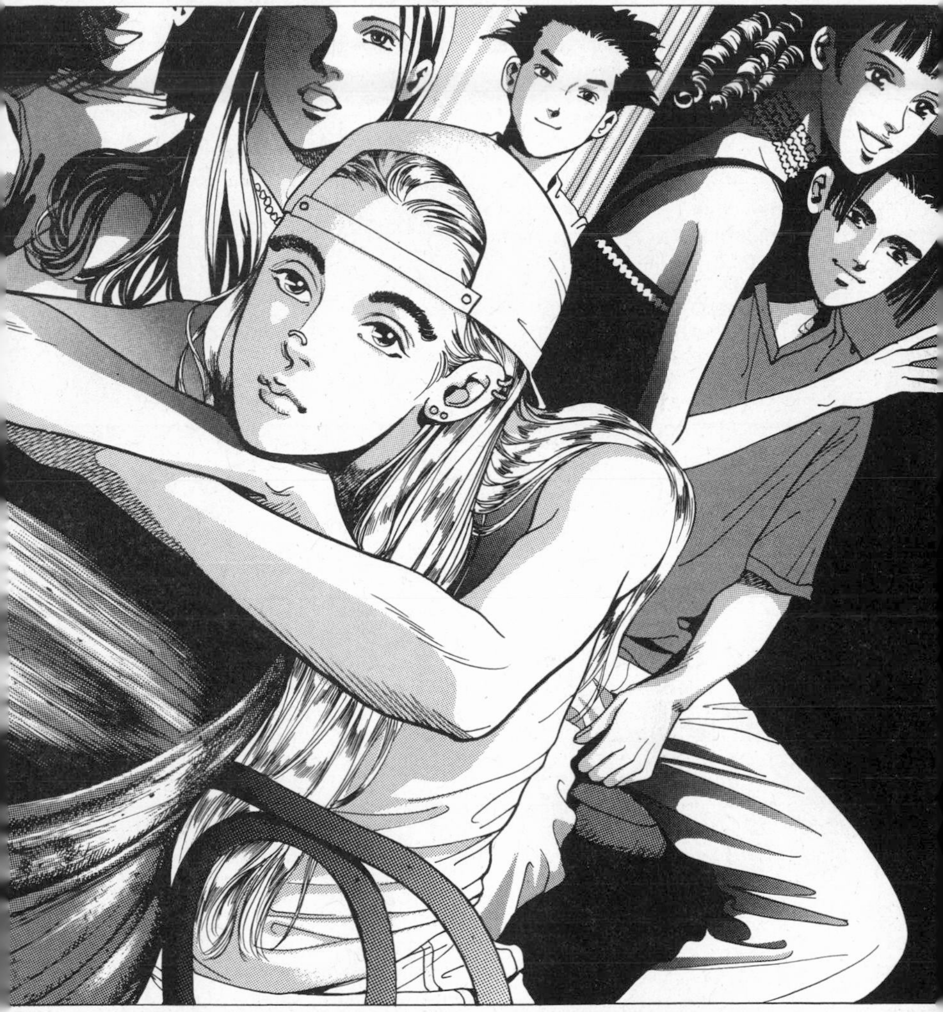

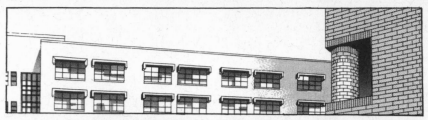

CLASS, LET ME INTRODUCE THE NEW STUDENT WHO TRANSFERRED TO OUR SCHOOL TODAY.

TO MAKE IT SHORT, I BELIEVE HE CAN BE A GREAT ADDITION TO OUR CLASS AND WILL BE A DEPENDABLE STUDENT.

I GUESS HE'LL AT LEAST RAISE OUR CLASS AVERAGE FOR SURE, RIGHT?!

PBTBT KIKI

I HOPE YOU WELCOME HIM WITH AN OPEN MIND WITHOUT RESERVE.

MMM~

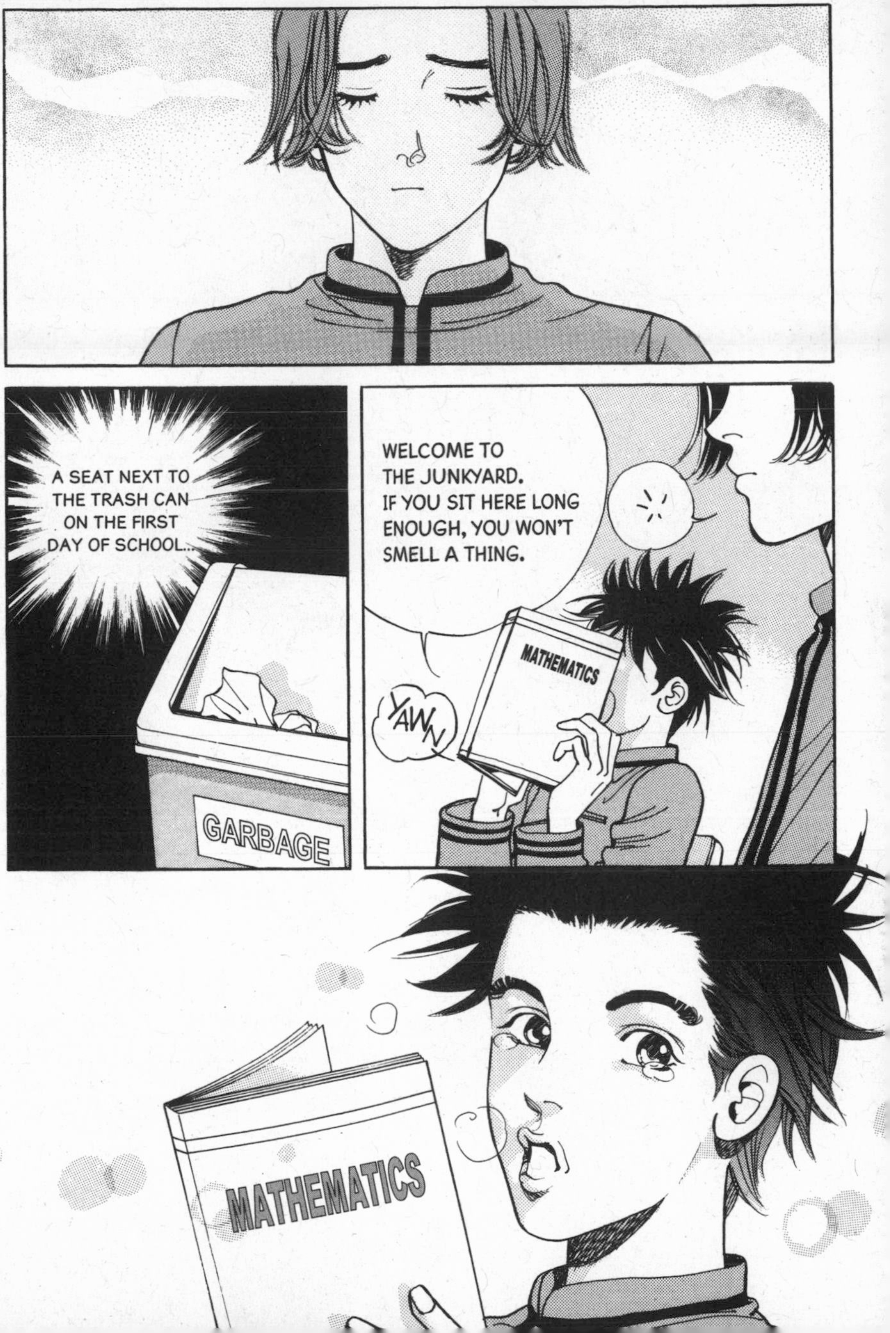
A SEAT NEXT TO THE TRASH CAN ON THE FIRST DAY OF SCHOOL...
GARBAGE
WELCOME TO THE JUNKYARD. IF YOU SIT HERE LONG ENOUGH, YOU WON'T SMELL A THING.
MATHEMATICS
YAWN
MATHEMATICS

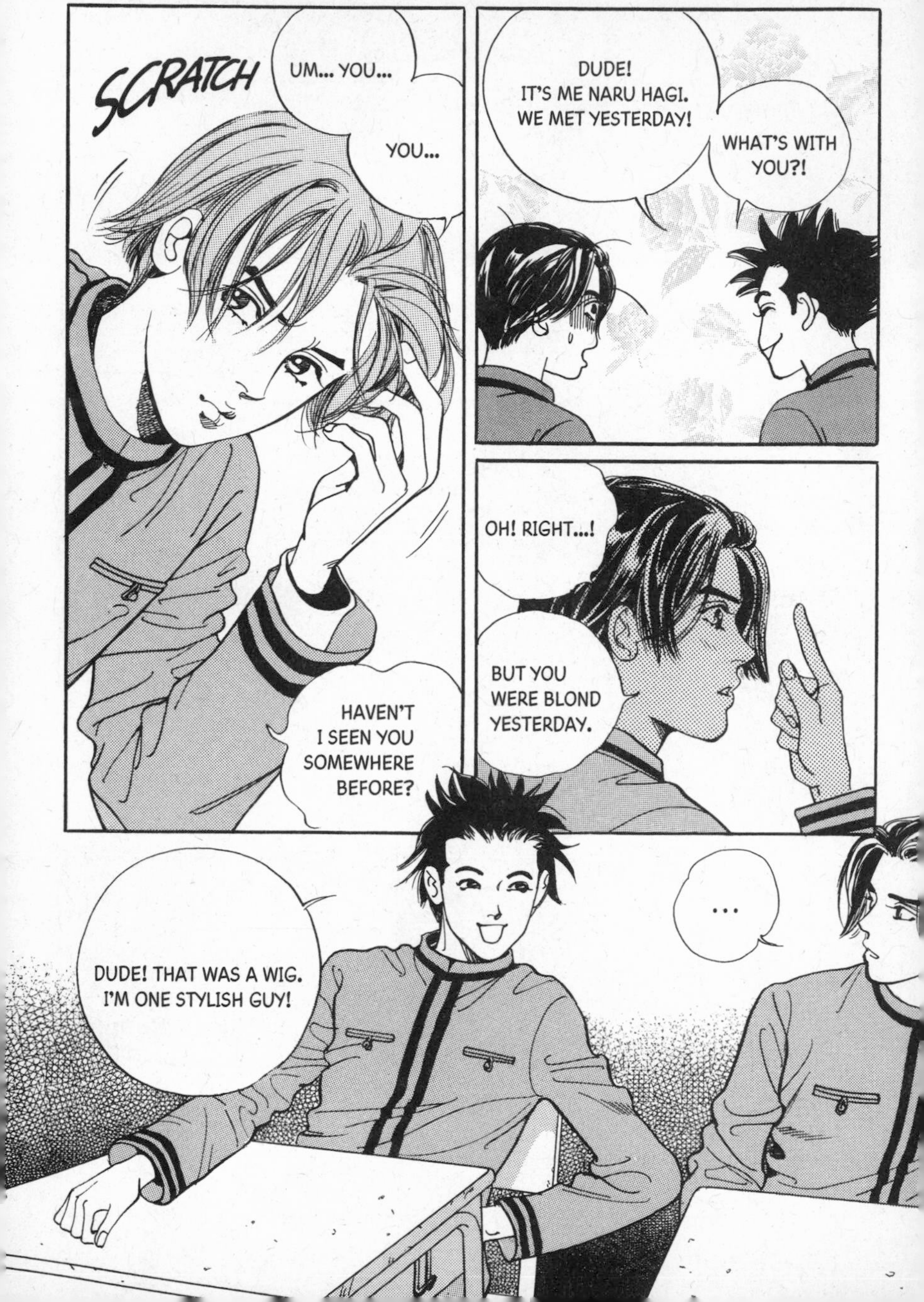
SCRATCH
UM... YOU...
YOU...
HAVEN'T I SEEN YOU SOMEWHERE BEFORE?
DUDE! IT'S ME NARU HAGI. WE MET YESTERDAY!
WHAT'S WITH YOU?!
OH! RIGHT...!
BUT YOU WERE BLOND YESTERDAY.
DUDE! THAT WAS A WIG. I'M ONE STYLISH GUY!
...

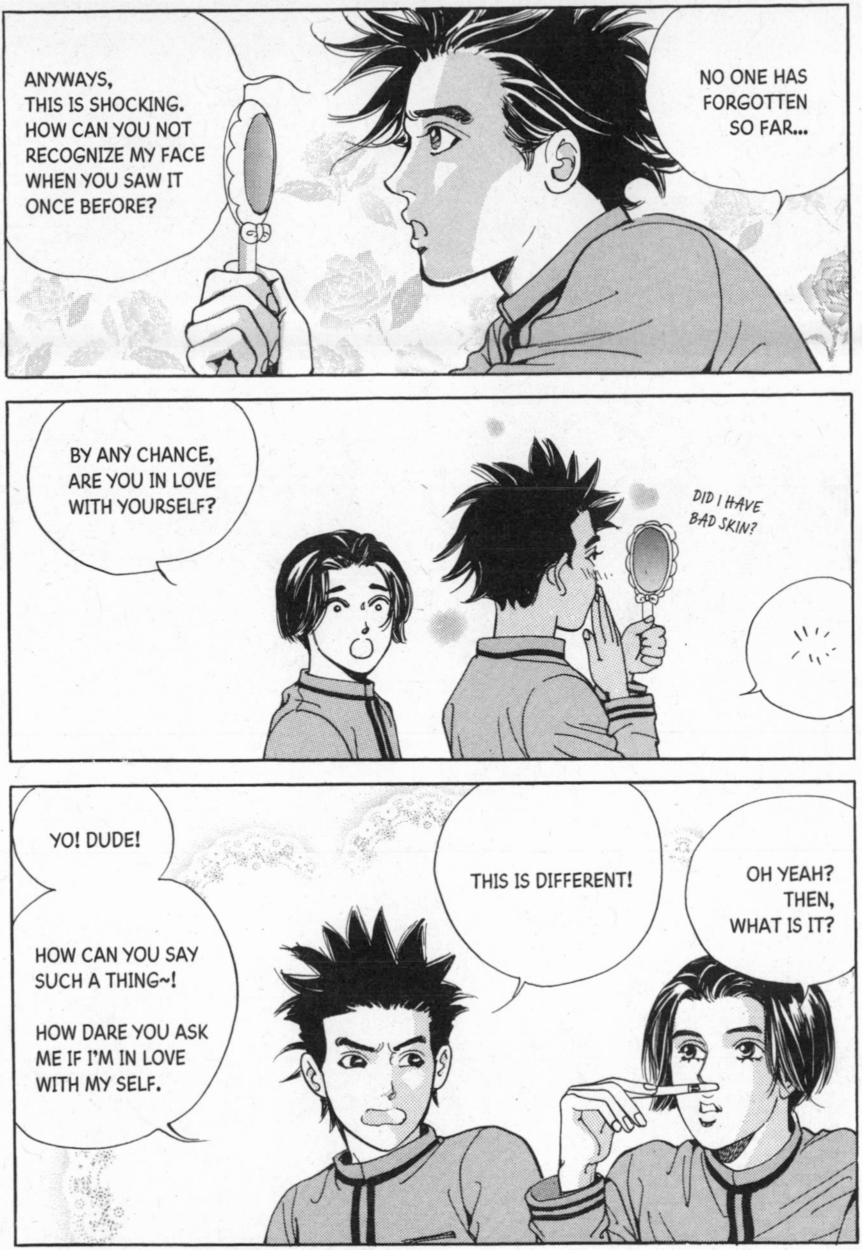
ANYWAYS, THIS IS SHOCKING. HOW CAN YOU NOT RECOGNIZE MY FACE WHEN YOU SAW IT ONCE BEFORE?
NO ONE HAS FORGOTTEN SO FAR...
BY ANY CHANCE, ARE YOU IN LOVE WITH YOURSELF?
DID I HAVE BAD SKIN?
YO! DUDE!
HOW CAN YOU SAY SUCH A THING~!
HOW DARE YOU ASK ME IF I'M IN LOVE WITH MY SELF.
THIS IS DIFFERENT!
OH YEAH? THEN, WHAT IS IT?

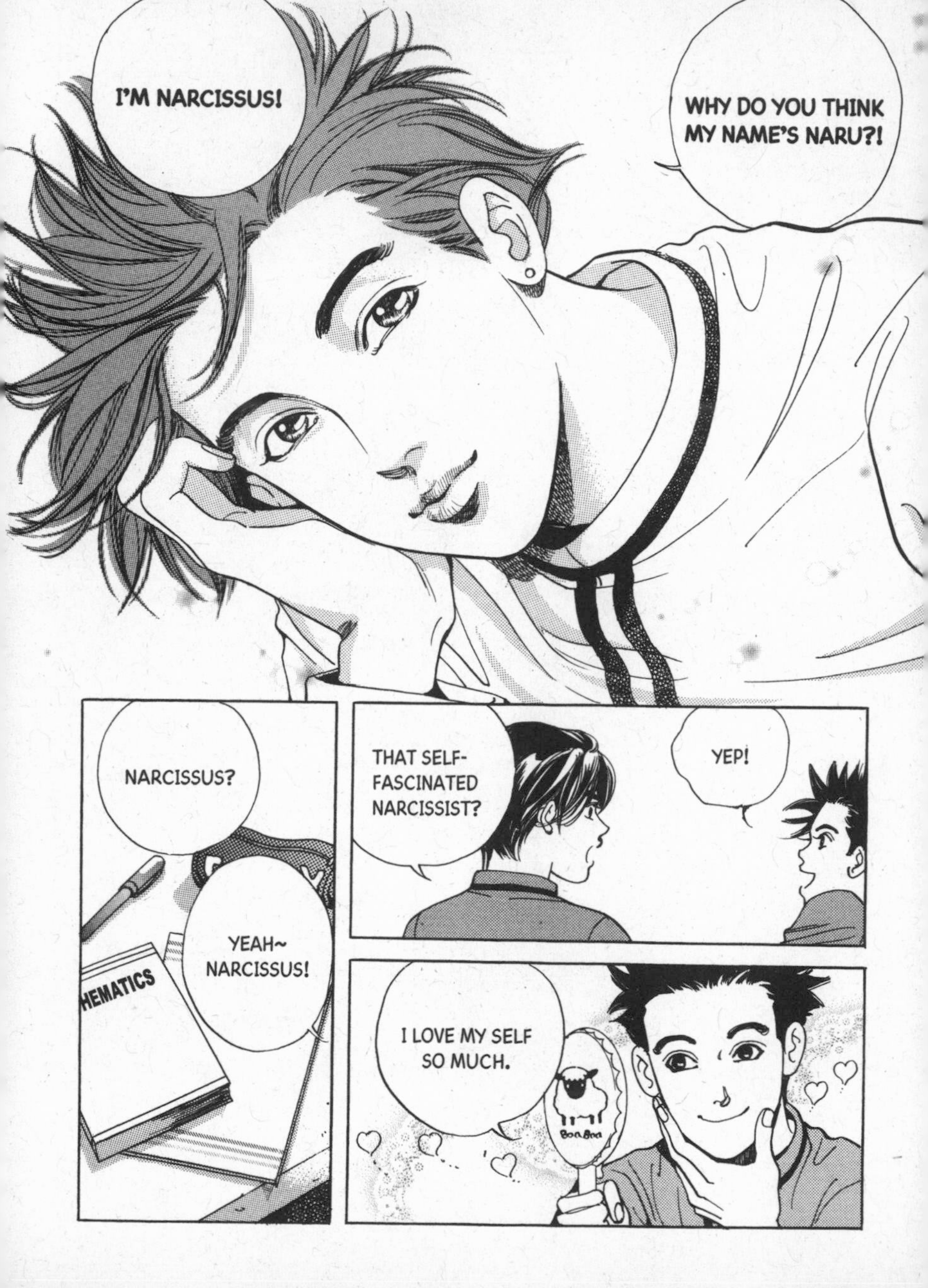
I'M NARCISSUS!
WHY DO YOU THINK MY NAME'S NARU?!
NARCISSUS?
YEAH~ NARCISSUS!
HEMATICS
THAT SELF-FASCINATED NARCISSIST?
YEP!
I LOVE MY SELF SO MUCH.

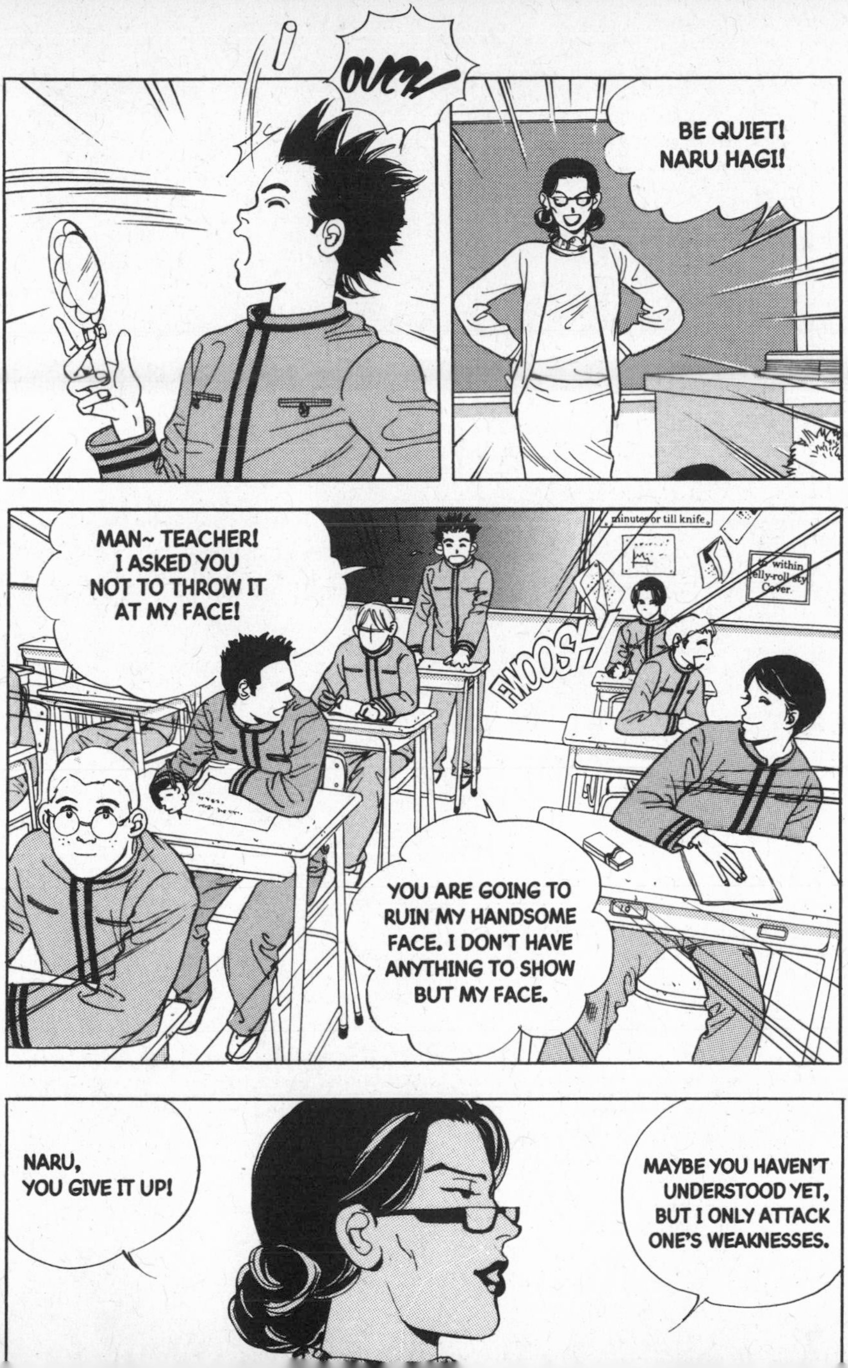
OUCH
BE QUIET! NARU HAGI!
MAN~ TEACHER! I ASKED YOU NOT TO THROW IT AT MY FACE!
WOOSH
YOU ARE GOING TO RUIN MY HANDSOME FACE. I DON'T HAVE ANYTHING TO SHOW BUT MY FACE.
NARU, YOU GIVE IT UP!
MAYBE YOU HAVEN'T UNDERSTOOD YET, BUT I ONLY ATTACK ONE'S WEAKNESSES.

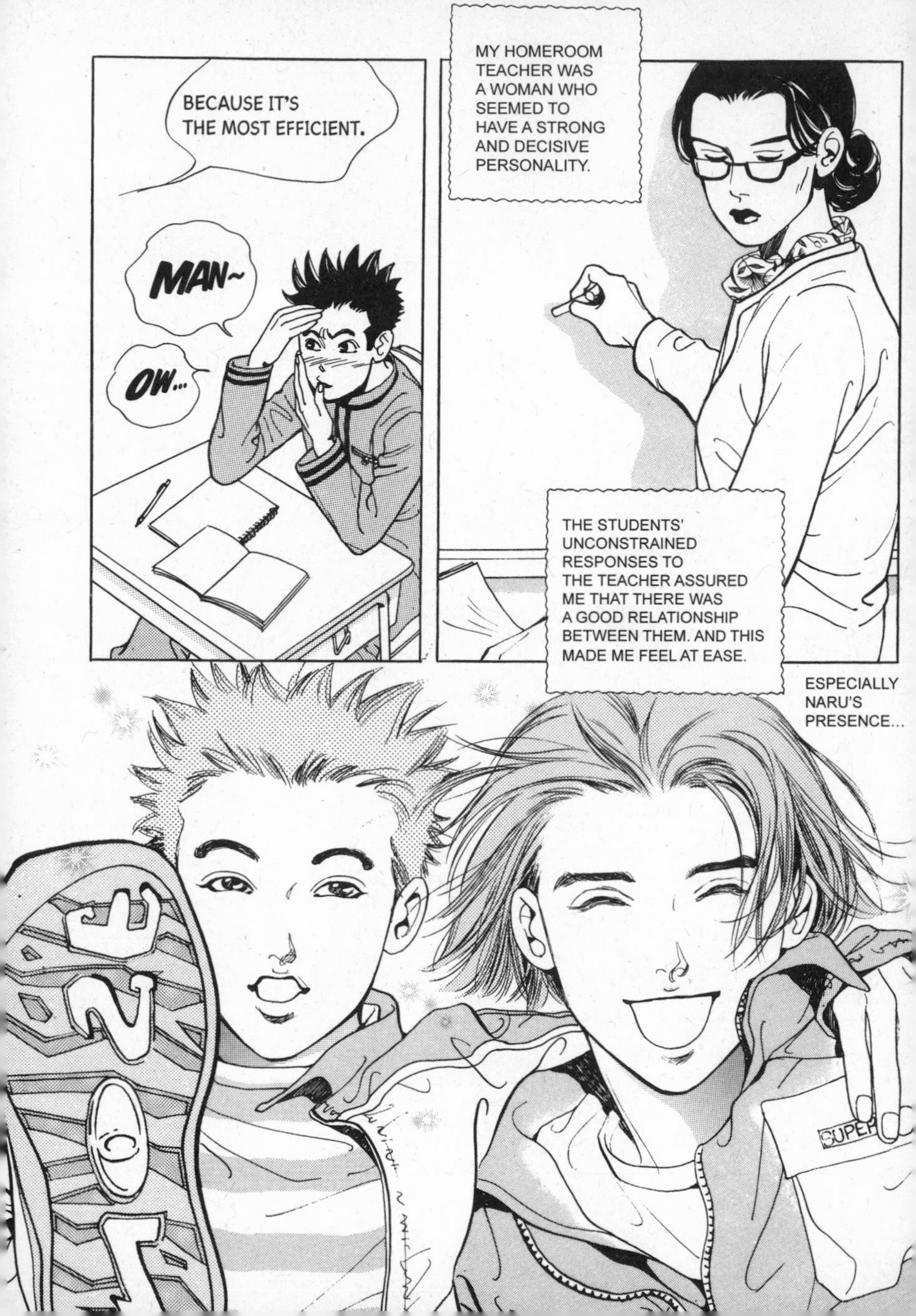
BECAUSE IT'S THE MOST EFFICIENT.
MAN~
OW...
MY HOMEROOM TEACHER WAS A WOMAN WHO SEEMED TO HAVE A STRONG AND DECISIVE PERSONALITY.
THE STUDENTS' UNCONSTRAINED RESPONSES TO THE TEACHER ASSURED ME THAT THERE WAS A GOOD RELATIONSHIP BETWEEN THEM. AND THIS MADE ME FEEL AT EASE.
ESPECIALLY NARU'S PRESENCE...
SUPER

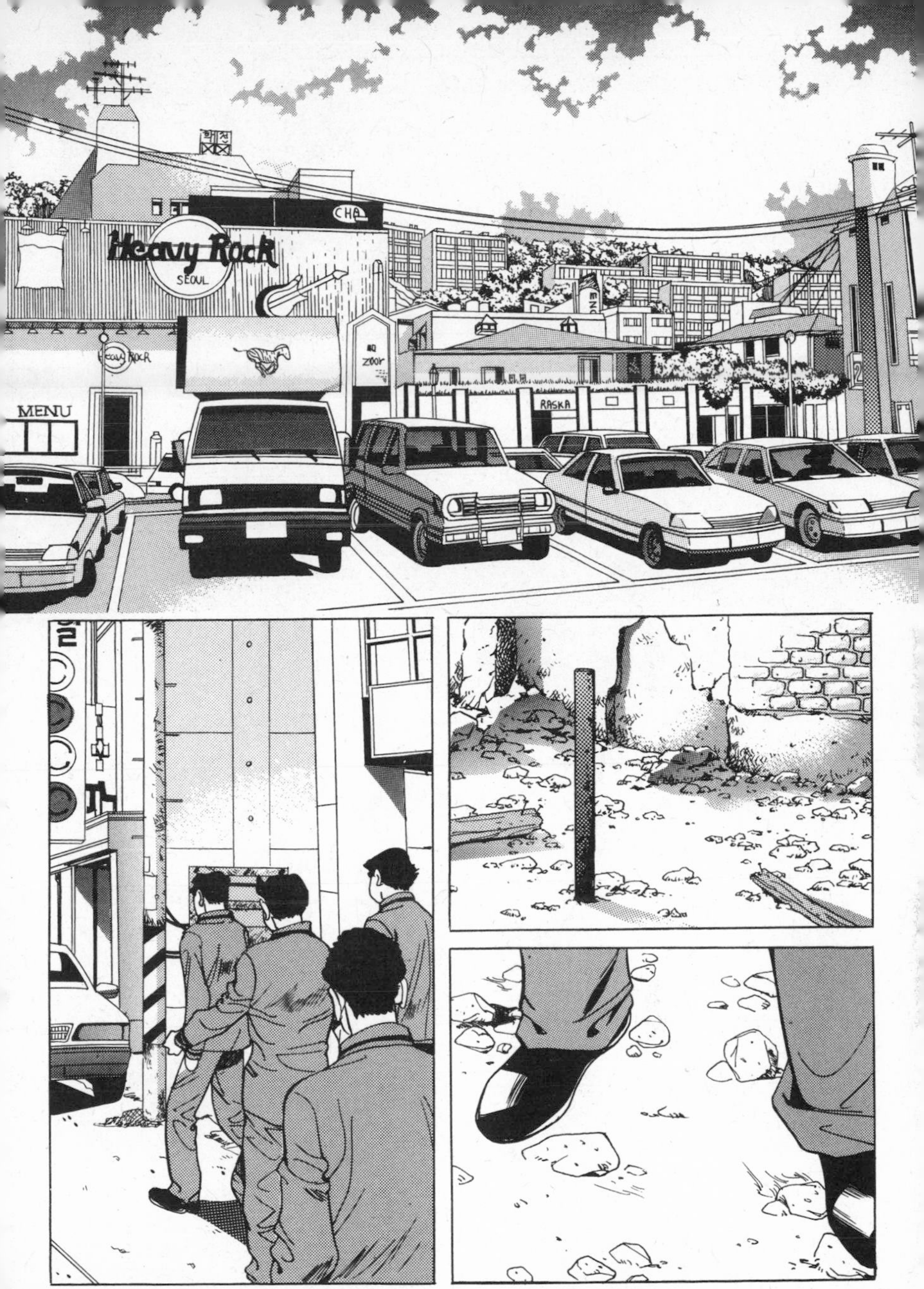
Heavy Rock
SEOUL
MENU
RASKA

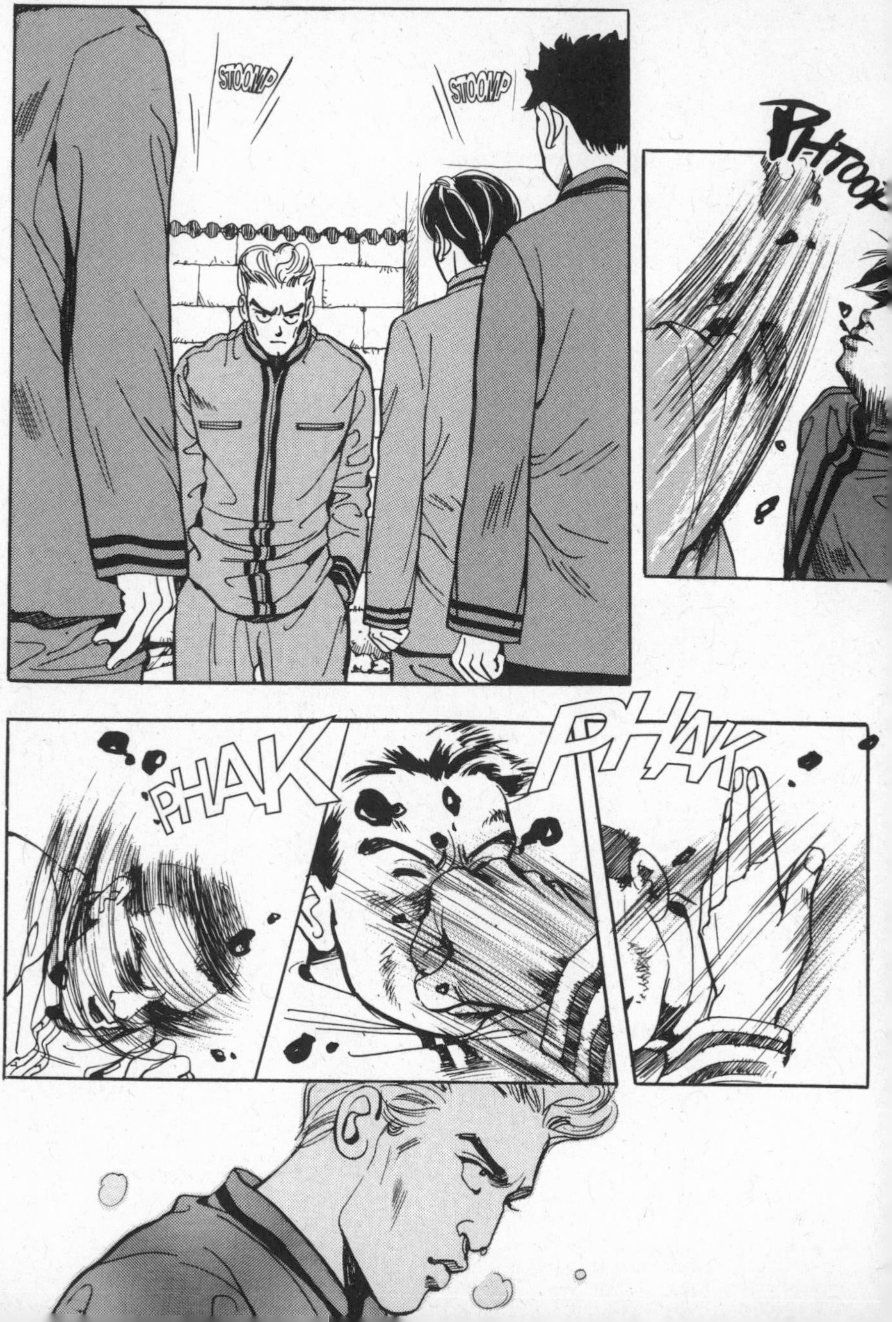
STOOMP
STOOMP
PHTOOK
PHAK
PHAK

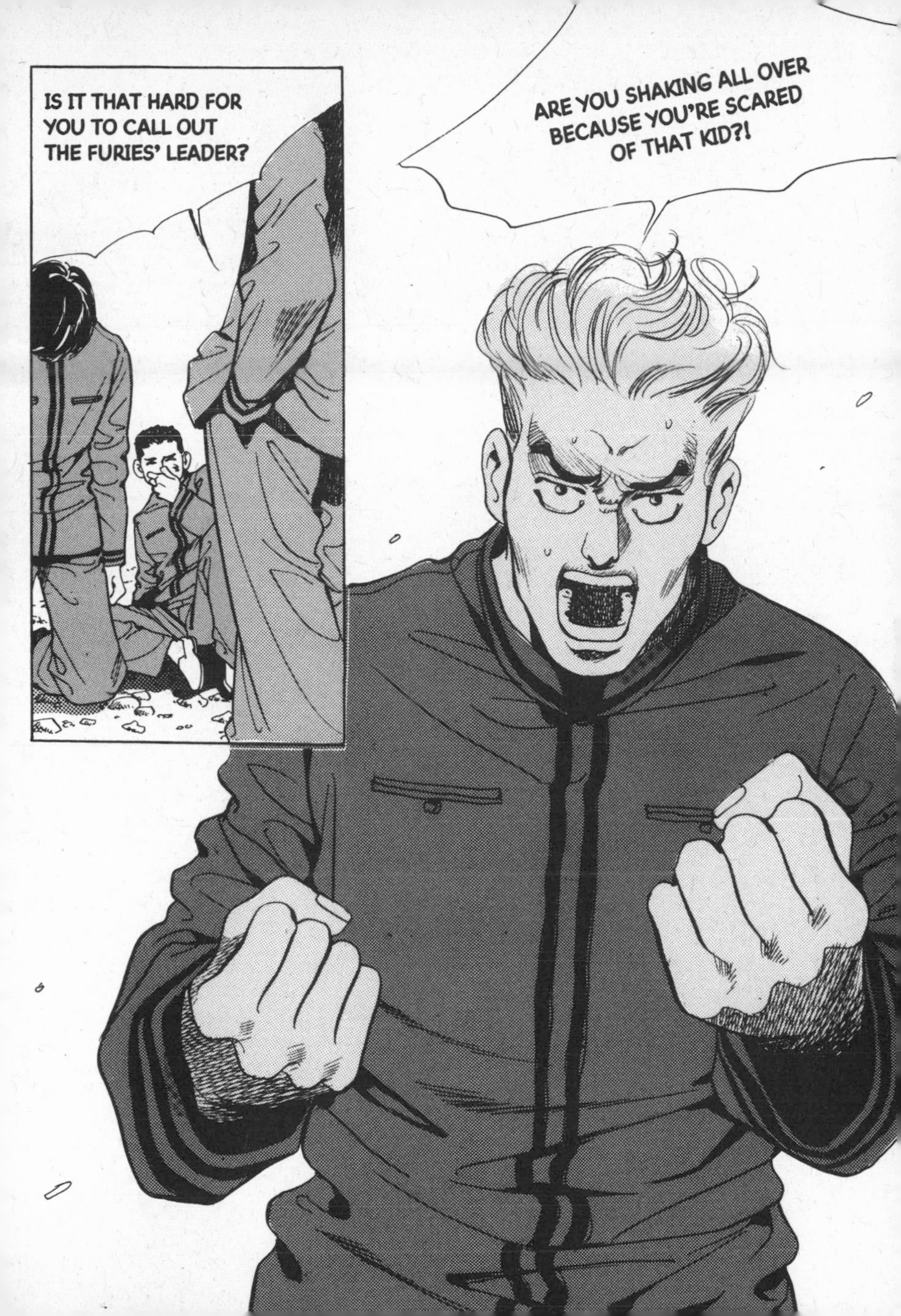
IS IT THAT HARD FOR YOU TO CALL OUT THE FURIES' LEADER?
ARE YOU SHAKING ALL OVER BECAUSE YOU'RE SCARED OF THAT KID?!

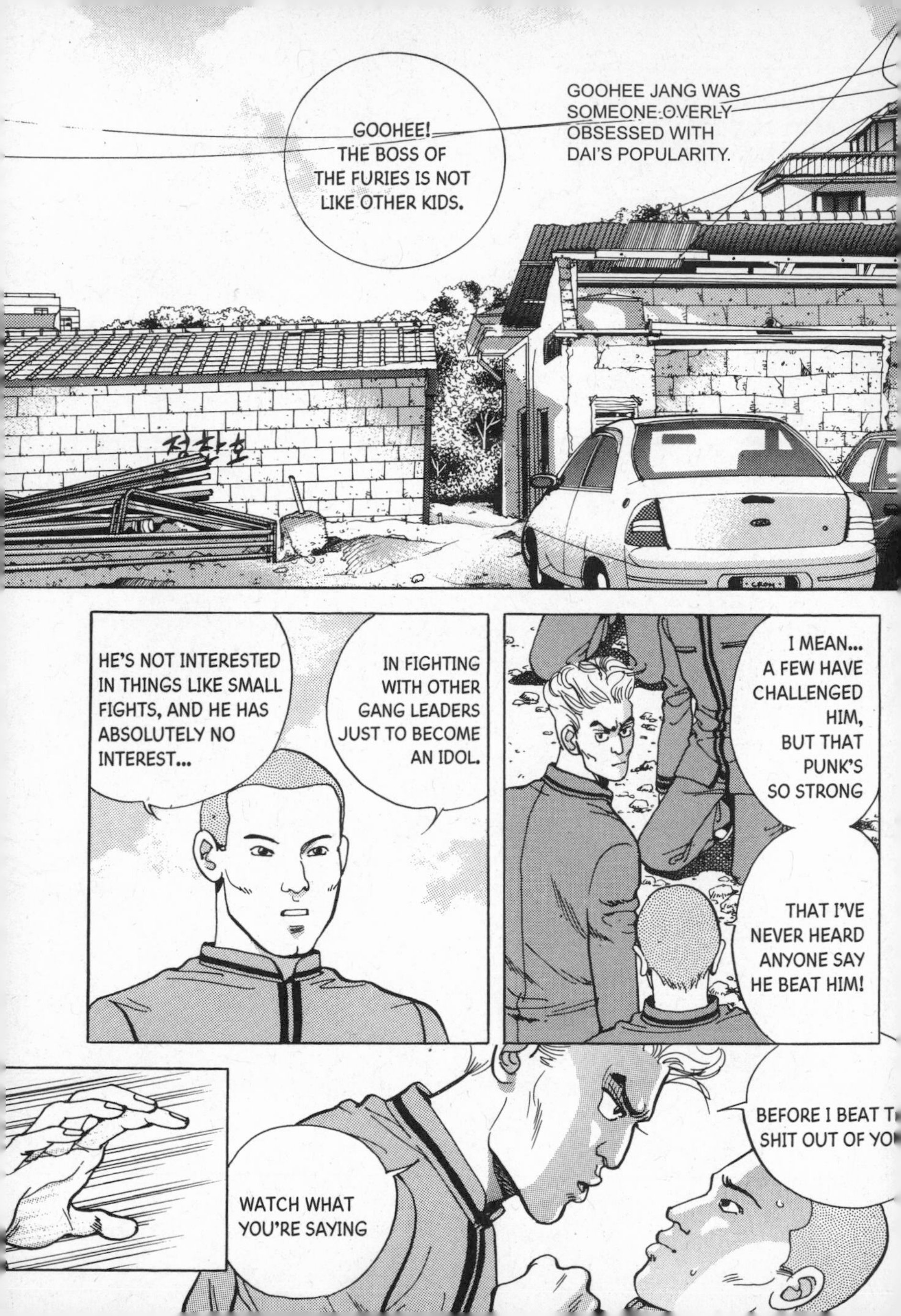
GOOHEE! THE BOSS OF THE FURIES IS NOT LIKE OTHER KIDS.
GOOHEE JANG WAS SOMEONE OVERLY OBSESSED WITH DAI'S POPULARITY.
HE'S NOT INTERESTED IN THINGS LIKE SMALL FIGHTS, AND HE HAS ABSOLUTELY NO INTEREST...
IN FIGHTING WITH OTHER GANG LEADERS JUST TO BECOME AN IDOL.
I MEAN... A FEW HAVE CHALLENGED HIM, BUT THAT PUNK'S SO STRONG
THAT I'VE NEVER HEARD ANYONE SAY HE BEAT HIM!
WATCH WHAT YOU'RE SAYING
BEFORE I BEAT T
SHIT OUT OF YO

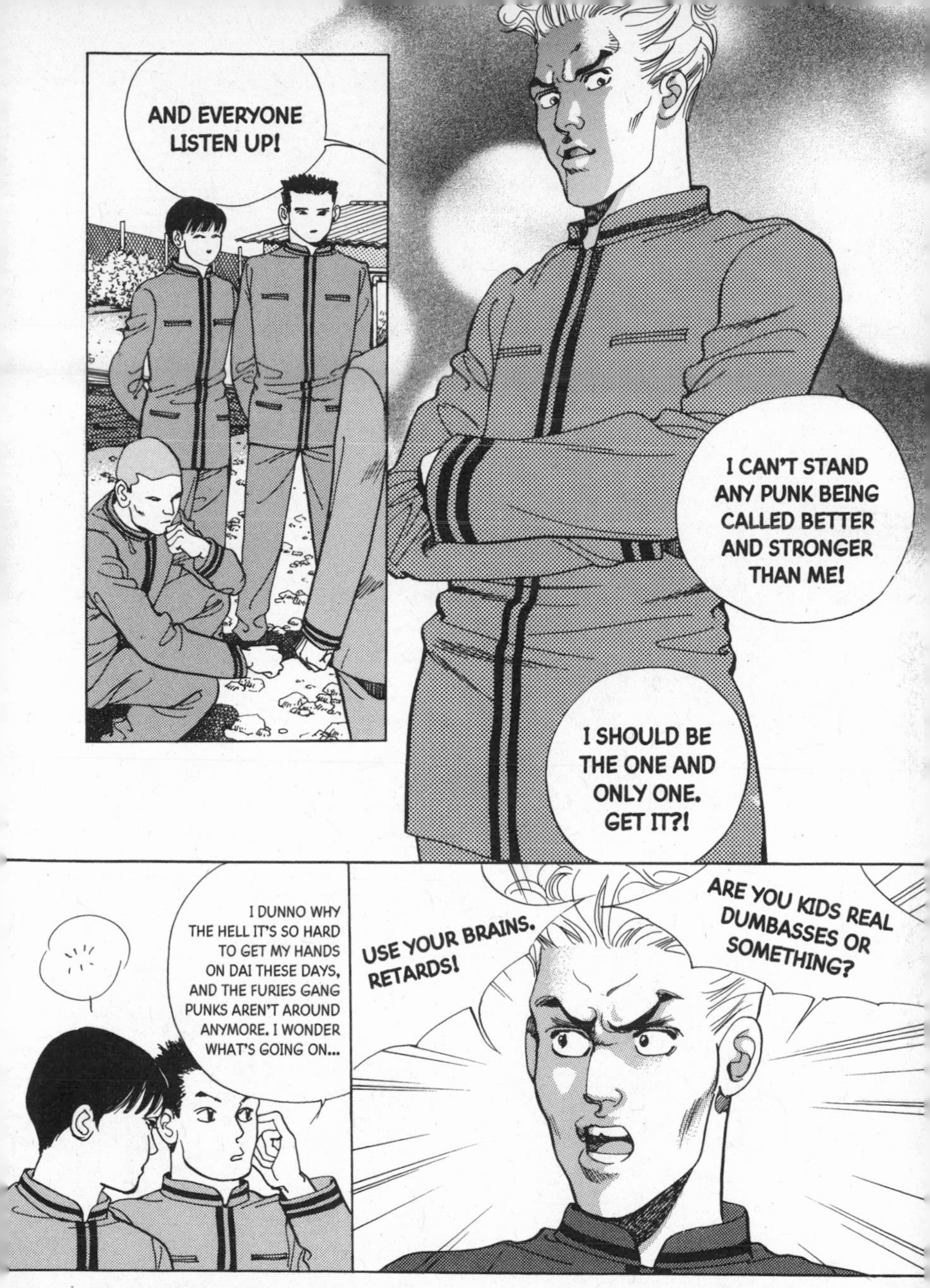
AND EVERYONE LISTEN UP!
I CAN'T STAND ANY PUNK BEING CALLED BETTER AND STRONGER THAN ME!
I SHOULD BE THE ONE AND ONLY ONE. GET IT?!
I DUNNO WHY THE HELL IT'S SO HARD TO GET MY HANDS ON DAI THESE DAYS, AND THE FURIES GANG PUNKS AREN'T AROUND ANYMORE. I WONDER WHAT'S GOING ON...
ARE YOU KIDS REAL DUMBASSES OR SOMETHING?
USE YOUR BRAINS. RETARDS!

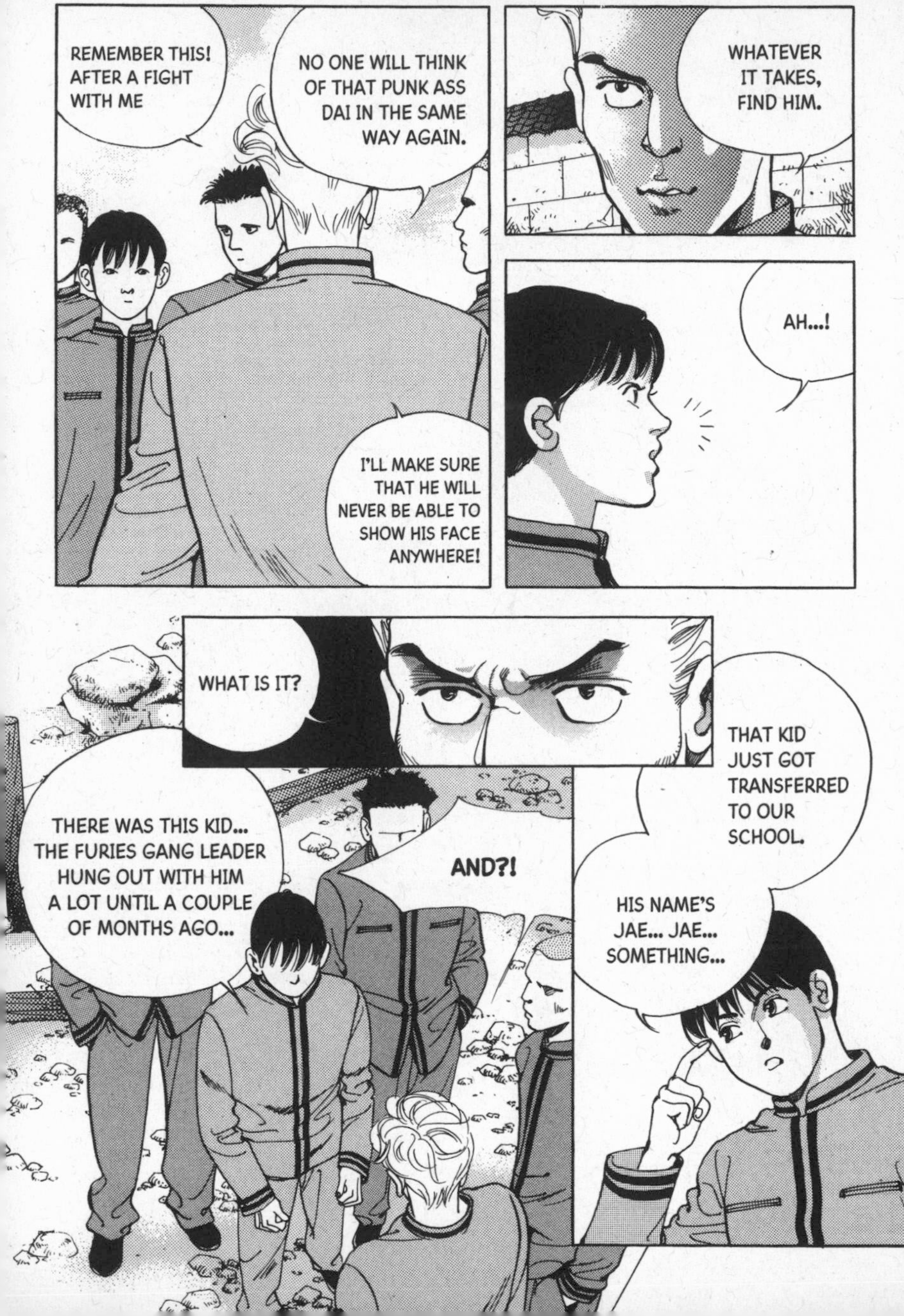
REMEMBER THIS! AFTER A FIGHT WITH ME
NO ONE WILL THINK OF THAT PUNK ASS DAI IN THE SAME WAY AGAIN.
I'LL MAKE SURE THAT HE WILL NEVER BE ABLE TO SHOW HIS FACE ANYWHERE!
WHATEVER IT TAKES, FIND HIM.
AH...!
WHAT IS IT?
THERE WAS THIS KID... THE FURIES GANG LEADER HUNG OUT WITH HIM A LOT UNTIL A COUPLE OF MONTHS AGO...
AND?!
THAT KID JUST GOT TRANSFERRED TO OUR SCHOOL.
HIS NAME'S JAE... JAE... SOMETHING...

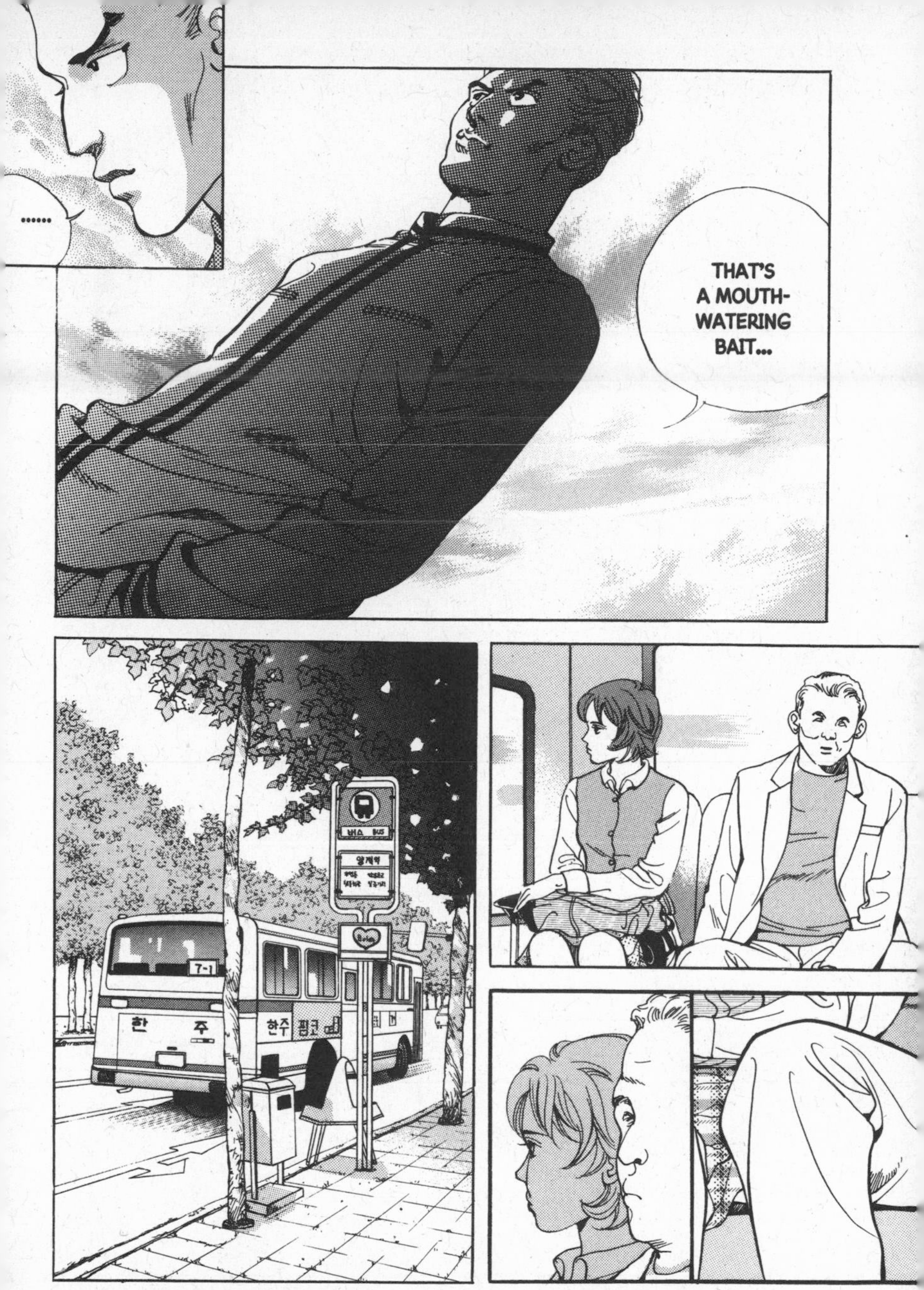
……
THAT'S A MOUTH-WATERING BAIT...
7-1

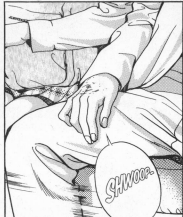

...

FILTHY...
THIS KIND
OF BODY HEAT
MAKES ME
FEEL SICK...

SHWOOP-

STAB

STAB

SHWOOP-

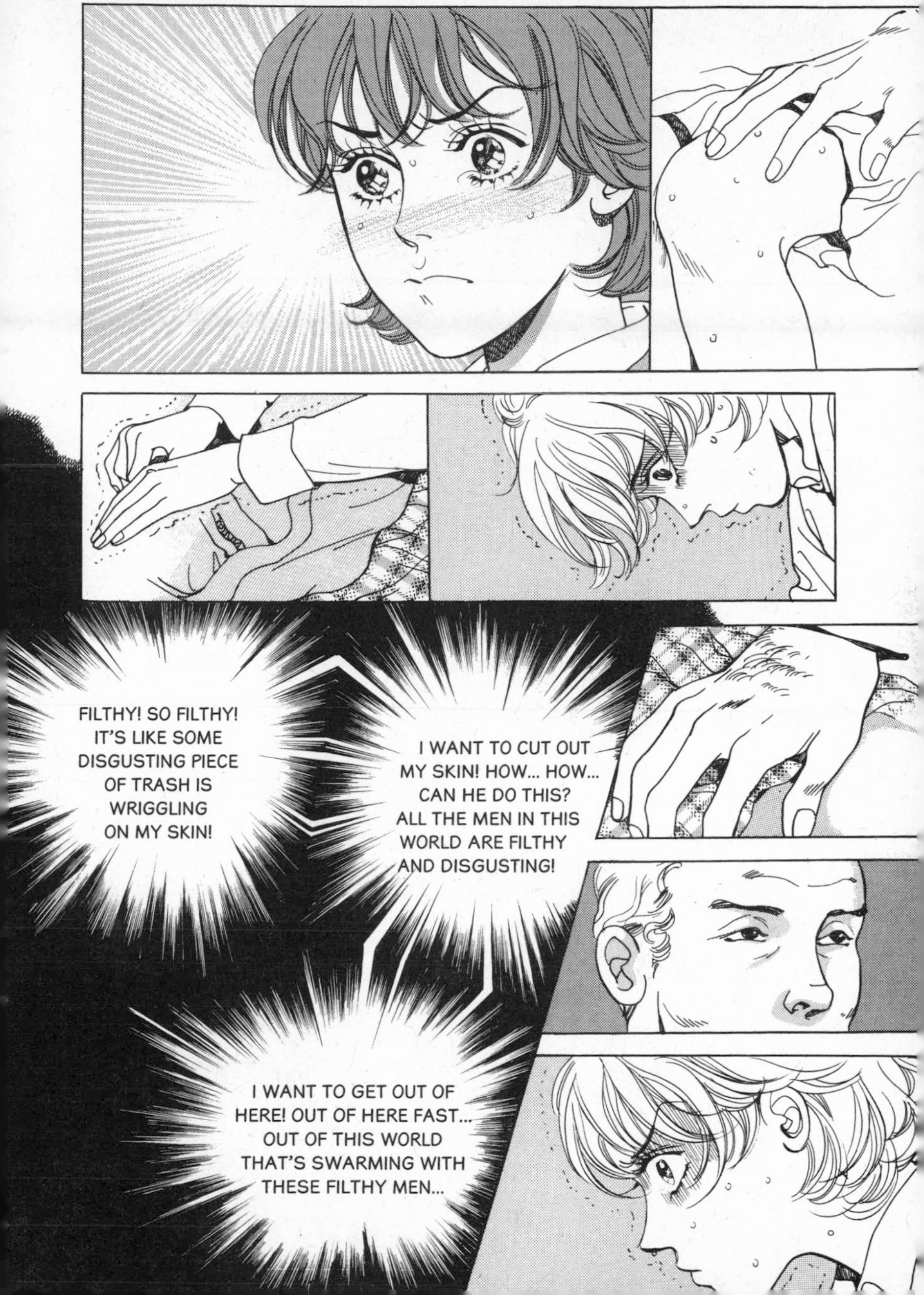
FILTHY! SO FILTHY! IT'S LIKE SOME DISGUSTING PIECE OF TRASH IS WRIGGLING ON MY SKIN!
I WANT TO CUT OUT MY SKIN! HOW... HOW... CAN HE DO THIS? ALL THE MEN IN THIS WORLD ARE FILTHY AND DISGUSTING!
I WANT TO GET OUT OF HERE! OUT OF HERE FAST... OUT OF THIS WORLD THAT'S SWARMING WITH THESE FILTHY MEN...

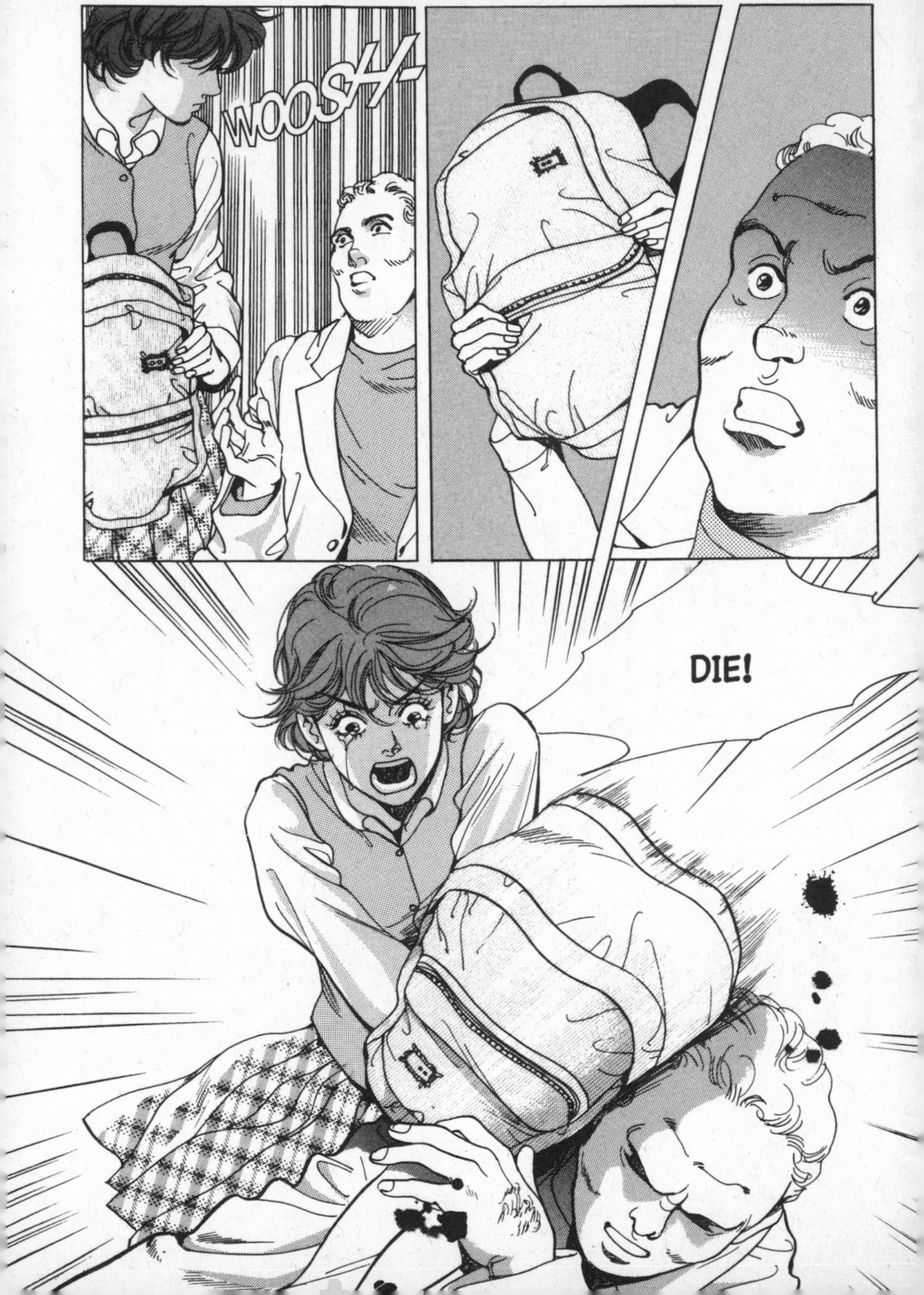
WOOSH-
DIE!

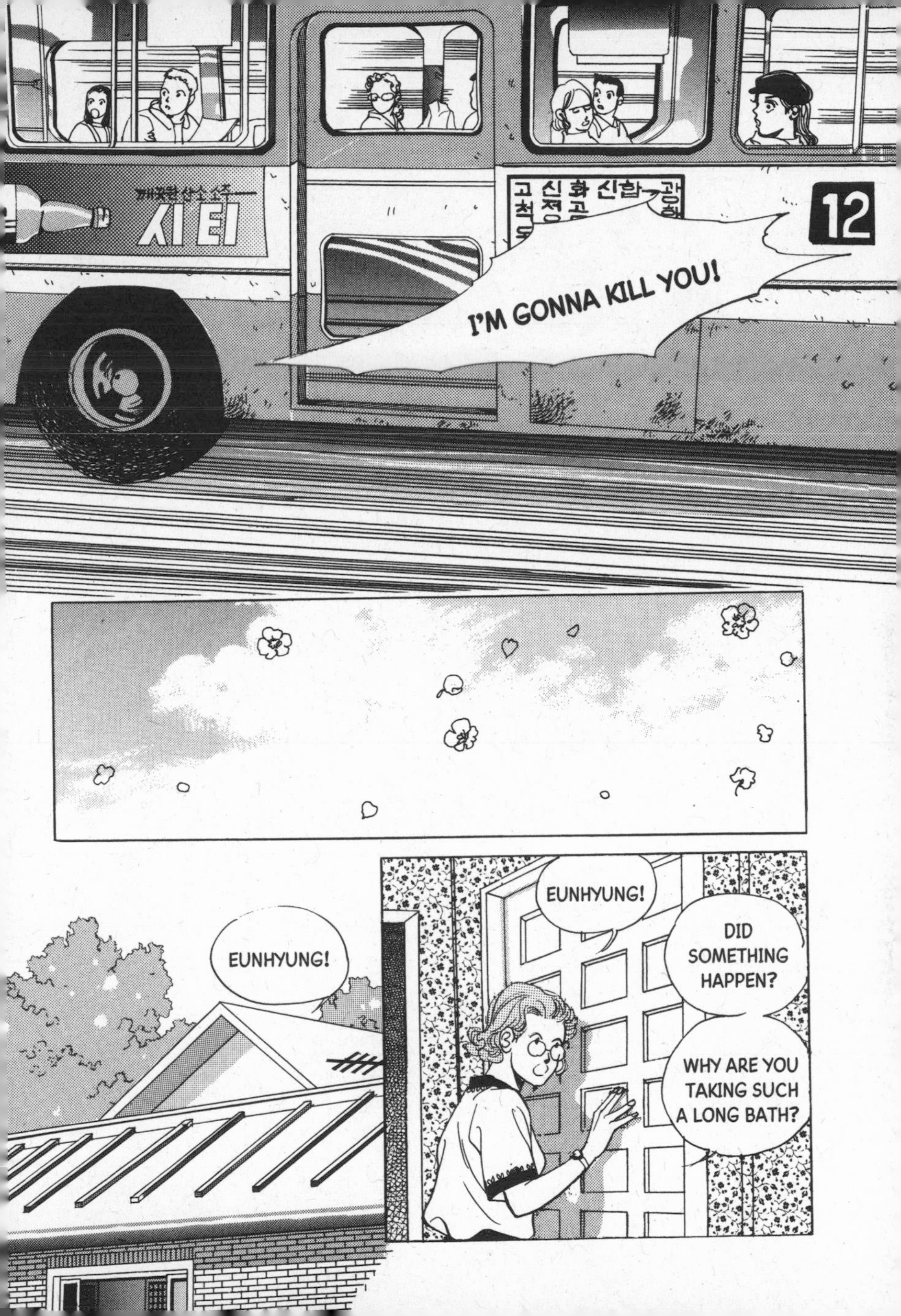
시티
12
I'M GONNA KILL YOU!
EUNHYUNG!
EUNHYUNG!
DID SOMETHING HAPPEN?
WHY ARE YOU TAKING SUCH A LONG BATH?

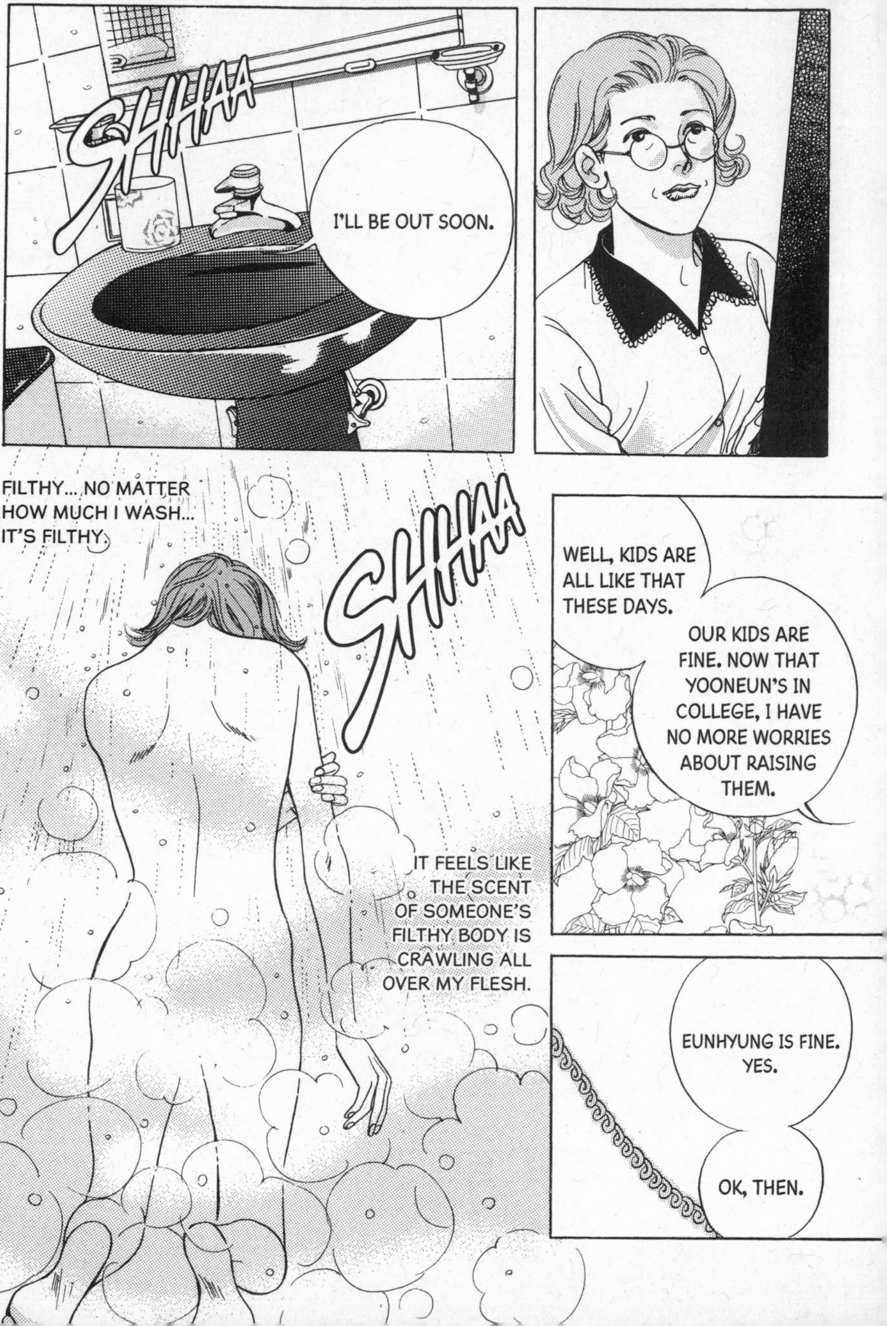
SHHAA
I'LL BE OUT SOON.
FILTHY... NO MATTER HOW MUCH I WASH... IT'S FILTHY.
SHHAA
IT FEELS LIKE THE SCENT OF SOMEONE'S FILTHY BODY IS CRAWLING ALL OVER MY FLESH.
WELL, KIDS ARE ALL LIKE THAT THESE DAYS.
OUR KIDS ARE FINE. NOW THAT YOONEUN'S IN COLLEGE, I HAVE NO MORE WORRIES ABOUT RAISING THEM.
EUNHYUNG IS FINE. YES.
OK, THEN.

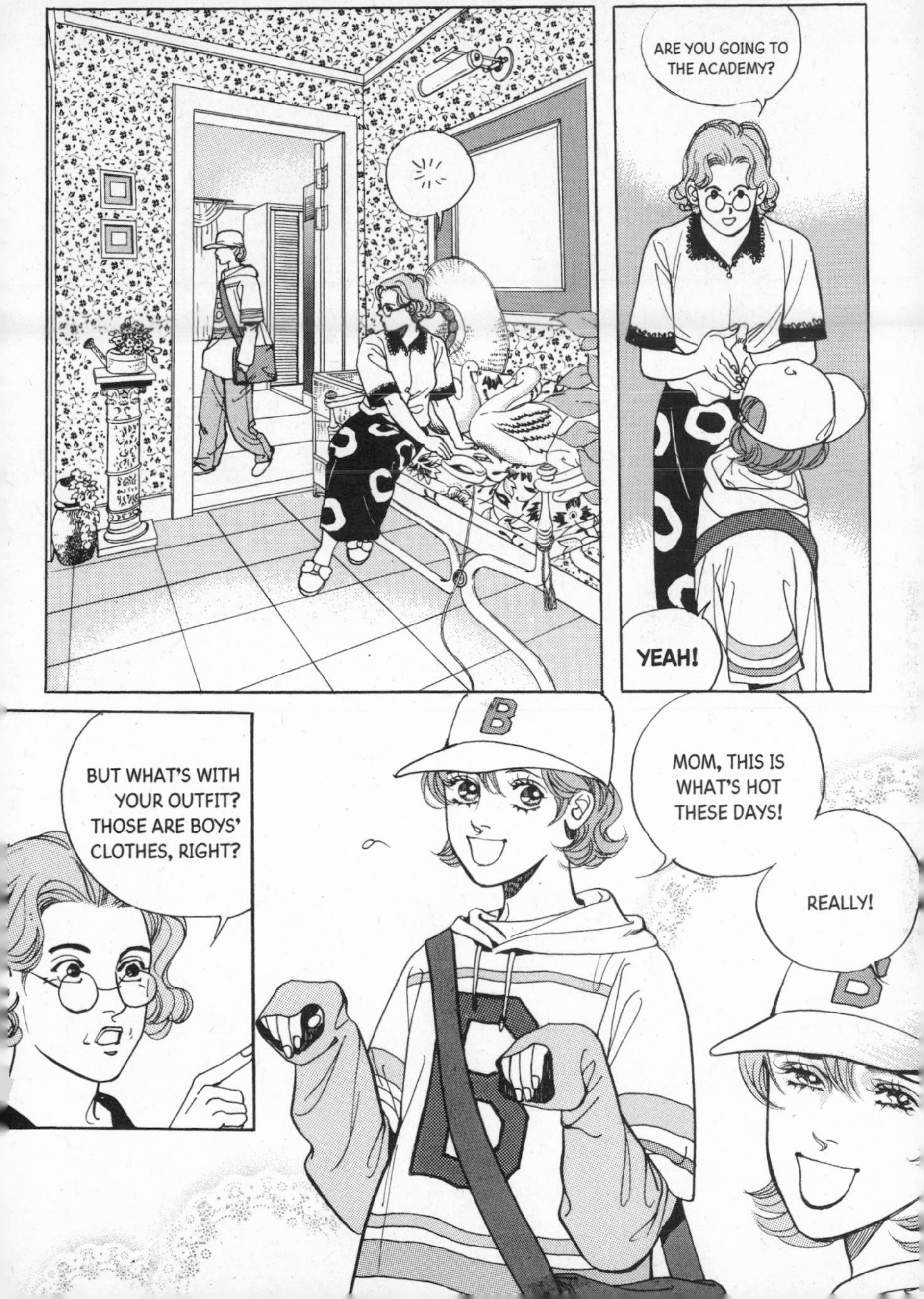
ARE YOU GOING TO THE ACADEMY?
YEAH!
BUT WHAT'S WITH YOUR OUTFIT? THOSE ARE BOYS' CLOTHES, RIGHT?
MOM, THIS IS WHAT'S HOT THESE DAYS!
REALLY!

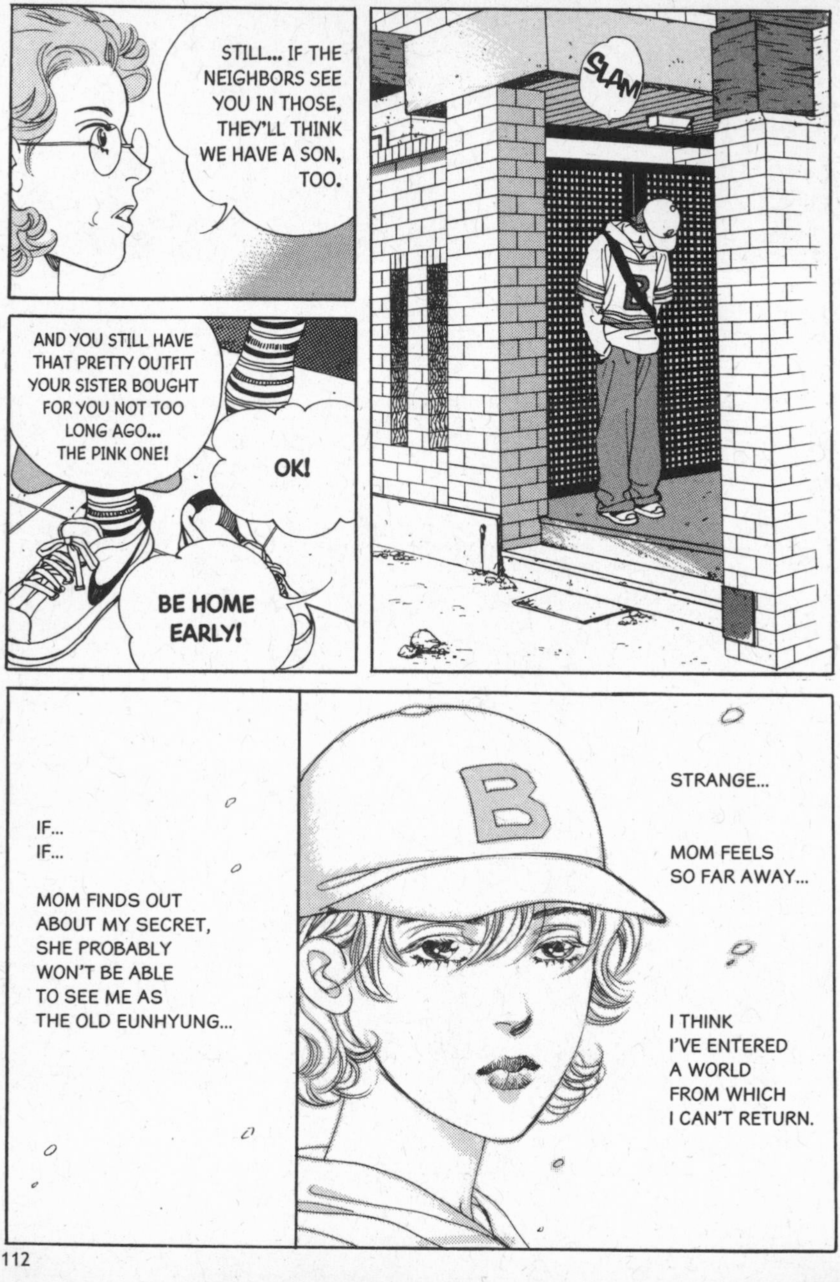
STILL... IF THE NEIGHBORS SEE YOU IN THOSE, THEY'LL THINK WE HAVE A SON, TOO.
SLAM
AND YOU STILL HAVE THAT PRETTY OUTFIT YOUR SISTER BOUGHT FOR YOU NOT TOO LONG AGO... THE PINK ONE!
OK!
BE HOME EARLY!
IF... IF...
MOM FINDS OUT ABOUT MY SECRET, SHE PROBABLY WON'T BE ABLE TO SEE ME AS THE OLD EUNHYUNG...
STRANGE...
MOM FEELS SO FAR AWAY...
I THINK I'VE ENTERED A WORLD FROM WHICH I CAN'T RETURN.

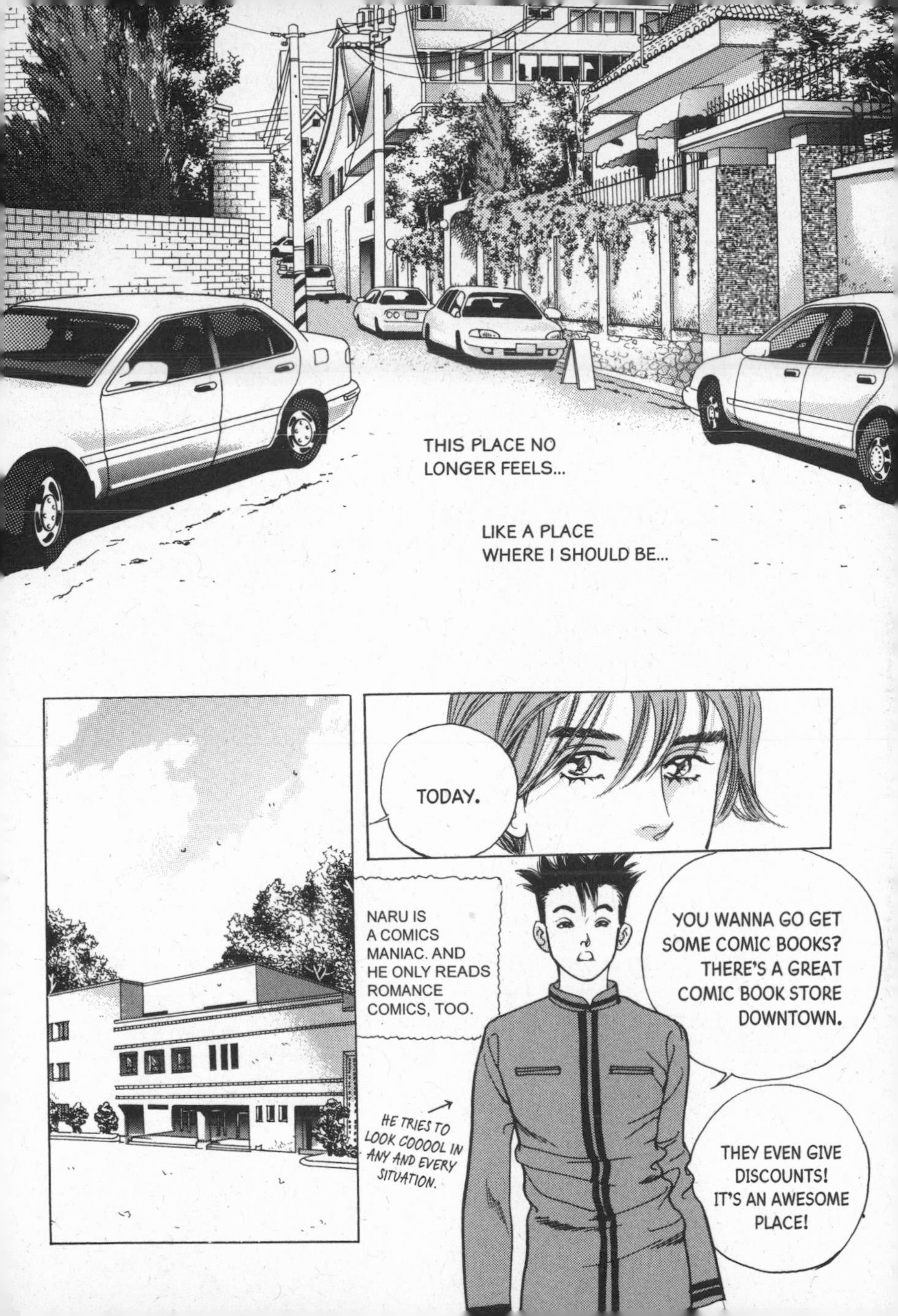
THIS PLACE NO LONGER FEELS...
LIKE A PLACE WHERE I SHOULD BE...
TODAY.
NARU IS A COMICS MANIAC. AND HE ONLY READS ROMANCE COMICS, TOO.
HE TRIES TO LOOK COOOOL IN ANY AND EVERY SITUATION.
YOU WANNA GO GET SOME COMIC BOOKS? THERE'S A GREAT COMIC BOOK STORE DOWNTOWN.
THEY EVEN GIVE DISCOUNTS! IT'S AN AWESOME PLACE!

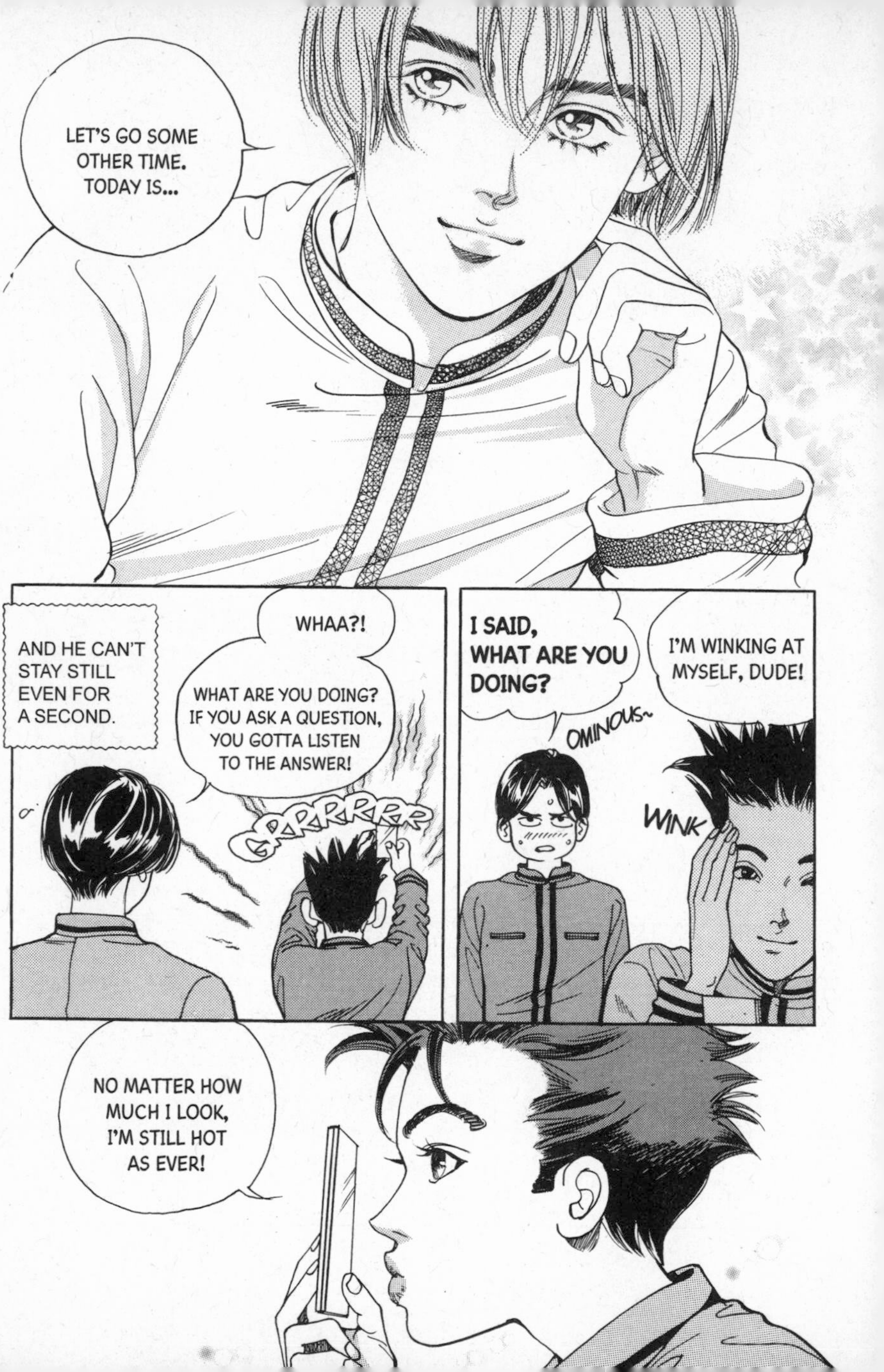
LET'S GO SOME OTHER TIME. TODAY IS...
AND HE CAN'T STAY STILL EVEN FOR A SECOND.
WHAA?!
WHAT ARE YOU DOING? IF YOU ASK A QUESTION, YOU GOTTA LISTEN TO THE ANSWER!
GRRRRRR
I SAID, WHAT ARE YOU DOING?
OMINOUS~
I'M WINKING AT MYSELF, DUDE!
WINK
NO MATTER HOW MUCH I LOOK, I'M STILL HOT AS EVER!

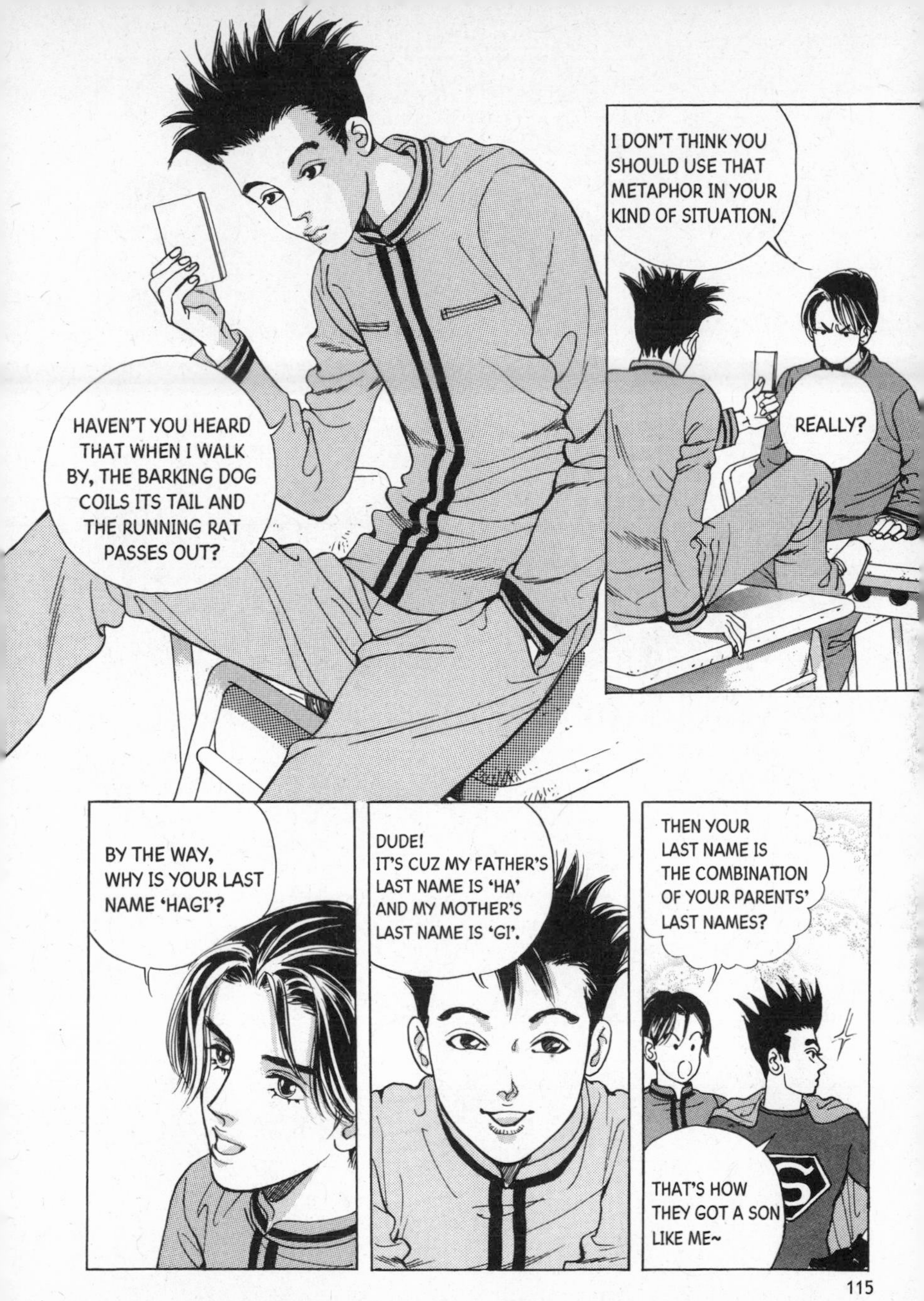
HAVEN'T YOU HEARD THAT WHEN I WALK BY, THE BARKING DOG COILS ITS TAIL AND THE RUNNING RAT PASSES OUT?
I DON'T THINK YOU SHOULD USE THAT METAPHOR IN YOUR KIND OF SITUATION.
REALLY?
BY THE WAY, WHY IS YOUR LAST NAME 'HAGI'?
DUDE! IT'S CUZ MY FATHER'S LAST NAME IS 'HA' AND MY MOTHER'S LAST NAME IS 'GI'.
THEN YOUR LAST NAME IS THE COMBINATION OF YOUR PARENTS' LAST NAMES?
THAT'S HOW THEY GOT A SON LIKE ME~

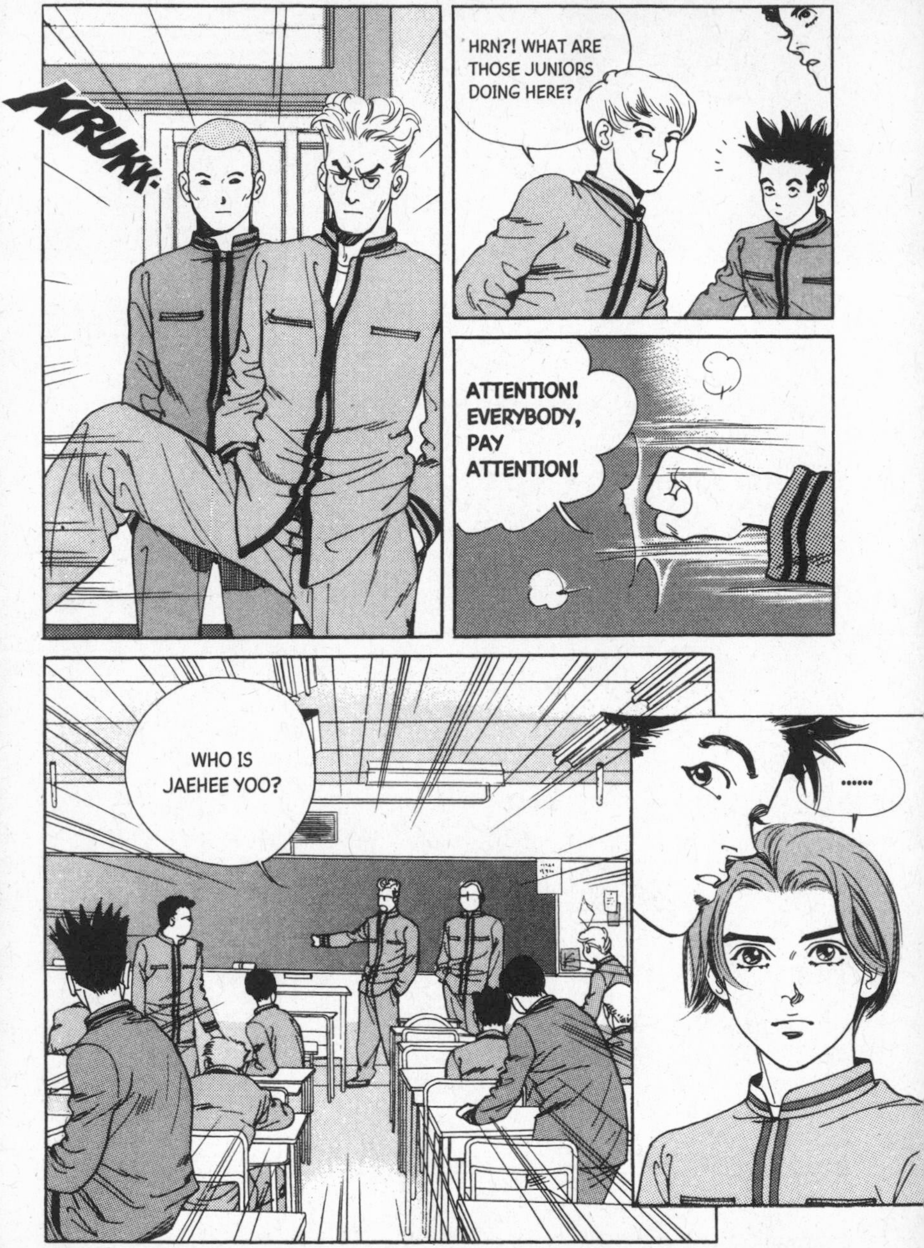
KRUKK
HRN?! WHAT ARE THOSE JUNIORS DOING HERE?
ATTENTION! EVERYBODY, PAY ATTENTION!
WHO IS JAEHEE YOO?
......

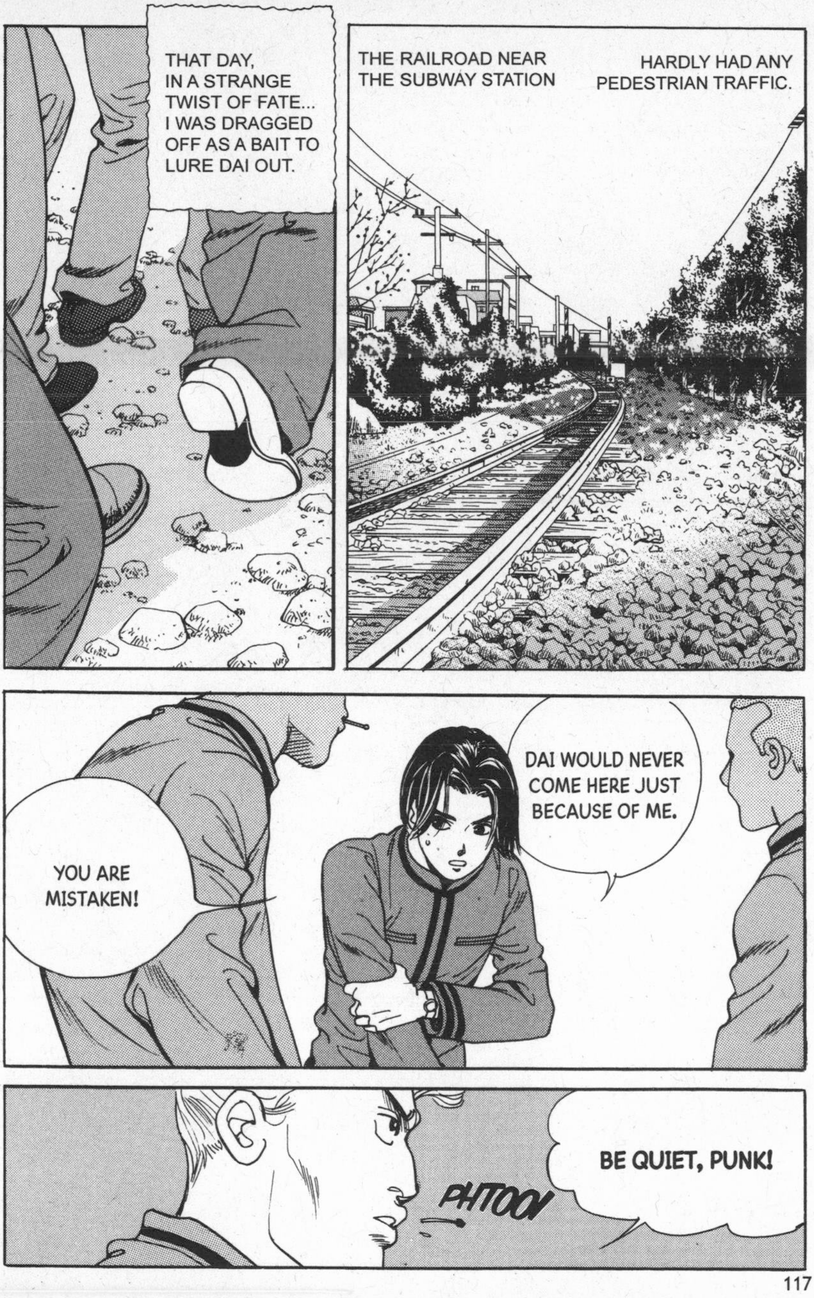
THAT DAY, IN A STRANGE TWIST OF FATE... I WAS DRAGGED OFF AS A BAIT TO LURE DAI OUT.
THE RAILROAD NEAR THE SUBWAY STATION
HARDLY HAD ANY PEDESTRIAN TRAFFIC.
YOU ARE MISTAKEN!
DAI WOULD NEVER COME HERE JUST BECAUSE OF ME.
PHTOO!
BE QUIET, PUNK!

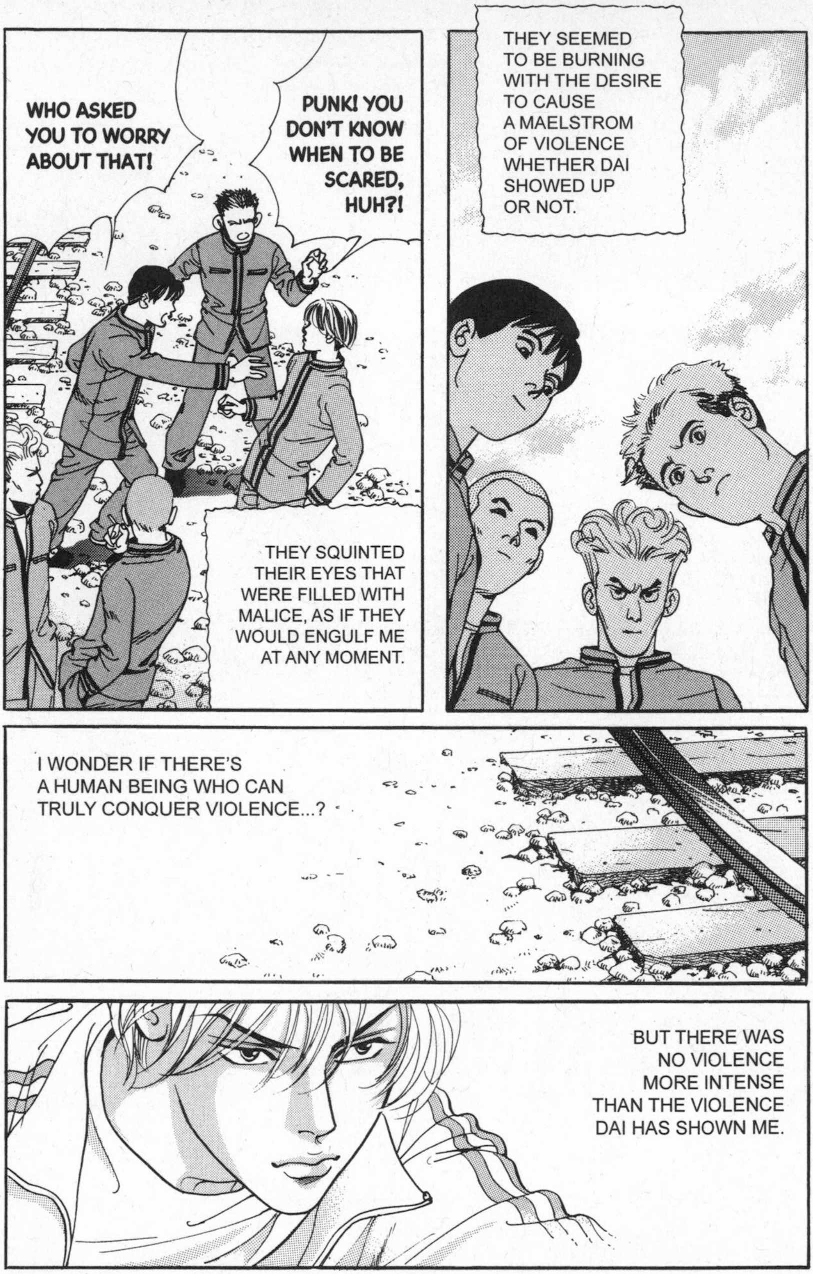
WHO ASKED YOU TO WORRY ABOUT THAT!
PUNK! YOU DON'T KNOW WHEN TO BE SCARED, HUH?!
THEY SQUINTED THEIR EYES THAT WERE FILLED WITH MALICE, AS IF THEY WOULD ENGULF ME AT ANY MOMENT.
THEY SEEMED TO BE BURNING WITH THE DESIRE TO CAUSE A MAELSTROM OF VIOLENCE WHETHER DAI SHOWED UP OR NOT.
I WONDER IF THERE'S A HUMAN BEING WHO CAN TRULY CONQUER VIOLENCE...?
BUT THERE WAS NO VIOLENCE MORE INTENSE THAN THE VIOLENCE DAI HAS SHOWN ME.

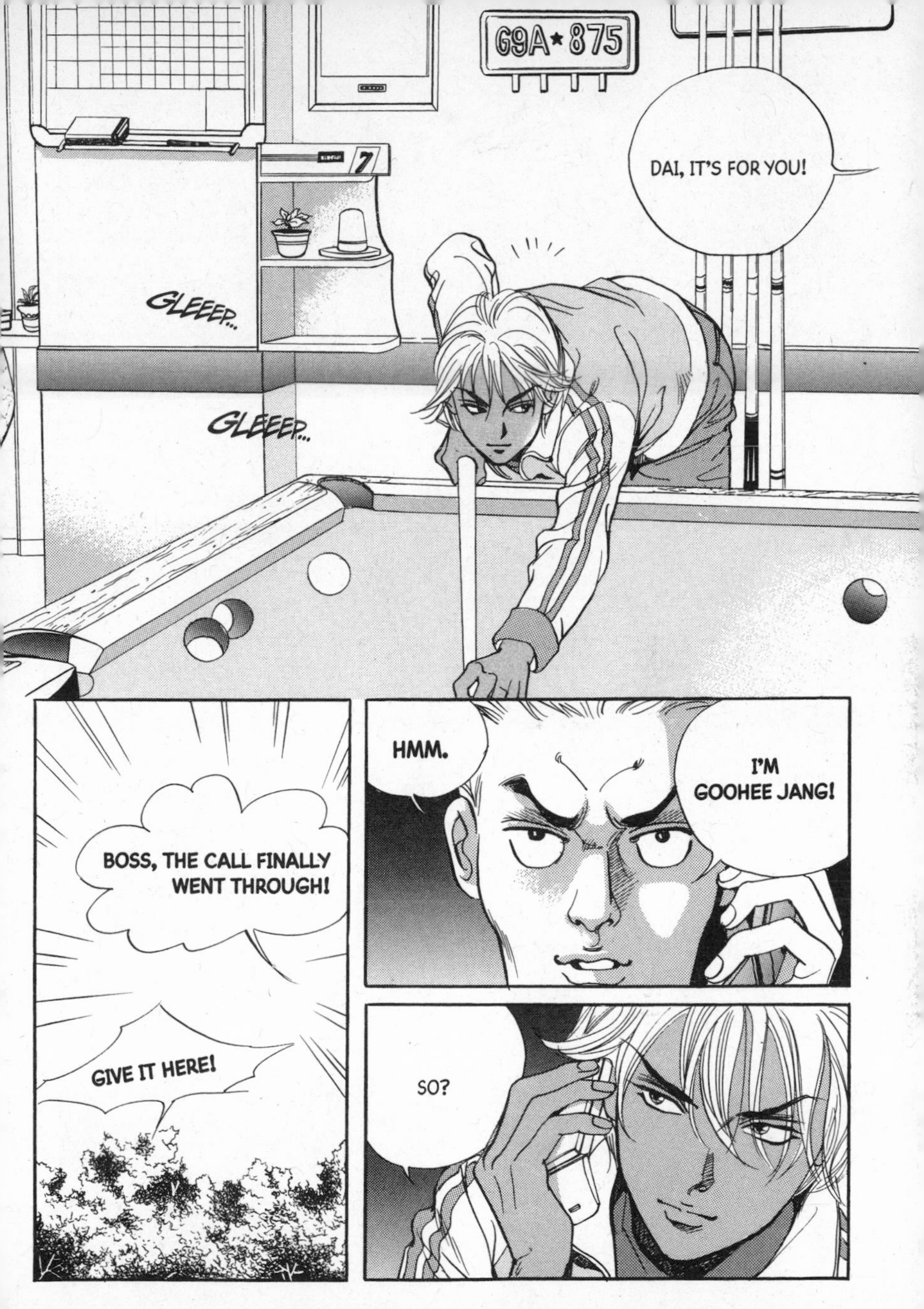
G9A★875
DAI, IT'S FOR YOU!
GLEEEP...
GLEEEP...
BOSS, THE CALL FINALLY WENT THROUGH!
GIVE IT HERE!
HMM.
I'M GOOHEE JANG!
SO?

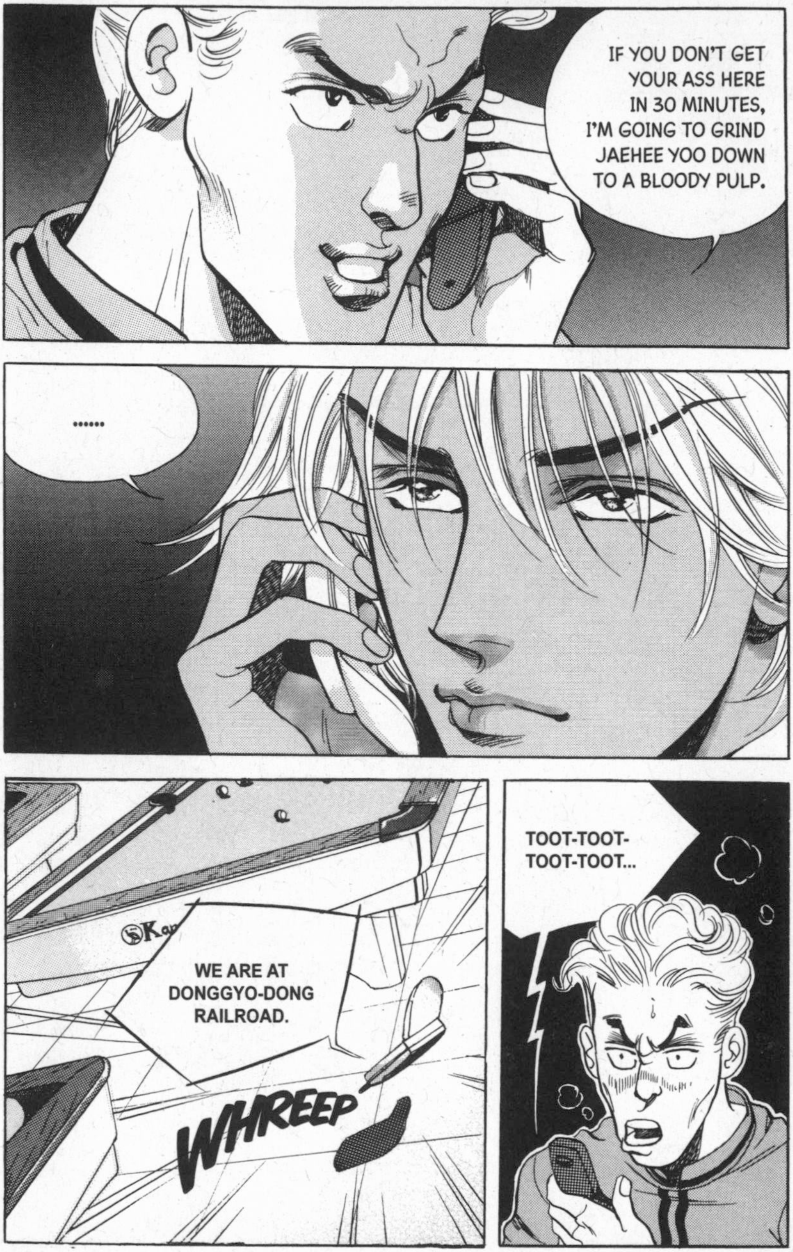
IF YOU DON'T GET YOUR ASS HERE IN 30 MINUTES, I'M GOING TO GRIND JAEHEE YOO DOWN TO A BLOODY PULP.
......
WE ARE AT DONGGYO-DONG RAILROAD.
WHREEP
TOOT-TOOT-TOOT-TOOT...

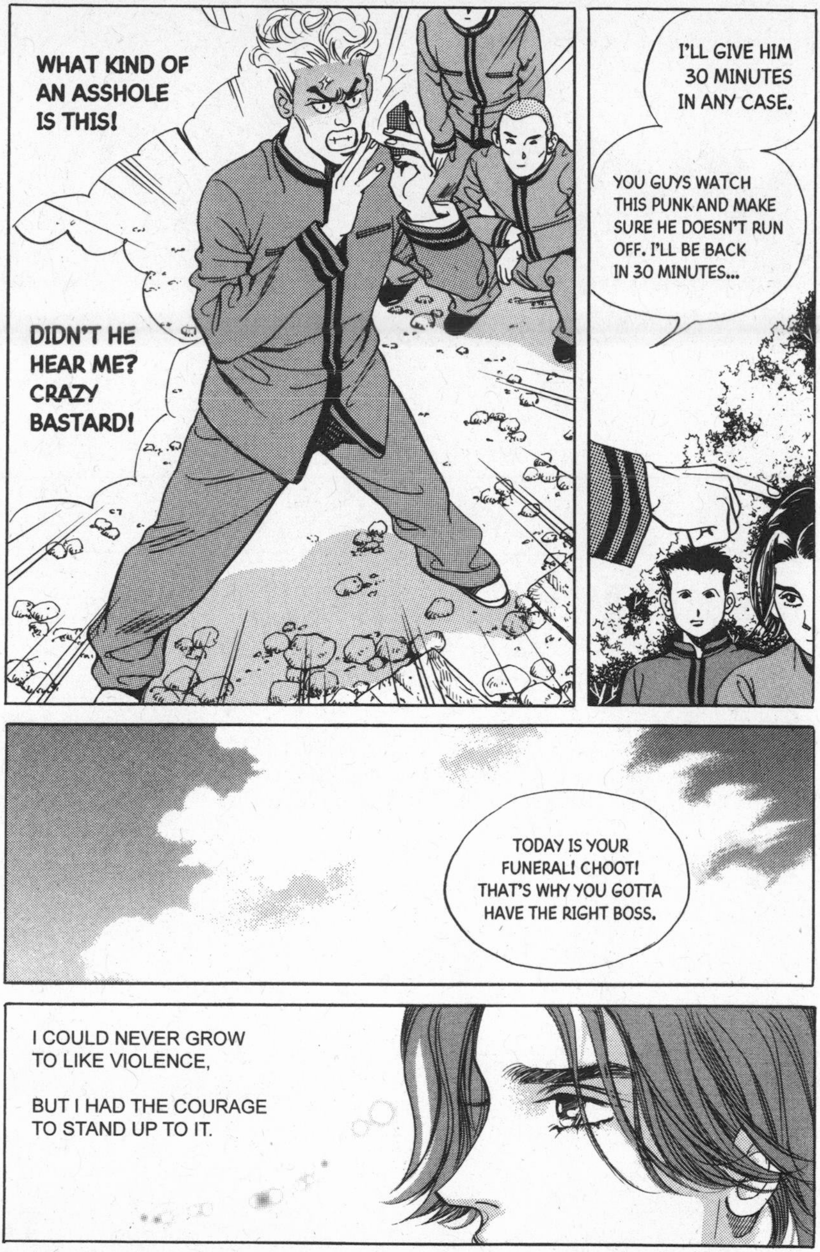
WHAT KIND OF AN ASSHOLE IS THIS!
DIDN'T HE HEAR ME? CRAZY BASTARD!
I'LL GIVE HIM 30 MINUTES IN ANY CASE.
YOU GUYS WATCH THIS PUNK AND MAKE SURE HE DOESN'T RUN OFF. I'LL BE BACK IN 30 MINUTES...
TODAY IS YOUR FUNERAL! CHOOT! THAT'S WHY YOU GOTTA HAVE THE RIGHT BOSS.
I COULD NEVER GROW TO LIKE VIOLENCE,
BUT I HAD THE COURAGE TO STAND UP TO IT.

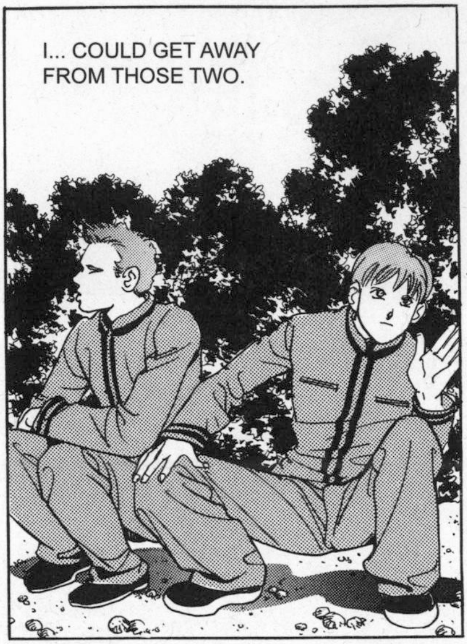
I... COULD GET AWAY FROM THOSE TWO.

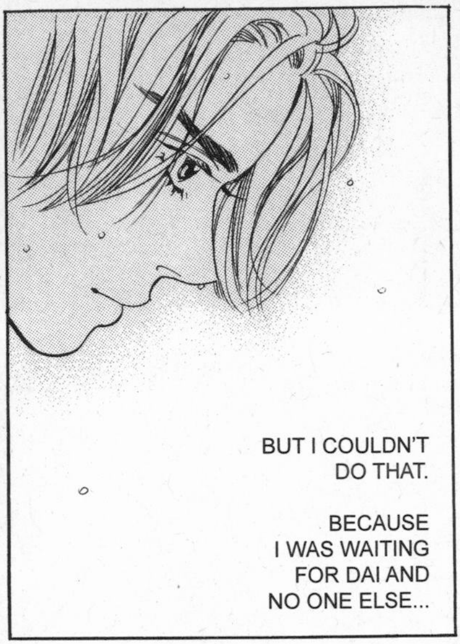
BUT I COULDN'T DO THAT.
BECAUSE I WAS WAITING FOR DAI AND NO ONE ELSE...

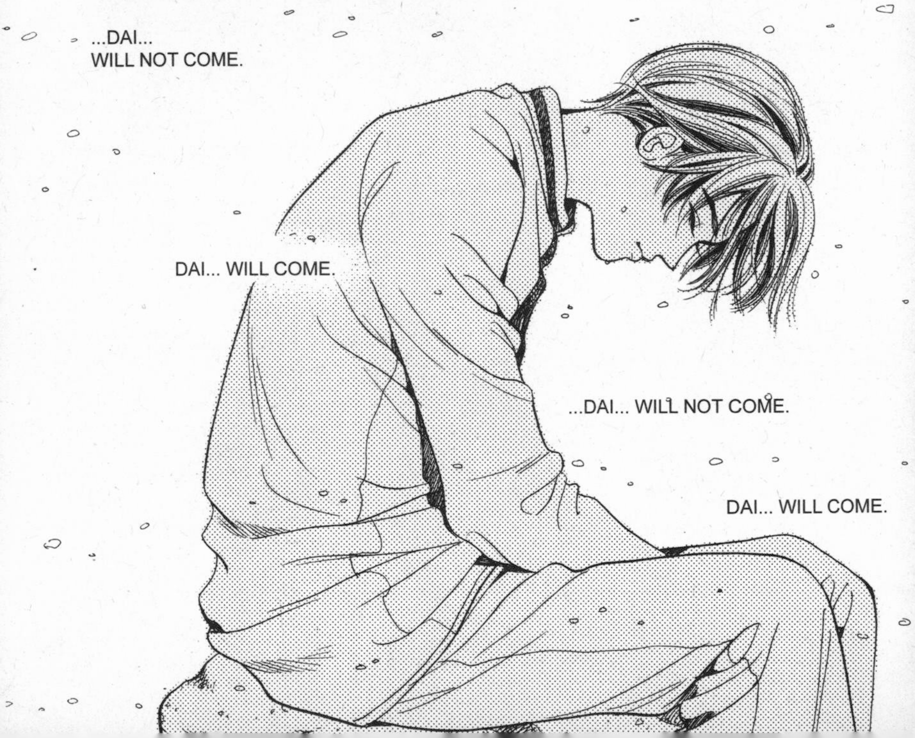
...DAI... WILL NOT COME.
DAI... WILL COME.
...DAI... WILL NOT COME.
DAI... WILL COME.

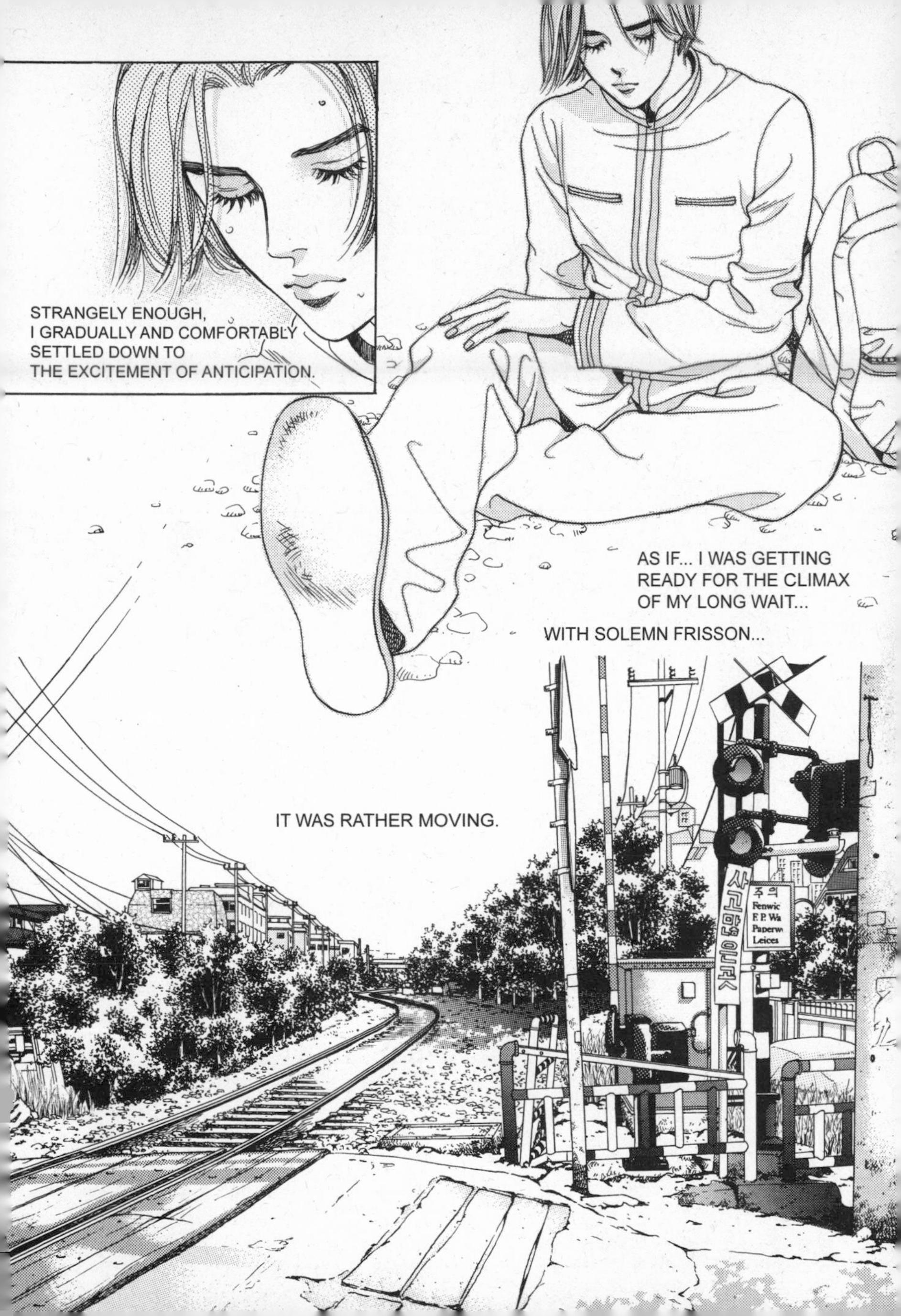
STRANGELY ENOUGH,
I GRADUALLY AND COMFORTABLY
SETTLED DOWN TO
THE EXCITEMENT OF ANTICIPATION.
AS IF... I WAS GETTING
READY FOR THE CLIMAX
OF MY LONG WAIT...
WITH SOLEMN FRISSON...
IT WAS RATHER MOVING.
사고많은곳
주의

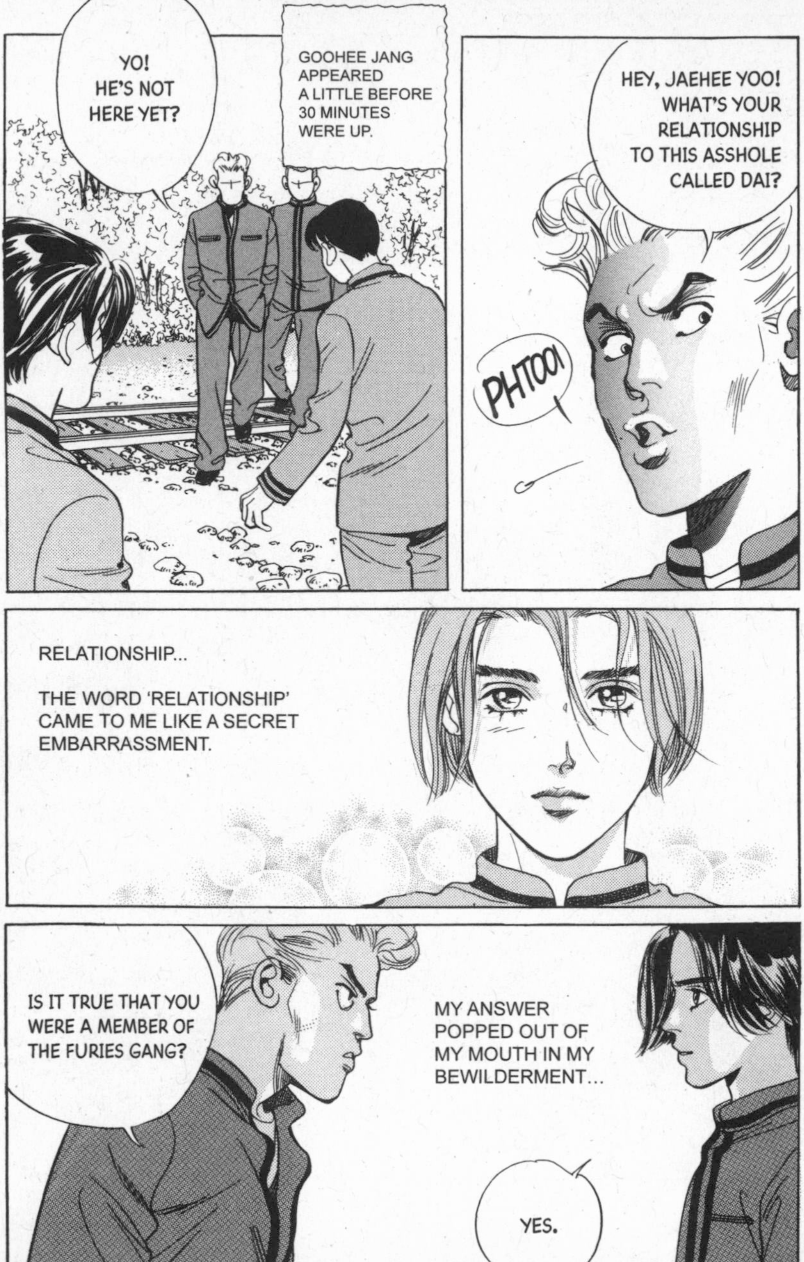
YO!
HE'S NOT HERE YET?
GOOHEE JANG APPEARED A LITTLE BEFORE 30 MINUTES WERE UP.
HEY, JAEHEE YOO! WHAT'S YOUR RELATIONSHIP TO THIS ASSHOLE CALLED DAI?
PHTOO!
RELATIONSHIP...
THE WORD 'RELATIONSHIP' CAME TO ME LIKE A SECRET EMBARRASSMENT.
IS IT TRUE THAT YOU WERE A MEMBER OF THE FURIES GANG?
MY ANSWER POPPED OUT OF MY MOUTH IN MY BEWILDERMENT...
YES.

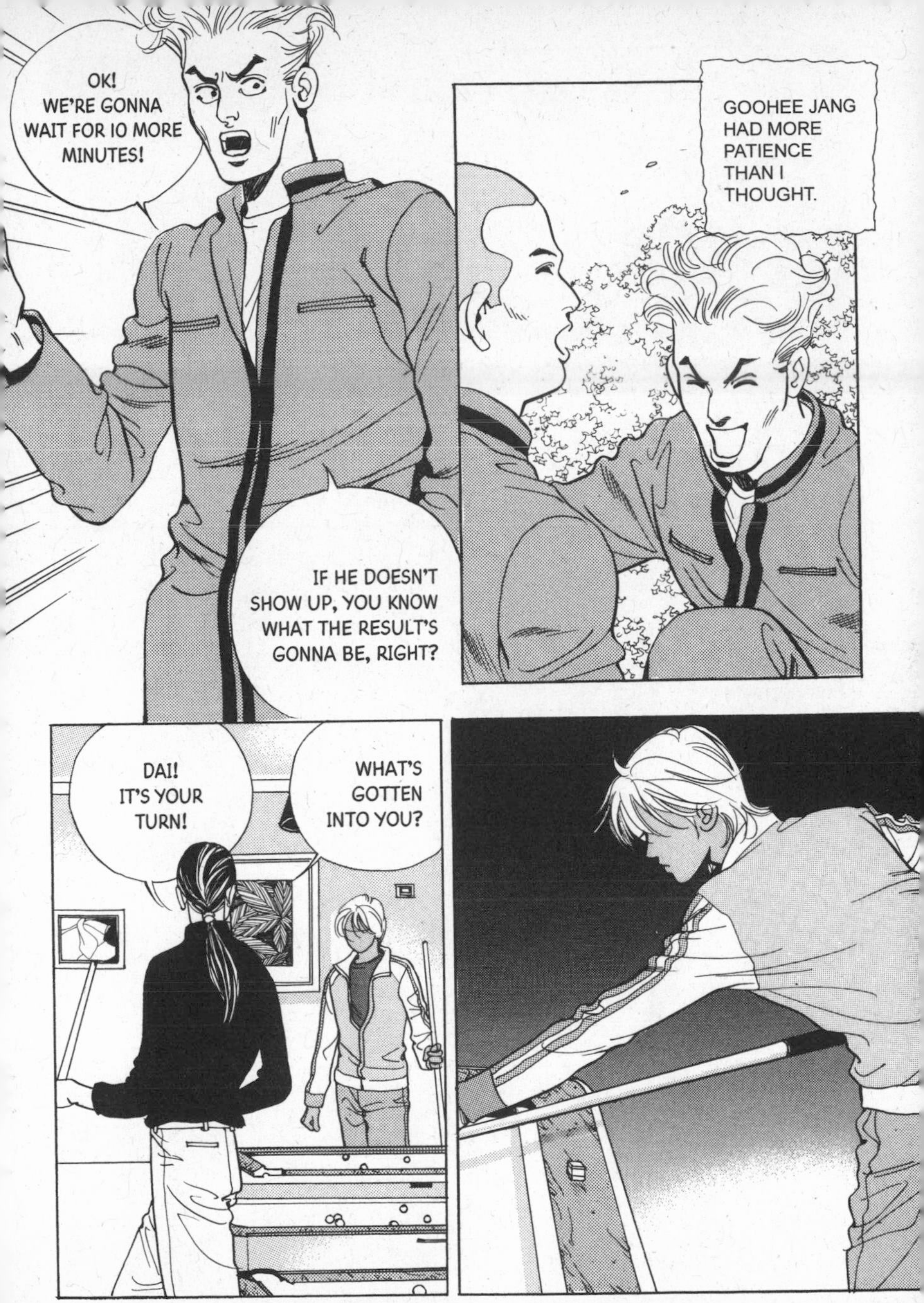
OK!
WE'RE GONNA
WAIT FOR 10 MORE
MINUTES!
IF HE DOESN'T
SHOW UP, YOU KNOW
WHAT THE RESULT'S
GONNA BE, RIGHT?
GOOHEE JANG
HAD MORE
PATIENCE
THAN I
THOUGHT.
DAI!
IT'S YOUR
TURN!
WHAT'S
GOTTEN
INTO YOU?

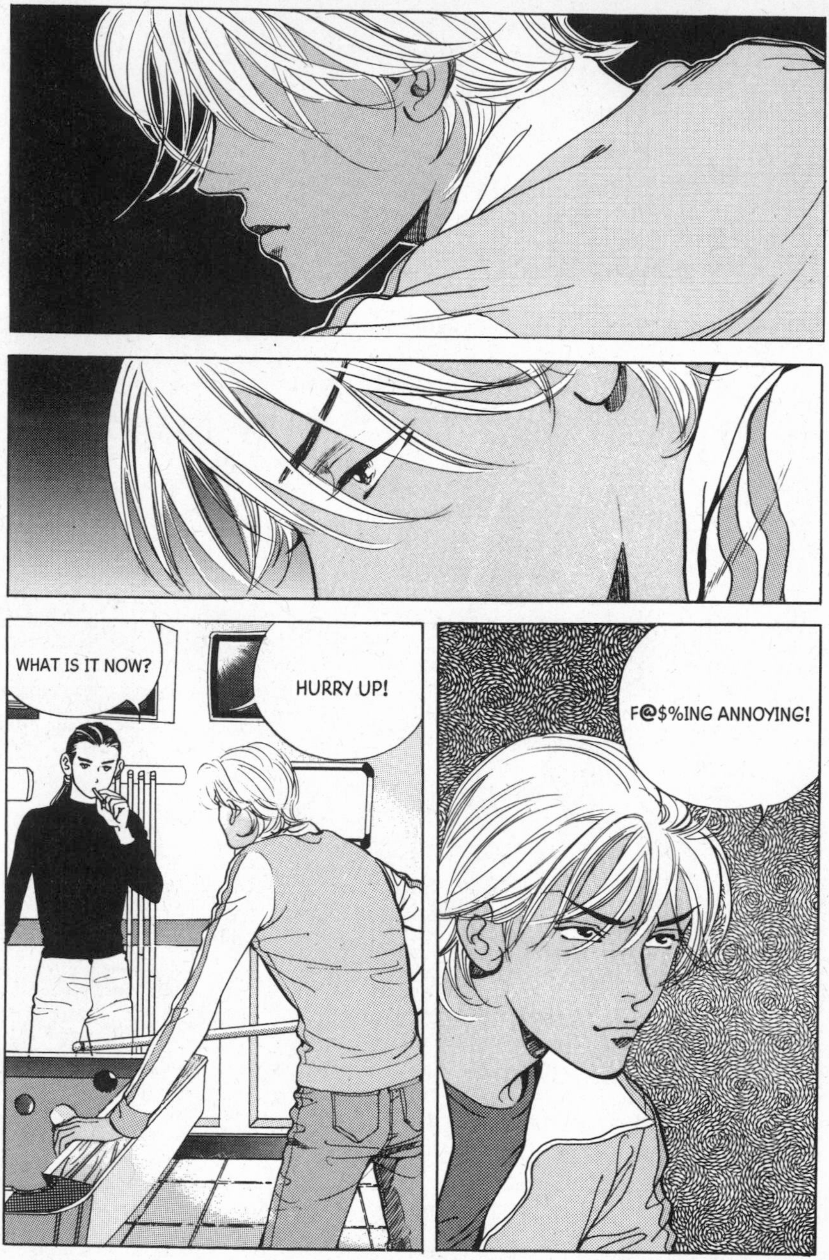
WHAT IS IT NOW?
HURRY UP!
F@$%ING ANNOYING!

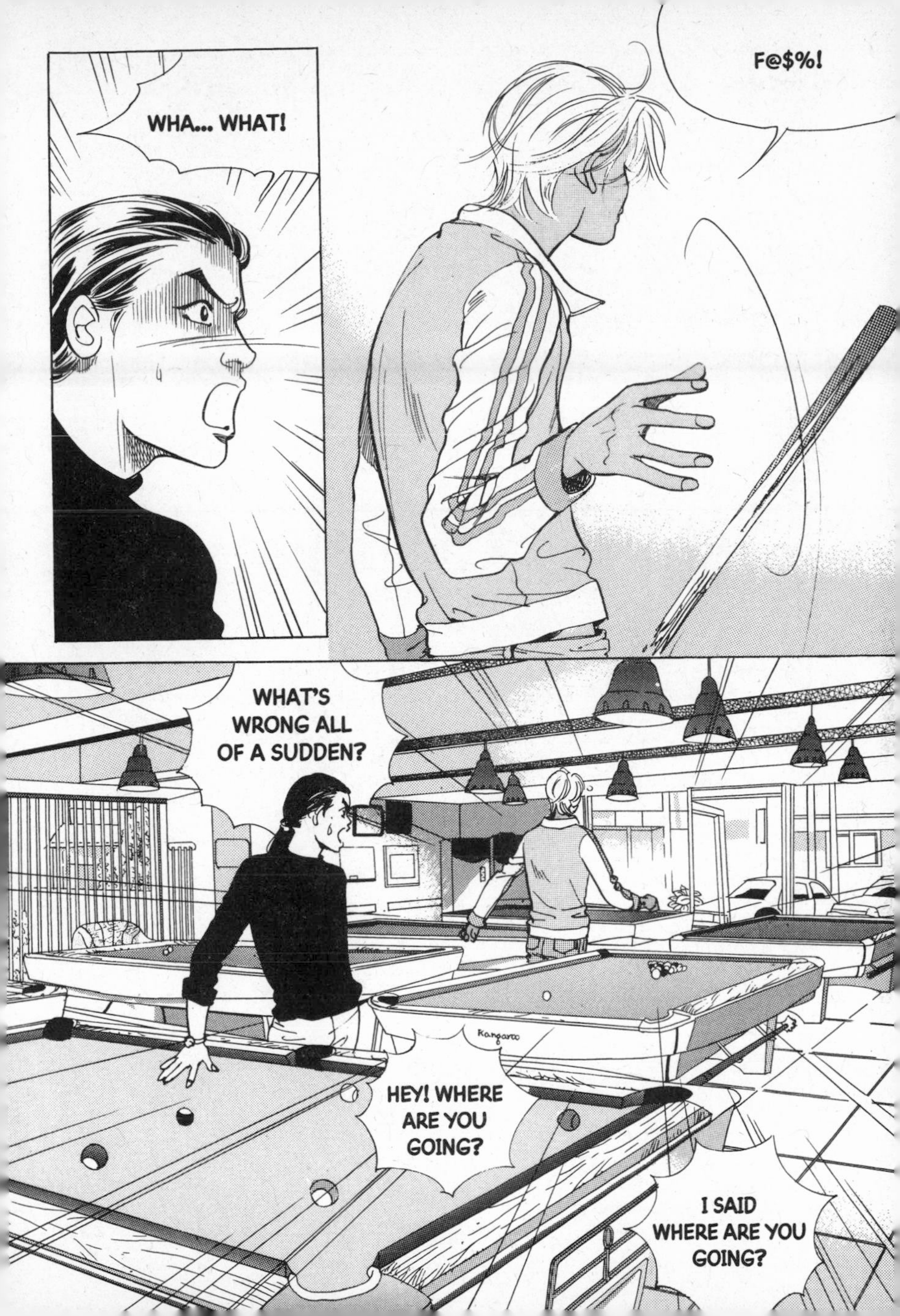
WHA... WHAT!
F@$%!
WHAT'S WRONG ALL OF A SUDDEN?
Kangaroo
HEY! WHERE ARE YOU GOING?
I SAID WHERE ARE YOU GOING?

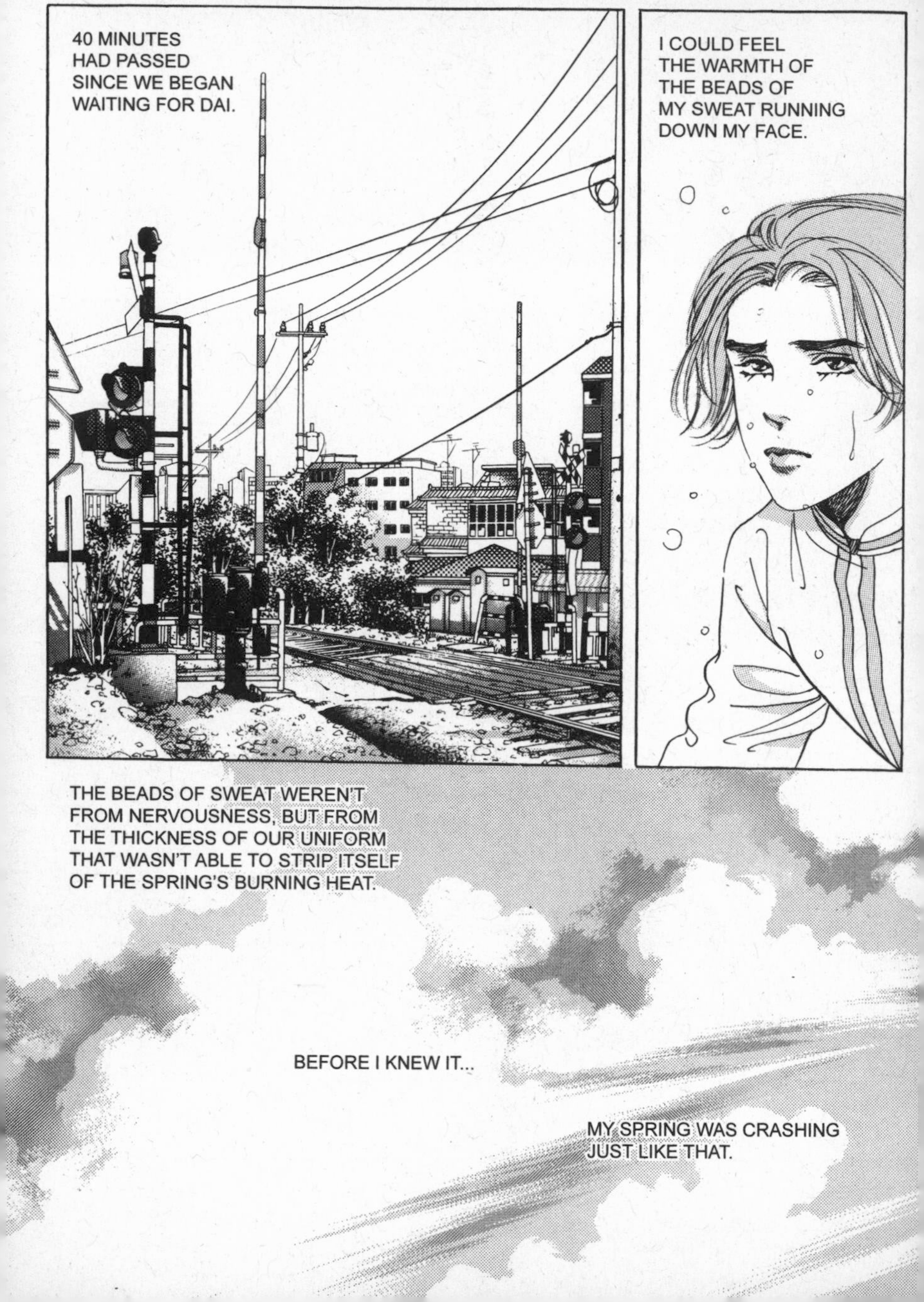
40 MINUTES HAD PASSED SINCE WE BEGAN WAITING FOR DAI.
I COULD FEEL THE WARMTH OF THE BEADS OF MY SWEAT RUNNING DOWN MY FACE.
THE BEADS OF SWEAT WEREN'T FROM NERVOUSNESS, BUT FROM THE THICKNESS OF OUR UNIFORM THAT WASN'T ABLE TO STRIP ITSELF OF THE SPRING'S BURNING HEAT.
BEFORE I KNEW IT...
MY SPRING WAS CRASHING JUST LIKE THAT.

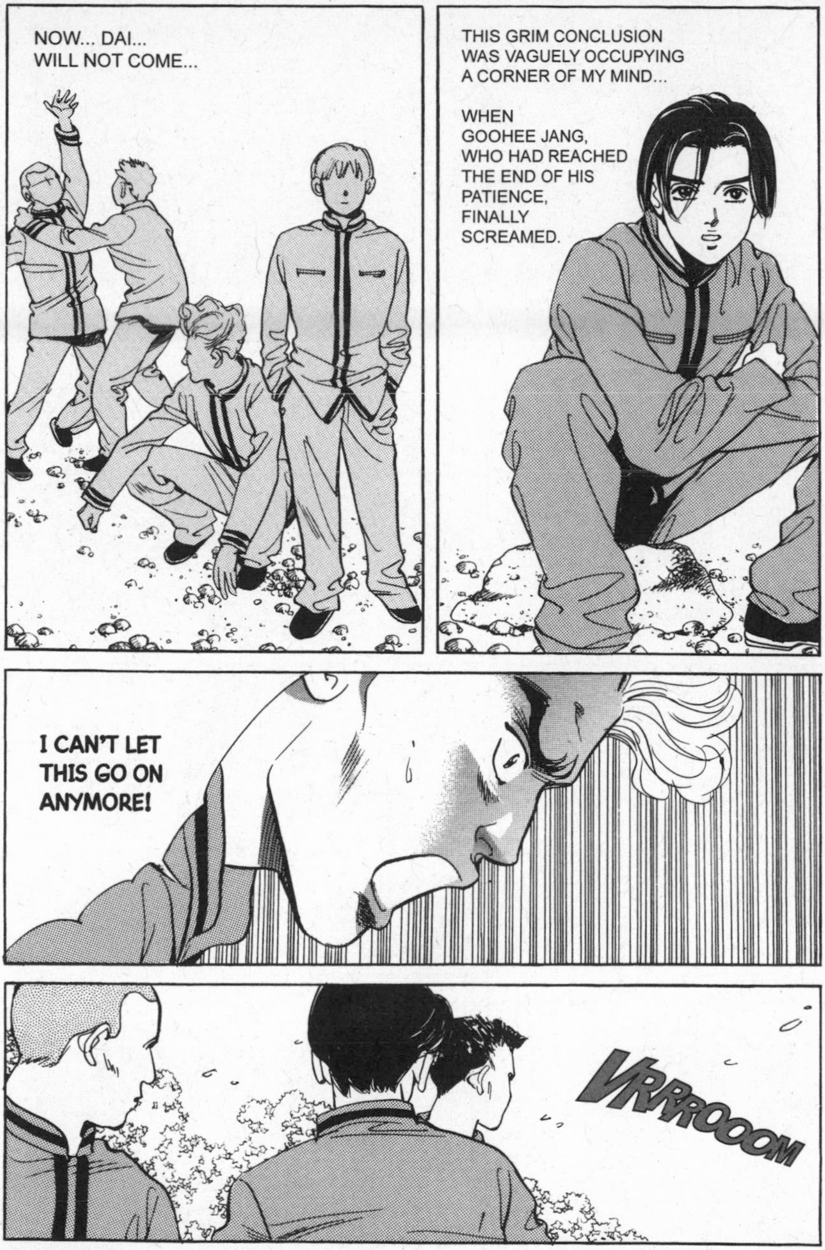
NOW... DAI...
WILL NOT COME...
THIS GRIM CONCLUSION WAS VAGUELY OCCUPYING A CORNER OF MY MIND...
WHEN GOOHEE JANG, WHO HAD REACHED THE END OF HIS PATIENCE, FINALLY SCREAMED.
I CAN'T LET THIS GO ON ANYMORE!
VRRROOOOM

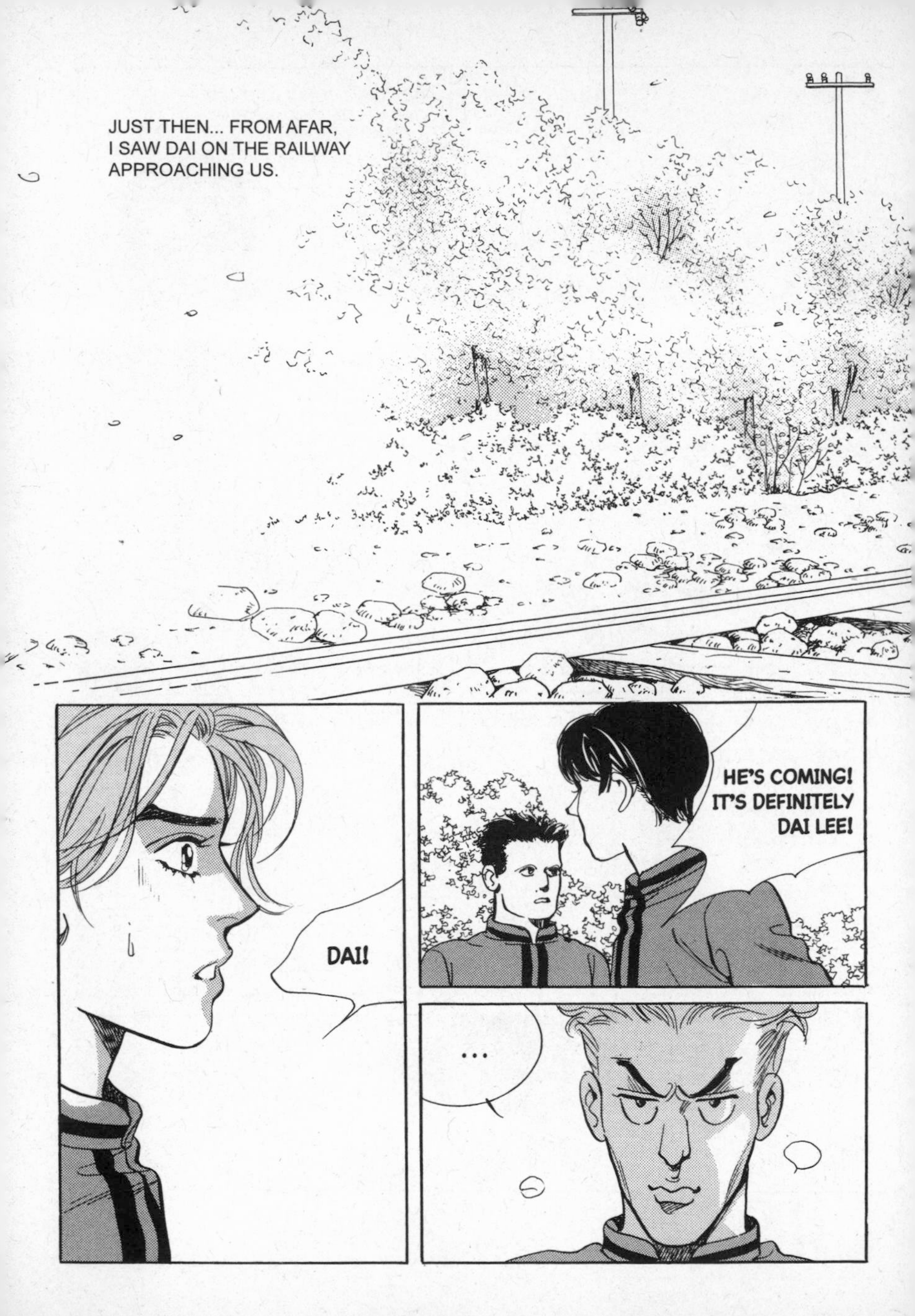
JUST THEN... FROM AFAR, I SAW DAI ON THE RAILWAY APPROACHING US.
DAI!
HE'S COMING! IT'S DEFINITELY DAI LEE!
...

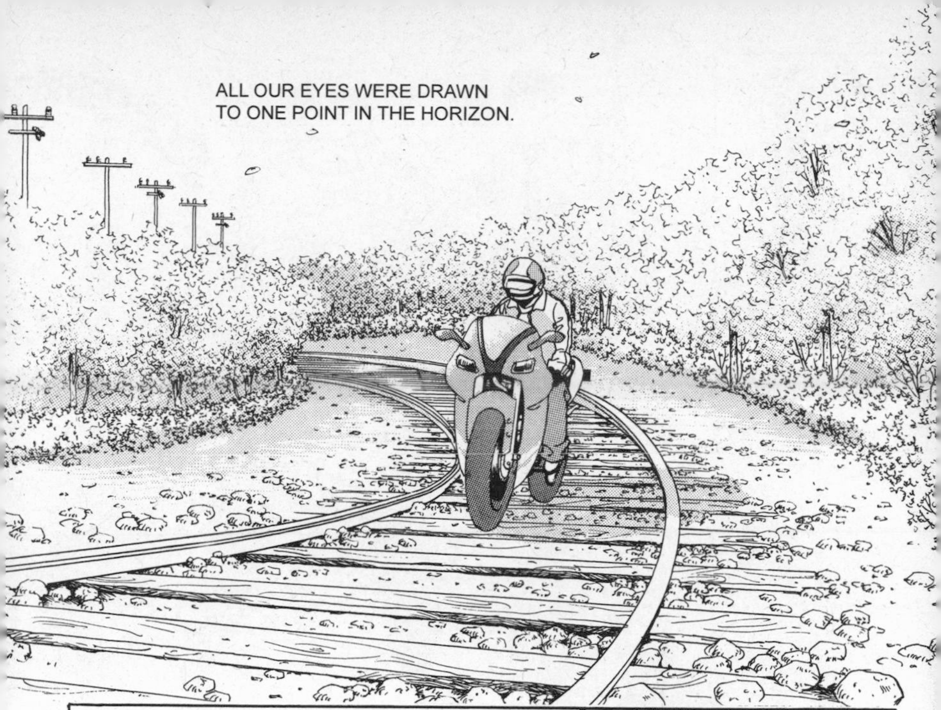
ALL OUR EYES WERE DRAWN
TO ONE POINT IN THE HORIZON.
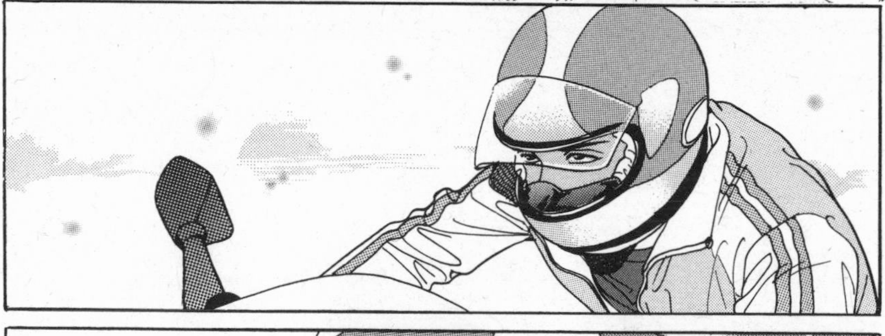
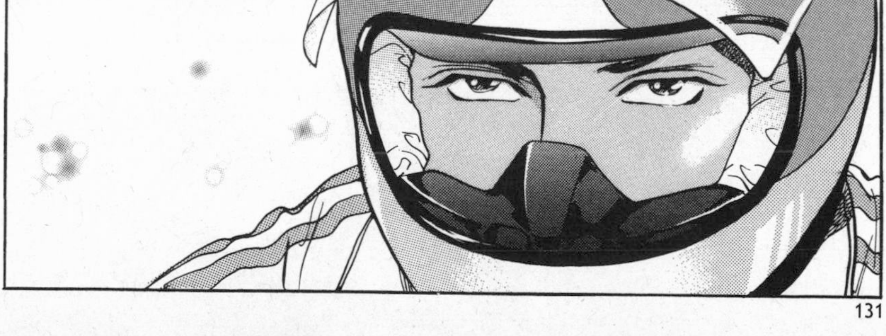

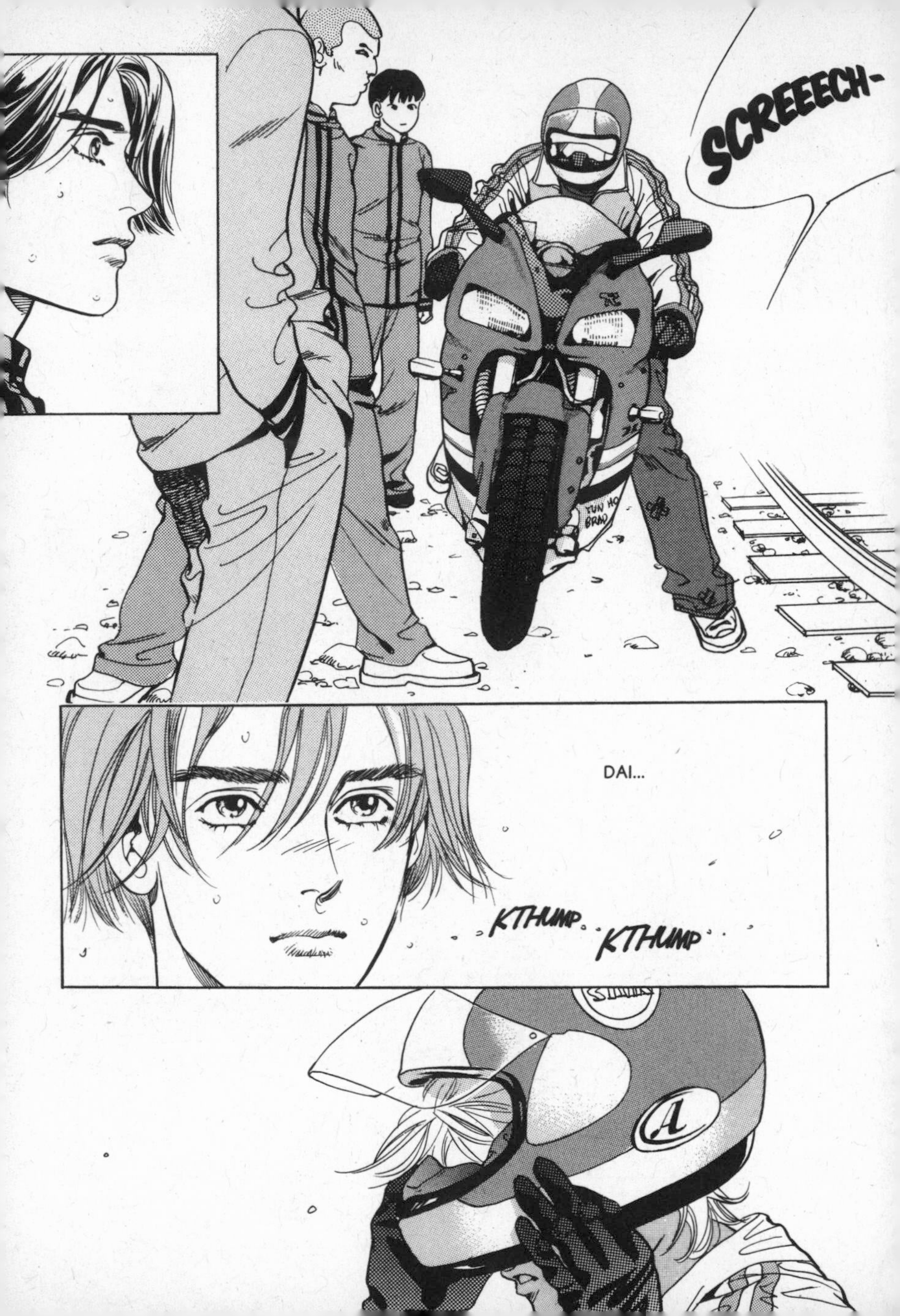

SCREEECH-
YUN HO
BRAD
DAI...
KTHUMP
KTHUMP

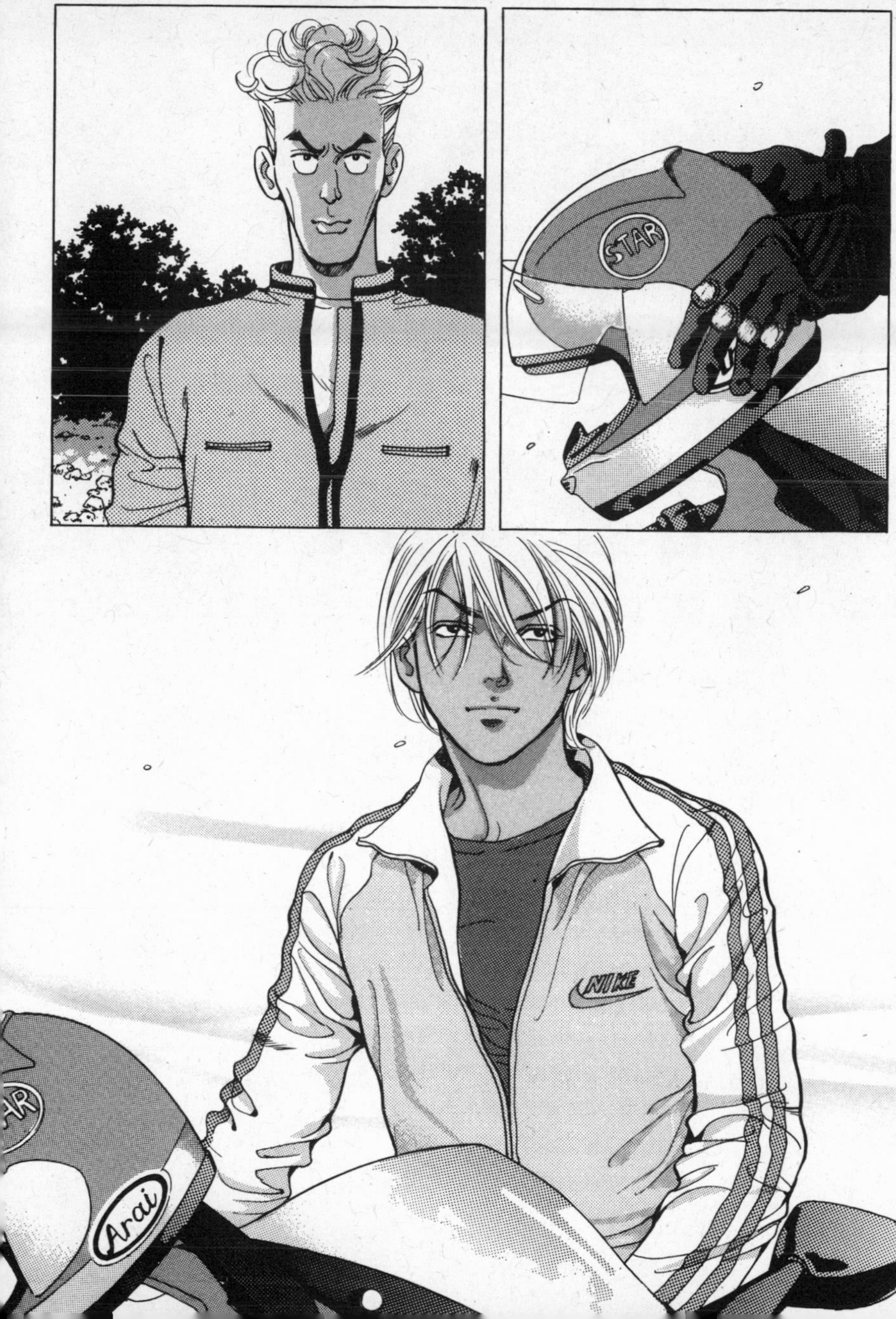
STAR
NIKE
Arai

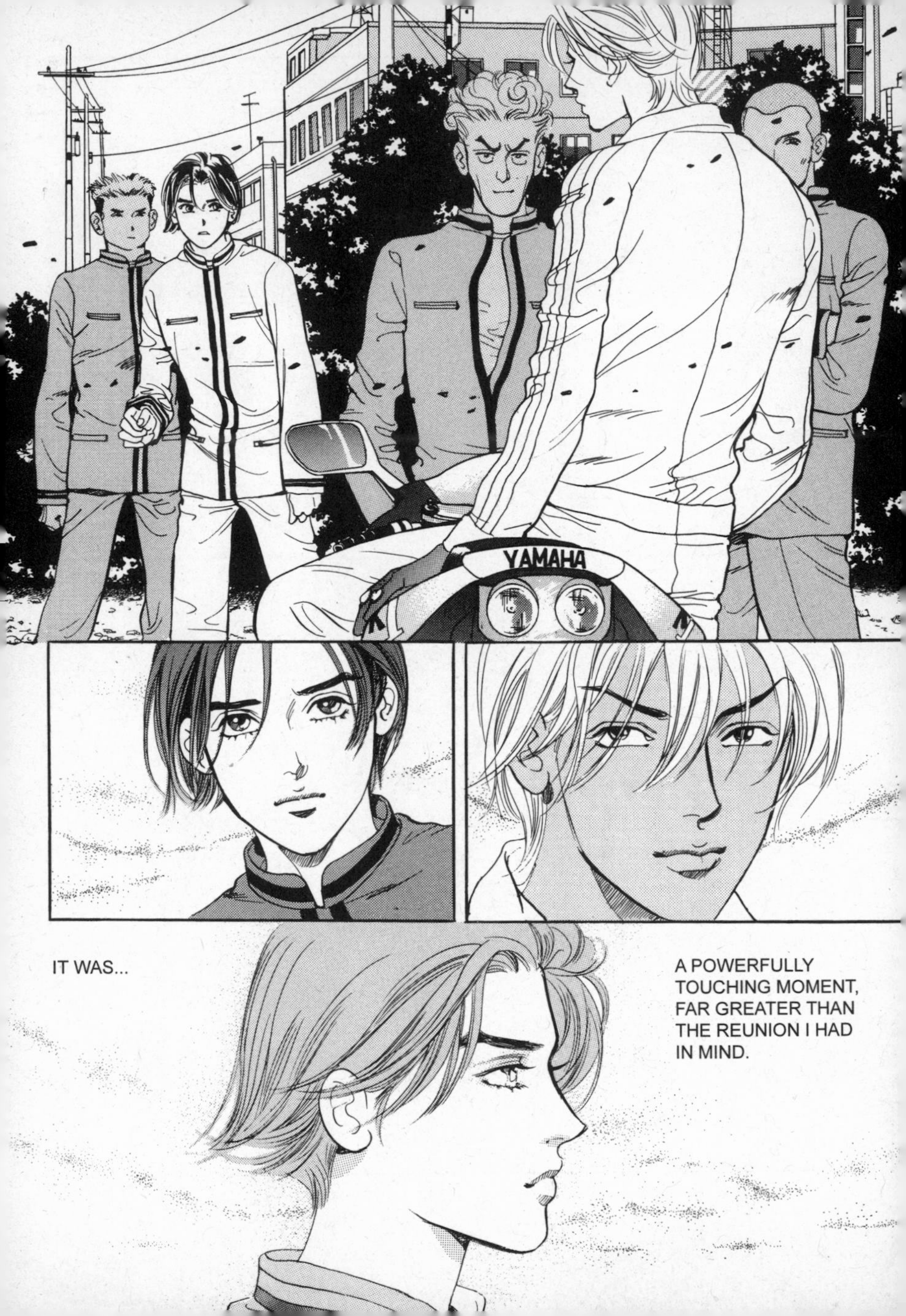
YAMAHA
IT WAS...
A POWERFULLY TOUCHING MOMENT, FAR GREATER THAN THE REUNION I HAD IN MIND.

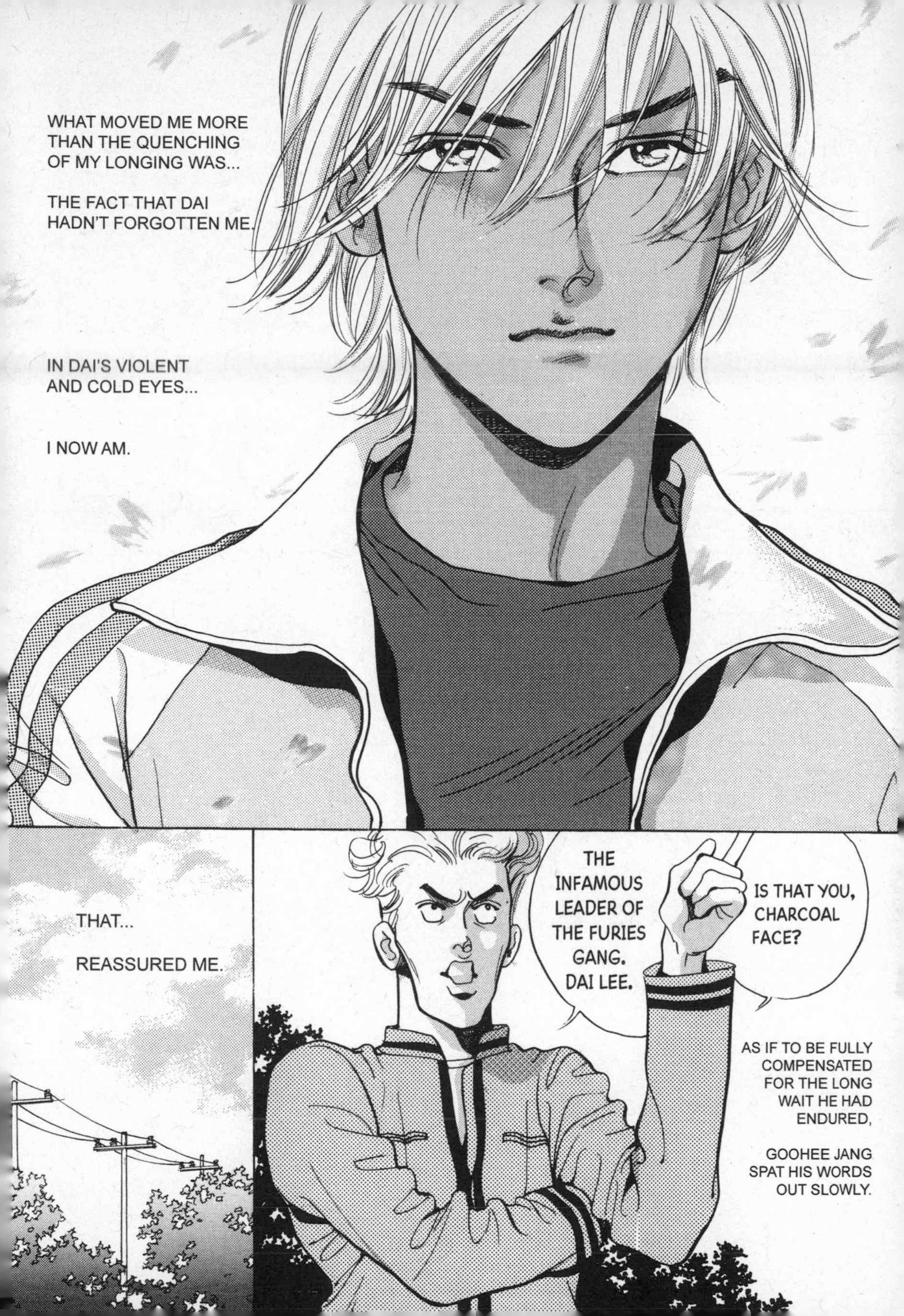
WHAT MOVED ME MORE THAN THE QUENCHING OF MY LONGING WAS...
THE FACT THAT DAI HADN'T FORGOTTEN ME.
IN DAI'S VIOLENT AND COLD EYES...
I NOW AM.
THAT...
REASSURED ME.
THE INFAMOUS LEADER OF THE FURIES GANG. DAI LEE.
IS THAT YOU, CHARCOAL FACE?
AS IF TO BE FULLY COMPENSATED FOR THE LONG WAIT HE HAD ENDURED,
GOOHEE JANG SPAT HIS WORDS OUT SLOWLY.

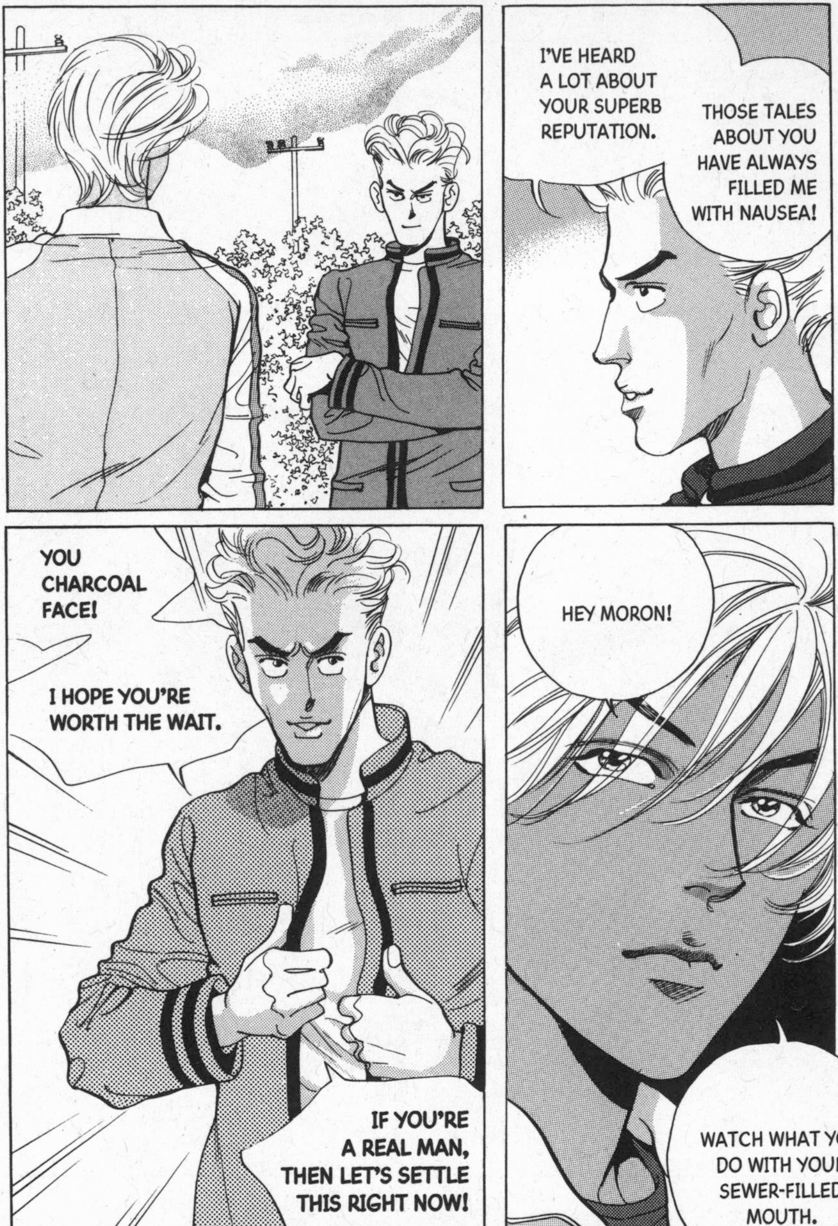
I'VE HEARD A LOT ABOUT YOUR SUPERB REPUTATION.
THOSE TALES ABOUT YOU HAVE ALWAYS FILLED ME WITH NAUSEA!
YOU CHARCOAL FACE!
I HOPE YOU'RE WORTH THE WAIT.
IF YOU'RE A REAL MAN, THEN LET'S SETTLE THIS RIGHT NOW!
HEY MORON!
WATCH WHAT YOU DO WITH YOUR SEWER-FILLED MOUTH.

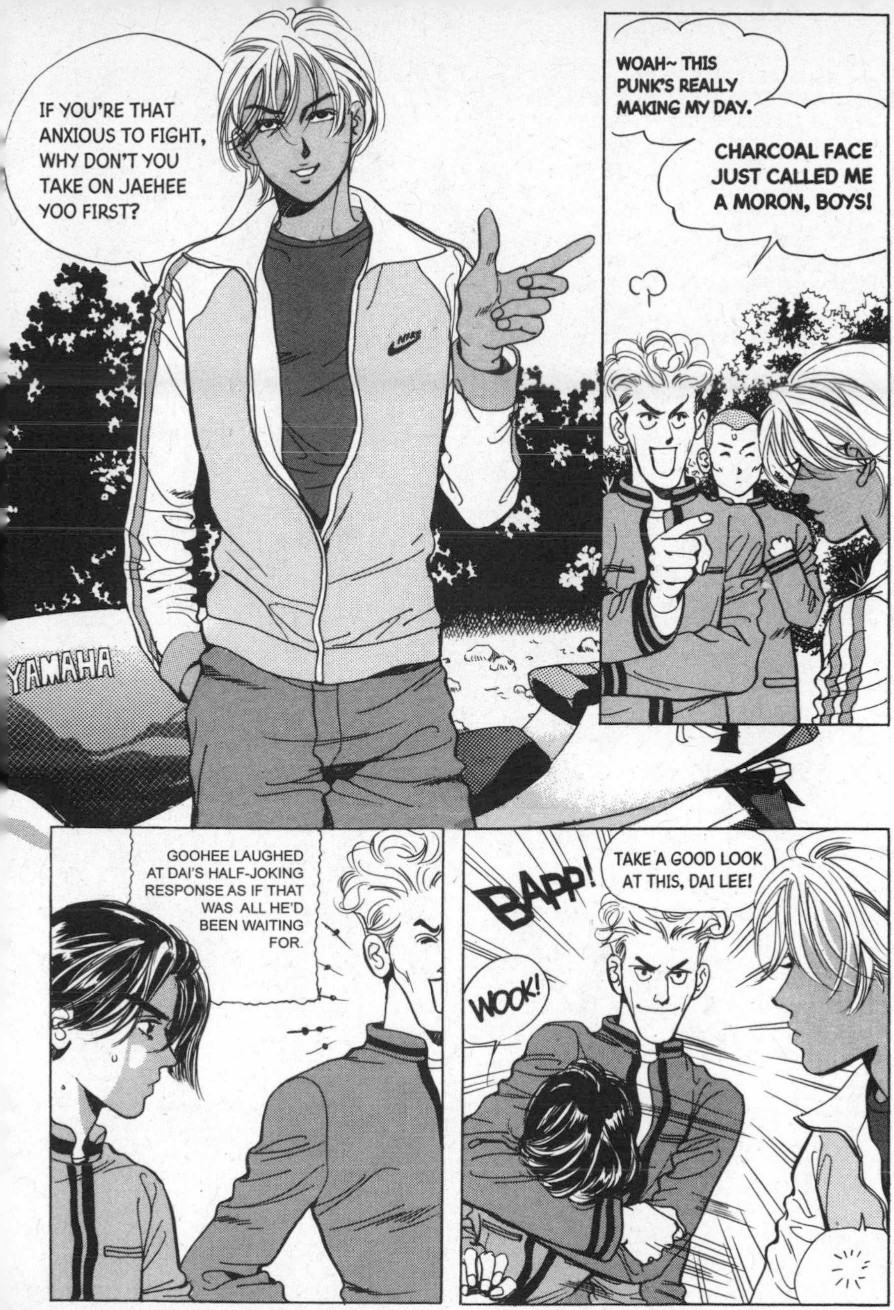

IF YOU'RE THAT ANXIOUS TO FIGHT, WHY DON'T YOU TAKE ON JAEHEE YOO FIRST?
YAMAHA
WOAH~ THIS PUNK'S REALLY MAKING MY DAY.
CHARCOAL FACE JUST CALLED ME A MORON, BOYS!
GOOHEE LAUGHED AT DAI'S HALF-JOKING RESPONSE AS IF THAT WAS ALL HE'D BEEN WAITING FOR.
BAPP!
TAKE A GOOD LOOK AT THIS, DAI LEE!
WOOK!

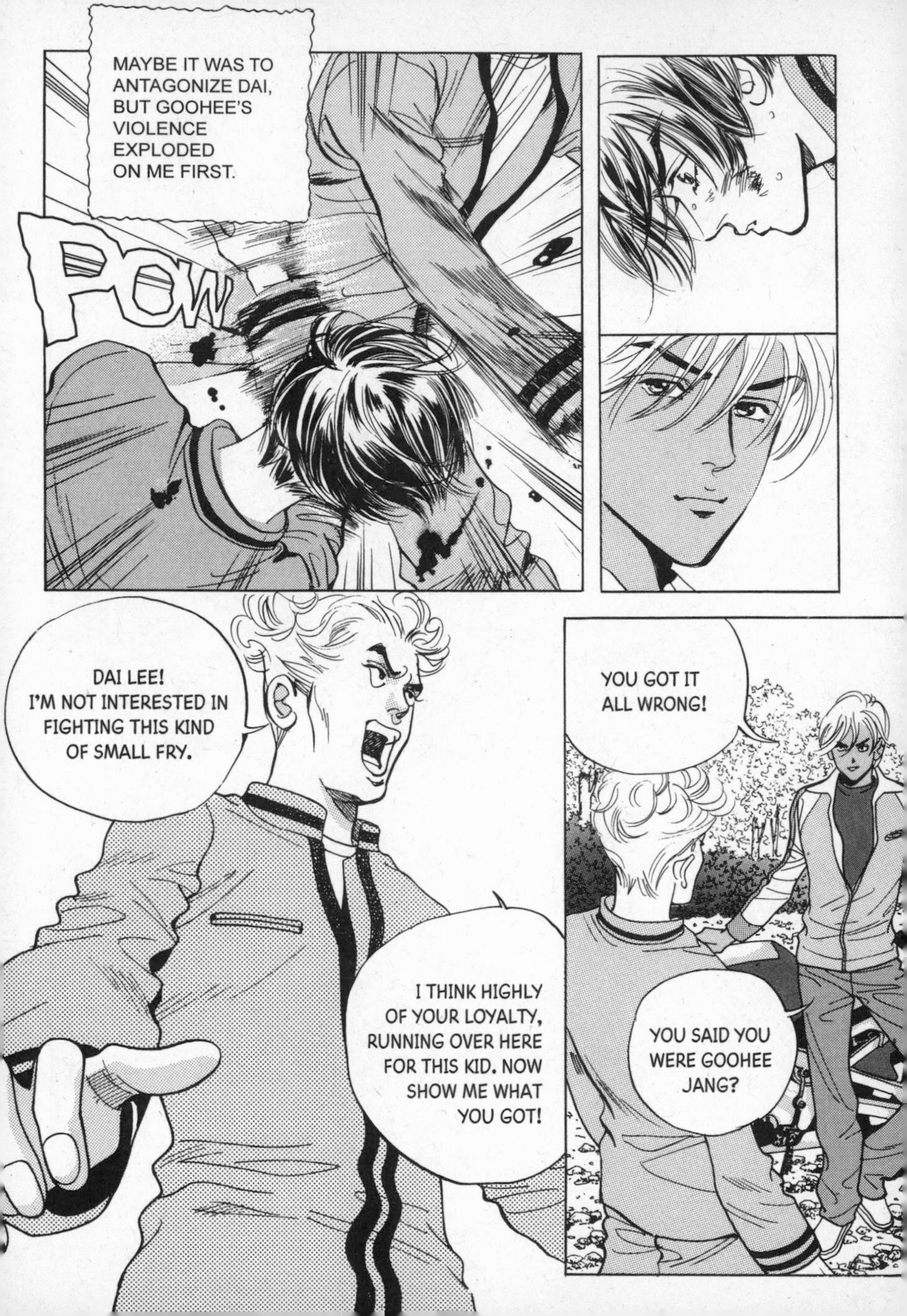
MAYBE IT WAS TO ANTAGONIZE DAI, BUT GOOHEE'S VIOLENCE EXPLODED ON ME FIRST.
POW
DAI LEE! I'M NOT INTERESTED IN FIGHTING THIS KIND OF SMALL FRY.
I THINK HIGHLY OF YOUR LOYALTY, RUNNING OVER HERE FOR THIS KID. NOW SHOW ME WHAT YOU GOT!
YOU GOT IT ALL WRONG!
YOU SAID YOU WERE GOOHEE JANG?

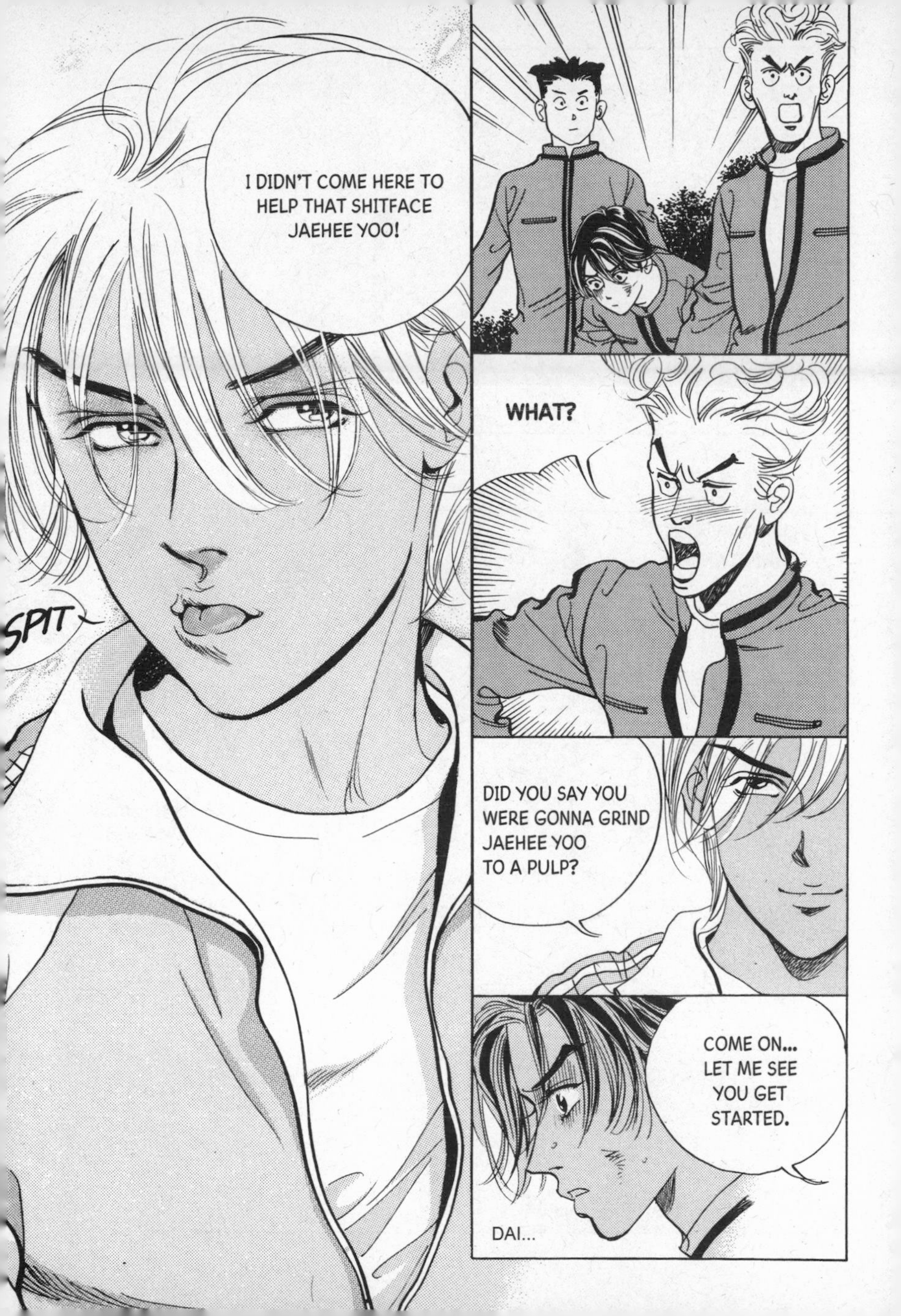
I DIDN'T COME HERE TO HELP THAT SHITFACE JAEHEE YOO!
SPIT
WHAT?
DID YOU SAY YOU WERE GONNA GRIND JAEHEE YOO TO A PULP?
COME ON... LET ME SEE YOU GET STARTED.
DAI...

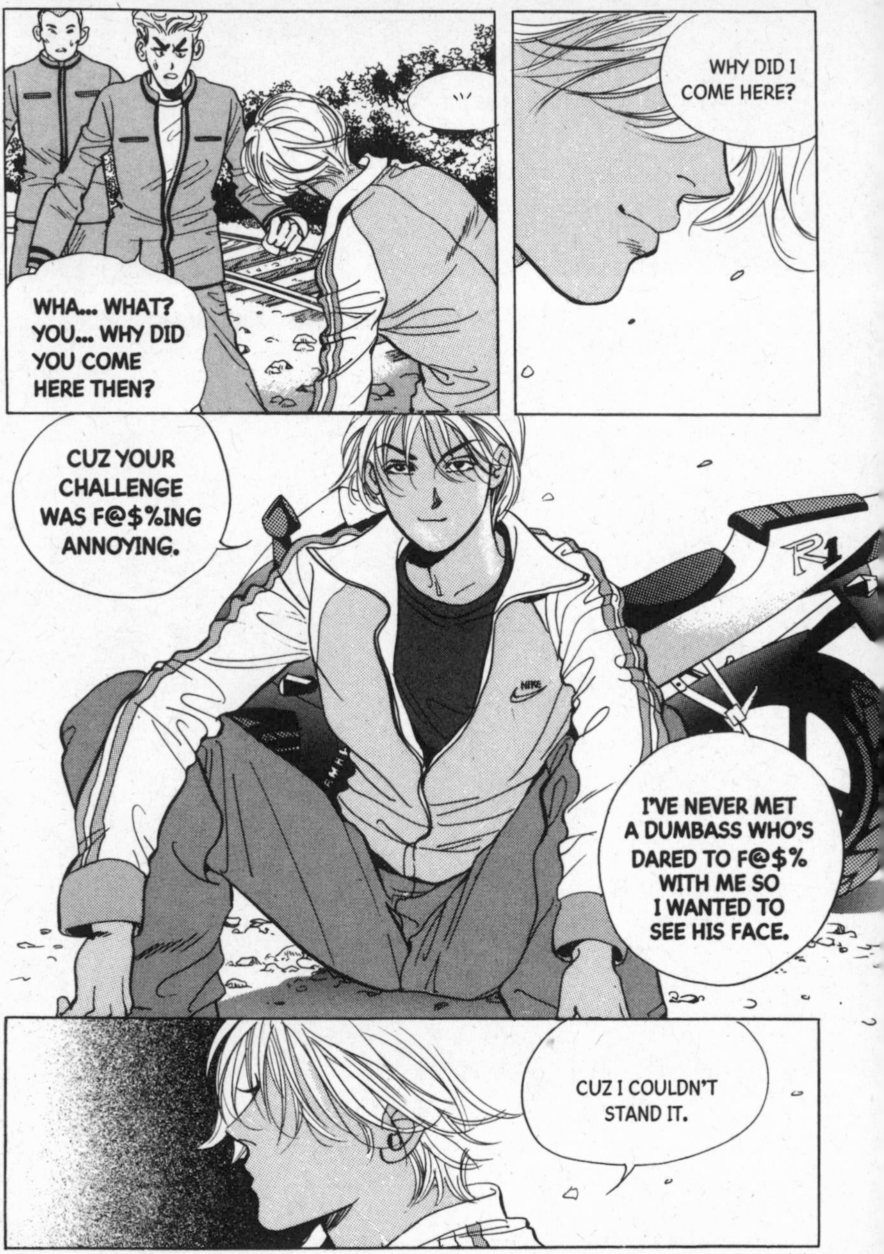
WHA... WHAT? YOU... WHY DID YOU COME HERE THEN?
WHY DID I COME HERE?
CUZ YOUR CHALLENGE WAS F@$%ING ANNOYING.
I'VE NEVER MET A DUMBASS WHO'S DARED TO F@$% WITH ME SO I WANTED TO SEE HIS FACE.
CUZ I COULDN'T STAND IT.

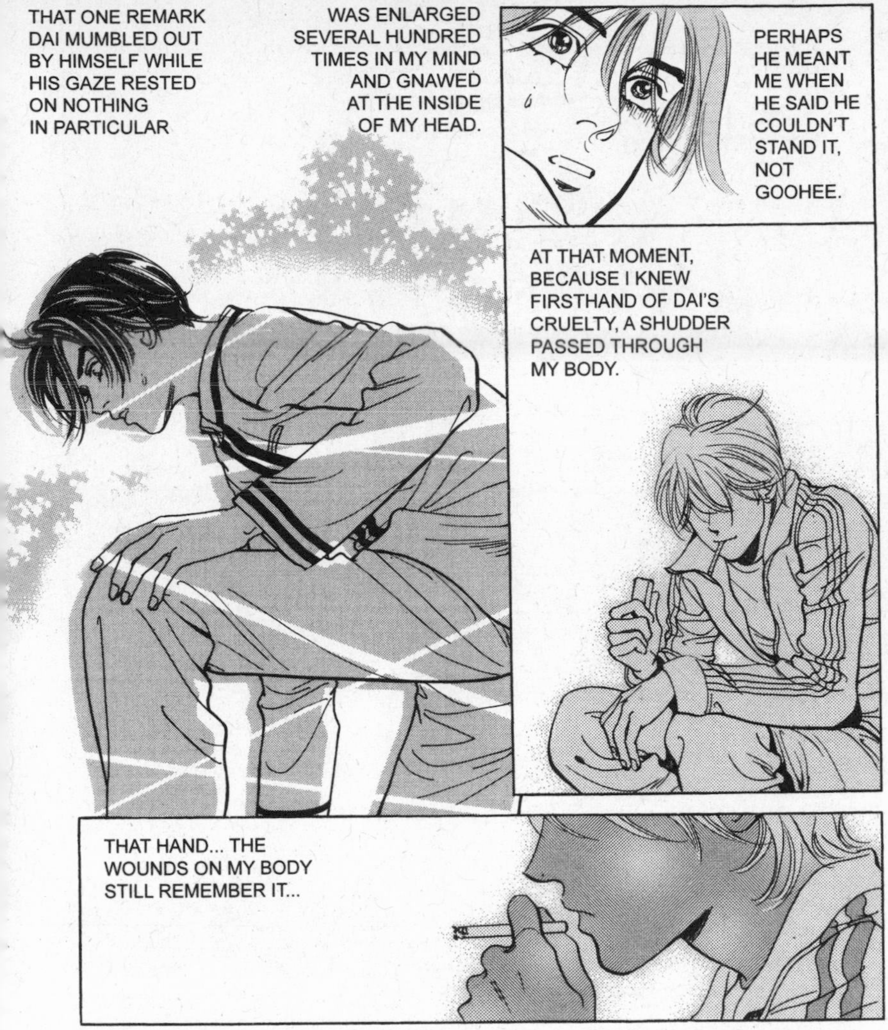
THAT ONE REMARK DAI MUMBLED OUT BY HIMSELF WHILE HIS GAZE RESTED ON NOTHING IN PARTICULAR
WAS ENLARGED SEVERAL HUNDRED TIMES IN MY MIND AND GNAWED AT THE INSIDE OF MY HEAD.
PERHAPS HE MEANT ME WHEN HE SAID HE COULDN'T STAND IT, NOT GOOHEE.
AT THAT MOMENT, BECAUSE I KNEW FIRSTHAND OF DAI'S CRUELTY, A SHUDDER PASSED THROUGH MY BODY.
THAT HAND... THE WOUNDS ON MY BODY STILL REMEMBER IT...
THAT MOUTH THAT PUFFS OUT GRAY CIGARETTE SMOKE...
ALWAYS CROOKED WITH A CRUEL SMILE.

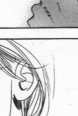

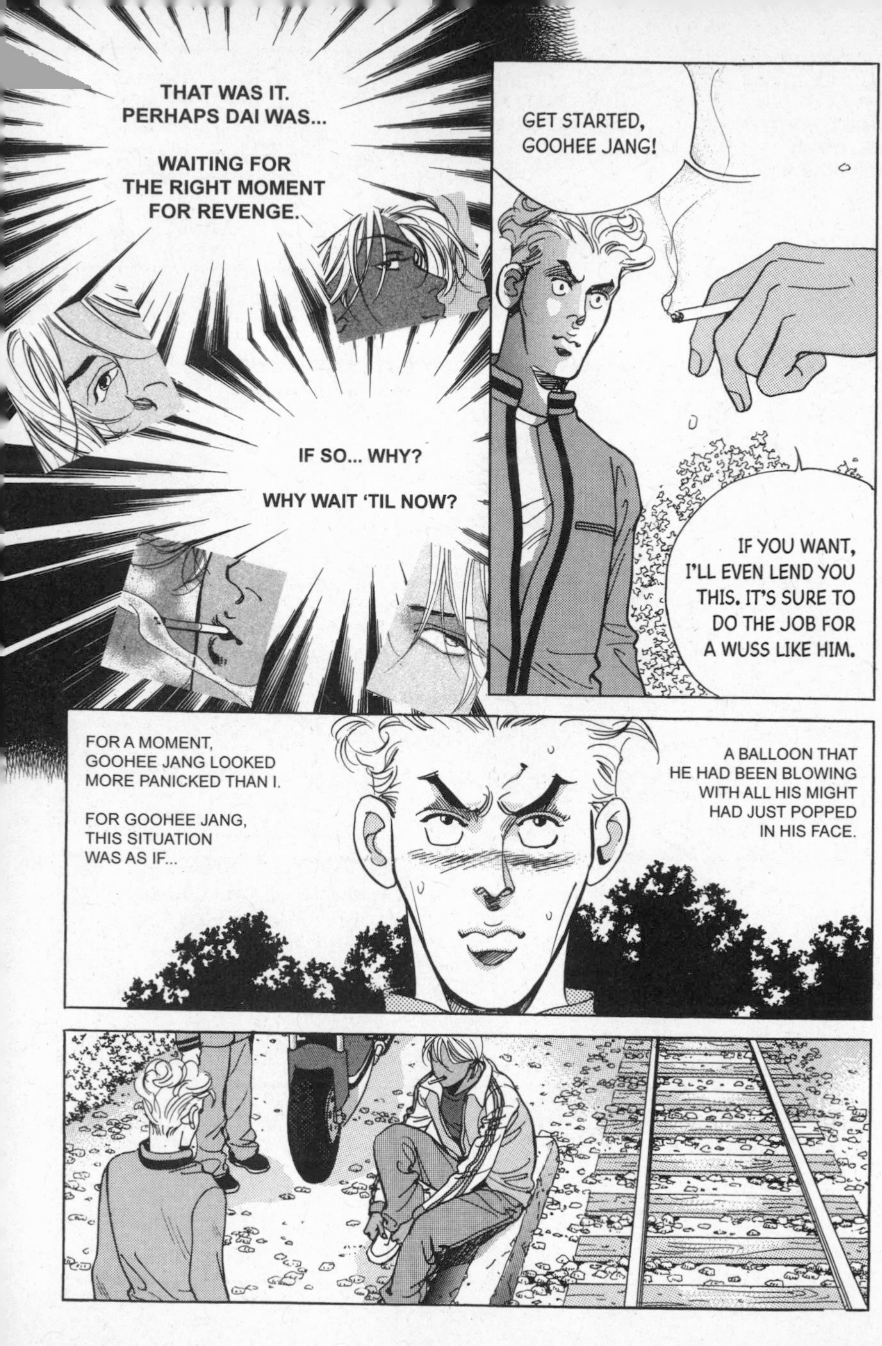
THAT WAS IT.
PERHAPS DAI WAS...
WAITING FOR THE RIGHT MOMENT FOR REVENGE.
IF SO... WHY?
WHY WAIT 'TIL NOW?
GET STARTED, GOOHEE JANG!
IF YOU WANT, I'LL EVEN LEND YOU THIS. IT'S SURE TO DO THE JOB FOR A WUSS LIKE HIM.
FOR A MOMENT, GOOHEE JANG LOOKED MORE PANICKED THAN I.
FOR GOOHEE JANG, THIS SITUATION WAS AS IF...
A BALLOON THAT HE HAD BEEN BLOWING WITH ALL HIS MIGHT HAD JUST POPPED IN HIS FACE.

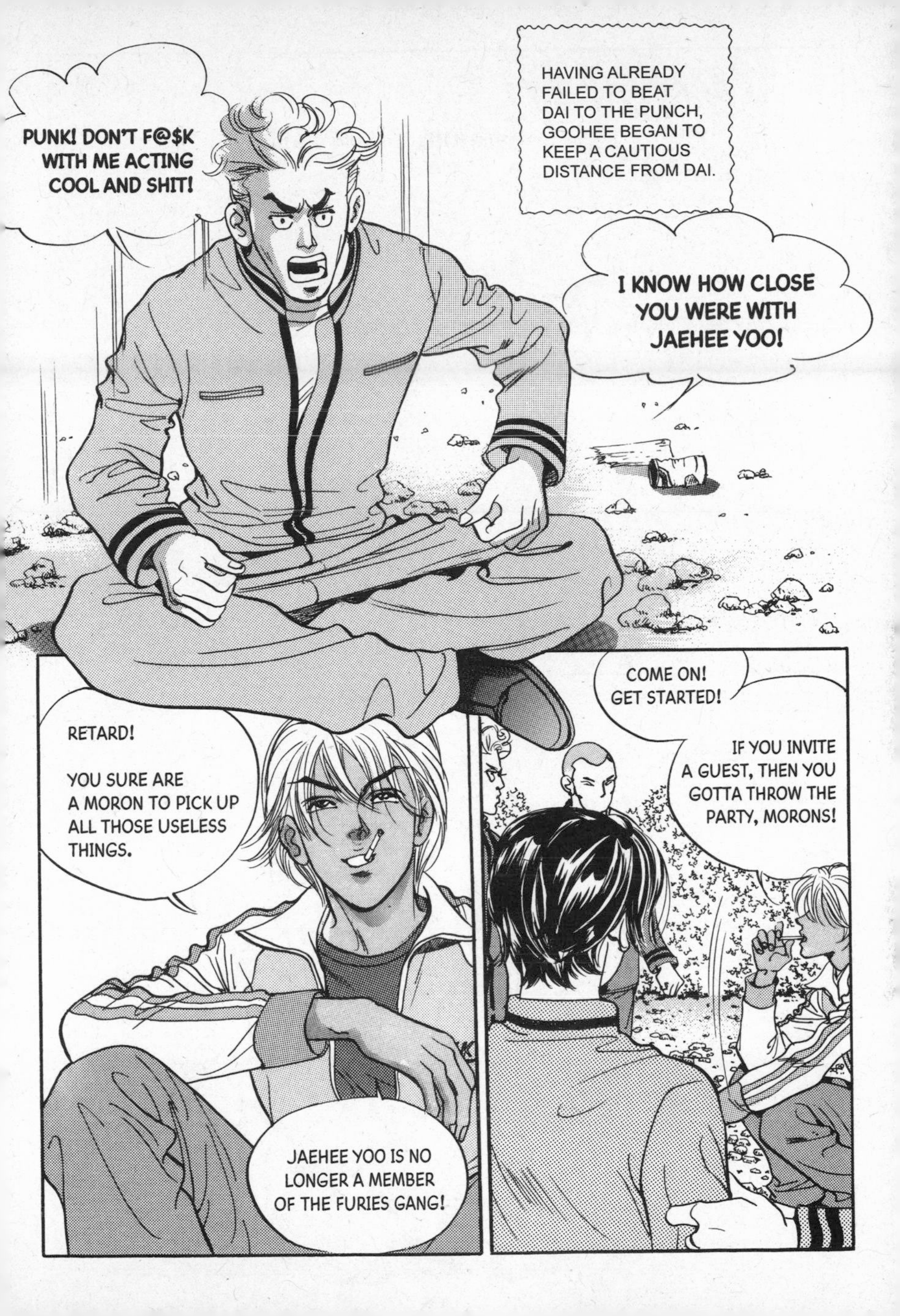
PUNK! DON'T F@$K WITH ME ACTING COOL AND SHIT!
HAVING ALREADY FAILED TO BEAT DAI TO THE PUNCH, GOOHEE BEGAN TO KEEP A CAUTIOUS DISTANCE FROM DAI.
I KNOW HOW CLOSE YOU WERE WITH JAEHEE YOO!
RETARD!
YOU SURE ARE A MORON TO PICK UP ALL THOSE USELESS THINGS.
JAEHEE YOO IS NO LONGER A MEMBER OF THE FURIES GANG!
COME ON! GET STARTED!
IF YOU INVITE A GUEST, THEN YOU GOTTA THROW THE PARTY, MORONS!

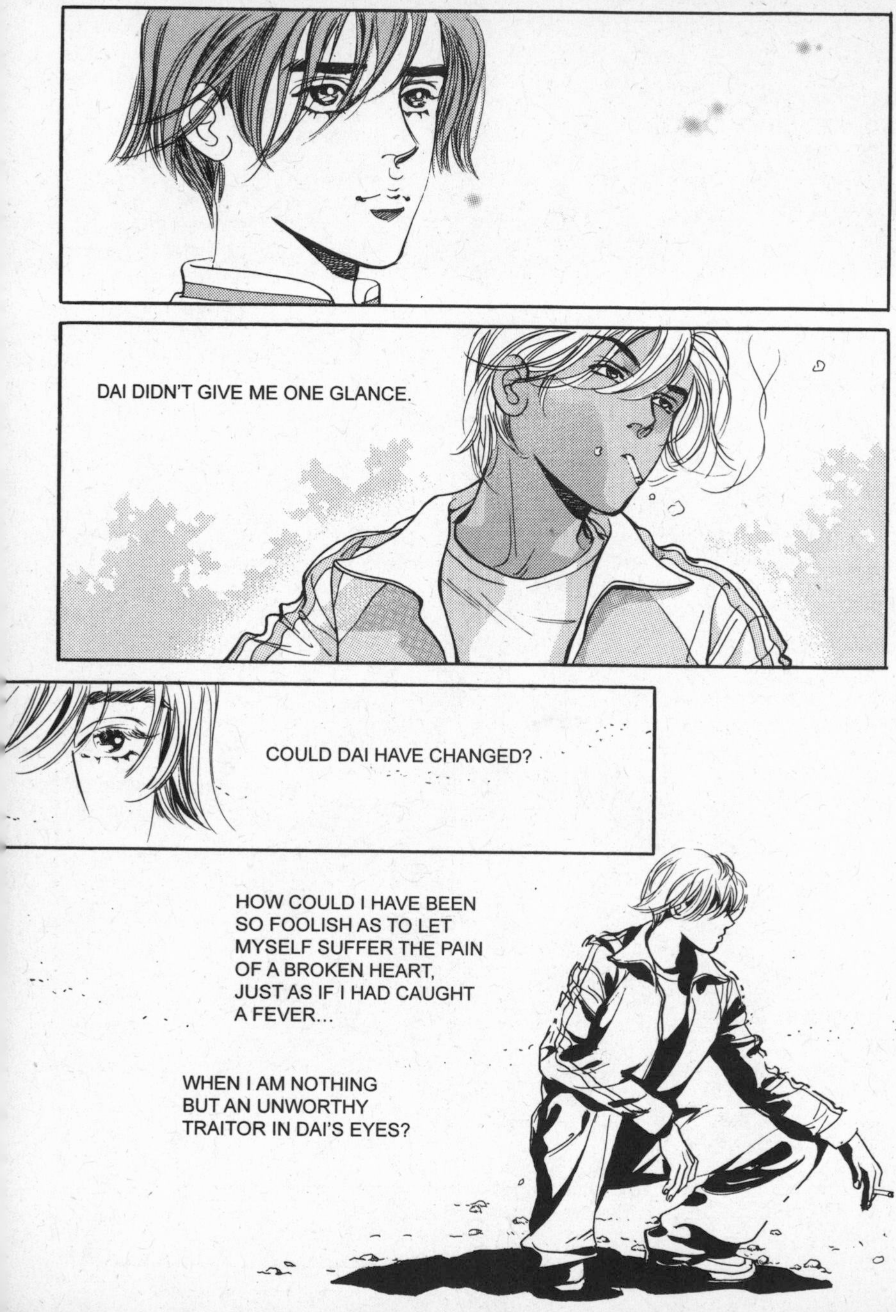
DAI DIDN'T GIVE ME ONE GLANCE.
COULD DAI HAVE CHANGED?
HOW COULD I HAVE BEEN SO FOOLISH AS TO LET MYSELF SUFFER THE PAIN OF A BROKEN HEART, JUST AS IF I HAD CAUGHT A FEVER...
WHEN I AM NOTHING BUT AN UNWORTHY TRAITOR IN DAI'S EYES?

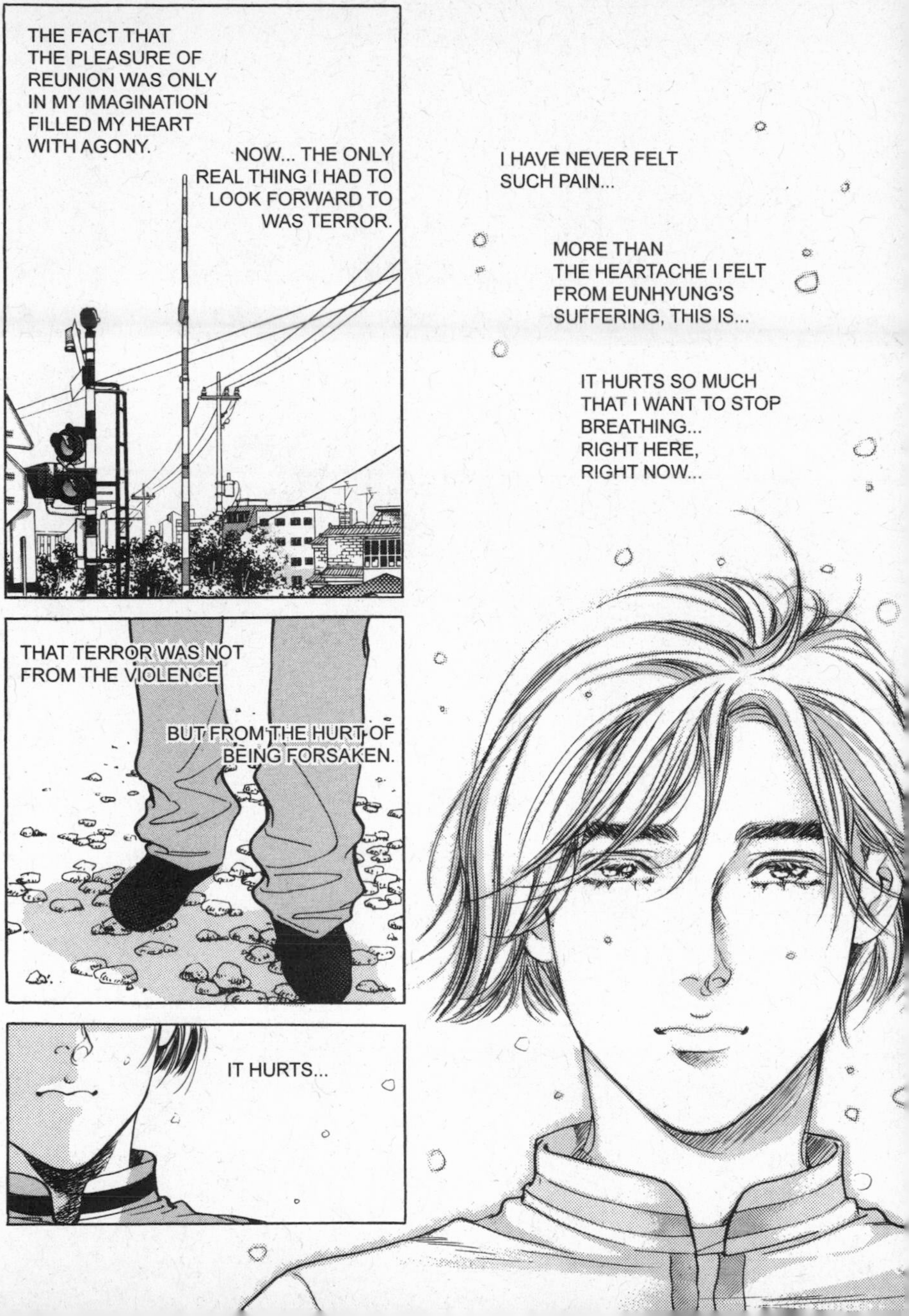
THE FACT THAT THE PLEASURE OF REUNION WAS ONLY IN MY IMAGINATION FILLED MY HEART WITH AGONY.
NOW... THE ONLY REAL THING I HAD TO LOOK FORWARD TO WAS TERROR.
THAT TERROR WAS NOT FROM THE VIOLENCE
BUT FROM THE HURT OF BEING FORSAKEN.
IT HURTS...
I HAVE NEVER FELT SUCH PAIN...
MORE THAN THE HEARTACHE I FELT FROM EUNHYUNG'S SUFFERING, THIS IS...
IT HURTS SO MUCH THAT I WANT TO STOP BREATHING... RIGHT HERE, RIGHT NOW...

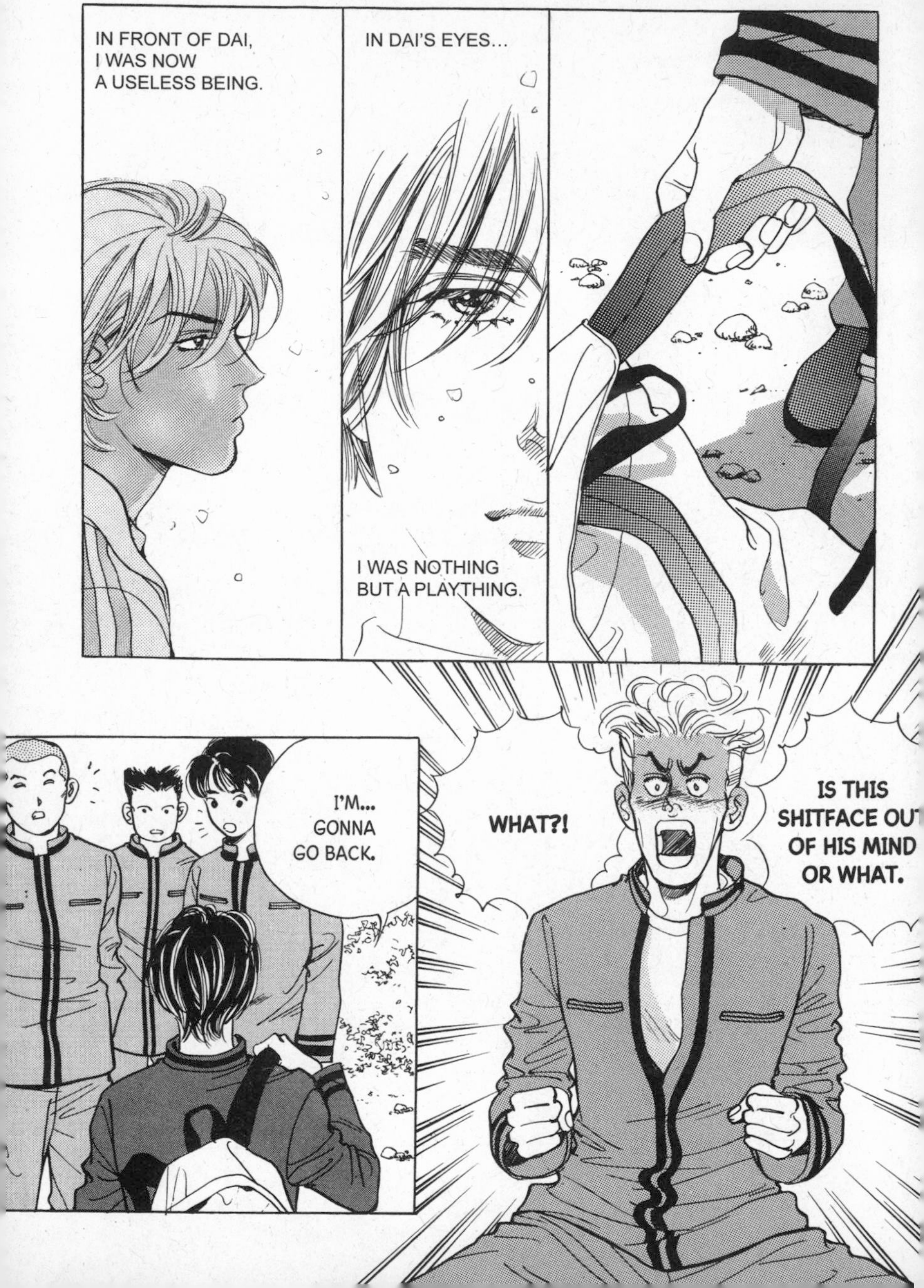
IN FRONT OF DAI,
I WAS NOW
A USELESS BEING.
IN DAI'S EYES…
I WAS NOTHING
BUT A PLAYTHING.
I'M... GONNA GO BACK.
WHAT?!
IS THIS SHITFACE OUT OF HIS MIND OR WHAT.

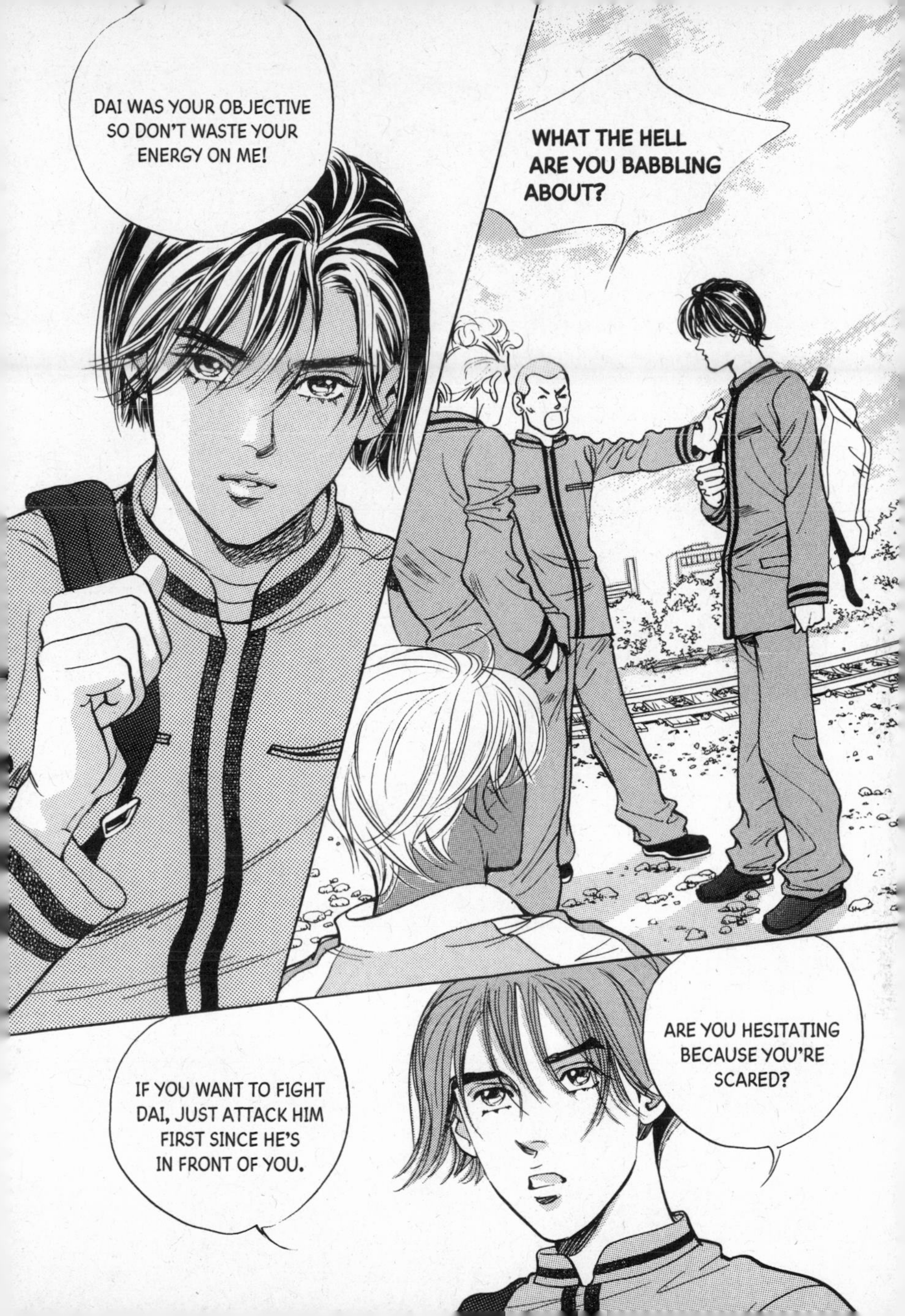
DAI WAS YOUR OBJECTIVE SO DON'T WASTE YOUR ENERGY ON ME!
WHAT THE HELL ARE YOU BABBLING ABOUT?
IF YOU WANT TO FIGHT DAI, JUST ATTACK HIM FIRST SINCE HE'S IN FRONT OF YOU.
ARE YOU HESITATING BECAUSE YOU'RE SCARED?

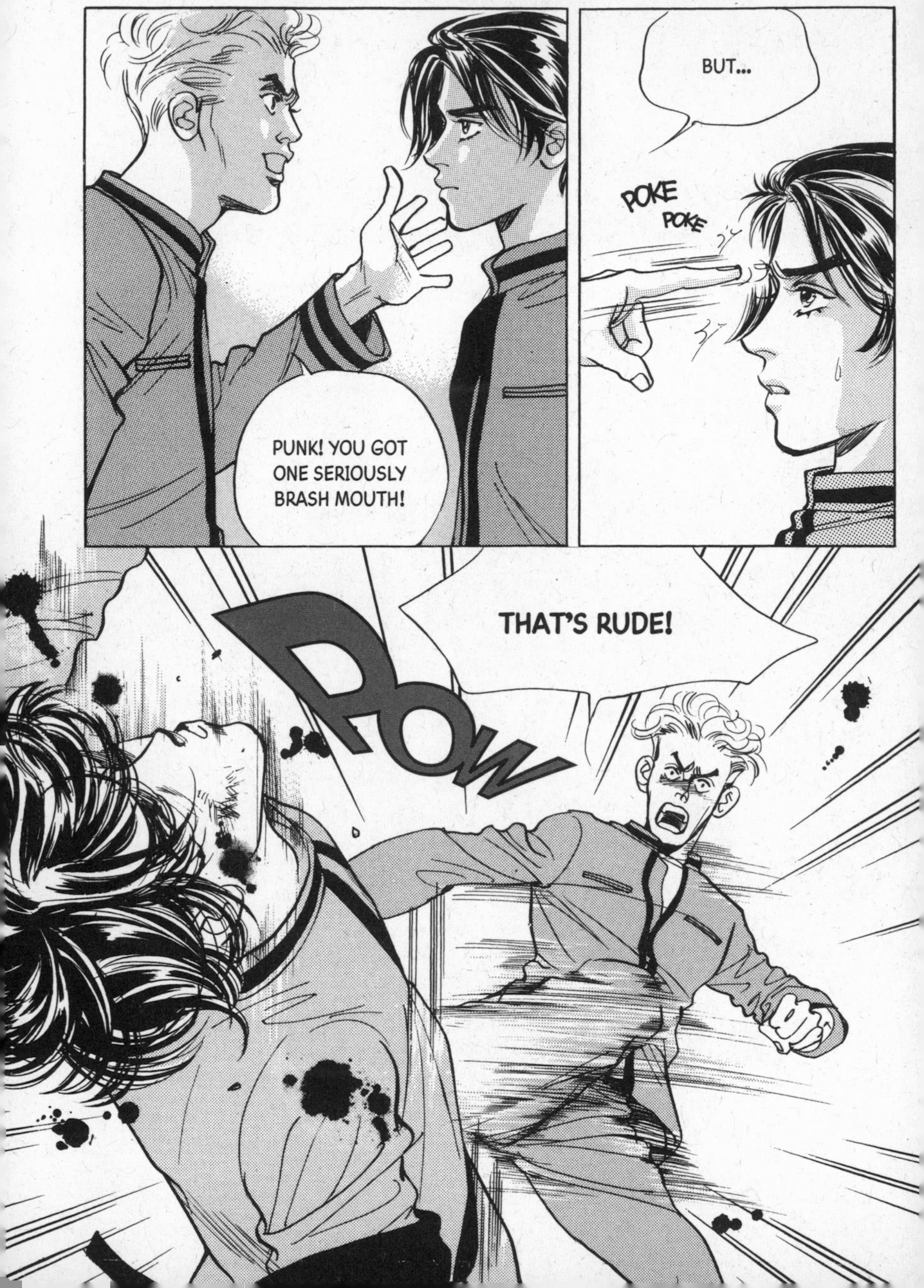
PUNK! YOU GOT ONE SERIOUSLY BRASH MOUTH!
BUT...
POKE
POKE
THAT'S RUDE!
POW

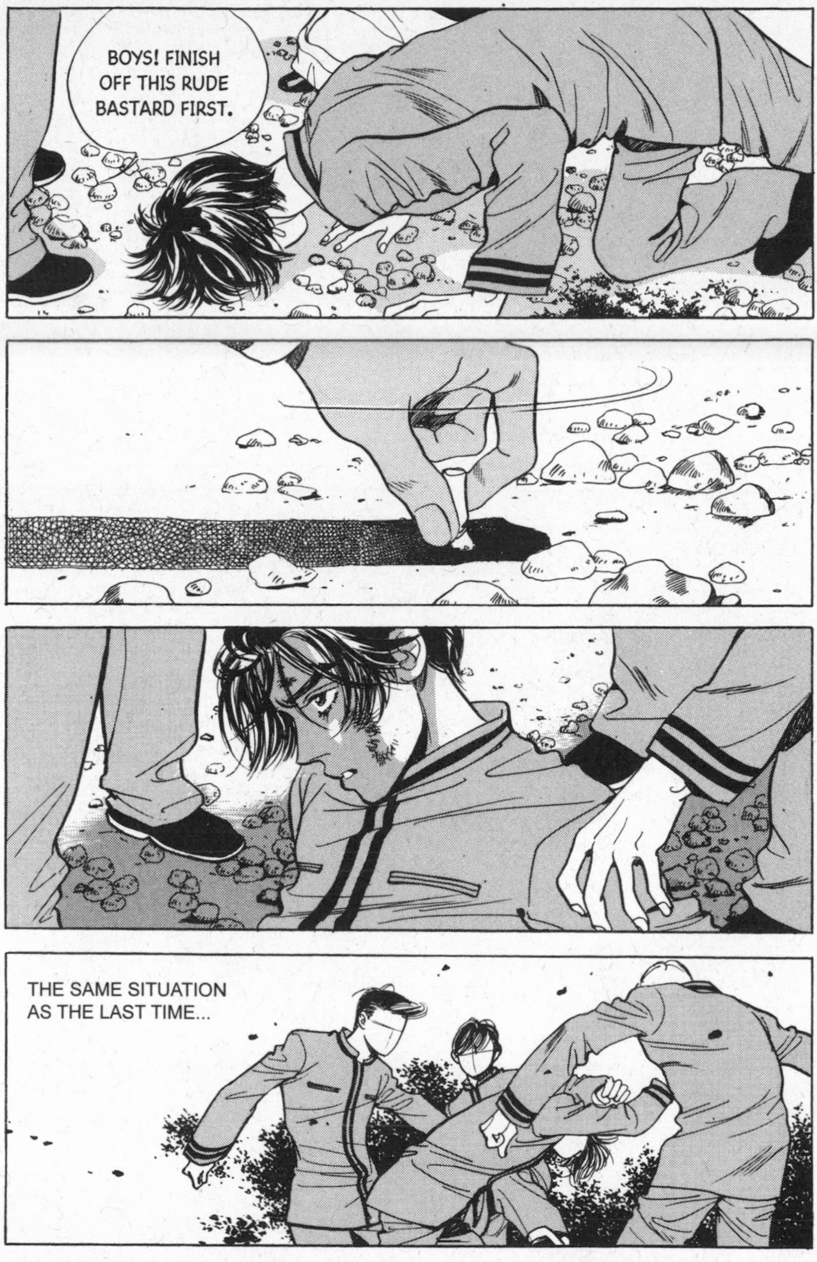
BOYS! FINISH OFF THIS RUDE BASTARD FIRST.
THE SAME SITUATION AS THE LAST TIME...

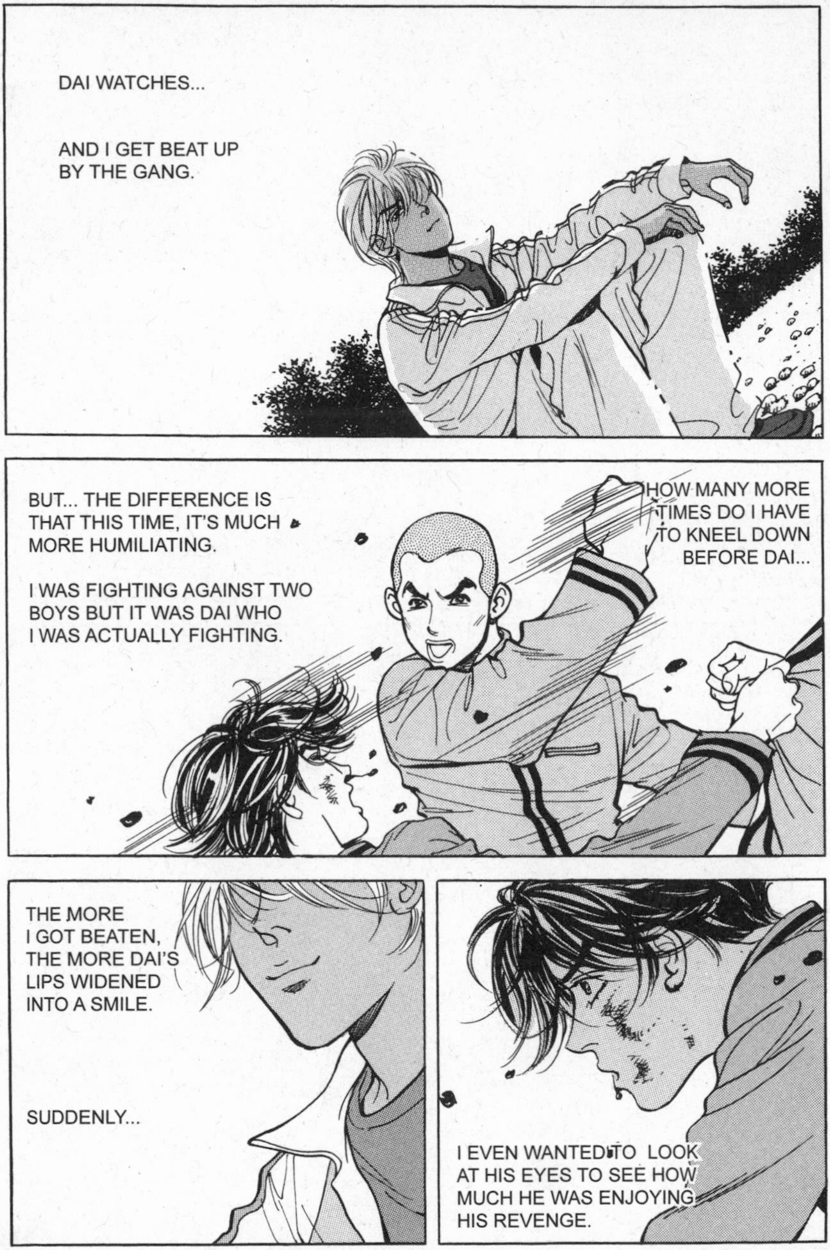
DAI WATCHES...
AND I GET BEAT UP BY THE GANG.
BUT... THE DIFFERENCE IS THAT THIS TIME, IT'S MUCH MORE HUMILIATING.
I WAS FIGHTING AGAINST TWO BOYS BUT IT WAS DAI WHO I WAS ACTUALLY FIGHTING.
HOW MANY MORE TIMES DO I HAVE TO KNEEL DOWN BEFORE DAI...
THE MORE I GOT BEATEN, THE MORE DAI'S LIPS WIDENED INTO A SMILE.
SUDDENLY...
I EVEN WANTED TO LOOK AT HIS EYES TO SEE HOW MUCH HE WAS ENJOYING HIS REVENGE.

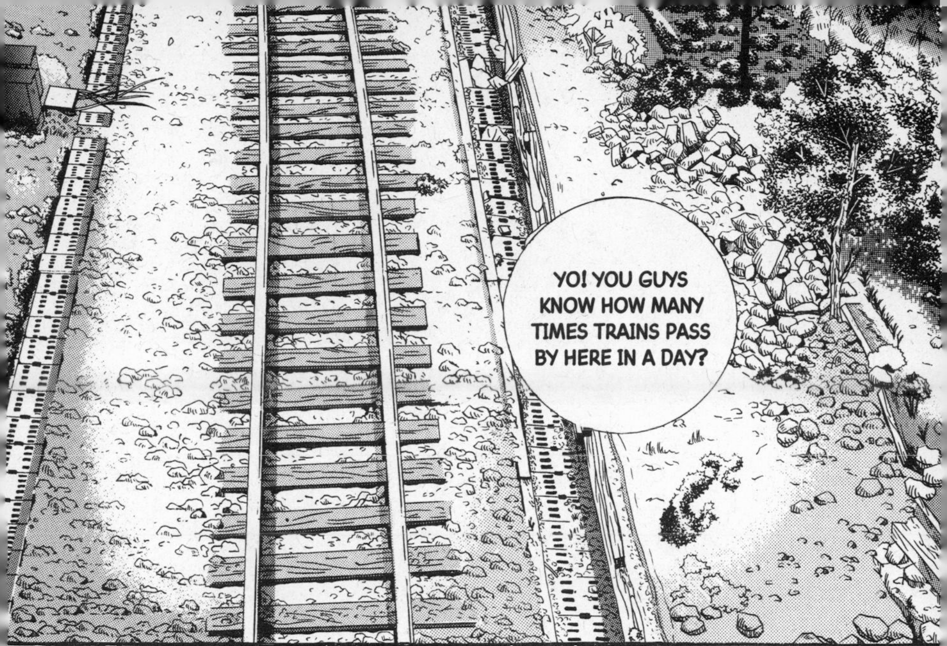
YO! YOU GUYS KNOW HOW MANY TIMES TRAINS PASS BY HERE IN A DAY?

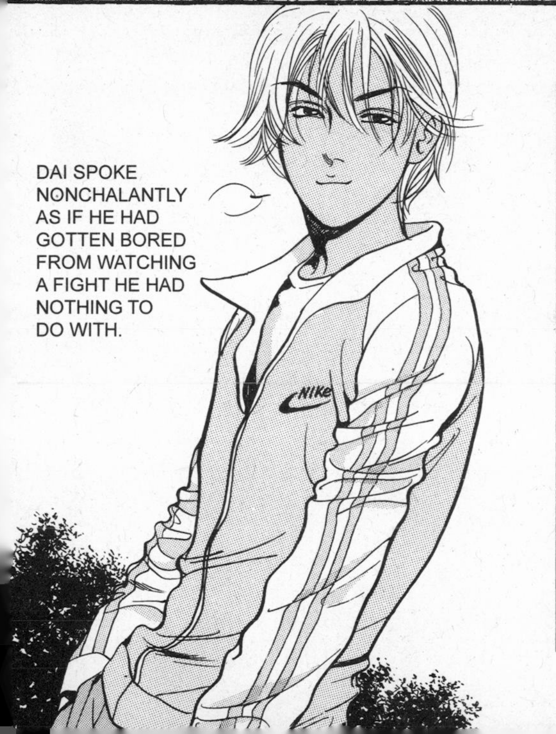
DAI SPOKE NONCHALANTLY AS IF HE HAD GOTTEN BORED FROM WATCHING A FIGHT HE HAD NOTHING TO DO WITH.
NIKE

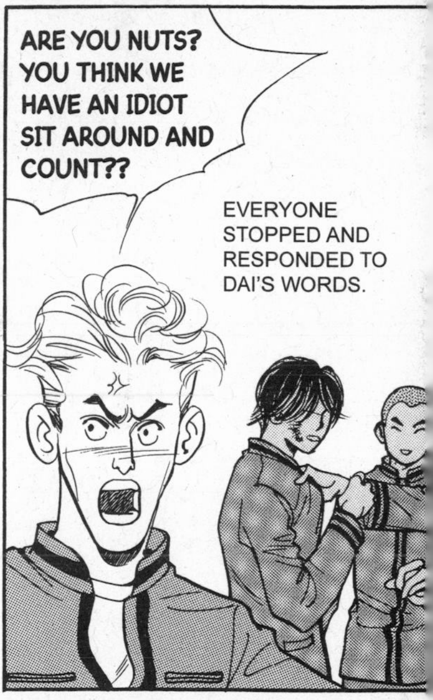
ARE YOU NUTS? YOU THINK WE HAVE AN IDIOT SIT AROUND AND COUNT??
EVERYONE STOPPED AND RESPONDED TO DAI'S WORDS.

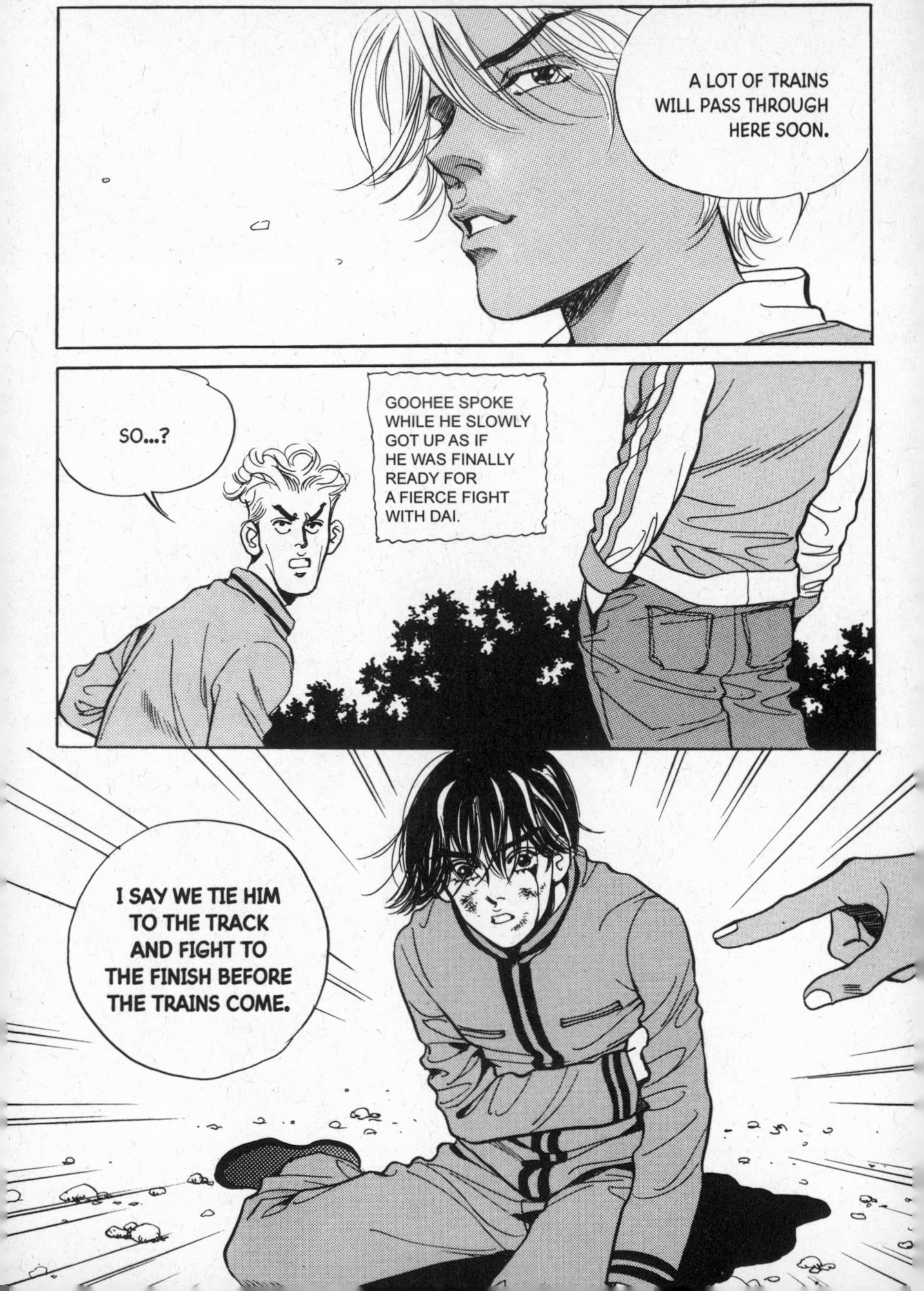
A LOT OF TRAINS WILL PASS THROUGH HERE SOON.
SO...?
GOOHEE SPOKE WHILE HE SLOWLY GOT UP AS IF HE WAS FINALLY READY FOR A FIERCE FIGHT WITH DAI.
I SAY WE TIE HIM TO THE TRACK AND FIGHT TO THE FINISH BEFORE THE TRAINS COME.

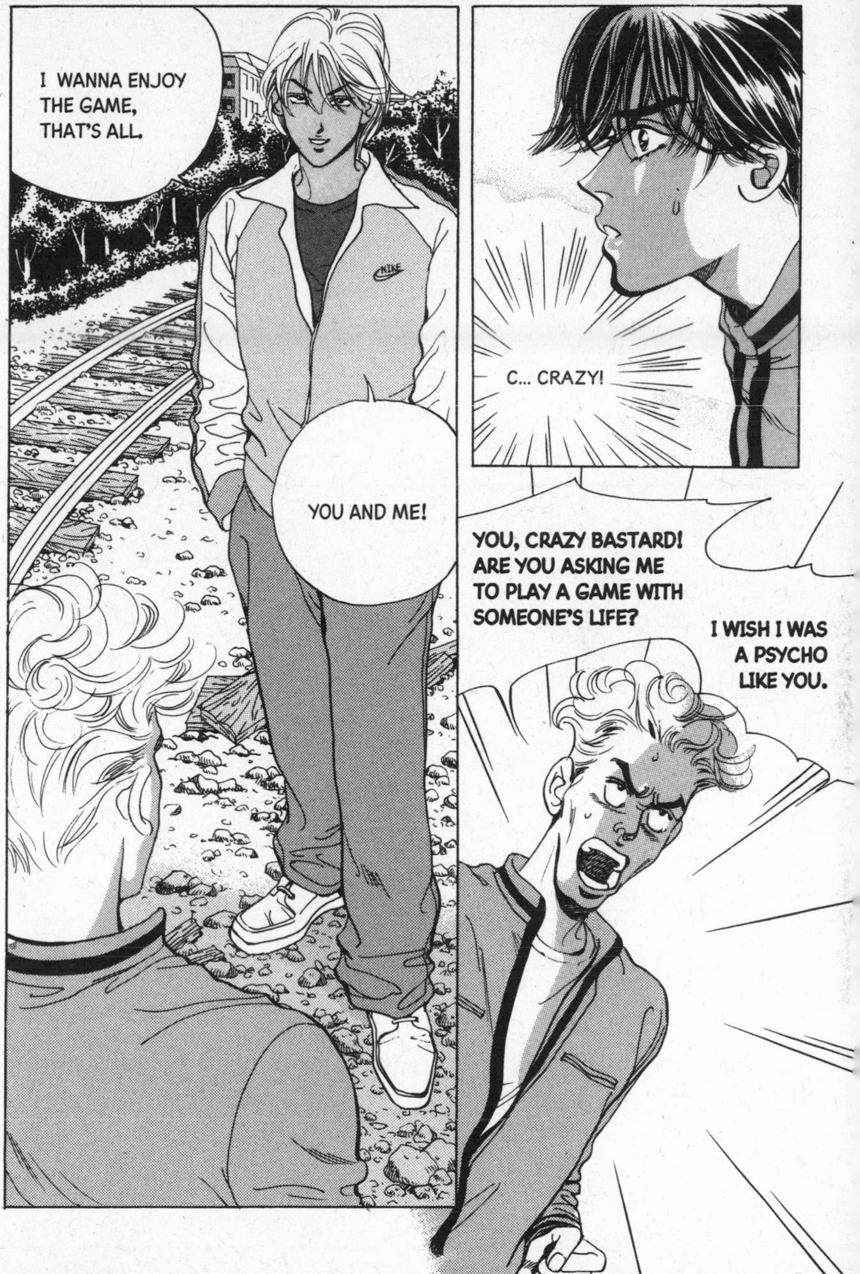
I WANNA ENJOY THE GAME, THAT'S ALL.
YOU AND ME!
C... CRAZY!
YOU, CRAZY BASTARD! ARE YOU ASKING ME TO PLAY A GAME WITH SOMEONE'S LIFE?
I WISH I WAS A PSYCHO LIKE YOU.

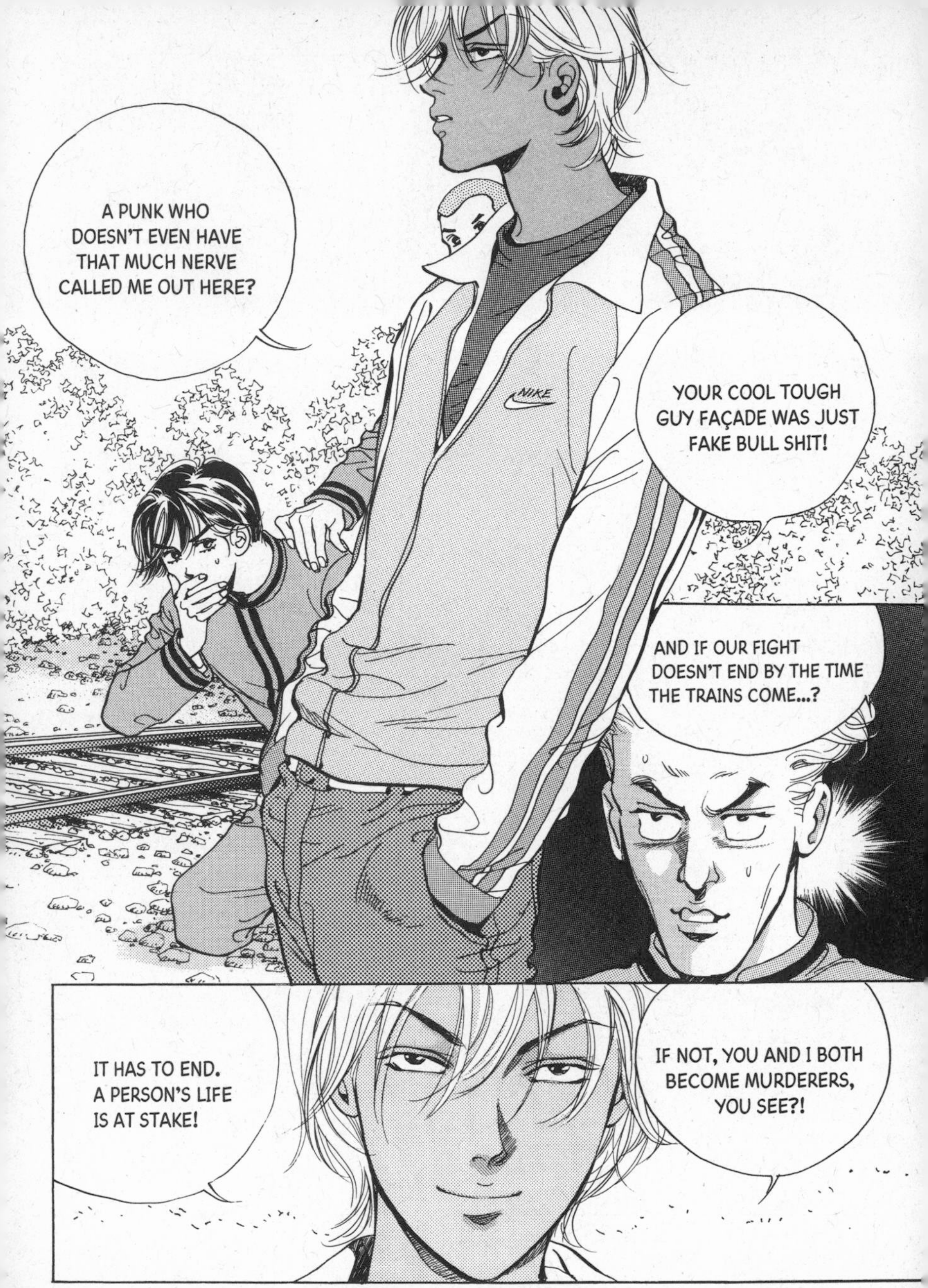
A PUNK WHO DOESN'T EVEN HAVE THAT MUCH NERVE CALLED ME OUT HERE?
NIKE
YOUR COOL TOUGH GUY FAÇADE WAS JUST FAKE BULL SHIT!
AND IF OUR FIGHT DOESN'T END BY THE TIME THE TRAINS COME...?
IT HAS TO END. A PERSON'S LIFE IS AT STAKE!
IF NOT, YOU AND I BOTH BECOME MURDERERS, YOU SEE?!

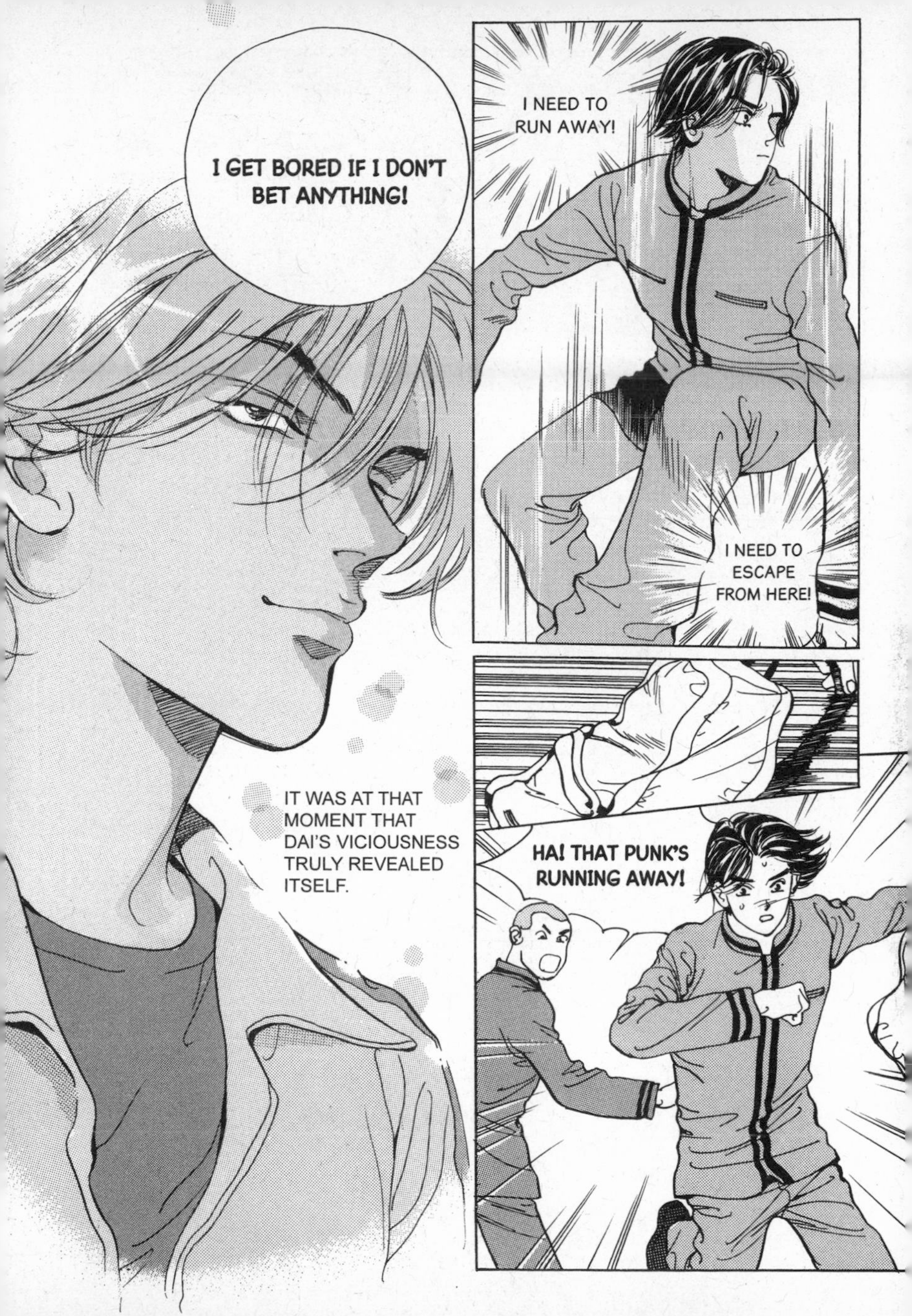
I GET BORED IF I DON'T BET ANYTHING!
IT WAS AT THAT MOMENT THAT DAI'S VICIOUSNESS TRULY REVEALED ITSELF.
I NEED TO RUN AWAY!
I NEED TO ESCAPE FROM HERE!
HA! THAT PUNK'S RUNNING AWAY!

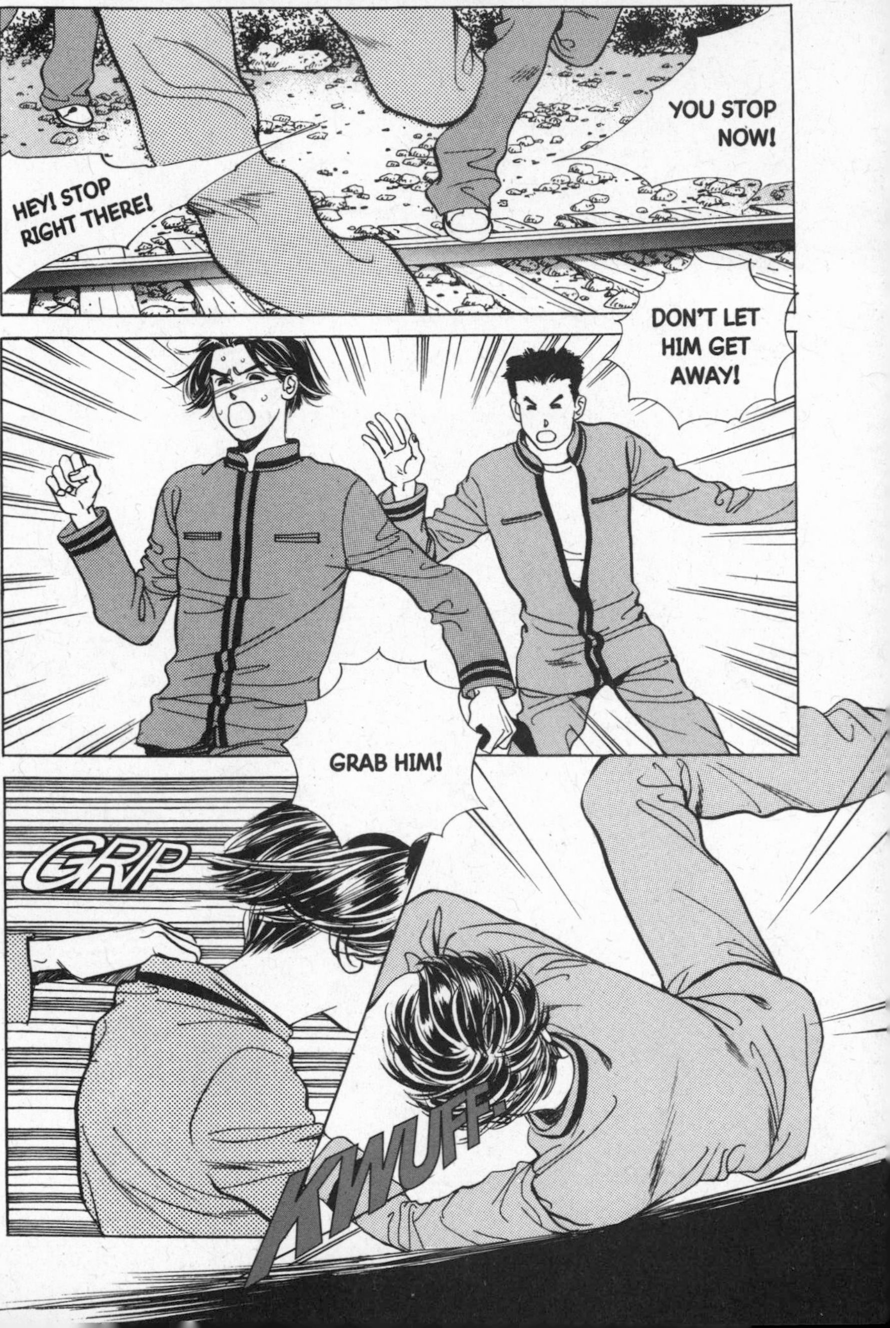
HEY! STOP RIGHT THERE!
YOU STOP NOW!
DON'T LET HIM GET AWAY!
GRAB HIM!
GRIP
KWUFF

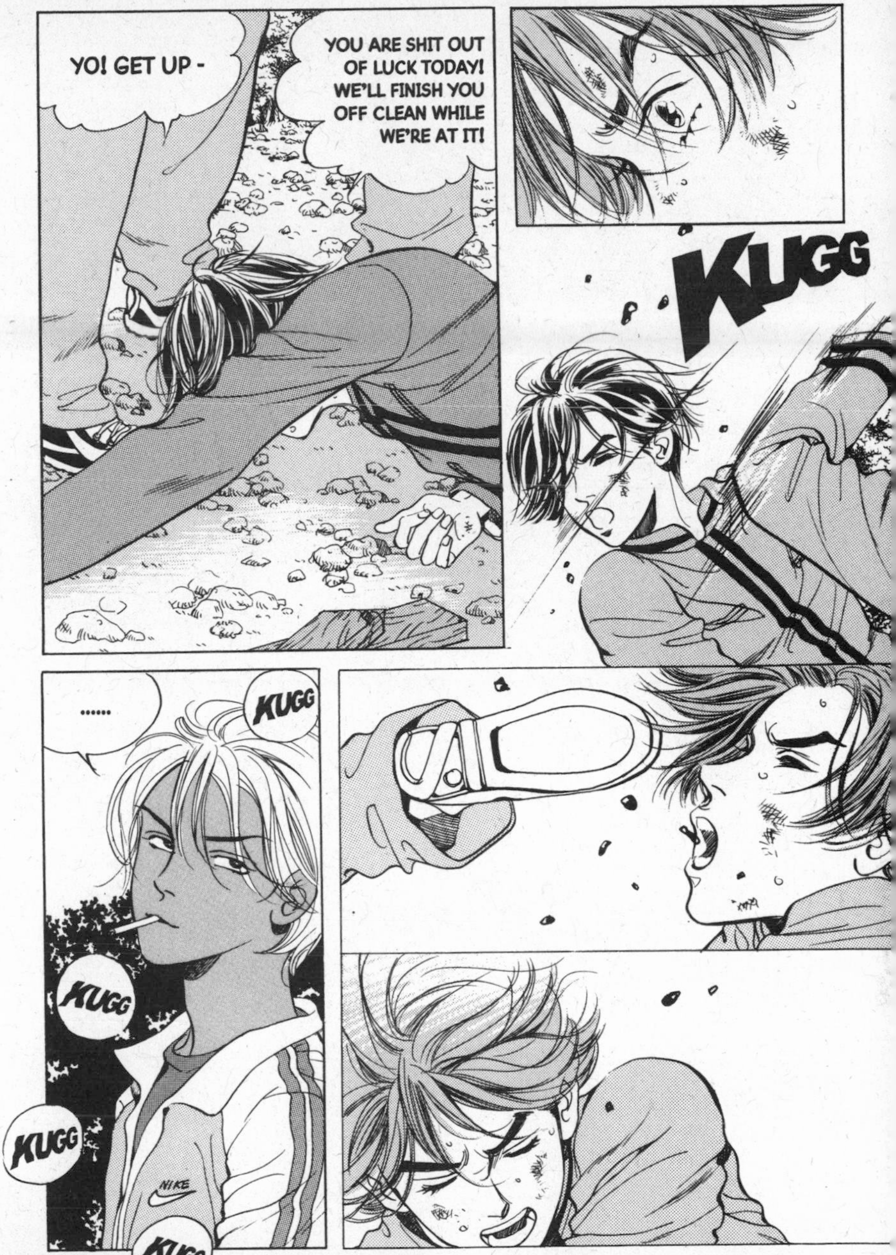
YO! GET UP -
YOU ARE SHIT OUT OF LUCK TODAY! WE'LL FINISH YOU OFF CLEAN WHILE WE'RE AT IT!
KUGG
......
KUGG
KUGG
KUGG
KUGG
NIKE

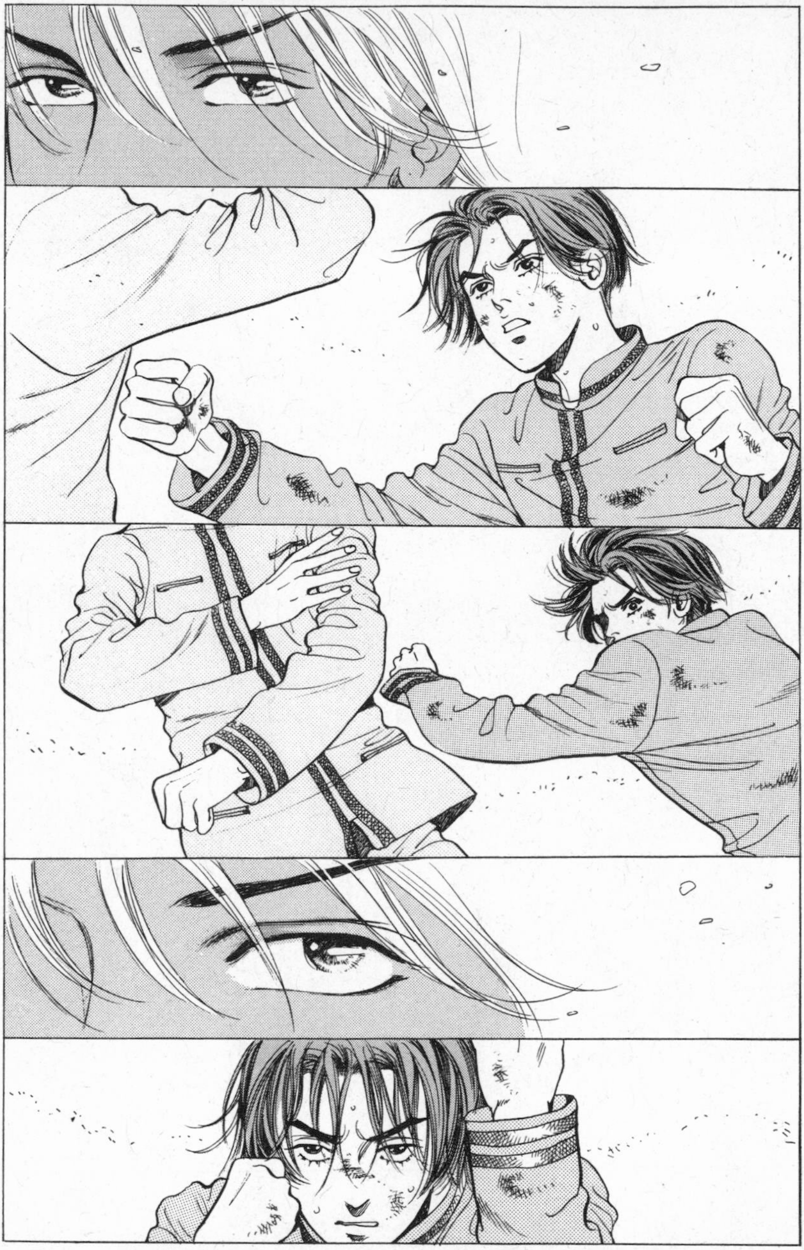

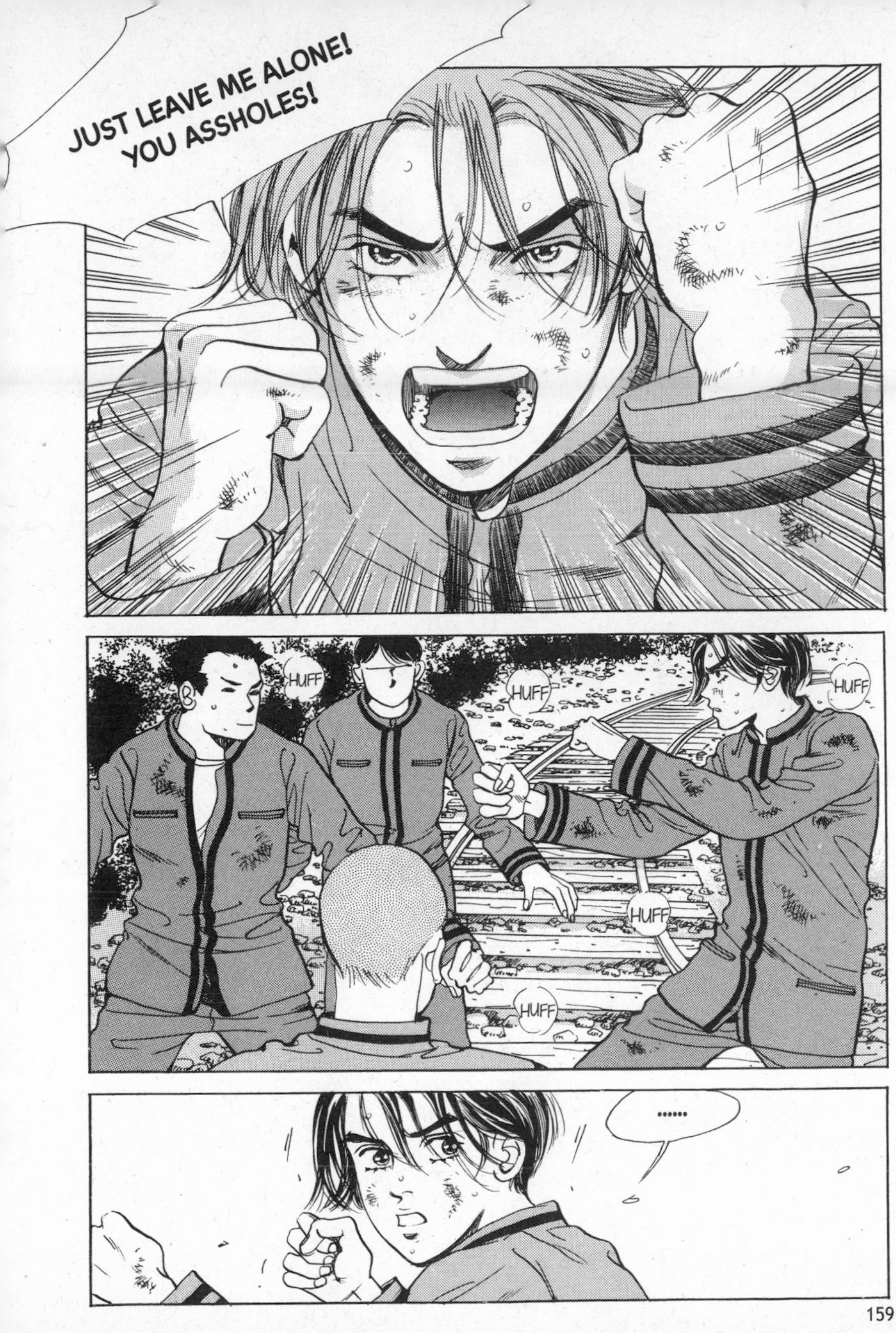
JUST LEAVE ME ALONE! YOU ASSHOLES!
HUFF
HUFF
HUFF
HUFF
HUFF
......

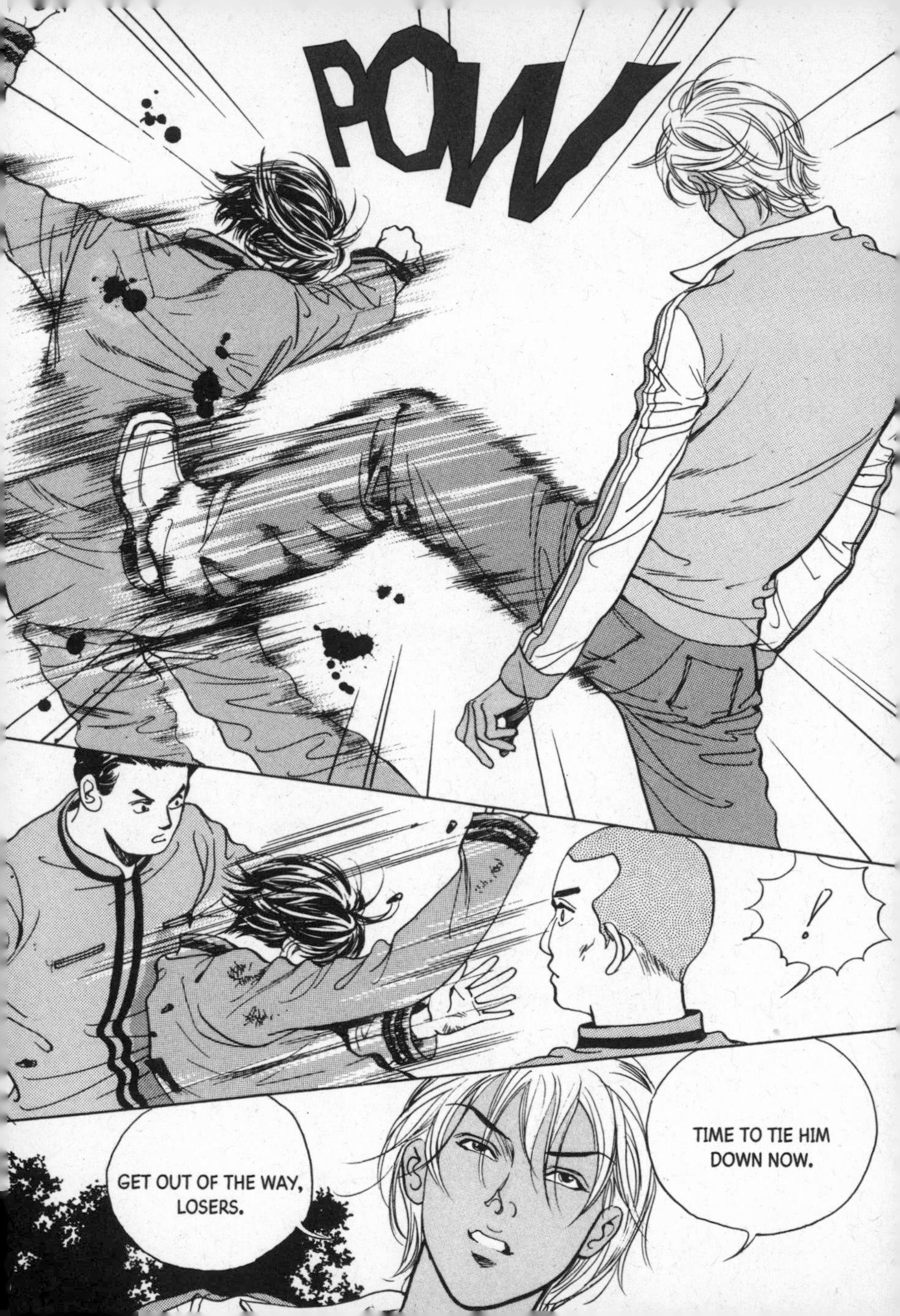
POW
!
GET OUT OF THE WAY, LOSERS.
TIME TO TIE HIM DOWN NOW.

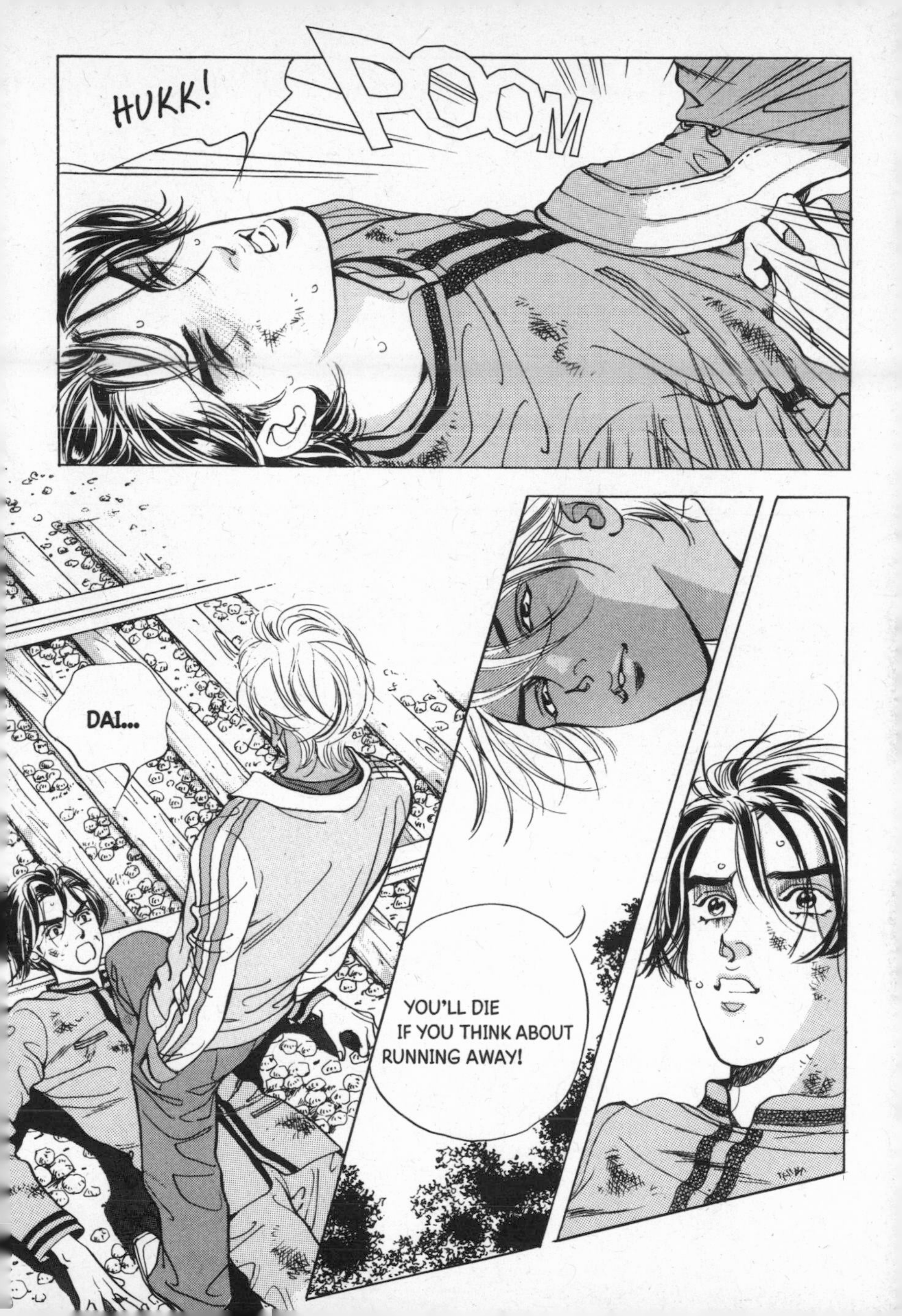
HUKK!
POOM
DAI...
YOU'LL DIE
IF YOU THINK ABOUT
RUNNING AWAY!

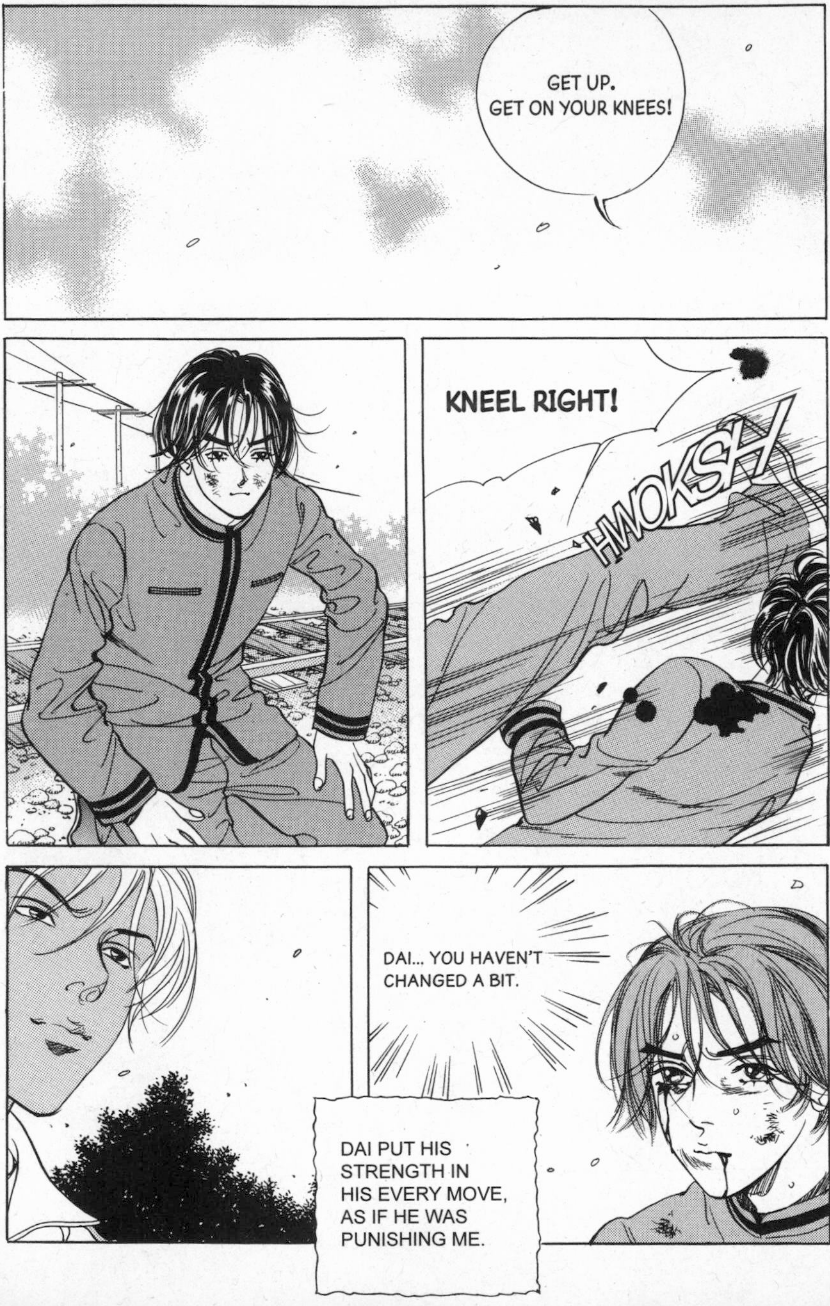
GET UP.
GET ON YOUR KNEES!
KNEEL RIGHT!
HWOKSH
DAI... YOU HAVEN'T CHANGED A BIT.
DAI PUT HIS STRENGTH IN HIS EVERY MOVE, AS IF HE WAS PUNISHING ME.

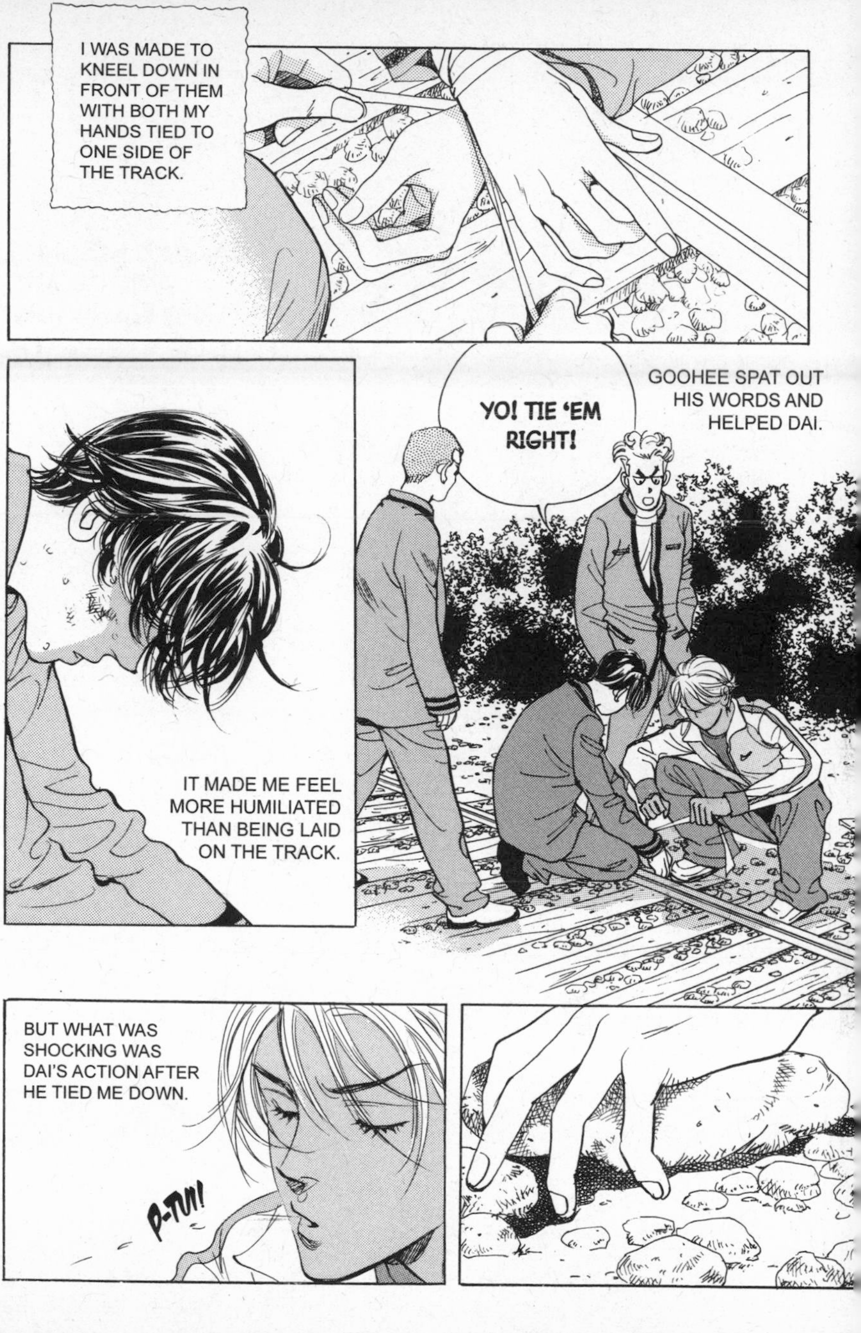
I WAS MADE TO KNEEL DOWN IN FRONT OF THEM WITH BOTH MY HANDS TIED TO ONE SIDE OF THE TRACK.
IT MADE ME FEEL MORE HUMILIATED THAN BEING LAID ON THE TRACK.
YO! TIE 'EM RIGHT!
GOOHEE SPAT OUT HIS WORDS AND HELPED DAI.
BUT WHAT WAS SHOCKING WAS DAI'S ACTION AFTER HE TIED ME DOWN.
P-TUI!

NO ONE HAD ANTICIPATED IT.

DAI WAS HOLDING
A ROCK AND
HIS HAND WAS
FULL OF STRENGTH.

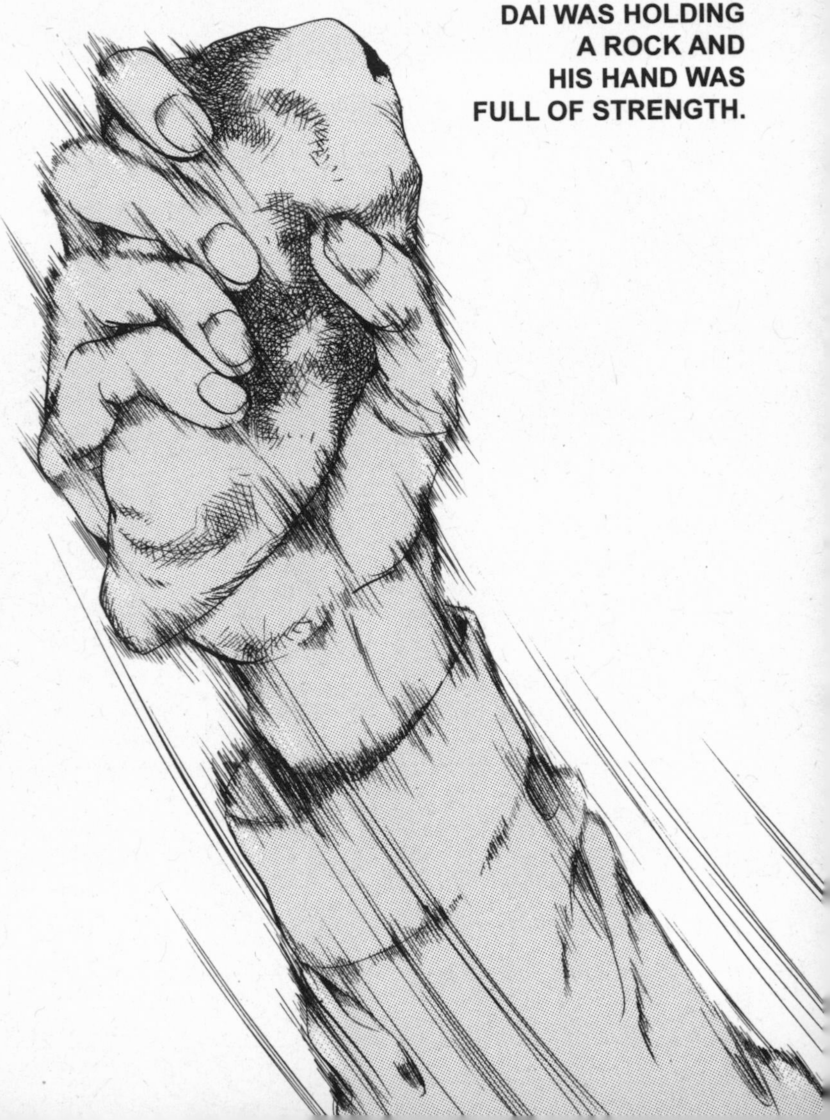

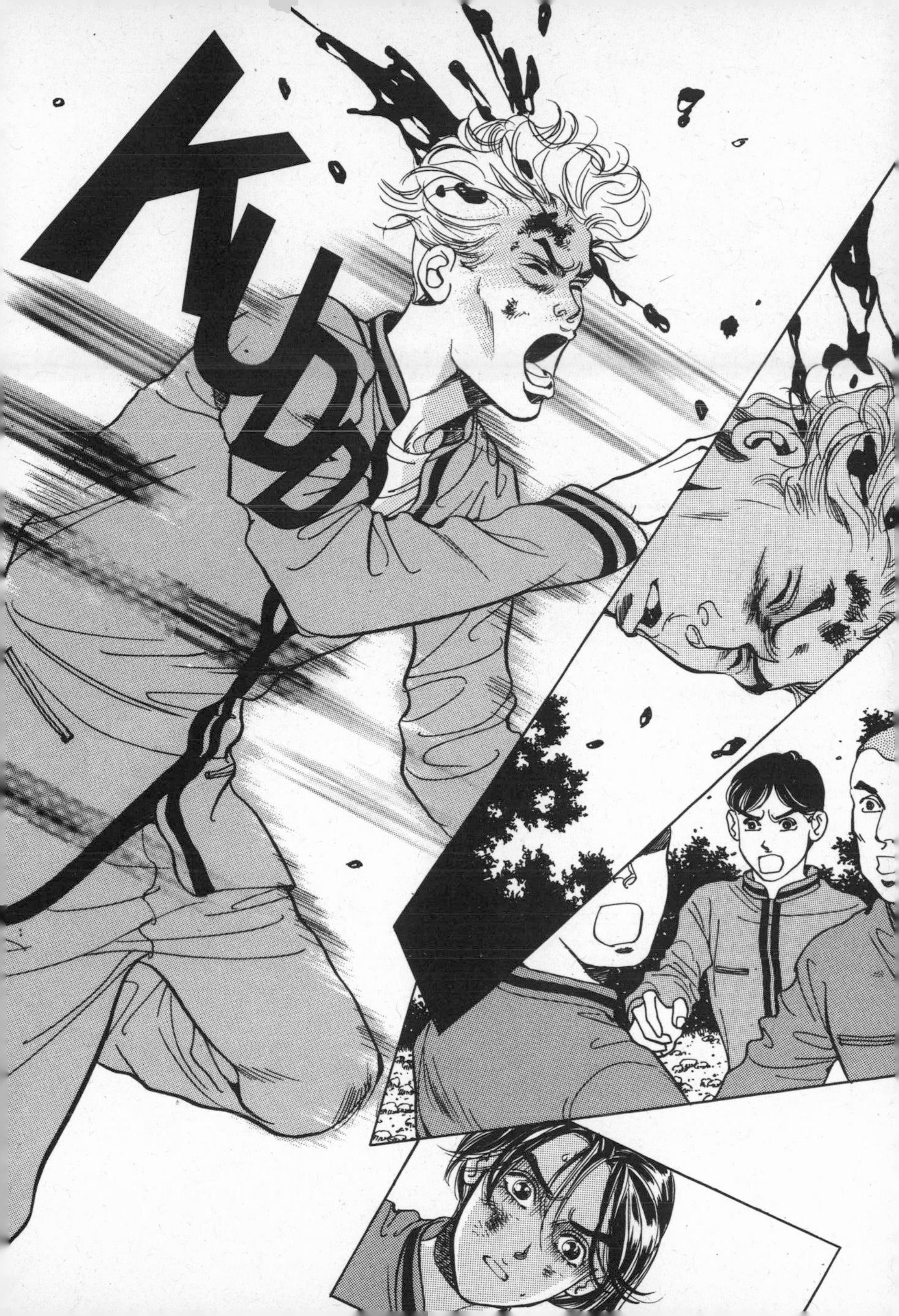
KUDD

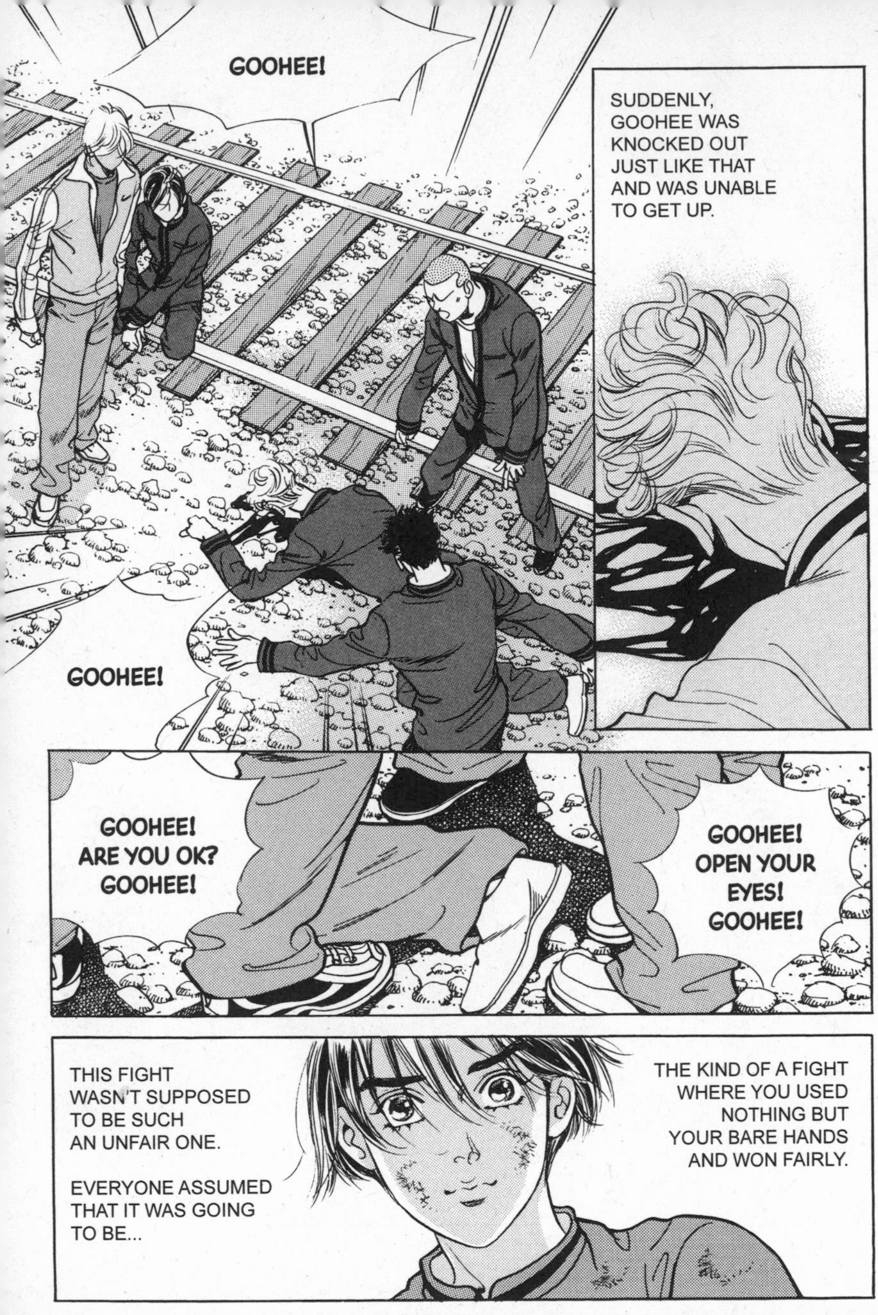
GOOHEE!
GOOHEE!
SUDDENLY, GOOHEE WAS KNOCKED OUT JUST LIKE THAT AND WAS UNABLE TO GET UP.
GOOHEE! ARE YOU OK? GOOHEE!
GOOHEE! OPEN YOUR EYES! GOOHEE!
THIS FIGHT WASN'T SUPPOSED TO BE SUCH AN UNFAIR ONE.
EVERYONE ASSUMED THAT IT WAS GOING TO BE...
THE KIND OF A FIGHT WHERE YOU USED NOTHING BUT YOUR BARE HANDS AND WON FAIRLY.

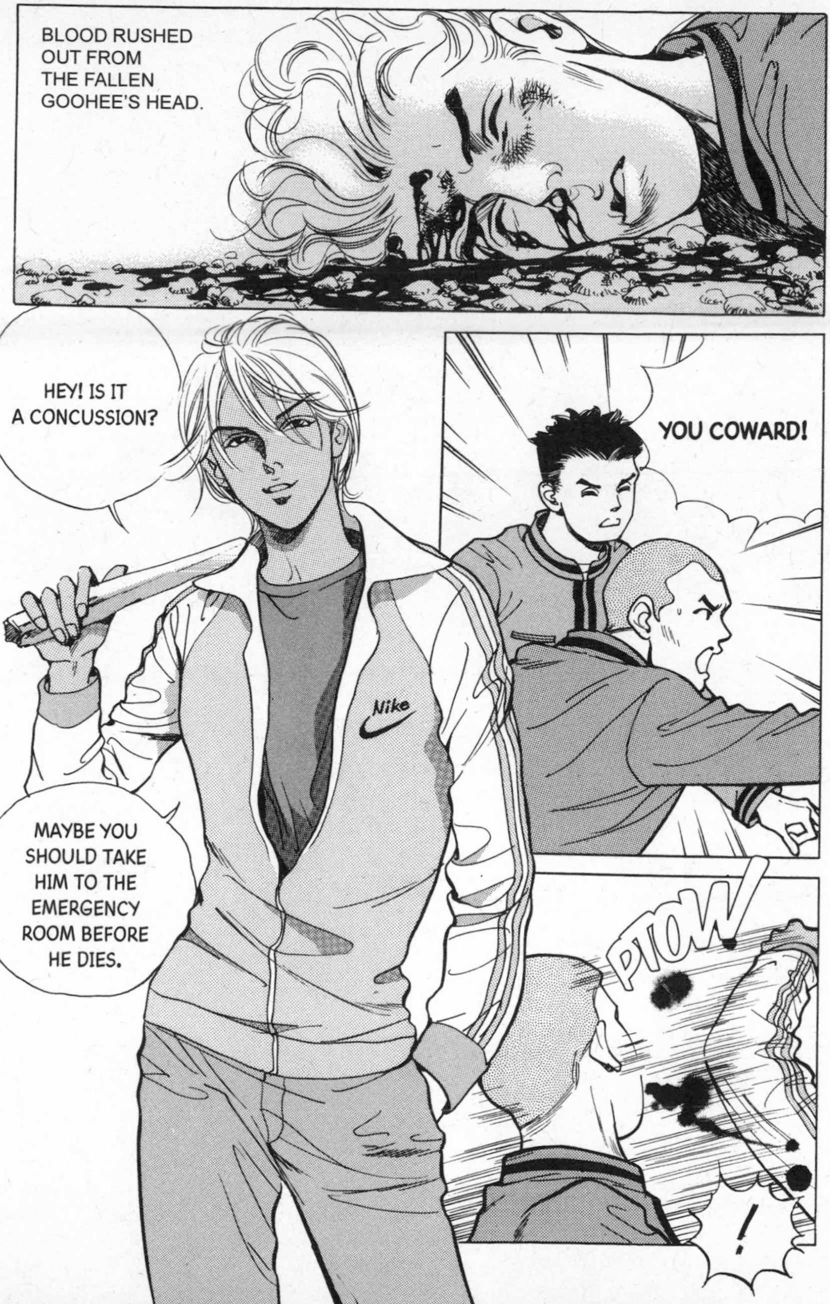
BLOOD RUSHED OUT FROM THE FALLEN GOOHEE'S HEAD.
HEY! IS IT A CONCUSSION?
MAYBE YOU SHOULD TAKE HIM TO THE EMERGENCY ROOM BEFORE HE DIES.
YOU COWARD!
PTOW!
!

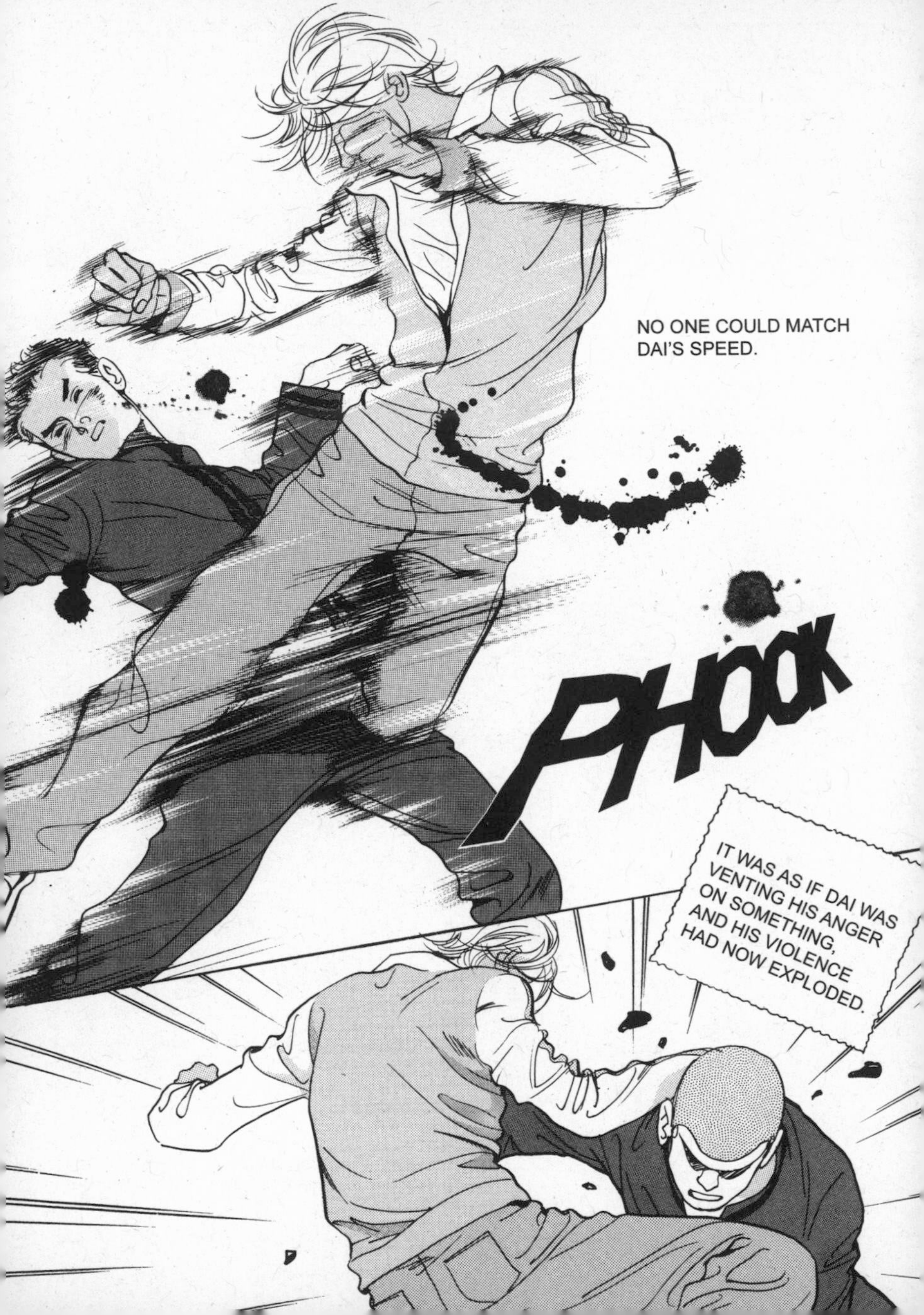
NO ONE COULD MATCH DAI'S SPEED.
PHOOK
IT WAS AS IF DAI WAS VENTING HIS ANGER ON SOMETHING, AND HIS VIOLENCE HAD NOW EXPLODED.

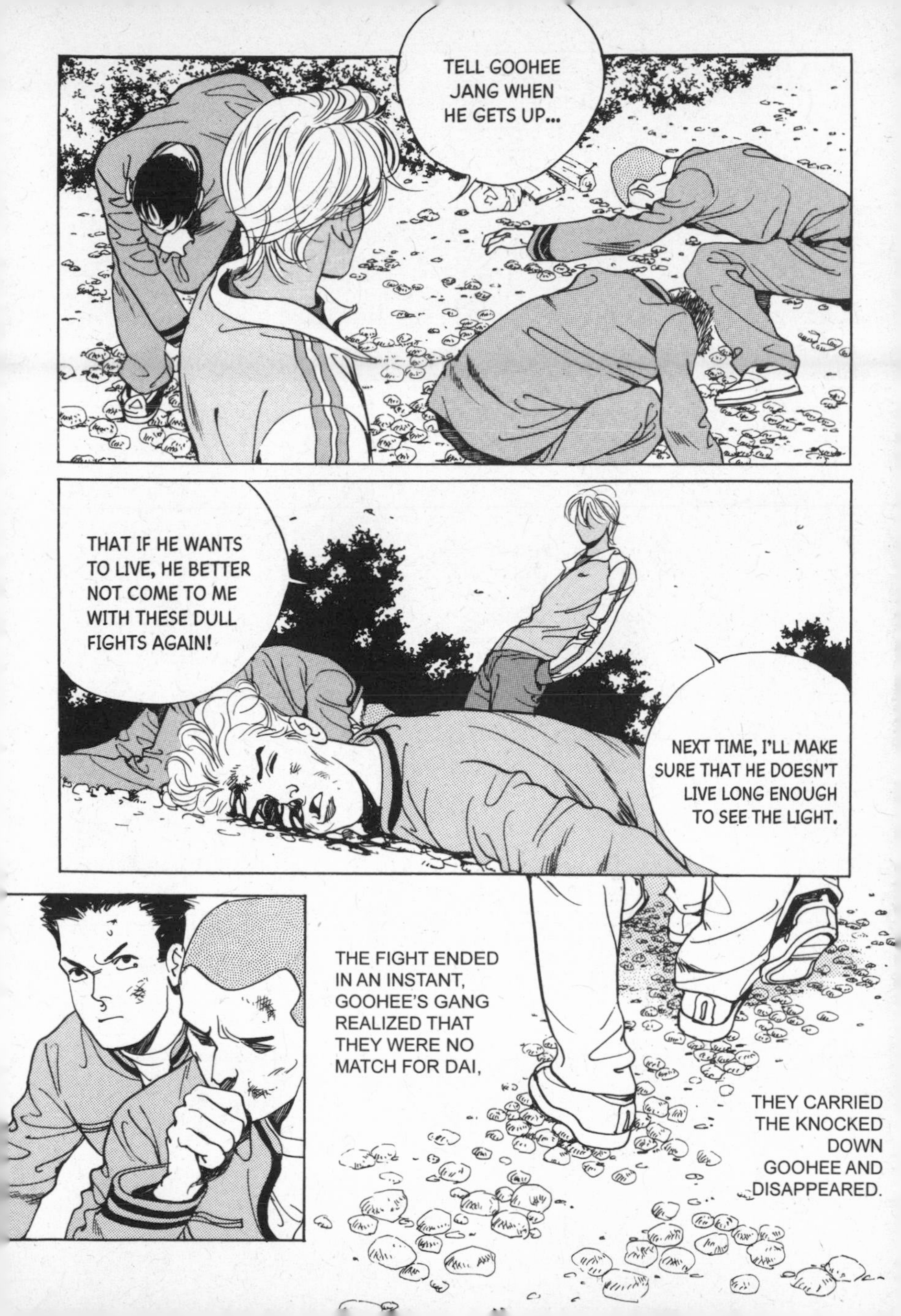
TELL GOOHEE JANG WHEN HE GETS UP...
THAT IF HE WANTS TO LIVE, HE BETTER NOT COME TO ME WITH THESE DULL FIGHTS AGAIN!
NEXT TIME, I'LL MAKE SURE THAT HE DOESN'T LIVE LONG ENOUGH TO SEE THE LIGHT.
THE FIGHT ENDED IN AN INSTANT, GOOHEE'S GANG REALIZED THAT THEY WERE NO MATCH FOR DAI,
THEY CARRIED THE KNOCKED DOWN GOOHEE AND DISAPPEARED.

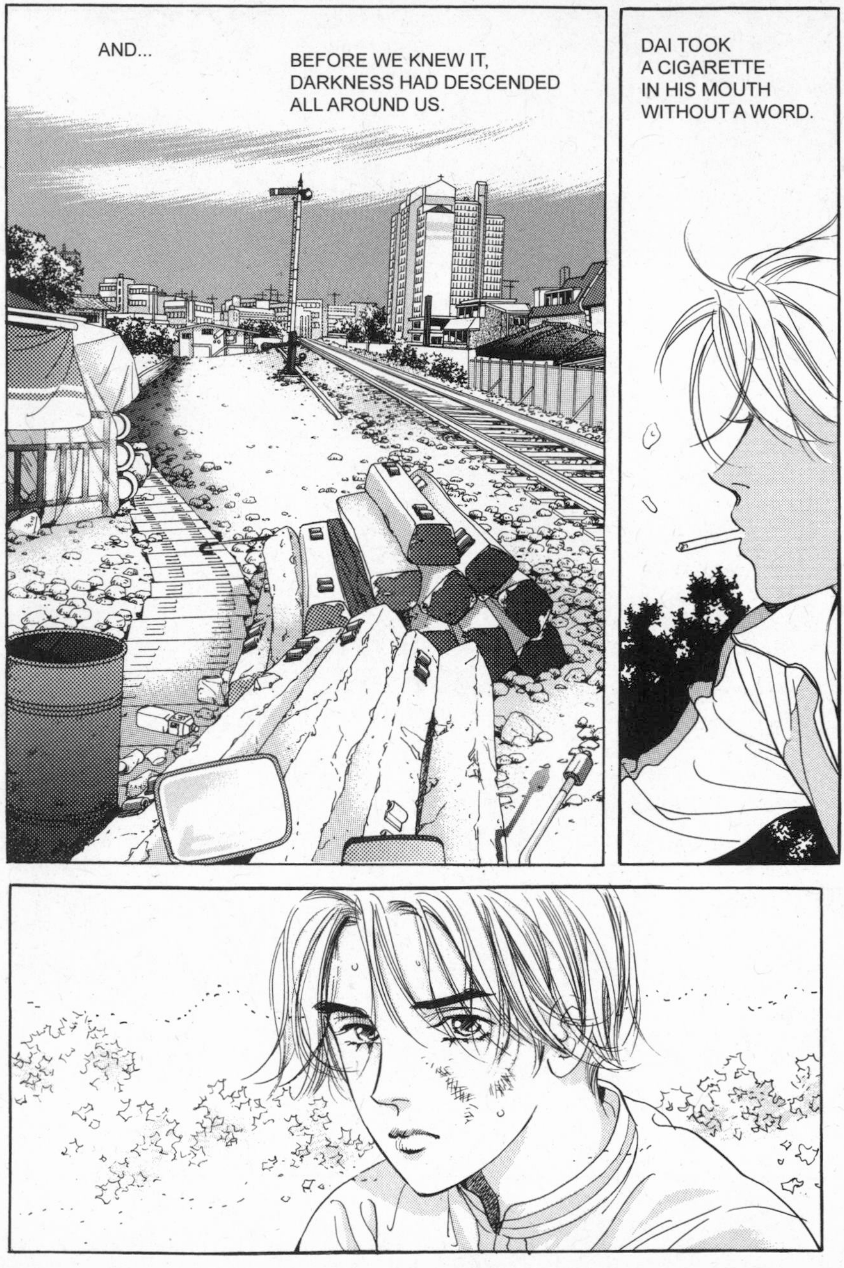
AND...
BEFORE WE KNEW IT, DARKNESS HAD DESCENDED ALL AROUND US.
DAI TOOK A CIGARETTE IN HIS MOUTH WITHOUT A WORD.

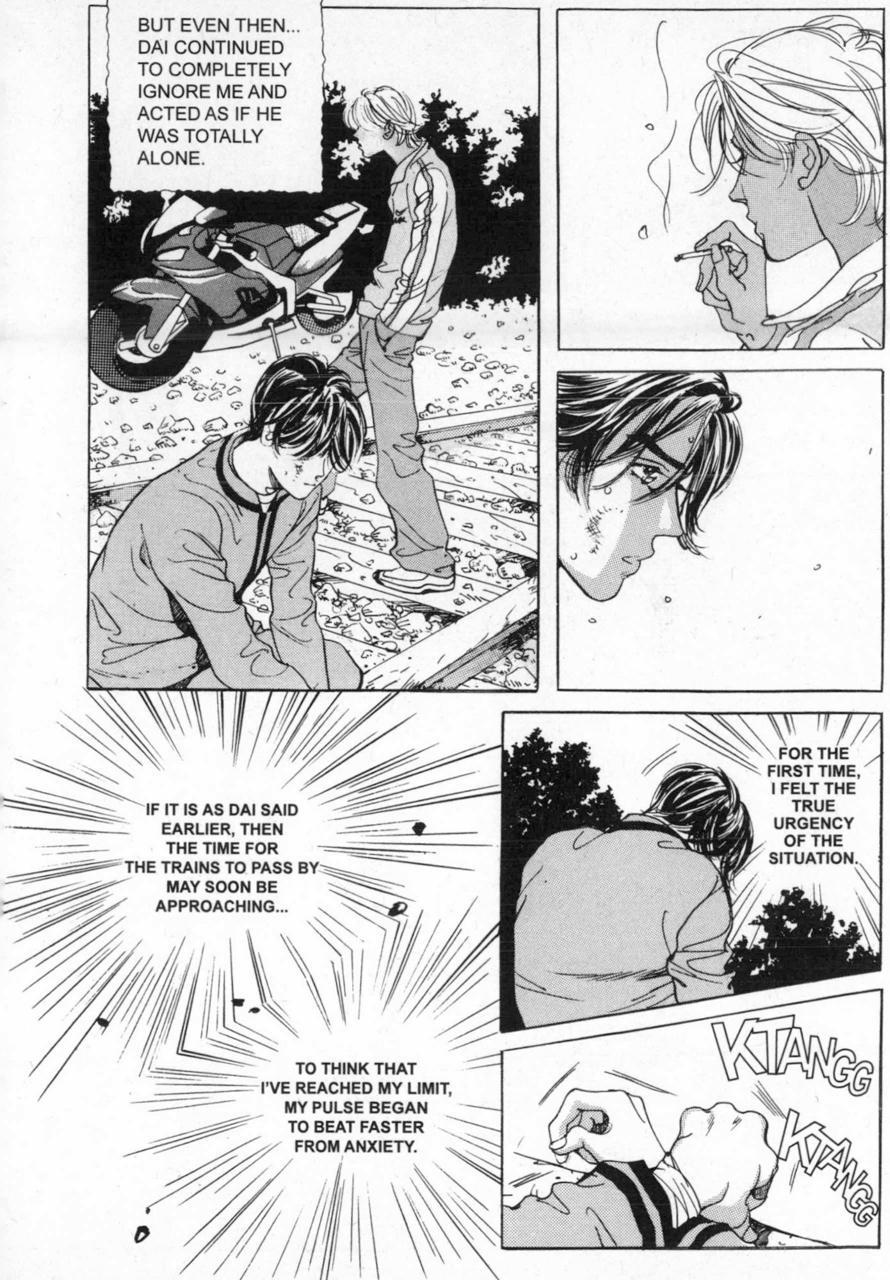
BUT EVEN THEN... DAI CONTINUED TO COMPLETELY IGNORE ME AND ACTED AS IF HE WAS TOTALLY ALONE.
IF IT IS AS DAI SAID EARLIER, THEN THE TIME FOR THE TRAINS TO PASS BY MAY SOON BE APPROACHING...
FOR THE FIRST TIME, I FELT THE TRUE URGENCY OF THE SITUATION.
TO THINK THAT I'VE REACHED MY LIMIT, MY PULSE BEGAN TO BEAT FASTER FROM ANXIETY.
KTANGG
KTANGG

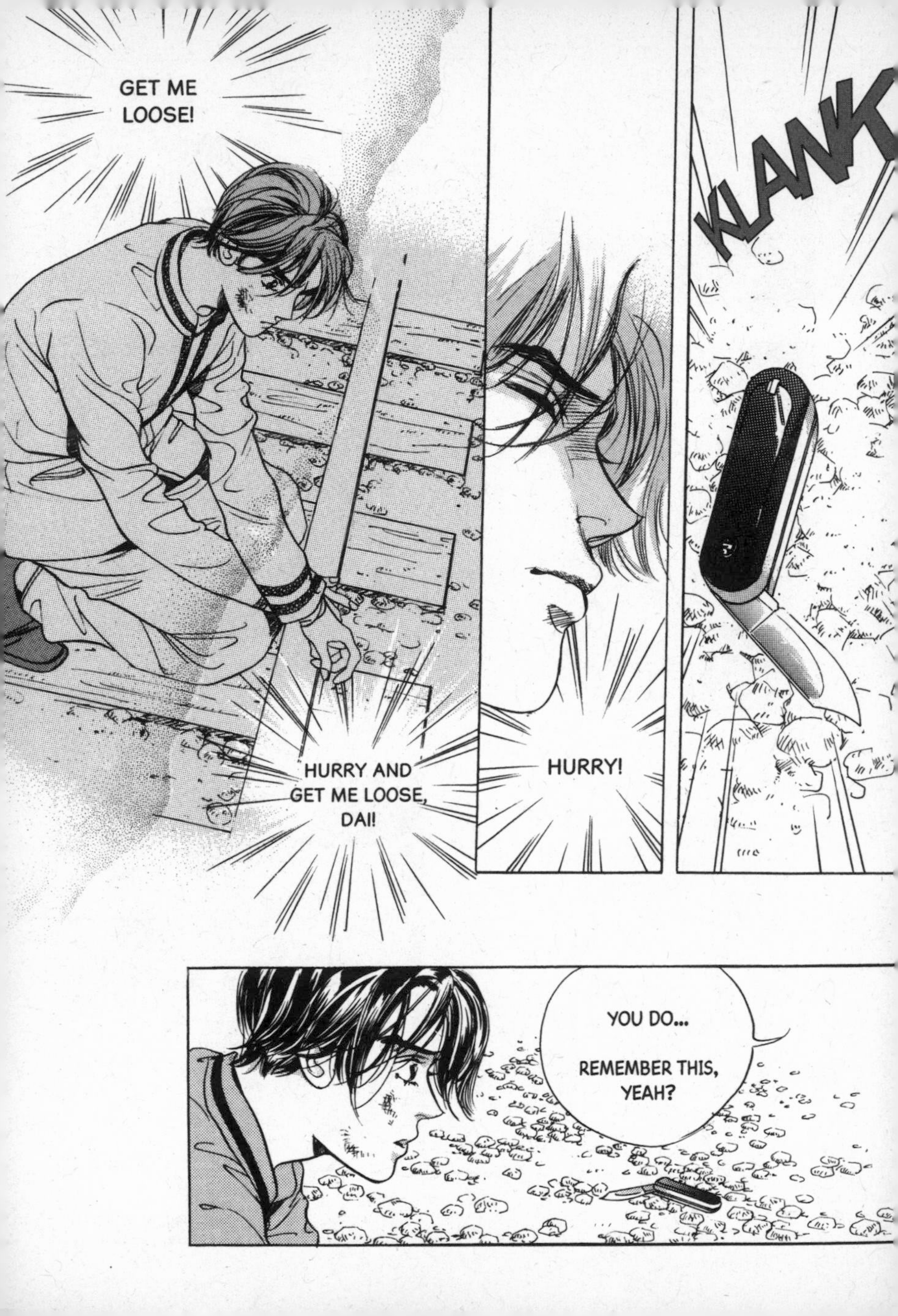
GET ME LOOSE!
HURRY AND GET ME LOOSE, DAI!
HURRY!
KLANK
YOU DO... REMEMBER THIS, YEAH?

IT WAS... THE KNIFE THAT I USED TO STAB DAI'S RATHER THICK SKIN TO FREE MYSELF FROM HIM.

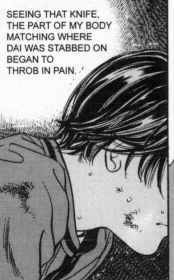

SEEING THAT KNIFE, THE PART OF MY BODY MATCHING WHERE DAI WAS STABBED ON BEGAN TO THROB IN PAIN.

ANSWER ME!

YES! OF COURSE I REMEMBER...

HOW... COULD I FORGET.

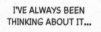

I'VE ALWAYS BEEN THINKING ABOUT IT...

FOR A VERY LONG TIME.

OTHER THOUGHTS...

WERE THERE BUT ONLY BRIEFLY.

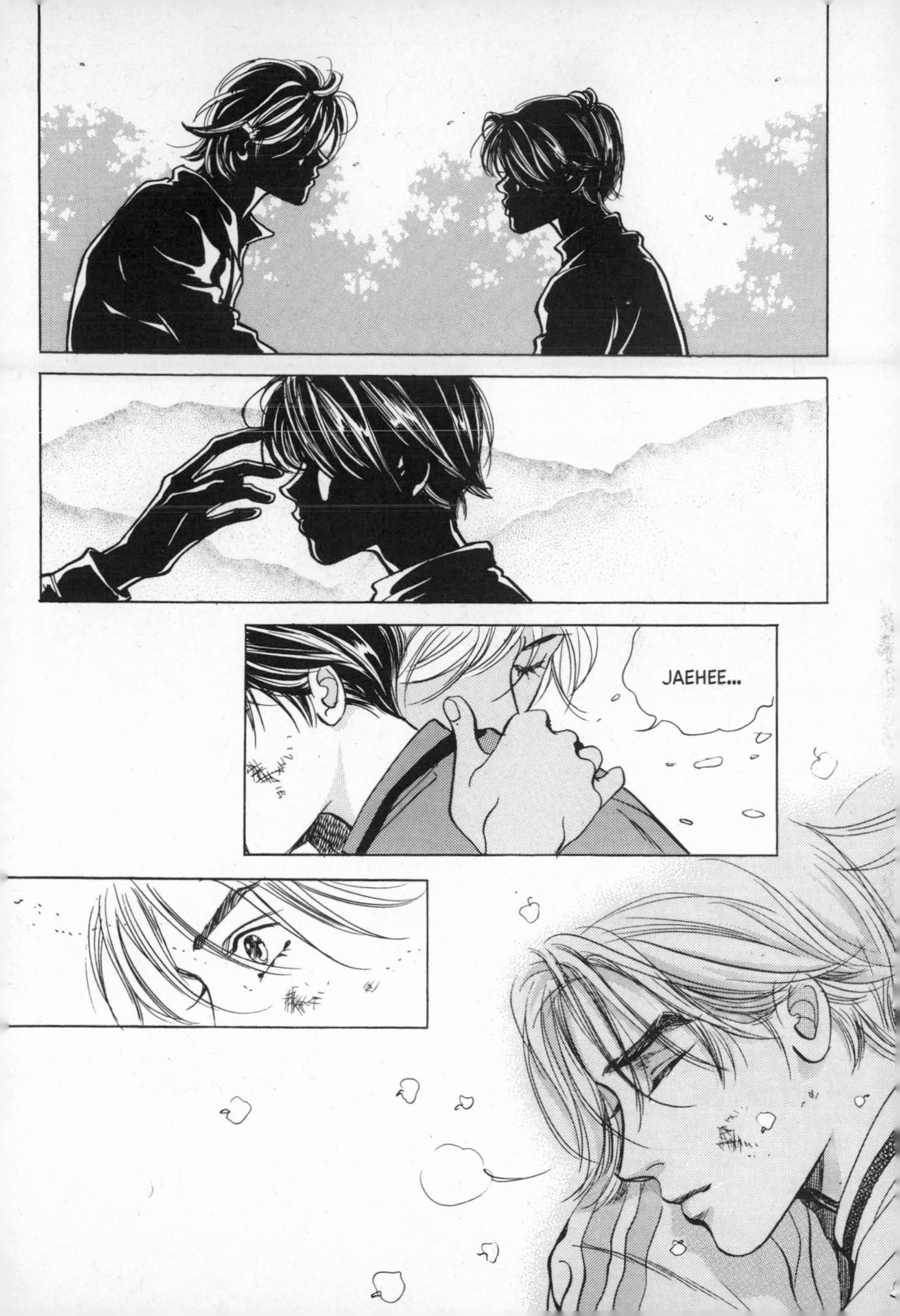
JAEHEE...

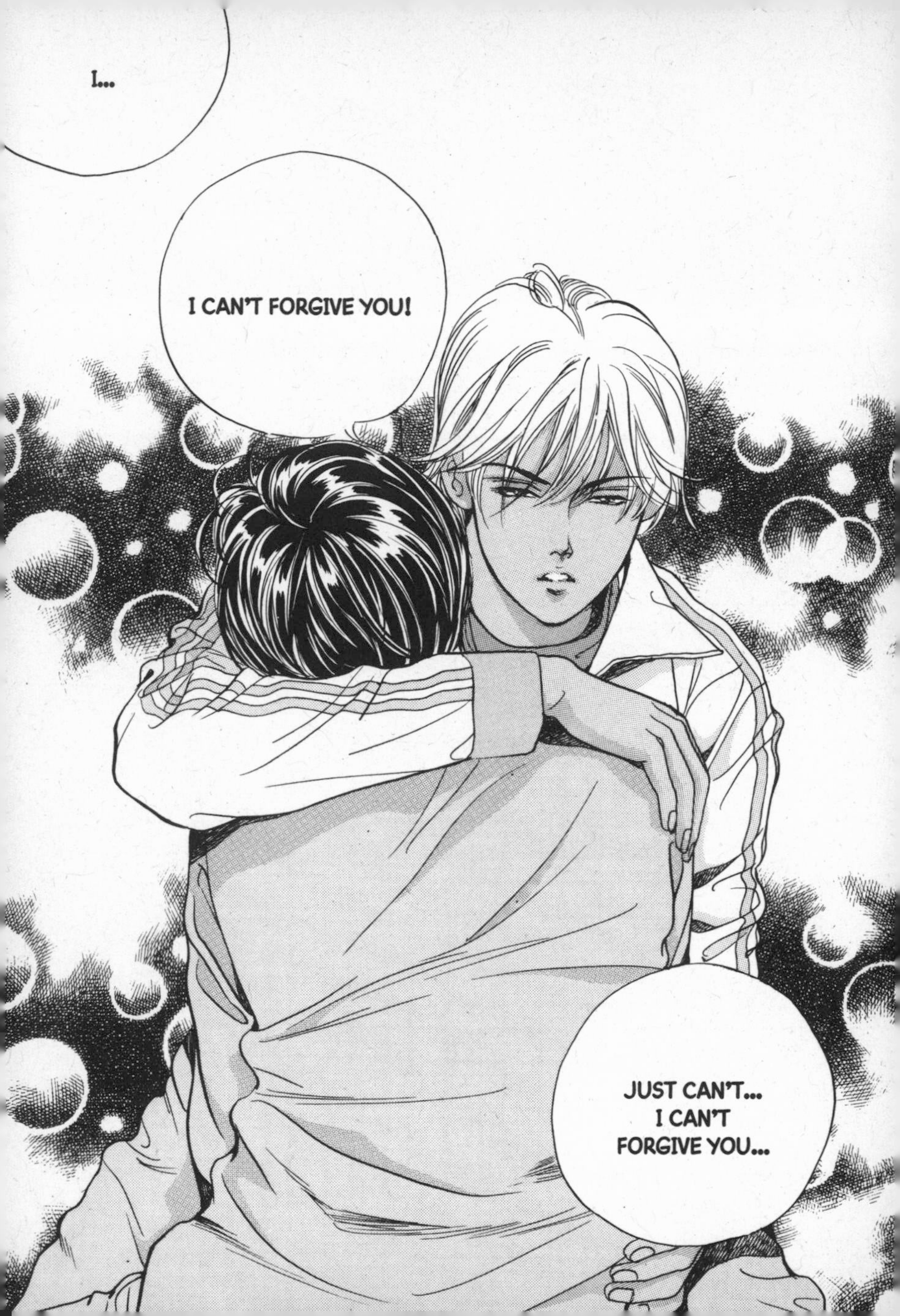
I...
I CAN'T FORGIVE YOU!
JUST CAN'T... I CAN'T FORGIVE YOU...

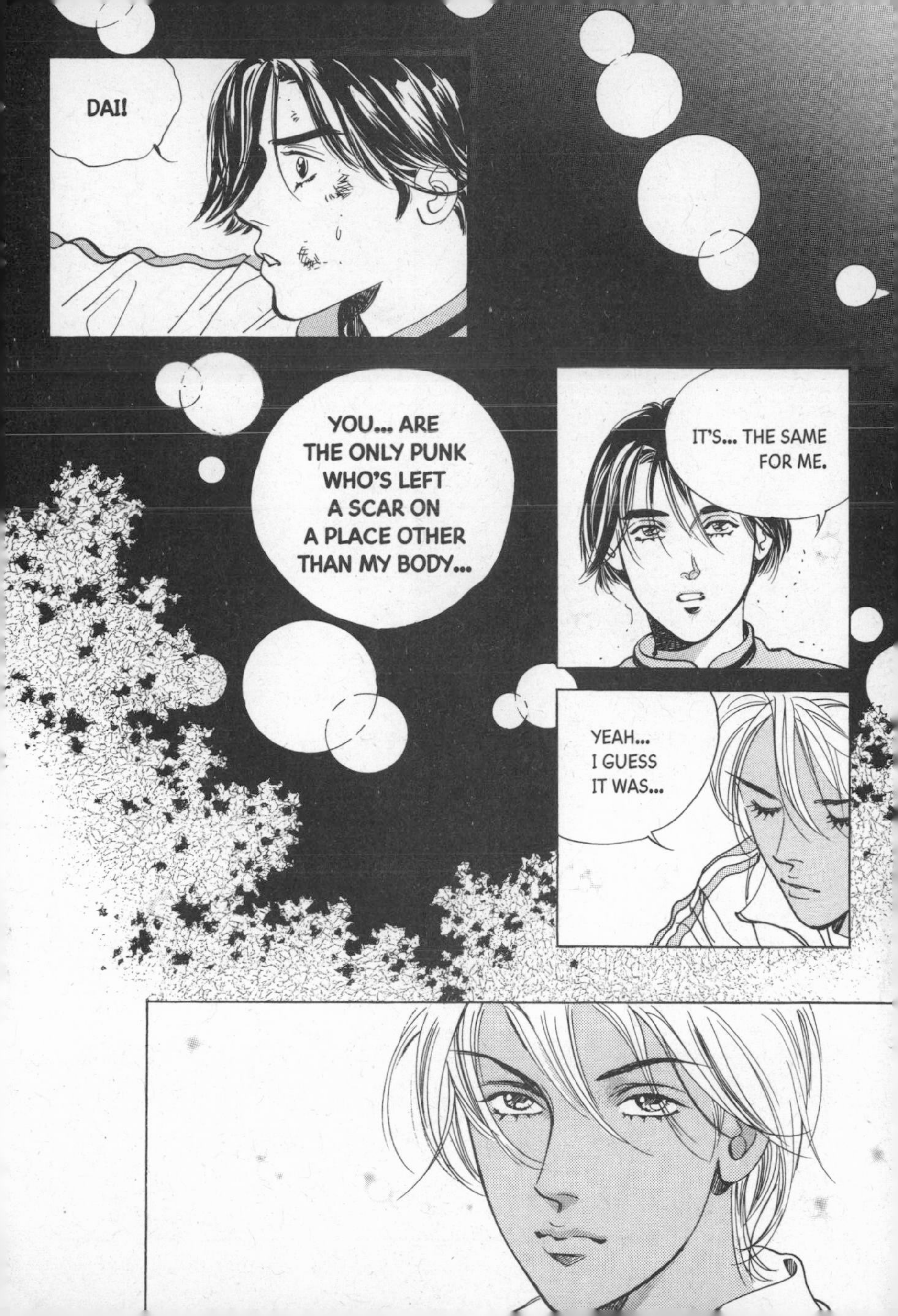
DAI!
YOU... ARE THE ONLY PUNK WHO'S LEFT A SCAR ON A PLACE OTHER THAN MY BODY...
IT'S... THE SAME FOR ME.
YEAH... I GUESS IT WAS...

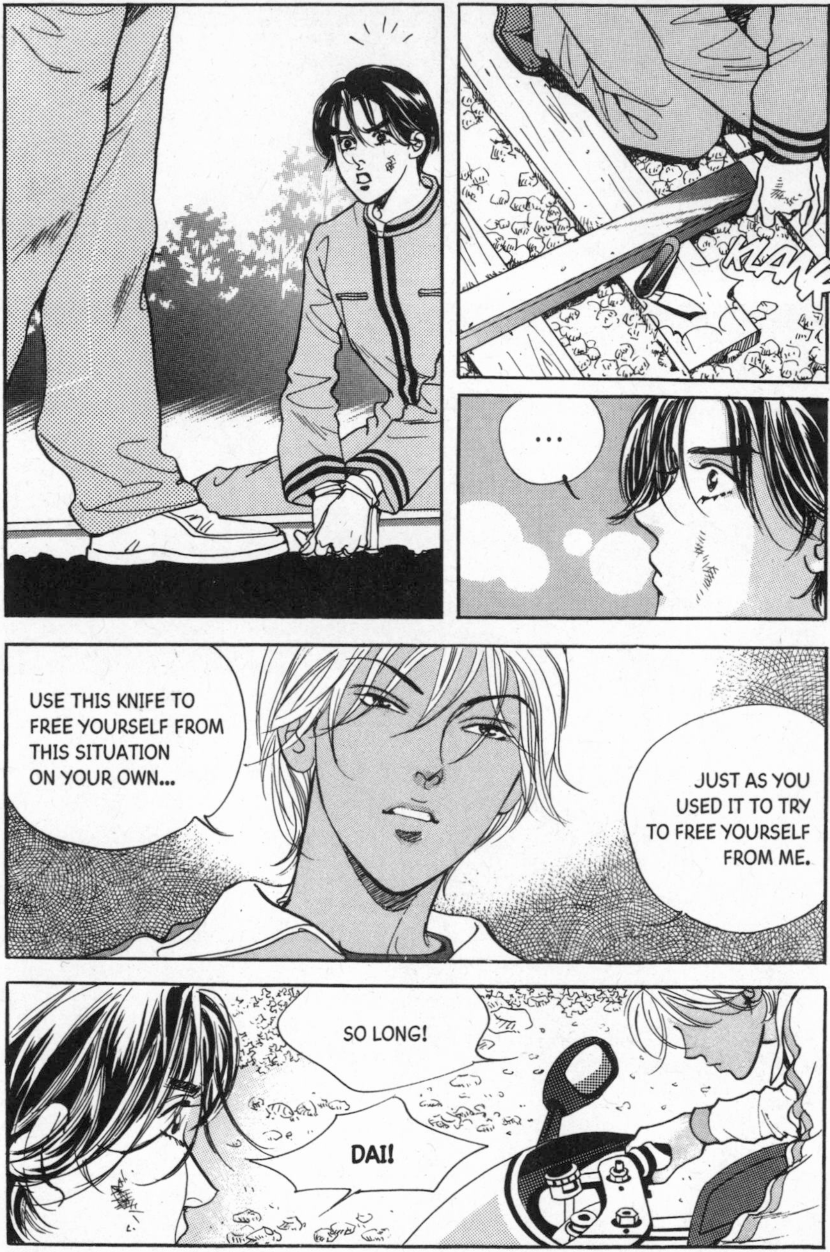
KLANK
...
USE THIS KNIFE TO FREE YOURSELF FROM THIS SITUATION ON YOUR OWN...
JUST AS YOU USED IT TO TRY TO FREE YOURSELF FROM ME.
SO LONG!
DAI!

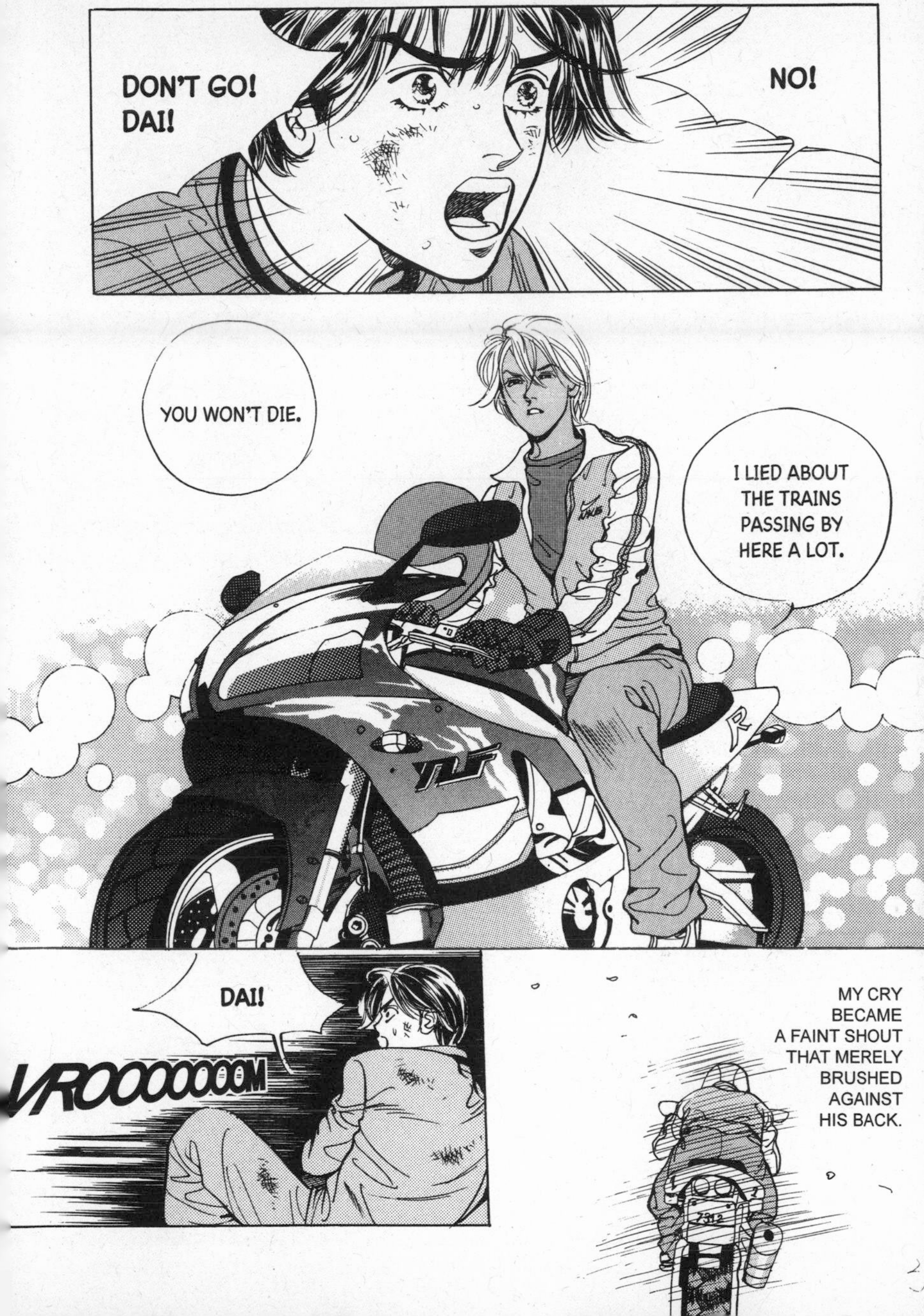
DON'T GO! DAI!
NO!
YOU WON'T DIE.
I LIED ABOUT THE TRAINS PASSING BY HERE A LOT.
DAI!
VROOOOOOOM
MY CRY BECAME A FAINT SHOUT THAT MERELY BRUSHED AGAINST HIS BACK.

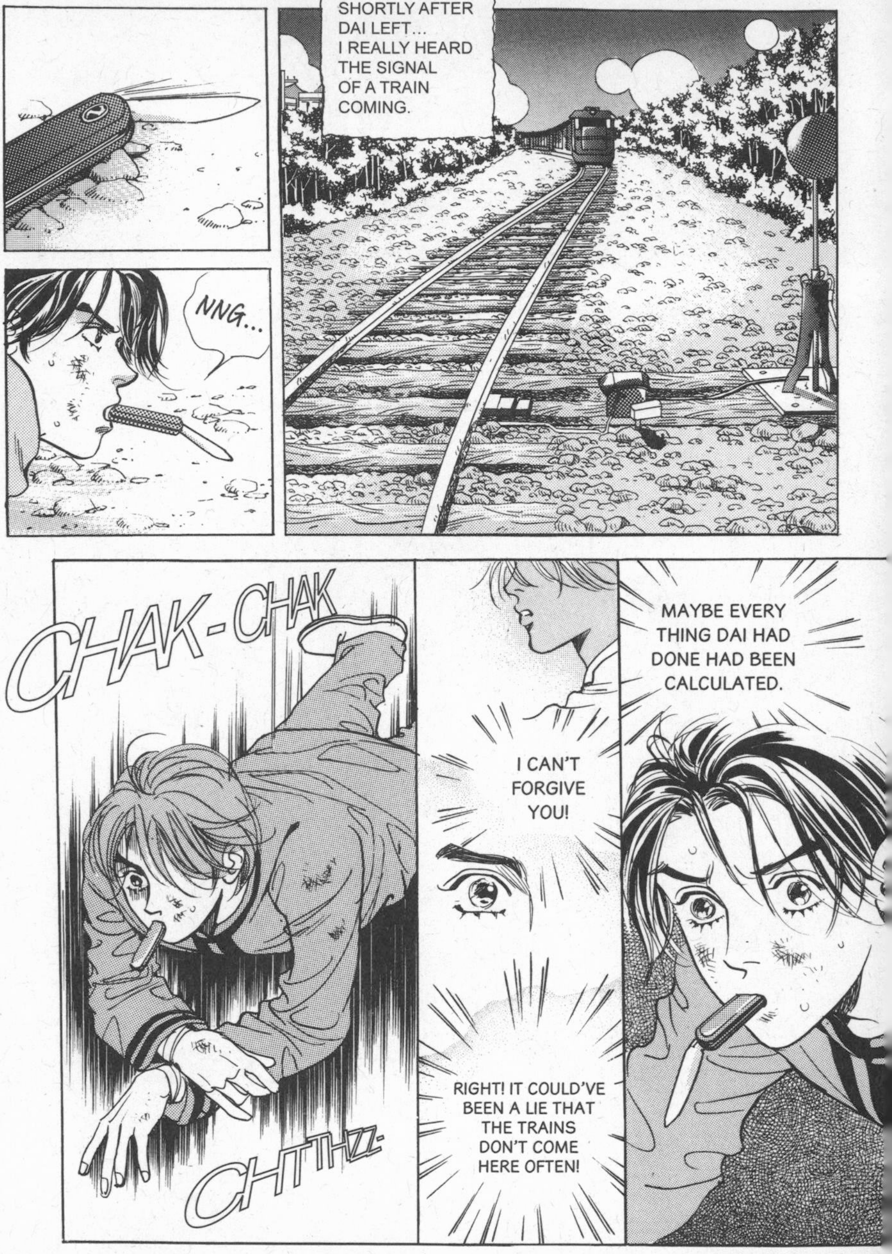
SHORTLY AFTER DAI LEFT... I REALLY HEARD THE SIGNAL OF A TRAIN COMING.
NNG...
CHAK-CHAK
CHITTHZZ-
I CAN'T FORGIVE YOU!
RIGHT! IT COULD'VE BEEN A LIE THAT THE TRAINS DON'T COME HERE OFTEN!
MAYBE EVERY THING DAI HAD DONE HAD BEEN CALCULATED.

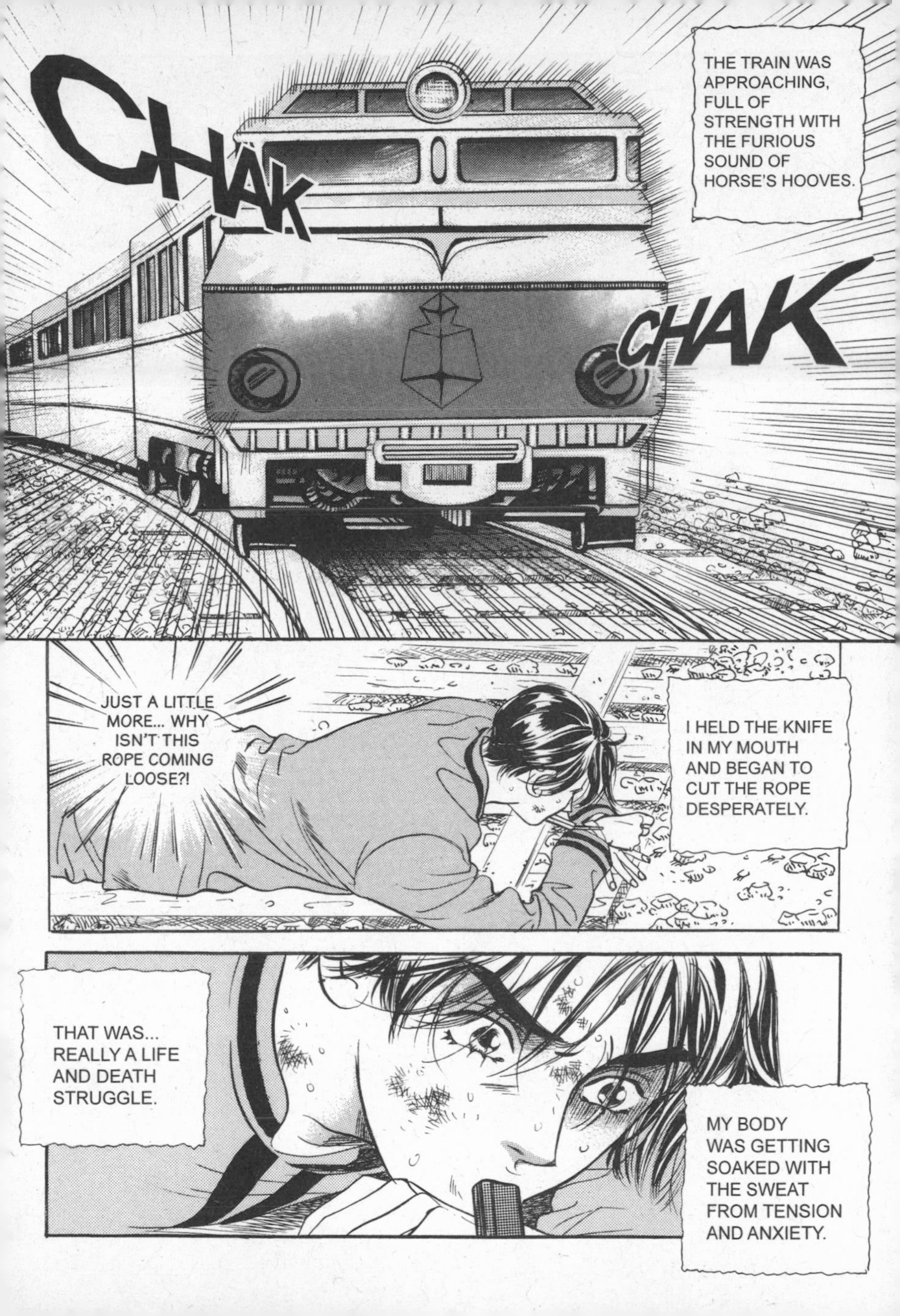
CHAK
THE TRAIN WAS APPROACHING, FULL OF STRENGTH WITH THE FURIOUS SOUND OF HORSE'S HOOVES.
CHAK
JUST A LITTLE MORE... WHY ISN'T THIS ROPE COMING LOOSE?!
I HELD THE KNIFE IN MY MOUTH AND BEGAN TO CUT THE ROPE DESPERATELY.
THAT WAS... REALLY A LIFE AND DEATH STRUGGLE.
MY BODY WAS GETTING SOAKED WITH THE SWEAT FROM TENSION AND ANXIETY.

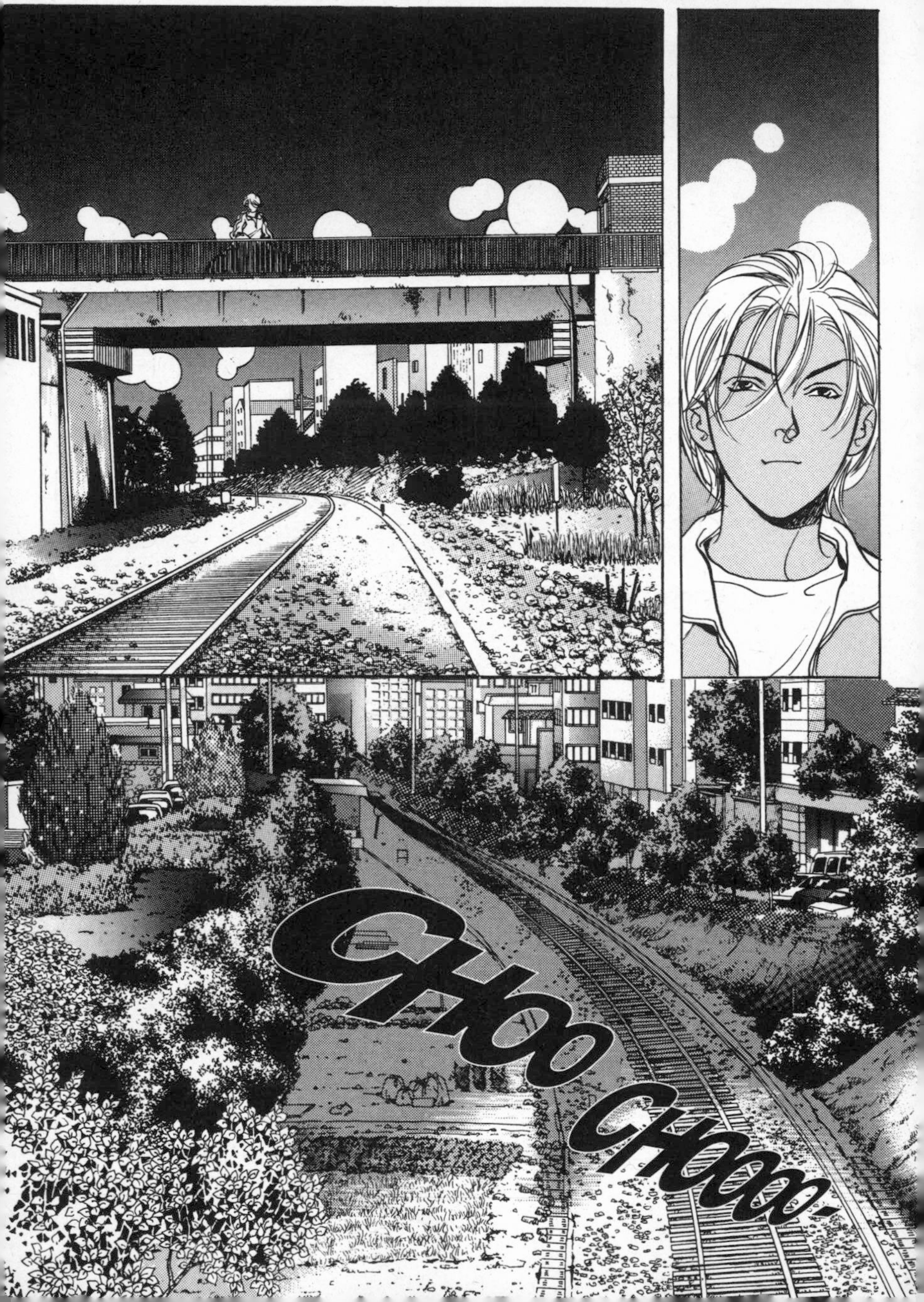
CHOO CHOOO-

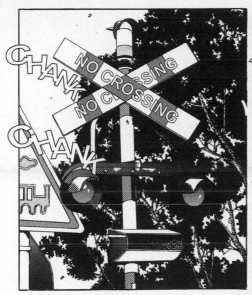

CHANK CHANK CHANK

NO CROSSING NO CROSSING

KA-ROOOOOSH

NO! I CAN'T DIE LIKE THIS!

MY BLOOD BEGAN TO BOIL AS IF IN A RUSH OF POWER.

LITTLE MORE... LITTLE BIT MORE...

MY PULSE STIMULATED MY HEART AT A FRENETIC SPEED.

RIP

KUMP

KUMP

KUMP

LITTLE...!

KUMP

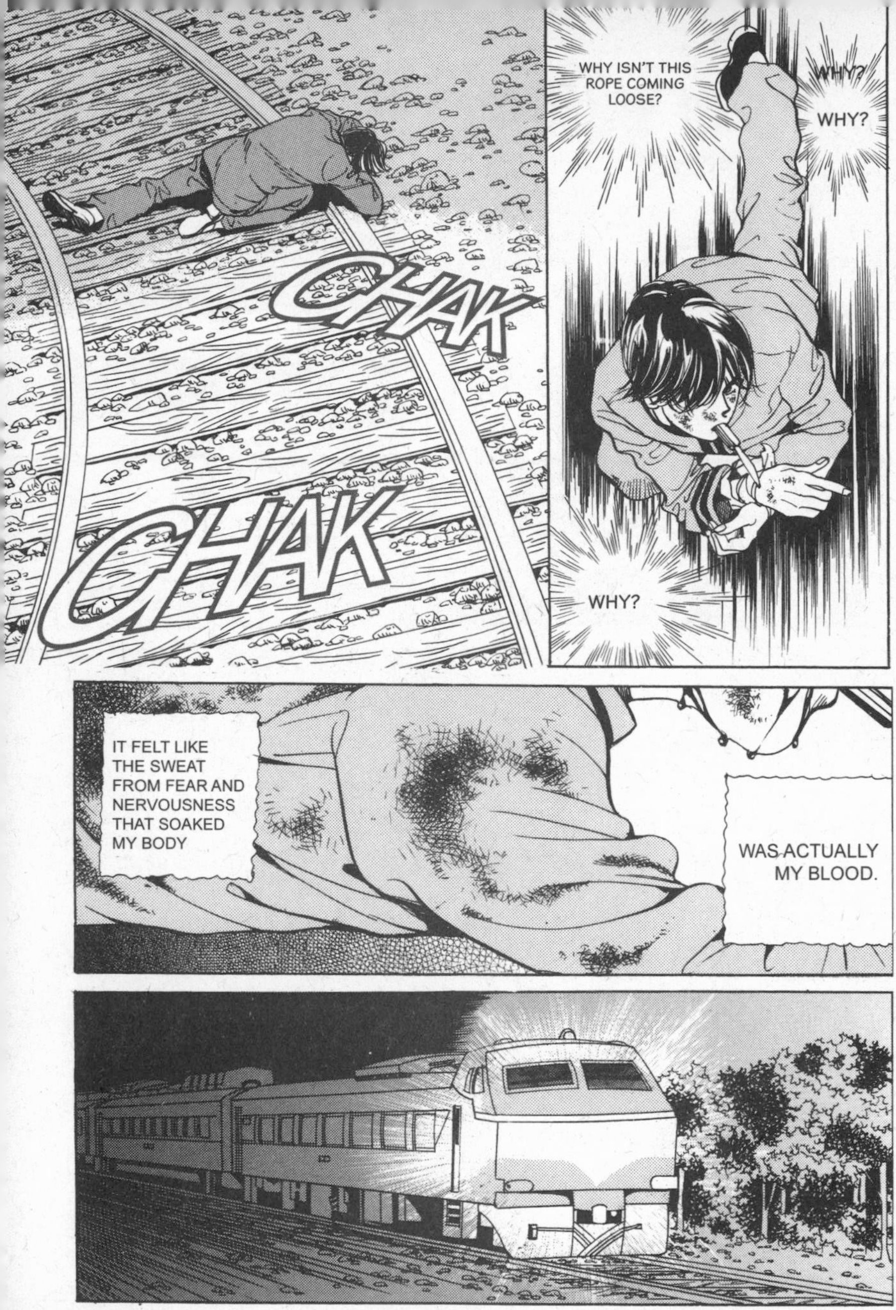
CHAK
CHAK
WHY ISN'T THIS ROPE COMING LOOSE?
WHY?
WHY?
WHY?
IT FELT LIKE THE SWEAT FROM FEAR AND NERVOUSNESS THAT SOAKED MY BODY
WAS ACTUALLY MY BLOOD.

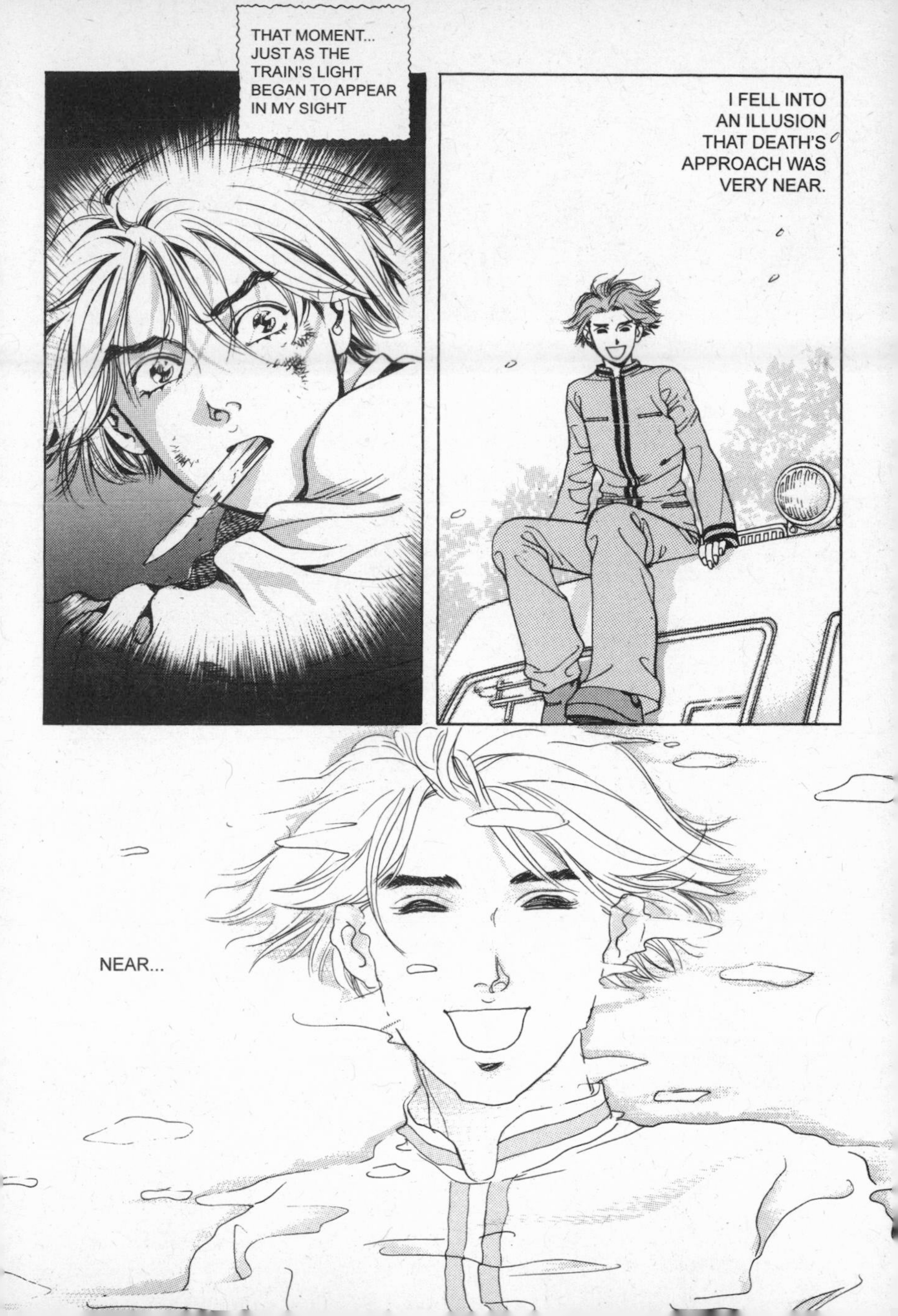
THAT MOMENT... JUST AS THE TRAIN'S LIGHT BEGAN TO APPEAR IN MY SIGHT
I FELL INTO AN ILLUSION THAT DEATH'S APPROACH WAS VERY NEAR.
NEAR...

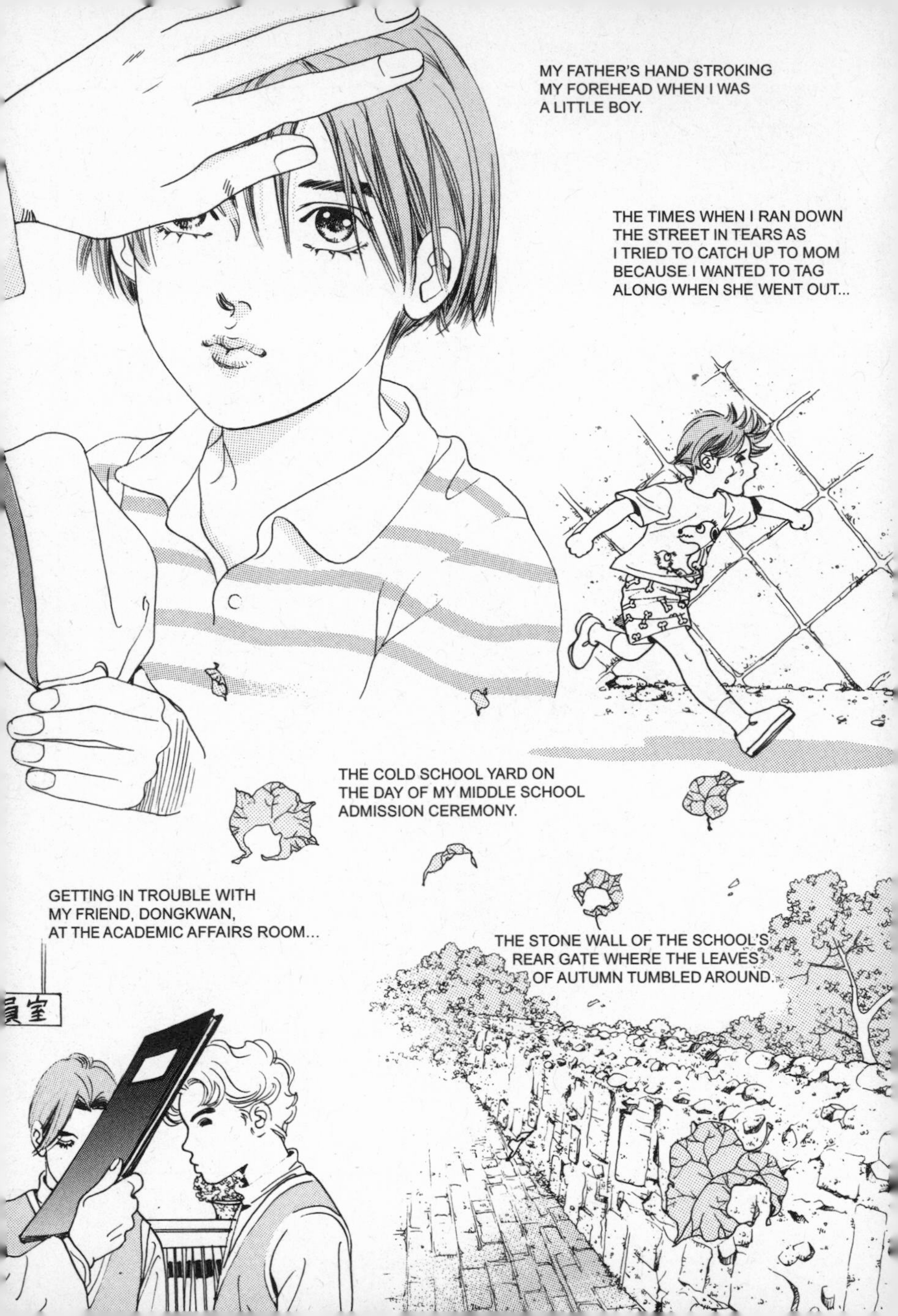
MY FATHER'S HAND STROKING MY FOREHEAD WHEN I WAS A LITTLE BOY.
THE TIMES WHEN I RAN DOWN THE STREET IN TEARS AS I TRIED TO CATCH UP TO MOM BECAUSE I WANTED TO TAG ALONG WHEN SHE WENT OUT...
THE COLD SCHOOL YARD ON THE DAY OF MY MIDDLE SCHOOL ADMISSION CEREMONY.
GETTING IN TROUBLE WITH MY FRIEND, DONGKWAN, AT THE ACADEMIC AFFAIRS ROOM...
THE STONE WALL OF THE SCHOOL'S REAR GATE WHERE THE LEAVES OF AUTUMN TUMBLED AROUND.

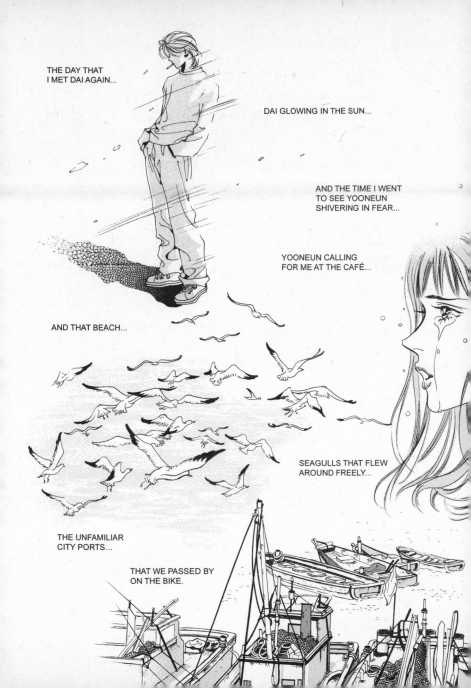

THE DAY THAT
I MET DAI AGAIN...

DAI GLOWING IN THE SUN...

AND THE TIME I WENT
TO SEE YOONEUN
SHIVERING IN FEAR...

YOONEUN CALLING
FOR ME AT THE CAFÉ...

AND THAT BEACH...

SEAGULLS THAT FLEW
AROUND FREELY...

THE UNFAMILIAR
CITY PORTS...

THAT WE PASSED BY
ON THE BIKE.

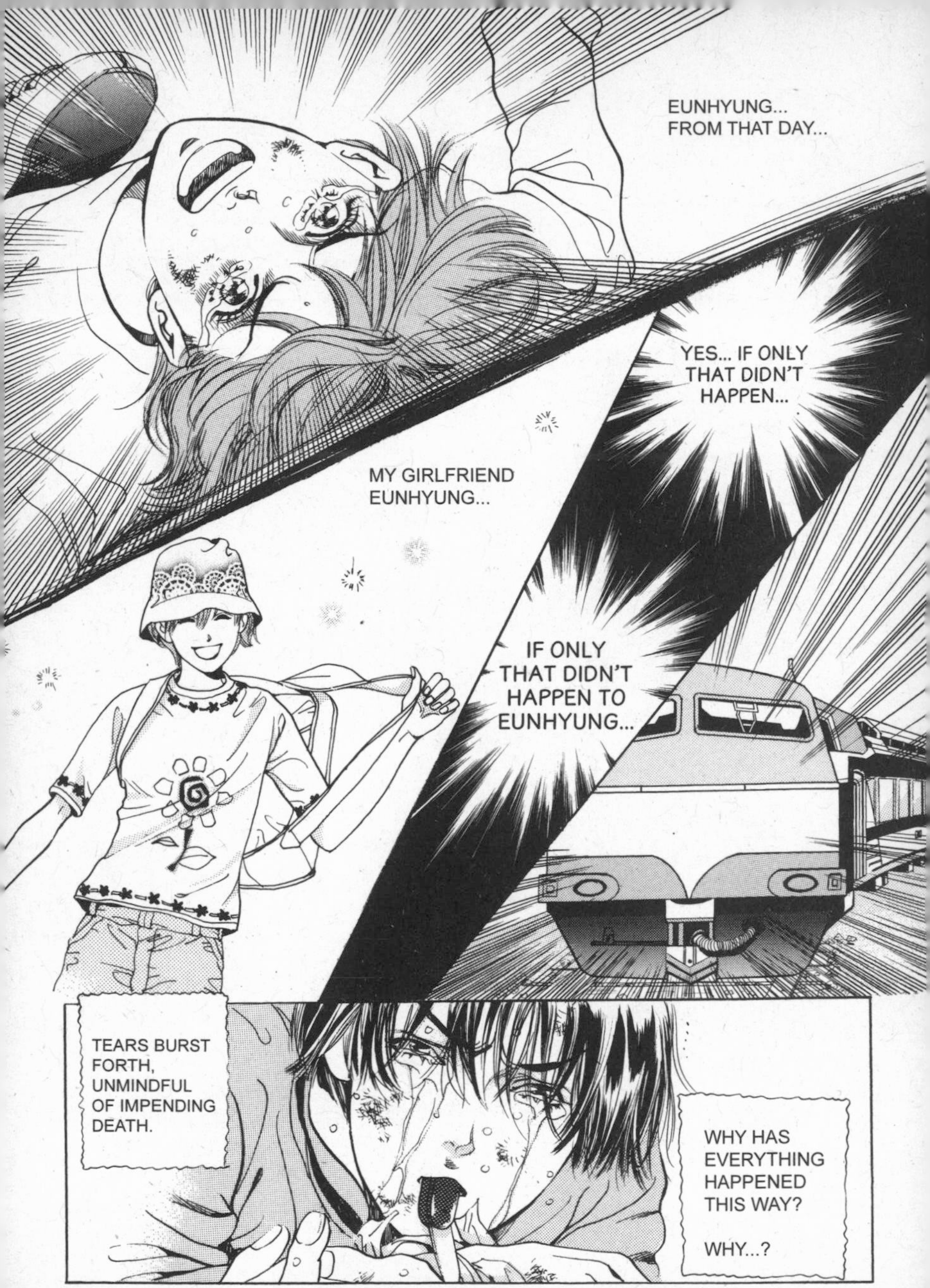
EUNHYUNG... FROM THAT DAY...
MY GIRLFRIEND EUNHYUNG...
YES... IF ONLY THAT DIDN'T HAPPEN...
IF ONLY THAT DIDN'T HAPPEN TO EUNHYUNG...
TEARS BURST FORTH, UNMINDFUL OF IMPENDING DEATH.
WHY HAS EVERYTHING HAPPENED THIS WAY?
WHY...?

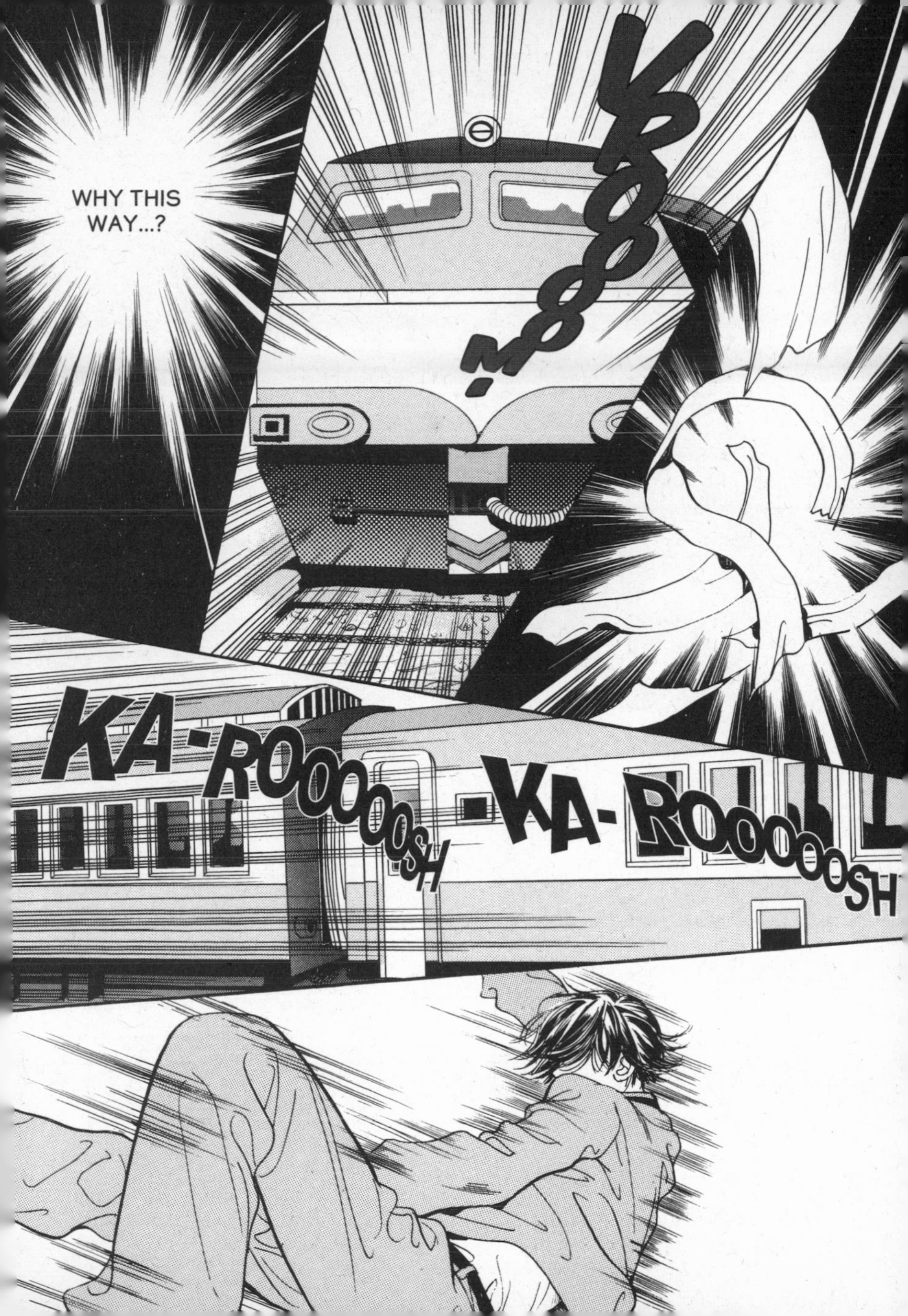
WHY THIS WAY...?
VROOOOM
KA-ROOOOOOSH
KA-ROOOOOOSH

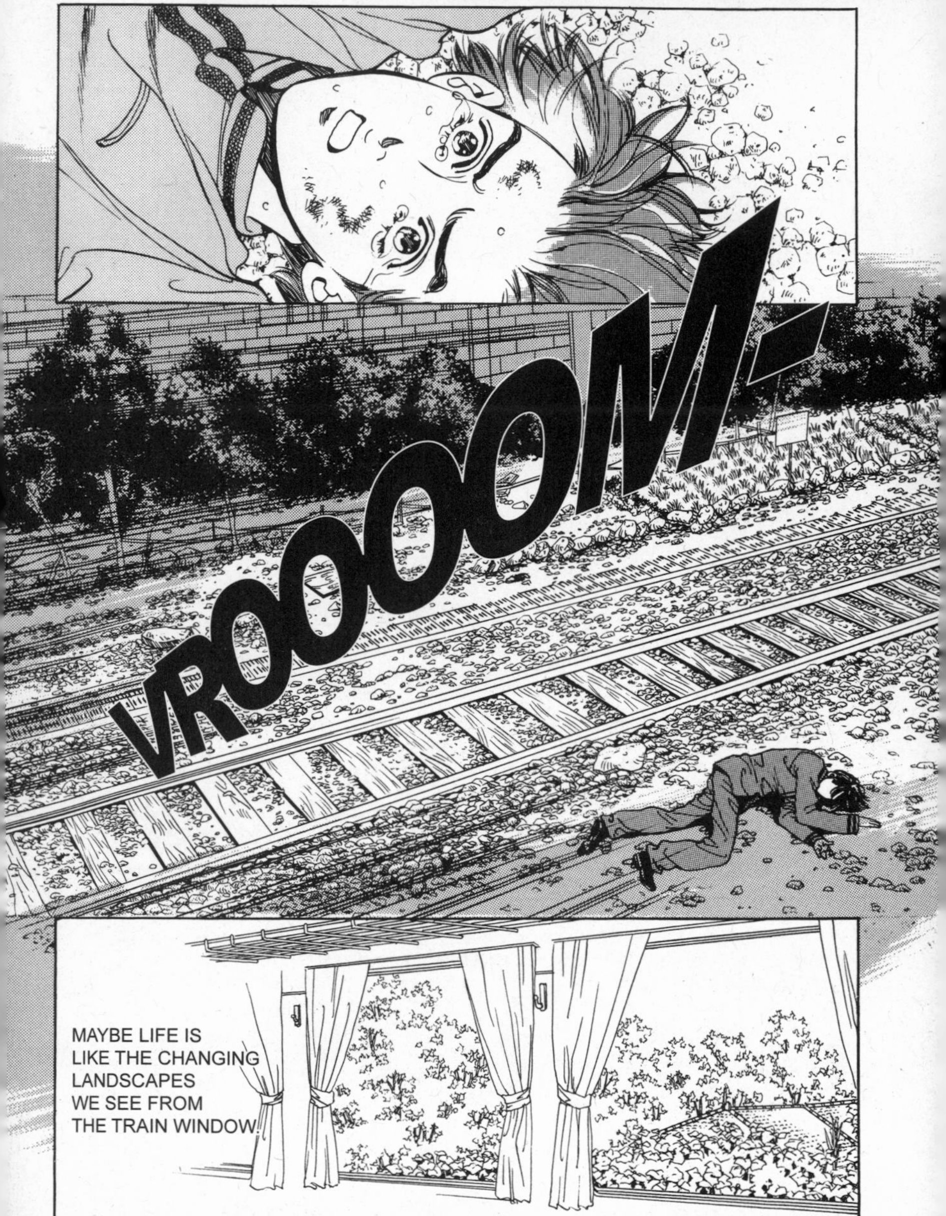
VROOOOOM-
MAYBE LIFE IS LIKE THE CHANGING LANDSCAPES WE SEE FROM THE TRAIN WINDOW.

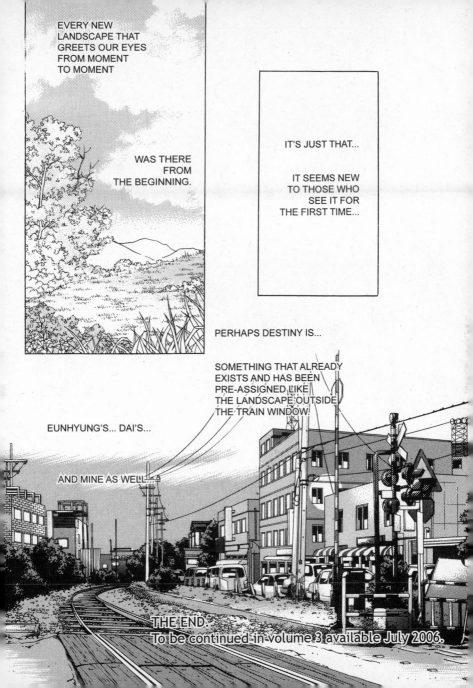

EVERY NEW LANDSCAPE THAT GREETS OUR EYES FROM MOMENT TO MOMENT

WAS THERE FROM THE BEGINNING.

IT'S JUST THAT...

IT SEEMS NEW TO THOSE WHO SEE IT FOR THE FIRST TIME...

PERHAPS DESTINY IS...

SOMETHING THAT ALREADY EXISTS AND HAS BEEN PRE-ASSIGNED LIKE THE LANDSCAPE OUTSIDE THE TRAIN WINDOW!

EUNHYUNG'S... DAI'S...

AND MINE AS WELL...

THE END.
To be continued in volume 3 available July 2006.

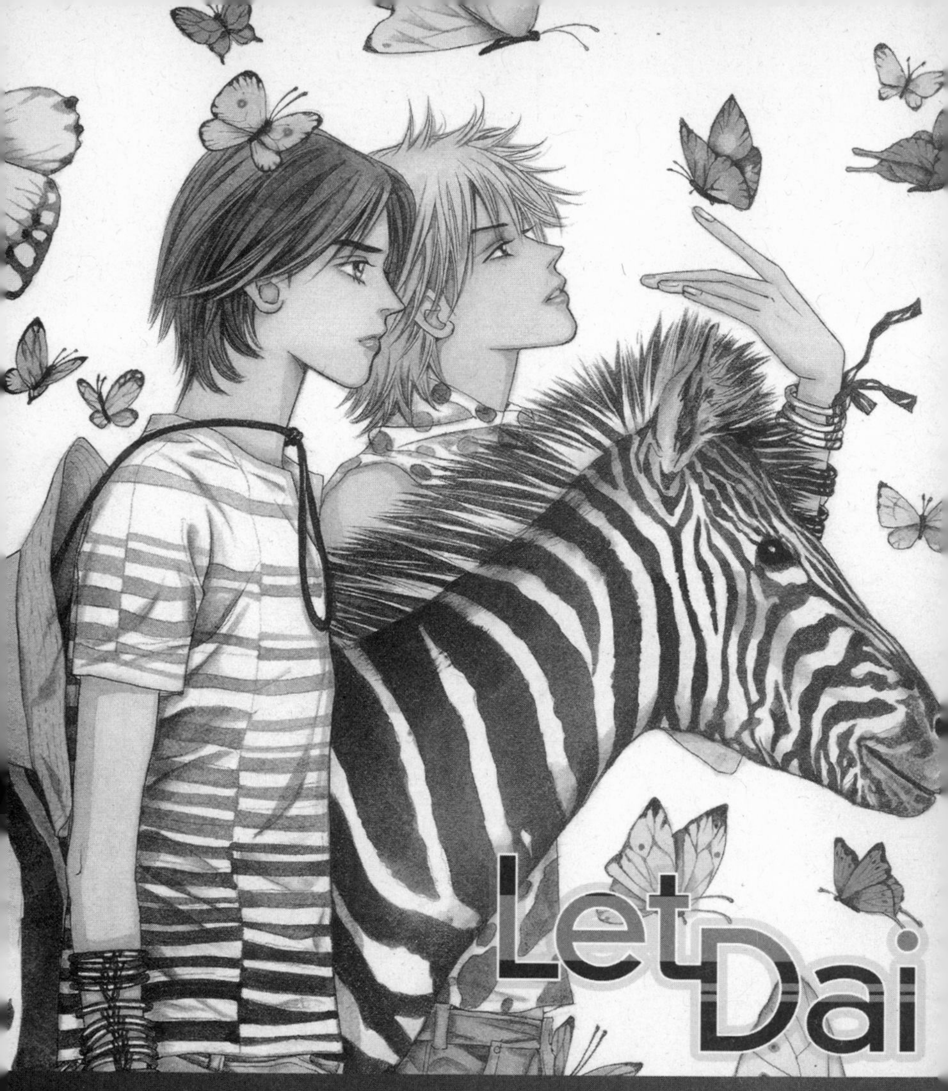
Let Dai

Vol. 3

Sooyeon Won

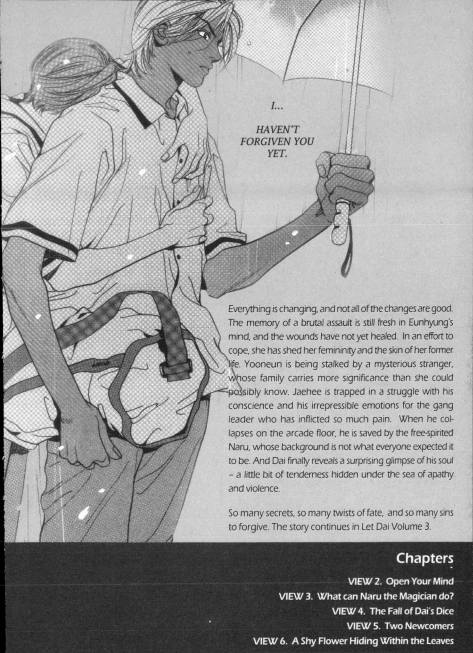

I...

*HAVEN'T
FORGIVEN YOU
YET.*

Everything is changing, and not all of the changes are good.
The memory of a brutal assault is still fresh in Eunhyung's
mind, and the wounds have not yet healed. In an effort to
cope, she has shed her femininity and the skin of her former
life. Yooneun is being stalked by a mysterious stranger,
whose family carries more significance than she could
possibly know. Jaehee is trapped in a struggle with his
conscience and his irrepressible emotions for the gang
leader who has inflicted so much pain. When he col-
lapses on the arcade floor, he is saved by the free-spirited
Naru, whose background is not what everyone expected it
to be. And Dai finally reveals a surprising glimpse of his soul
– a little bit of tenderness hidden under the sea of apathy
and violence.

So many secrets, so many twists of fate, and so many sins
to forgive. The story continues in Let Dai Volume 3.

Chapters

Hottest Shonen-ai
Boy Princess Vol. 2
finally in print!

Boy Princess Volume 2 will get your pulse racing from page one, as this story of complex convictions takes off right from where the last book left us arrested in suspense. Princess Elena returns to free her little brother from playing her stand-in in a strategic marriage of two kingdoms. But is it too late? Are the feelings ignited between the two princes too strong to be extinguished by her second thought gesture? When she finds herself unable to fulfill her obligations as his wife, suspicions begin to bubble to the surface and evildoers and transgressors emerge within her midst. As Prince Jed's sister contends for domination and the people of the forest gather their might, the future of the throne is not at all certain. Loyalties will crumble and passions will soar in Volume 2 of this heart-throbbing offbeat romance!

Seyoung Kim

Boy Princess 2

the great
CATSBY

 Vol. 1 Created by **Doha**

"The Great Catsby is twisted, funny and beautiful. Can't wait to read more."

Scott McCloud, Author, Understanding Comics

Winner of 3 most *prestigious awards for manhwa in 2005!*

MAY 2006 RELEASES!

Read Them Online at www.NETCOMICS.com

EUNHYE LEE
2
Pine Kiss

PINE KISS VOL. 2

Eunhye Lee

After the dramatic events of Eunhye Lee's first episode, we find the characters of *Pine Kiss* revealed again in bold and illustrious art. The story of Dali and her enigmatic history is depicted with passion while her connection to the beautiful new teacher Orion is finally explained. This connection, of course, only draws her and the sassy Sebin to a fierce confrontation. Mix in Sanghyung, the basketball-loving classmate who pines for Sebin, and the reader witnesses a web of drama and secret alliances. Will the relationships of Orion and his students jeopardize his position? Who will share their very first kiss with Orion? Lee's sometimes humorous, sometimes poignant tale continues and leaves the reader enamored with the skills of a master.

MIRA LEE
Land of Silver Rain
2

LAND OF SILVER RAIN VOL. 2

Mira Lee

Misty-Rain is deported to the land of her birth, and Sirius, the rich Prince of the Land of the Unicorns, tries to go to the world of humans to find her. Concerned for her charge, Nanny hatches a plot that causes the young prince to lose all his memories of Misty-Rain. With only a fox-witch as her companion in this strange new world, Misty-Rain gets into a car accident, and almost dies. Fortunately, she is given new life by the power of the "Tae-guek" spirit bestowed by the Great King of Darkness. Two years pass and Misty-Rain, a normal eighth-grader at Yulha Middle School, is now living with a human family. She has been placed under the charge of two brothers, one of whom is a handsome but obnoxious athlete, whose wicked personality has left him with no friends. As she lives out her new life, Misty- Rain seems to have all but forgotten the magical land where she was raised. Prince Sirius, however, is gradually snapping out of Nanny's spell and is slowly remembering...

Available now at your favorite bookstores
Read it online at www.NETCOMICS.com

MAY 2006 RELEASES!

Read Them Online at www.NETCOMICS.com

MADTOWN HOSPITAL VOL. 2
JTK

A fierce competition to win a town's respect ensues between Don Juan from Madtown Hospital and Kyungwan Ryoo from the Cemetery Hospital. Amidst broken bones, a clumsy chase through the rooftops, and the mad rush of ambulances, will the patients even emerge alive? A smothering heat has fallen on Madtown Hospital, and none of the air-conditioners work! Watch as the members of Madtown's staff try everything in their power to make their patients comfortable. From dressing up like ghosts and scaring them to shivers, to dressing up in colorful swimsuits in the operating room--all in the name of their patients' mental health! The staff of Madtown Hospital is back and they are ready to take you on another gut-busting rollercoaster adventure through operating room antics and crazy medical fun! Fasten your seatbelts; this is going to be one bumpy ride!

HOTEL CALIFORNIA
JTK

From Korea's legendary comedy writer and the creator of Madtown Hospital comes *Hotel California!* Somewhere in America, a place with plenty of rooms for anyone who gets himself in trouble exists. Free of charge and all-inclusive, The Collin Prison will take anyone who comes in, and will try to reform them to boot! Dallas Westcoast has taken revenge on his father's killer. Unfortunately, he has murdered the wrong person. Now he finds himself sucked into the vortex of what appears to be the twilight zone's demented sister--The Collin Prison: The *Hotel California*. Joy, the prison's only woman is actually a transsexual martial arts master. The warden is a country music fanatic who brainwashes his prisoners with the unceasing broadcast of country songs. Irving and Tom try to resist this musical communism by holding fast to hip hop. These are just a few of the bizarre cast of characters in this crazy place. Sit back and watch as they work up a non-stop series of absurd events guaranteed to have you rolling on the floor. Welcome to the *Hotel California!*

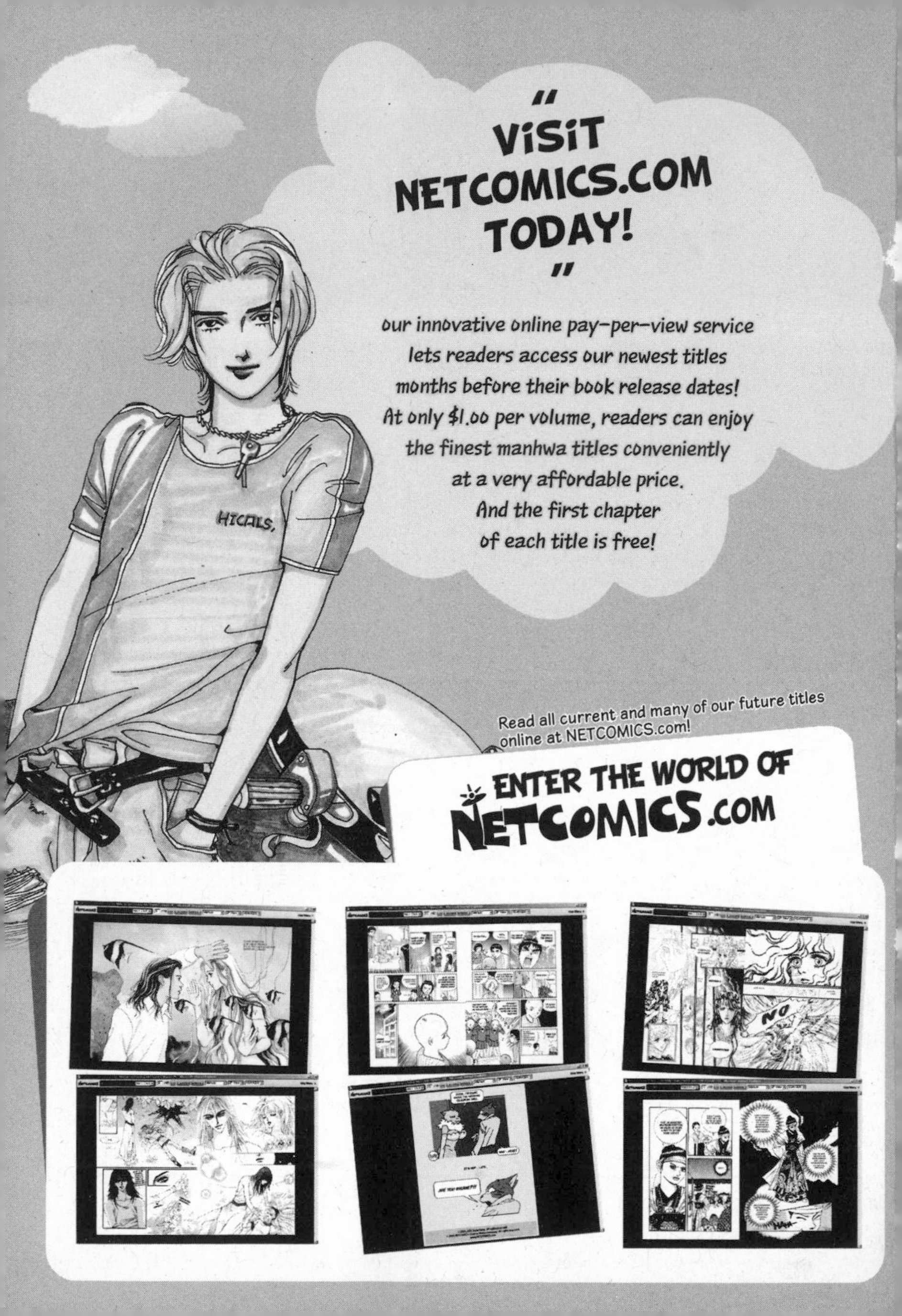
"
VISIT
NETCOMICS.COM
TODAY!
"
our innovative online pay-per-view service lets readers access our newest titles months before their book release dates! At only $1.00 per volume, readers can enjoy the finest manhwa titles conveniently at a very affordable price. And the first chapter of each title is free!
HICALS,
Read all current and many of our future titles online at NETCOMICS.com!
ENTER THE WORLD OF
NETCOMICS.COM
NO